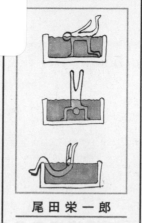

尾田栄一郎

They say that half-bathing is good for one's health! Time for volume 81 to begin!!

−Eiichiro Oda, 2016

iichiro Oda began his manga career at the age of 17, when his one-shot cowboy manga **Wanted!** won second place in the coveted Tezuka manga awards. Oda went on to work as an assistant to some of the biggest manga artists in the industry, including Nobuhiro Watsuki, before winning the Hop Step Award for new artists. His pirate adventure **One Piece**, which debuted in **Weekly Shonen Jump** in 1997, quickly became one of the most popular manga in Japan.

ONE PIECE VOL. 81
NEW WORLD PART 21

SHONEN JUMP Manga Edition

STORY AND ART BY EIICHIRO ODA

Translation/Stephen Paul
Touch-up Art & Lettering/Vanessa Satone
Design/Fawn Lau
Editor/Alexis Kirsch

Printed in the U.S.A.

Published by VIZ Media, LLC
P.O. Box 77010
San Francisco, CA 94107

10 9 8 7 6 5 4 3 2 1
First printing, February 2017

SHONEN JUMP MANGA

ONE PIECE

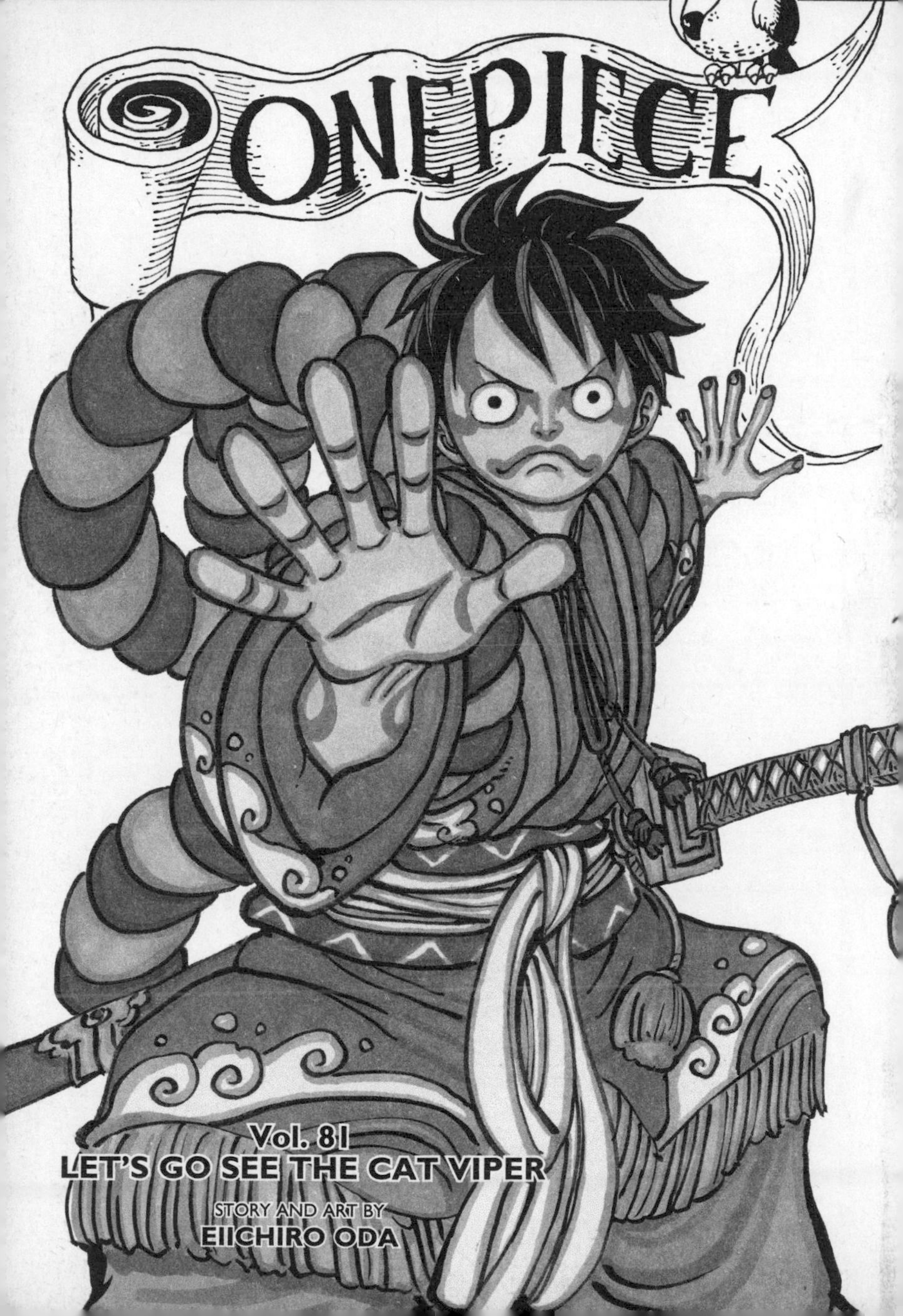

Vol. 81
LET'S GO SEE THE CAT VIPER

STORY AND ART BY
EIICHIRO ODA

The Straw Hat Crew

Tony Tony Chopper

After researching powerful medicine in Birdie Kingdom, he reunited with the rest of the crew.

Ship's Doctor, Bounty: 100 berries

Monkey D. Luffy

A young man who dreams of becoming the Pirate King. After training with Rayleigh, he and his crew head for the New World!

Captain, Bounty: 500 million berries

Nico Robin

She spent her time in Baltigo with the leader of the Revolutionary Army: Luffy's father, Dragon.

Archeologist, Bounty: 130 million berries

Roronoa Zolo

He swallowed his pride and asked to be trained by Mihawk on Gloom Island before reuniting with the rest of the crew.

Fighter, Bounty: 320 million berries

Franky

He modified himself in Future Land Baldimore and turned himself into Armored Franky before reuniting with the rest of the crew.

Shipwright, Bounty: 94 million berries

Nami

She studied the weather of the New World on the small Sky Island Weatheria, a place where weather is studied as a science.

Navigator, Bounty: 66 million berries

Brook

After being captured and used as a freak show by the Longarm Tribe, he became a famous rock star called "Soul King" Brook.

Musician, Bounty: 83 million berries

Usopp

He trained under Heracles at the Bowin Islands to become the King of Snipers.

Sniper, Bounty: 200 million berries

Shanks

One of the Four Emperors. Waits for Luffy in the "New World," the second half of the Grand Line.

Captain of the Red-Haired Pirates

Sanji

After fighting the New Kama Karate masters in the Kamabakka Kingdom, he returned to the crew.

Cook, Bounty: 177 million berries

kingdom from his control. After Luffy finally emerges victorious over their foe, he is forced into a ritual of cups with the other pirates they fought alongside. It's the creation of the Straw Hat Fleet!

As the powers of the world realign following the Navy's capture of Doflamingo, Luffy's crew sets off for Zou to catch up to Nami's group, which left earlier. Zou turns out to be a kingdom on the back of a gigantic elephant, but it's already destroyed when they arrive. Once they meet up with Nami, they learn that something has happened to Sanji...

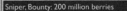

The story of ONE PIECE 1»81

Heart Pirates

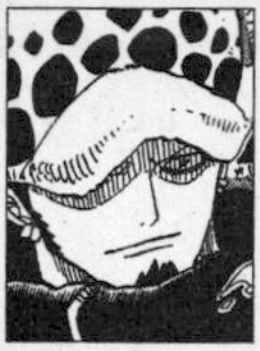
Trafalgar Law
Captain of the Heart Pirates

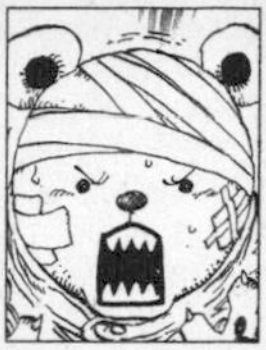
Bepo
Navigator of the Heart Pirates

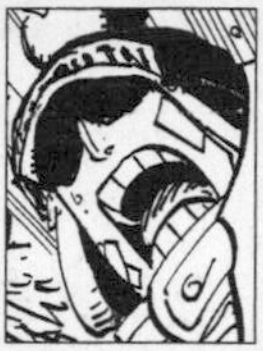
Penguin
Heart Pirates Crew

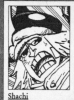

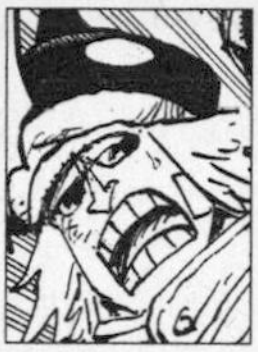
Shachi
Heart Pirates Crew

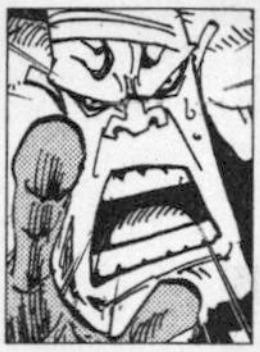
Jean Bart
Heart Pirates Crew

Wano Kingdom

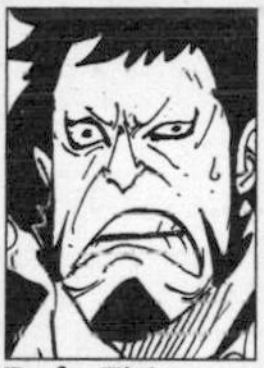
Foxfire Kin'emon
Samurai of Wano

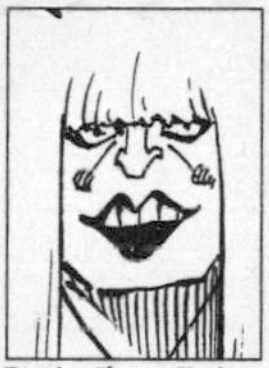
Evening Shower Kanjuro
Samurai of Wano

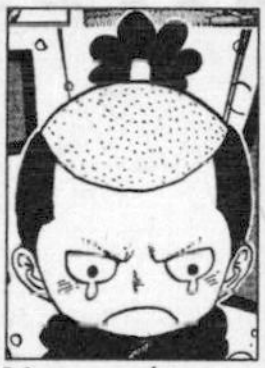
Momonosuke
Kin'emon's Son

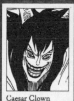

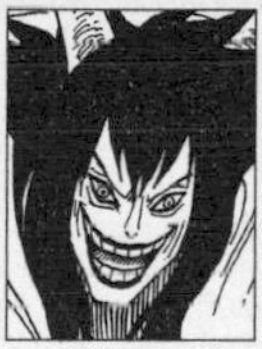
Caesar Clown
Former Govt Scientist

The Minks

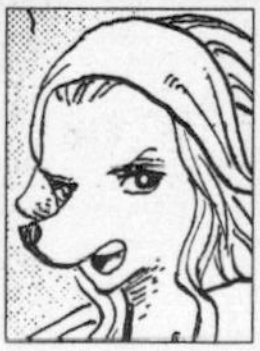
Wanda (Dog Mink)
Battlebeast Tribe

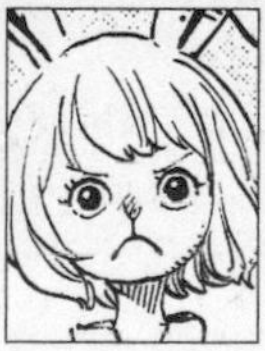
Carrot (Bunny Mink)
Battlebeast Tribe

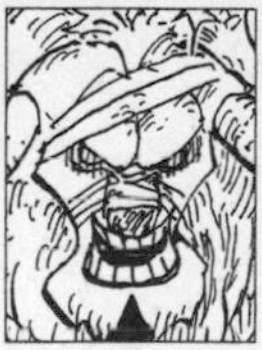
Roddy (Bull Mink)
Guardian of the Whale Forest

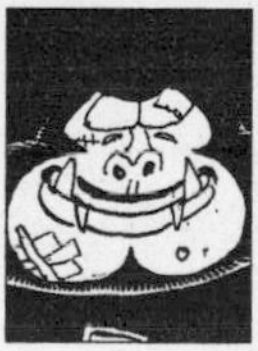
BB (Gorilla Mink)
Guardian of the Whale Forest

Story

After two years of hard training, the Straw Hat pirates are back together, first at the Sabaody Archipelago and then through Fish-Man Island to their next stage: the New World!!

The crew happens across Trafalgar Law on the island of Punk Hazard. At his suggestion, they form a new pirate alliance that seeks to take down one of the Four Emperors. The group infiltrates the kingdom of Dressrosa in an attempt to take down Doflamingo, Kaido's trading partner, and find themselves in a battle to liberate the

Vol. 81
LET'S GO SEE THE CAT VIPER

CONTENTS

Chapter 807:
TEN DAYS EARLIER

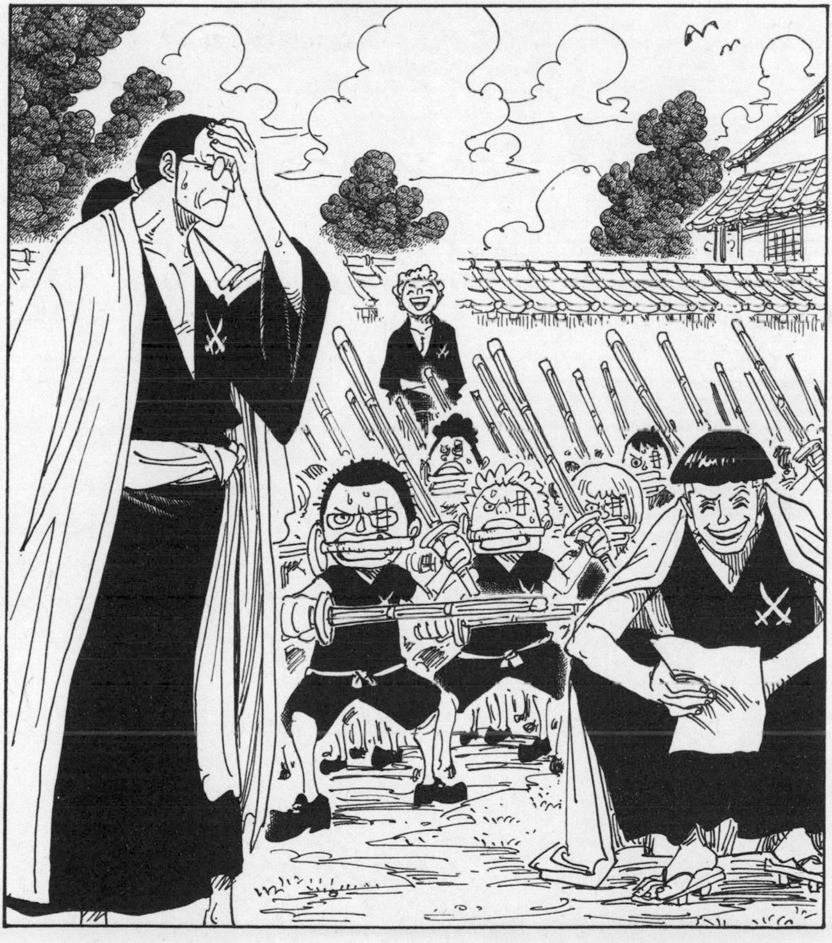

DECKS OF THE WORLD, 500-MILLION-MAN ARC,
VOL. 3: "FROST-MOON VILLAGE"

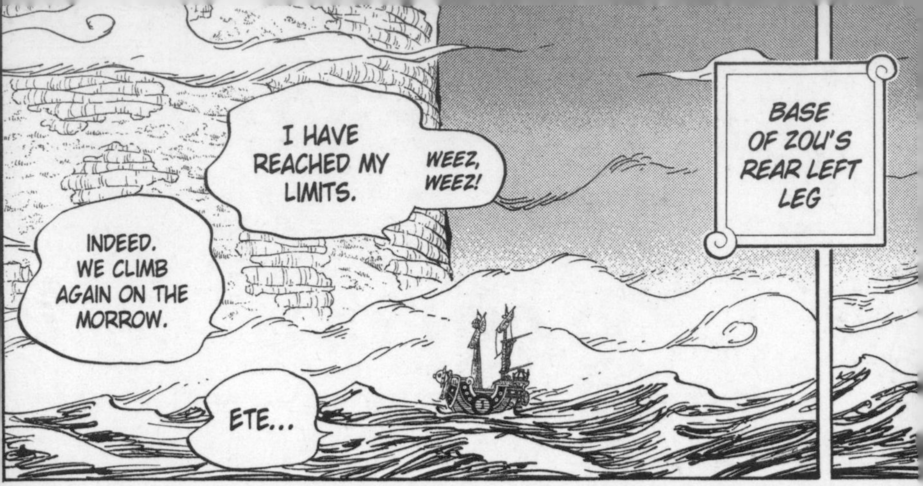
BASE OF ZOU'S REAR LEFT LEG
WEEZ, WEEZ!
I HAVE REACHED MY LIMITS.
INDEED. WE CLIMB AGAIN ON THE MORROW.
ETE...

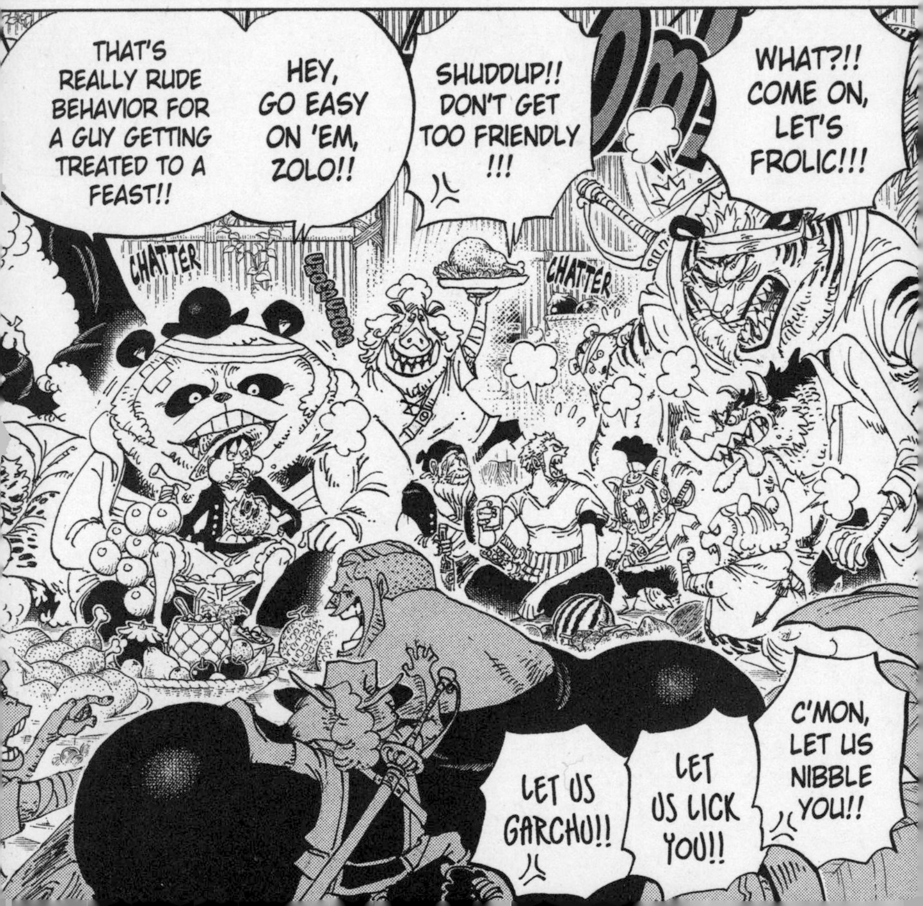
WHAT?!! COME ON, LET'S FROLIC!!!
SHUDDUP!! DON'T GET TOO FRIENDLY !!!
HEY, GO EASY ON 'EM, ZOLO!!
THAT'S REALLY RUDE BEHAVIOR FOR A GUY GETTING TREATED TO A FEAST!!
CHATTER
CHATTER
C'MON, LET US NIBBLE YOU!!
LET US LICK YOU!!
LET US GARCHU!!

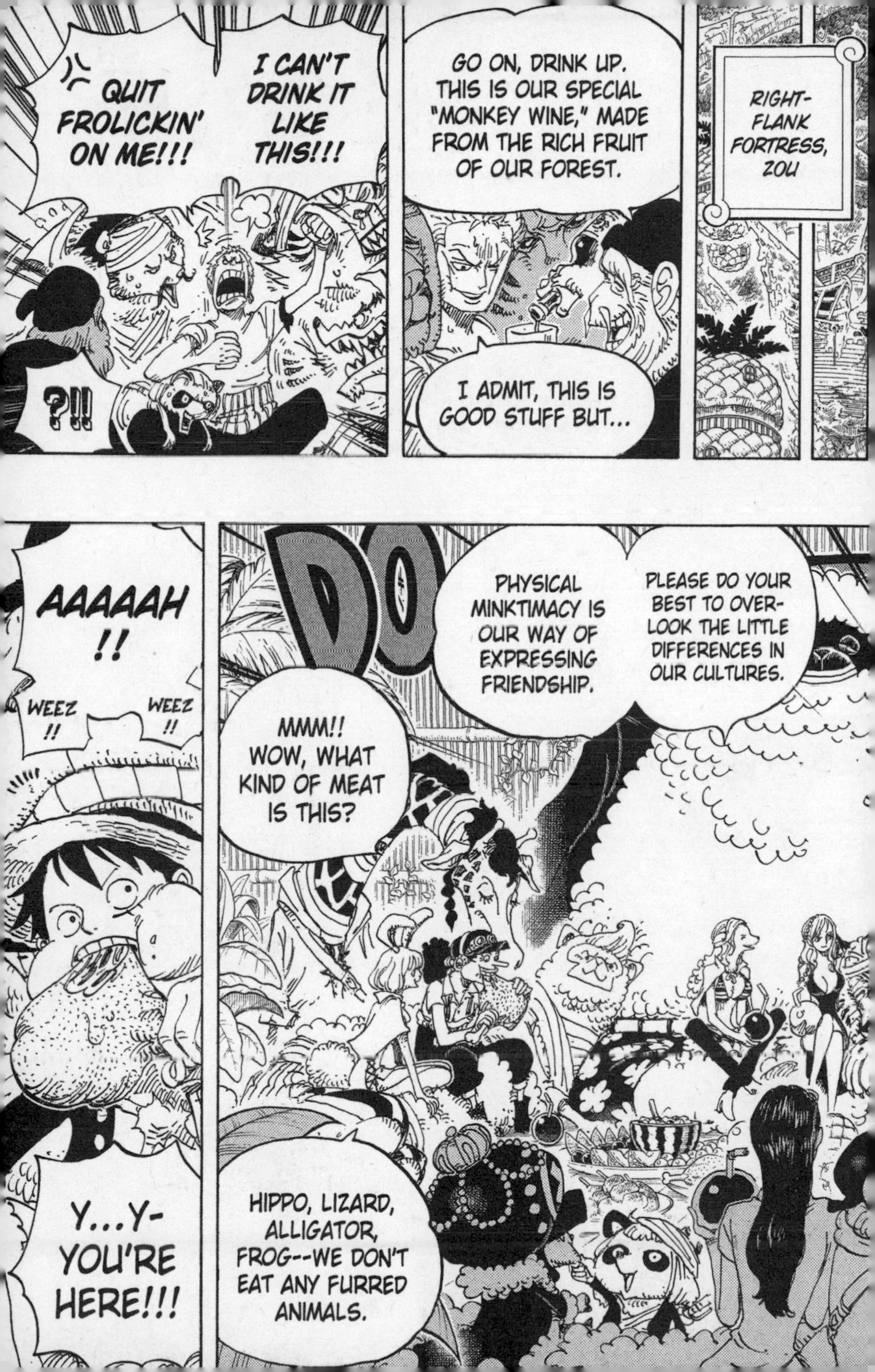
RIGHT-FLANK FORTRESS, ZOU
GO ON, DRINK UP. THIS IS OUR SPECIAL "MONKEY WINE," MADE FROM THE RICH FRUIT OF OUR FOREST.
I ADMIT, THIS IS GOOD STUFF BUT...
I CAN'T DRINK IT LIKE THIS!!!
QUIT FROLICKIN' ON ME!!!
?!!
DO
PLEASE DO YOUR BEST TO OVER-LOOK THE LITTLE DIFFERENCES IN OUR CULTURES.
PHYSICAL MINKTIMACY IS OUR WAY OF EXPRESSING FRIENDSHIP.
MMM!! WOW, WHAT KIND OF MEAT IS THIS?
HIPPO, LIZARD, ALLIGATOR, FROG--WE DON'T EAT ANY FURRED ANIMALS.
AAAAAH!!
WEEZ!!
WEEZ!!
Y...Y-YOU'RE HERE!!!

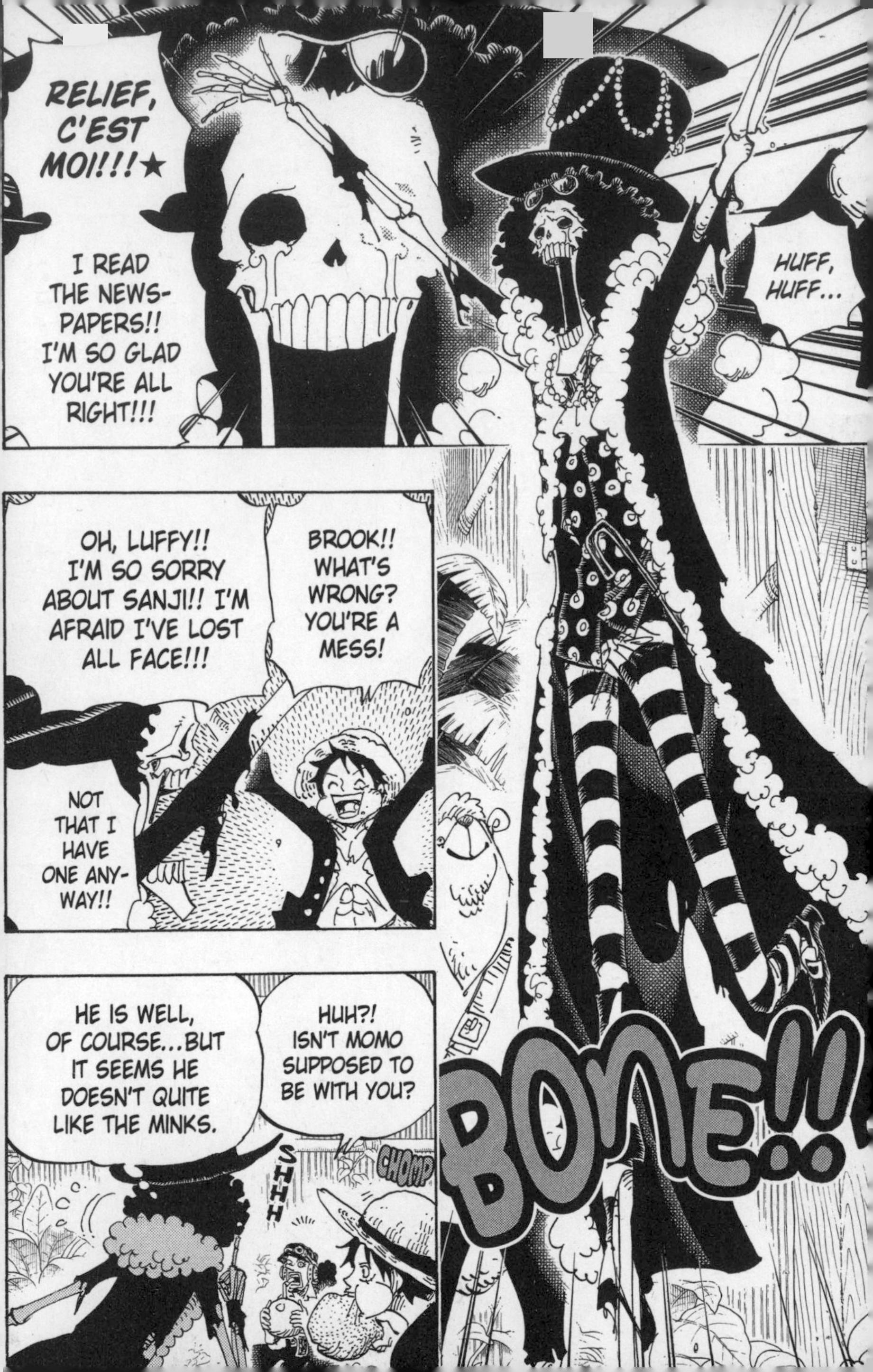
HUFF, HUFF...
BONE!!...
RELIEF, C'EST MOI!!!★
I READ THE NEWS-PAPERS!! I'M SO GLAD YOU'RE ALL RIGHT!!!
BROOK!! WHAT'S WRONG? YOU'RE A MESS!
OH, LUFFY!! I'M SO SORRY ABOUT SANJI!! I'M AFRAID I'VE LOST ALL FACE!!!
NOT THAT I HAVE ONE ANY-WAY!!
HUH?! ISN'T MOMO SUPPOSED TO BE WITH YOU?
HE IS WELL, OF COURSE...BUT IT SEEMS HE DOESN'T QUITE LIKE THE MINKS.
CHOMP
SHHH

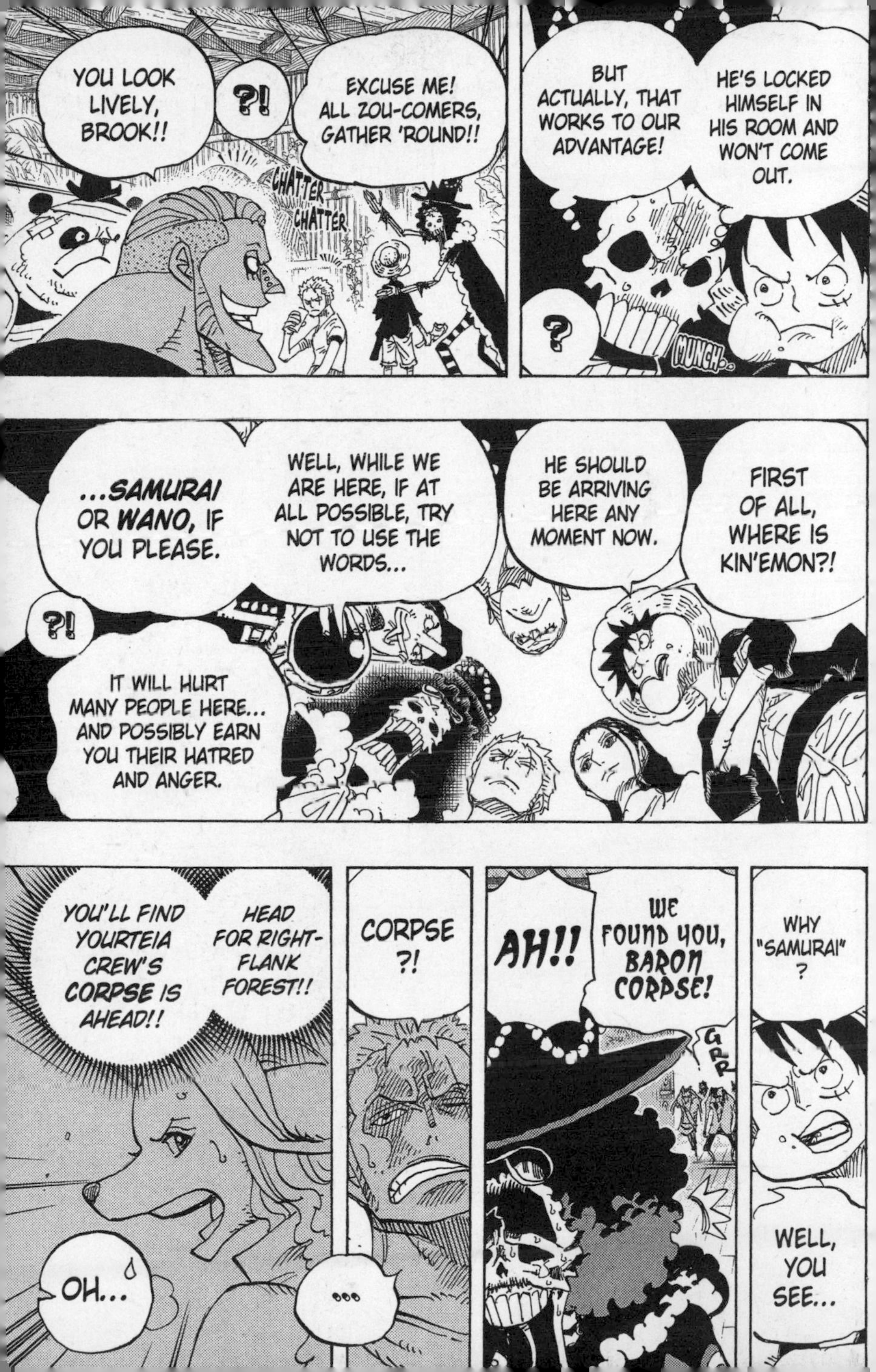
HE'S LOCKED HIMSELF IN HIS ROOM AND WON'T COME OUT.
BUT ACTUALLY, THAT WORKS TO OUR ADVANTAGE!
?
MUNCH
EXCUSE ME! ALL ZOU-COMERS, GATHER 'ROUND!!
?!
YOU LOOK LIVELY, BROOK!!
CHATTER CHATTER
FIRST OF ALL, WHERE IS KIN'EMON?!
HE SHOULD BE ARRIVING HERE ANY MOMENT NOW.
WELL, WHILE WE ARE HERE, IF AT ALL POSSIBLE, TRY NOT TO USE THE WORDS...
...SAMURAI OR WANO, IF YOU PLEASE.
?!
IT WILL HURT MANY PEOPLE HERE... AND POSSIBLY EARN YOU THEIR HATRED AND ANGER.
WHY "SAMURAI"?
WELL, YOU SEE...
WE FOUND YOU, BARON CORPSE!
AH!!
GRR
CORPSE?!
...
HEAD FOR RIGHT-FLANK FOREST!!
YOU'LL FIND YOURTEIA CREW'S CORPSE IS AHEAD!!
OH...

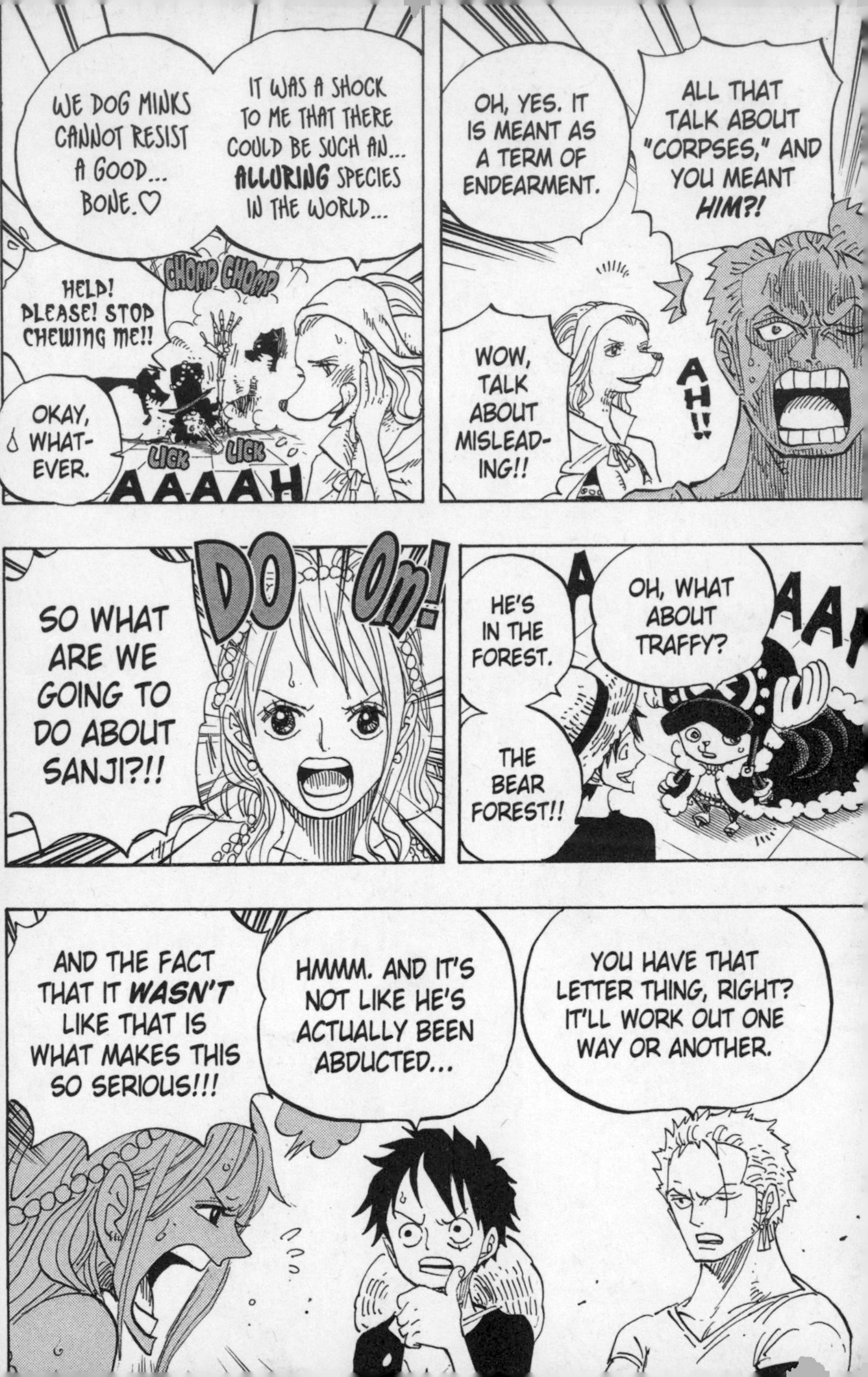
ALL THAT TALK ABOUT "CORPSES," AND YOU MEANT *HIM?!*
OH, YES. IT IS MEANT AS A TERM OF ENDEARMENT.
AH!!
WOW, TALK ABOUT MISLEADING!!
IT WAS A SHOCK TO ME THAT THERE COULD BE SUCH AN... **ALLURING** SPECIES IN THE WORLD...
WE DOG MINKS CANNOT RESIST A GOOD... BONE.♡
CHOMP CHOMP
HELP! PLEASE! STOP CHEWING ME!!
LICK LICK
AAAAH
OKAY, WHATEVER.
OH, WHAT ABOUT TRAFFY?
HE'S IN THE FOREST.
THE BEAR FOREST!!
DOOM!
SO WHAT ARE WE GOING TO DO ABOUT SANJI?!!
YOU HAVE THAT LETTER THING, RIGHT? IT'LL WORK OUT ONE WAY OR ANOTHER.
HMMM. AND IT'S NOT LIKE HE'S ACTUALLY BEEN ABDUCTED...
AND THE FACT THAT IT *WASN'T* LIKE THAT IS WHAT MAKES THIS SO SERIOUS!!!

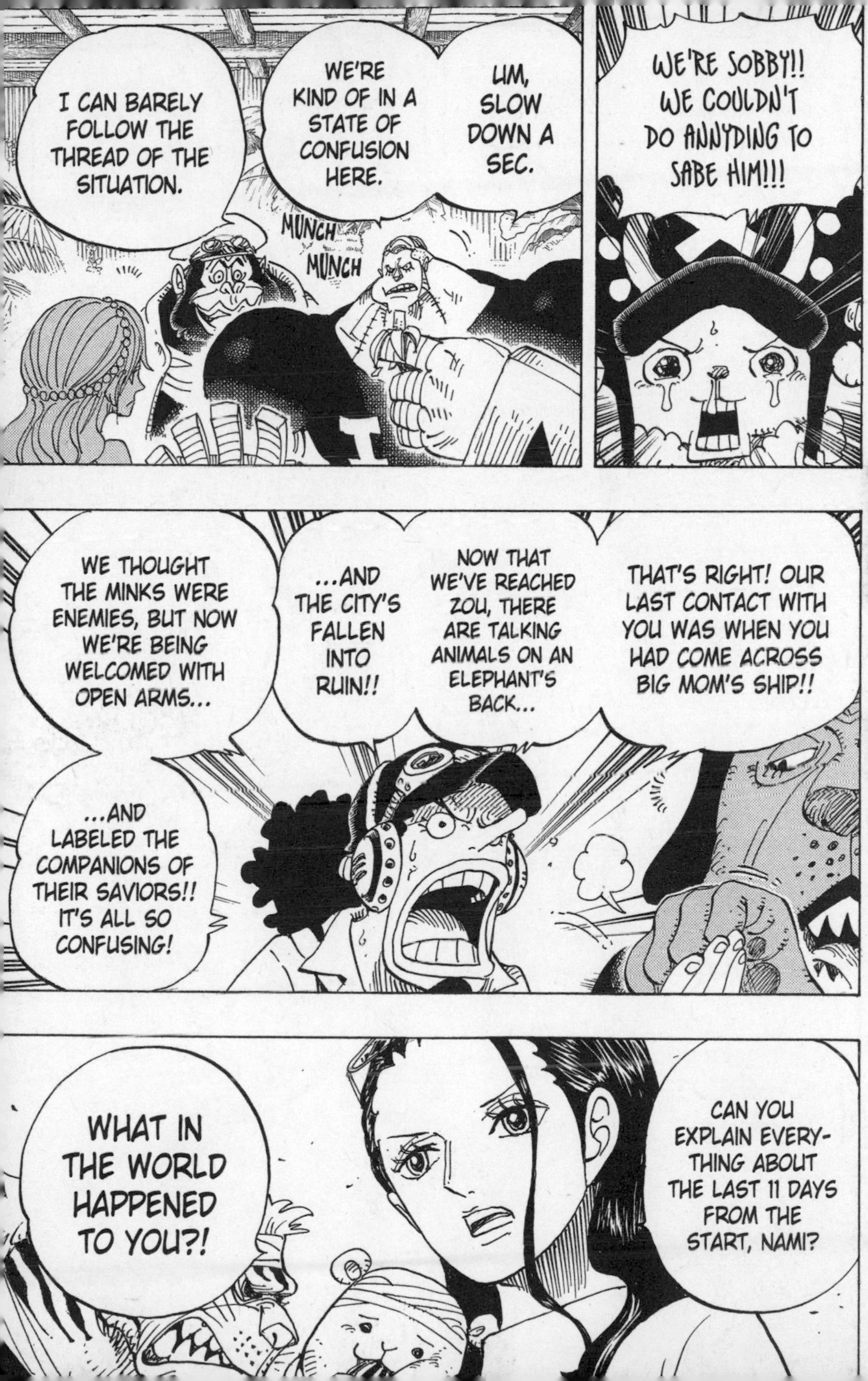
WE'RE SOBBY!! WE COULDN'T DO ANNYDING TO SABE HIM!!!
UM, SLOW DOWN A SEC.
WE'RE KIND OF IN A STATE OF CONFUSION HERE.
I CAN BARELY FOLLOW THE THREAD OF THE SITUATION.
MUNCH
MUNCH
THAT'S RIGHT! OUR LAST CONTACT WITH YOU WAS WHEN YOU HAD COME ACROSS BIG MOM'S SHIP!!
NOW THAT WE'VE REACHED ZOU, THERE ARE TALKING ANIMALS ON AN ELEPHANT'S BACK...
...AND THE CITY'S FALLEN INTO RUIN!!
WE THOUGHT THE MINKS WERE ENEMIES, BUT NOW WE'RE BEING WELCOMED WITH OPEN ARMS...
...AND LABELED THE COMPANIONS OF THEIR SAVIORS!! IT'S ALL SO CONFUSING!
CAN YOU EXPLAIN EVERY-THING ABOUT THE LAST 11 DAYS FROM THE START, NAMI?
WHAT IN THE WORLD HAPPENED TO YOU?!

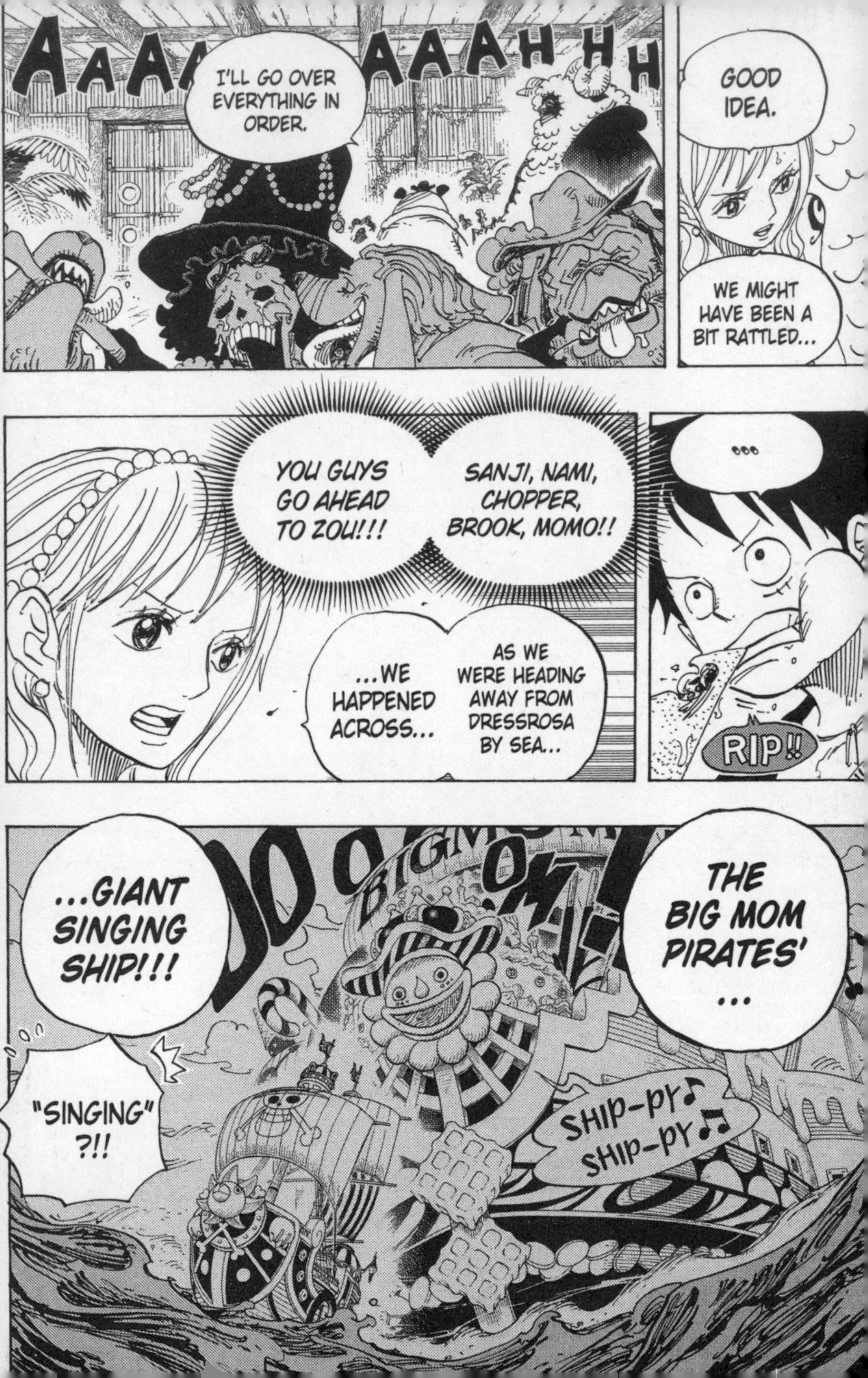
GOOD IDEA.
WE MIGHT HAVE BEEN A BIT RATTLED...
I'LL GO OVER EVERYTHING IN ORDER.
...
RIP!!
SANJI, NAMI, CHOPPER, BROOK, MOMO!!
YOU GUYS GO AHEAD TO ZOU!!!
AS WE WERE HEADING AWAY FROM DRESSROSA BY SEA...
...WE HAPPENED ACROSS...
THE BIG MOM PIRATES' ...
...GIANT SINGING SHIP!!!
SHIP-PY♪ SHIP-PY♪
"SINGING" ?!!

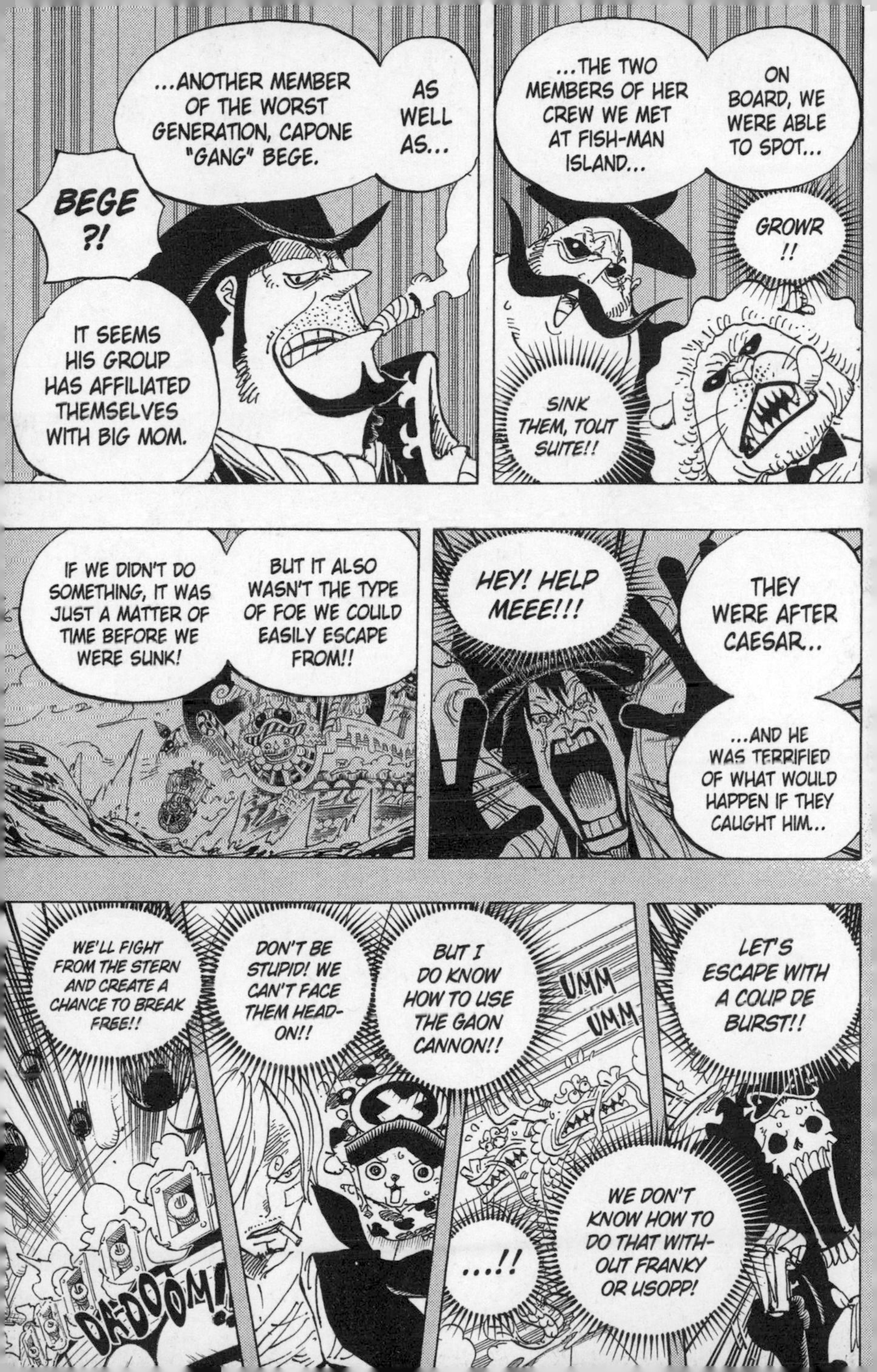
ON BOARD, WE WERE ABLE TO SPOT...
...THE TWO MEMBERS OF HER CREW WE MET AT FISH-MAN ISLAND...
GROWR!!
SINK THEM, TOUT SUITE!!
AS WELL AS...
...ANOTHER MEMBER OF THE WORST GENERATION, CAPONE "GANG" BEGE.
BEGE?!
IT SEEMS HIS GROUP HAS AFFILIATED THEMSELVES WITH BIG MOM.
THEY WERE AFTER CAESAR...
...AND HE WAS TERRIFIED OF WHAT WOULD HAPPEN IF THEY CAUGHT HIM...
HEY! HELP MEEE!!!
BUT IT ALSO WASN'T THE TYPE OF FOE WE COULD EASILY ESCAPE FROM!!
IF WE DIDN'T DO SOMETHING, IT WAS JUST A MATTER OF TIME BEFORE WE WERE SUNK!
LET'S ESCAPE WITH A COUP DE BURST!!
WE DON'T KNOW HOW TO DO THAT WITH-OUT FRANKY OR USOPP!
UMM
UMM
BUT I DO KNOW HOW TO USE THE GAON CANNON!!
...!!
DON'T BE STUPID! WE CAN'T FACE THEM HEAD-ON!!
WE'LL FIGHT FROM THE STERN AND CREATE A CHANCE TO BREAK FREE!!
DA-DOOM!!

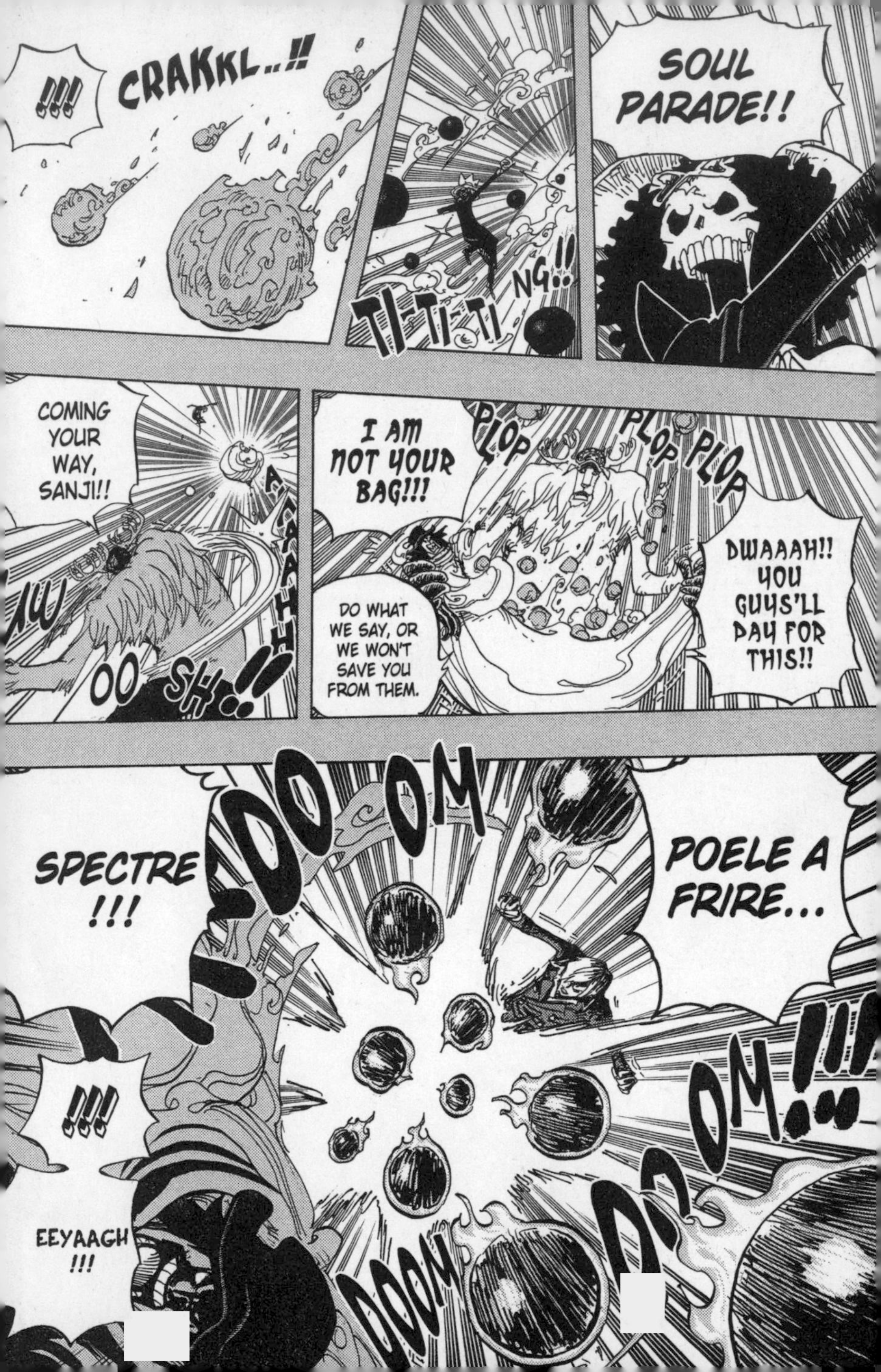
SOUL PARADE!!
TI-TI-TI NG!!
!!!
CRAKKL..!!
I AM NOT YOUR BAG!!!
PLOP PLOP PLOP
DWAAAH!! YOU GUYS'LL PAY FOR THIS!!
DO WHAT WE SAY, OR WE WON'T SAVE YOU FROM THEM.
COMING YOUR WAY, SANJI!!
OO SH..!!
POELE A FRIRE...
SPECTRE !!!
DOOM
!!!
EEYAAGH !!!
DOOM DOOM!!!

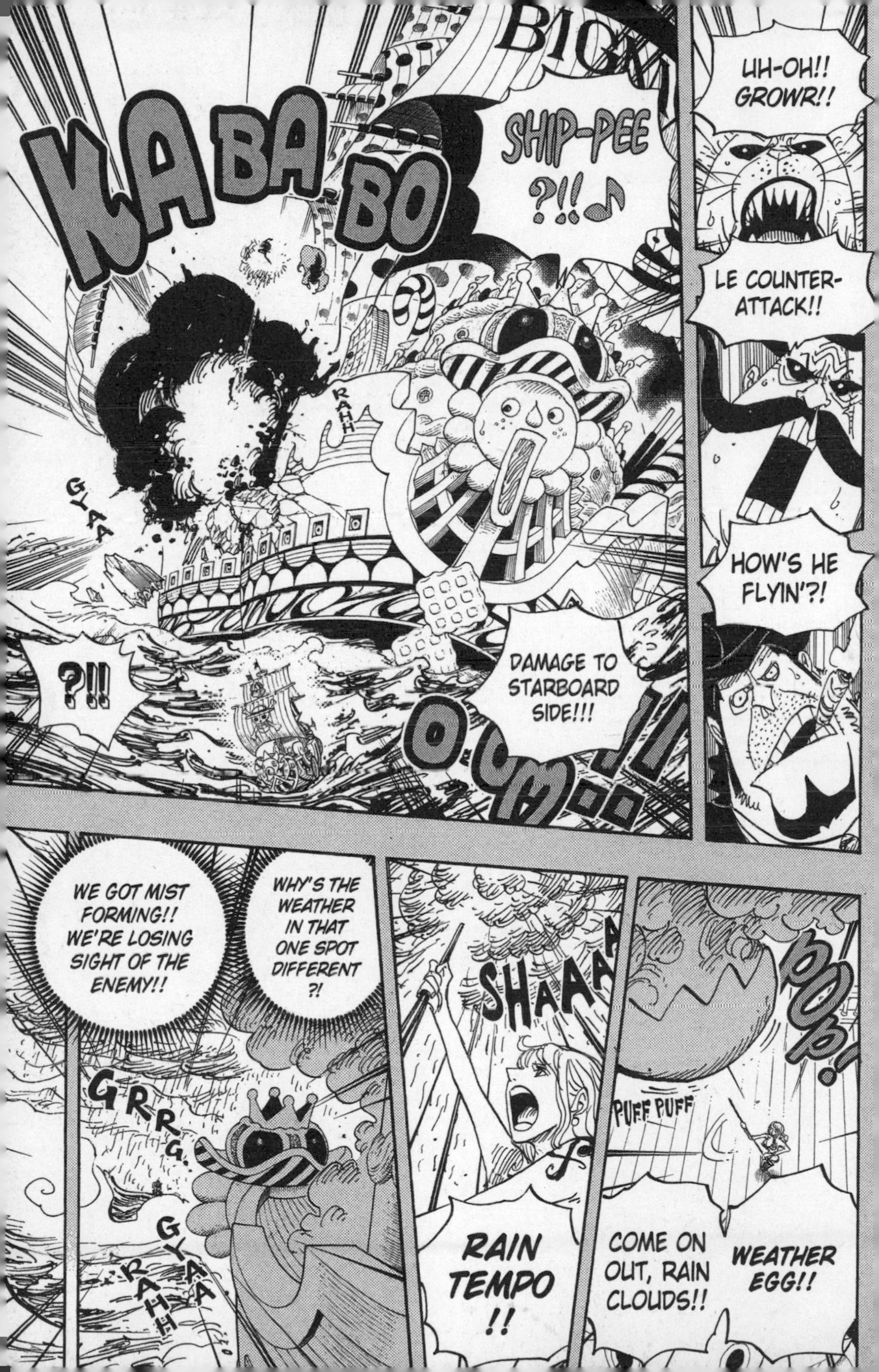
UH-OH!! GROWR!!
LE COUNTER-ATTACK!!
HOW'S HE FLYIN'?!
SHIP-PEE ?!!♪
KA BA BO
RAHH
GYAA
DAMAGE TO STARBOARD SIDE!!!
?!!
DOOM!!
POP!
PUFF PUFF
WEATHER EGG!!
COME ON OUT, RAIN CLOUDS!!
SHAAA
RAIN TEMPO!!
WHY'S THE WEATHER IN THAT ONE SPOT DIFFERENT?!
WE GOT MIST FORMING!! WE'RE LOSING SIGHT OF THE ENEMY!!
GRRRG
GYAA
RAHH

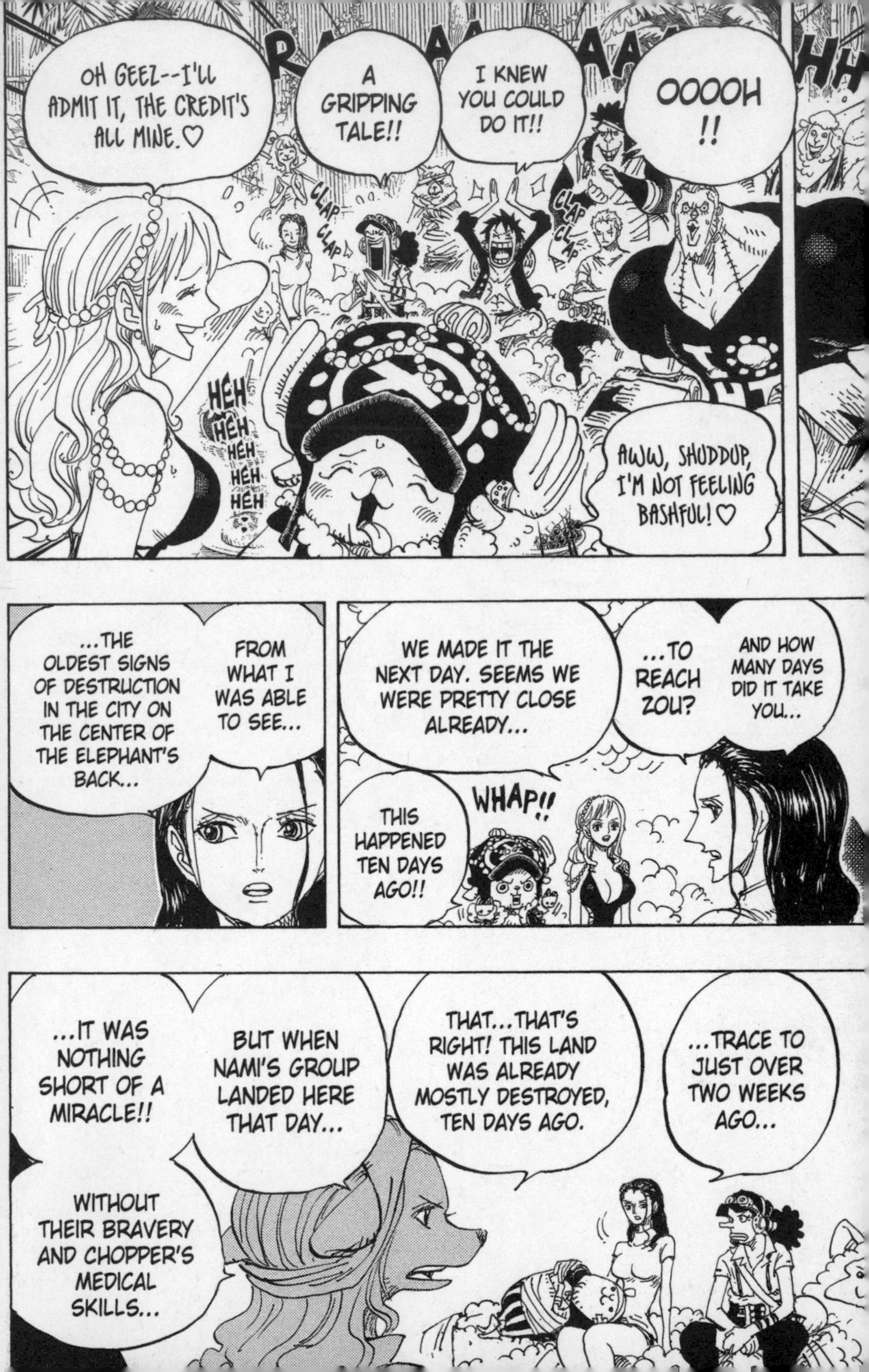
OOOOH!!
I KNEW YOU COULD DO IT!!
A GRIPPING TALE!!
OH GEEZ--I'LL ADMIT IT, THE CREDIT'S ALL MINE. ♡
CLAP CLAP CLAP
CLAP CLAP CLAP
AWW, SHUDDUP, I'M NOT FEELING BASHFUL! ♡
HEH HEH HEH HEH HEH
AND HOW MANY DAYS DID IT TAKE YOU...
...TO REACH ZOU?
WE MADE IT THE NEXT DAY. SEEMS WE WERE PRETTY CLOSE ALREADY...
WHAP!!
THIS HAPPENED TEN DAYS AGO!!
FROM WHAT I WAS ABLE TO SEE...
...THE OLDEST SIGNS OF DESTRUCTION IN THE CITY ON THE CENTER OF THE ELEPHANT'S BACK...
...TRACE TO JUST OVER TWO WEEKS AGO...
THAT...THAT'S RIGHT! THIS LAND WAS ALREADY MOSTLY DESTROYED, TEN DAYS AGO.
BUT WHEN NAMI'S GROUP LANDED HERE THAT DAY...
...IT WAS NOTHING SHORT OF A MIRACLE!!
WITHOUT THEIR BRAVERY AND CHOPPER'S MEDICAL SKILLS...

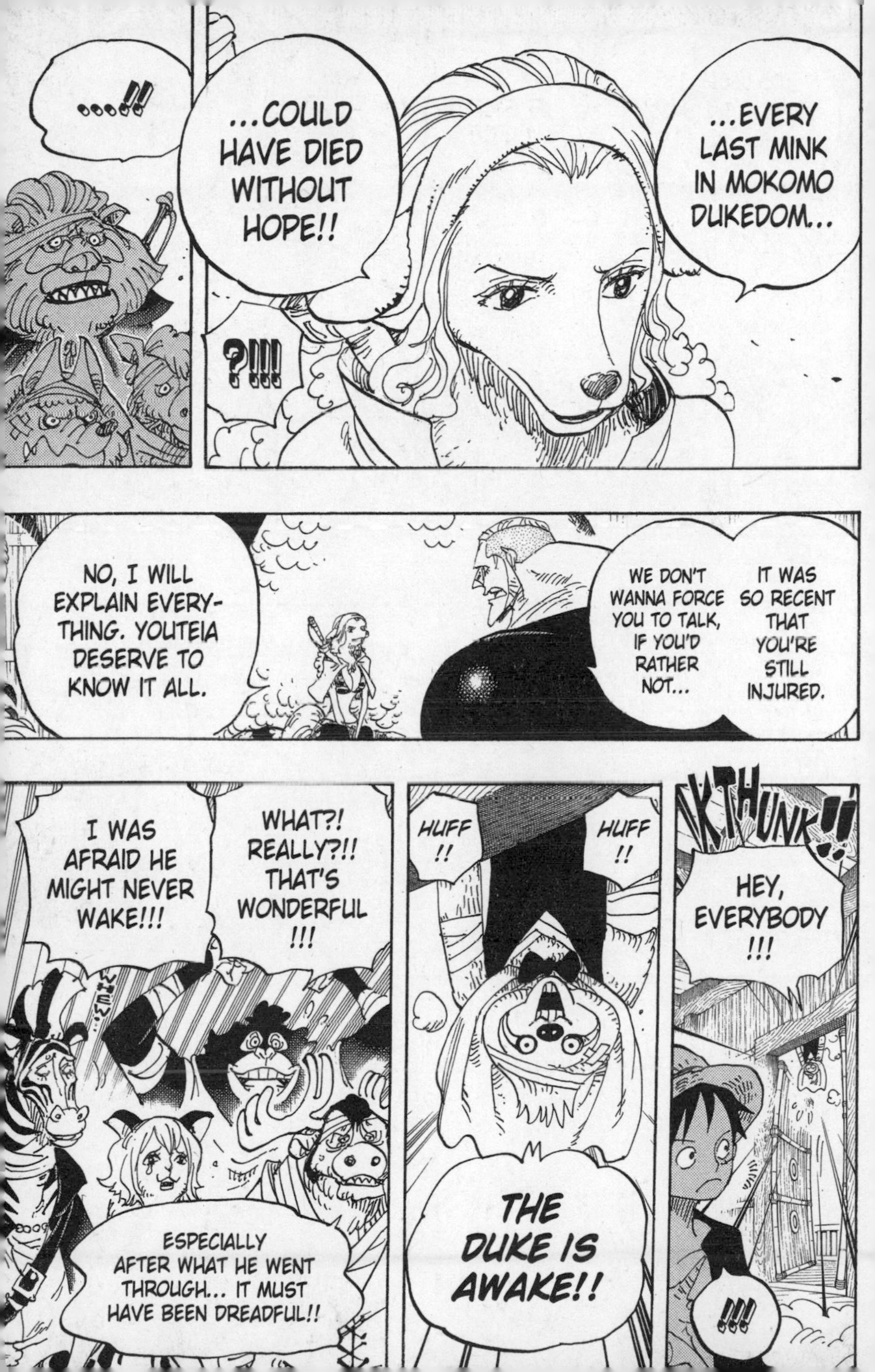
...EVERY LAST MINK IN MOKOMO DUKEDOM...
...COULD HAVE DIED WITHOUT HOPE!!
?!!!
....!!
IT WAS SO RECENT THAT YOU'RE STILL INJURED.
WE DON'T WANNA FORCE YOU TO TALK, IF YOU'D RATHER NOT...
NO, I WILL EXPLAIN EVERY-THING. YOUTEIA DESERVE TO KNOW IT ALL.
KTHUNK!!
HEY, EVERYBODY!!!
!!!
HUFF!!
HUFF!!
THE DUKE IS AWAKE!!
WHAT?! REALLY?!! THAT'S WONDERFUL!!!
I WAS AFRAID HE MIGHT NEVER WAKE!!!
WHEW...
ESPECIALLY AFTER WHAT HE WENT THROUGH... IT MUST HAVE BEEN DREADFUL!!

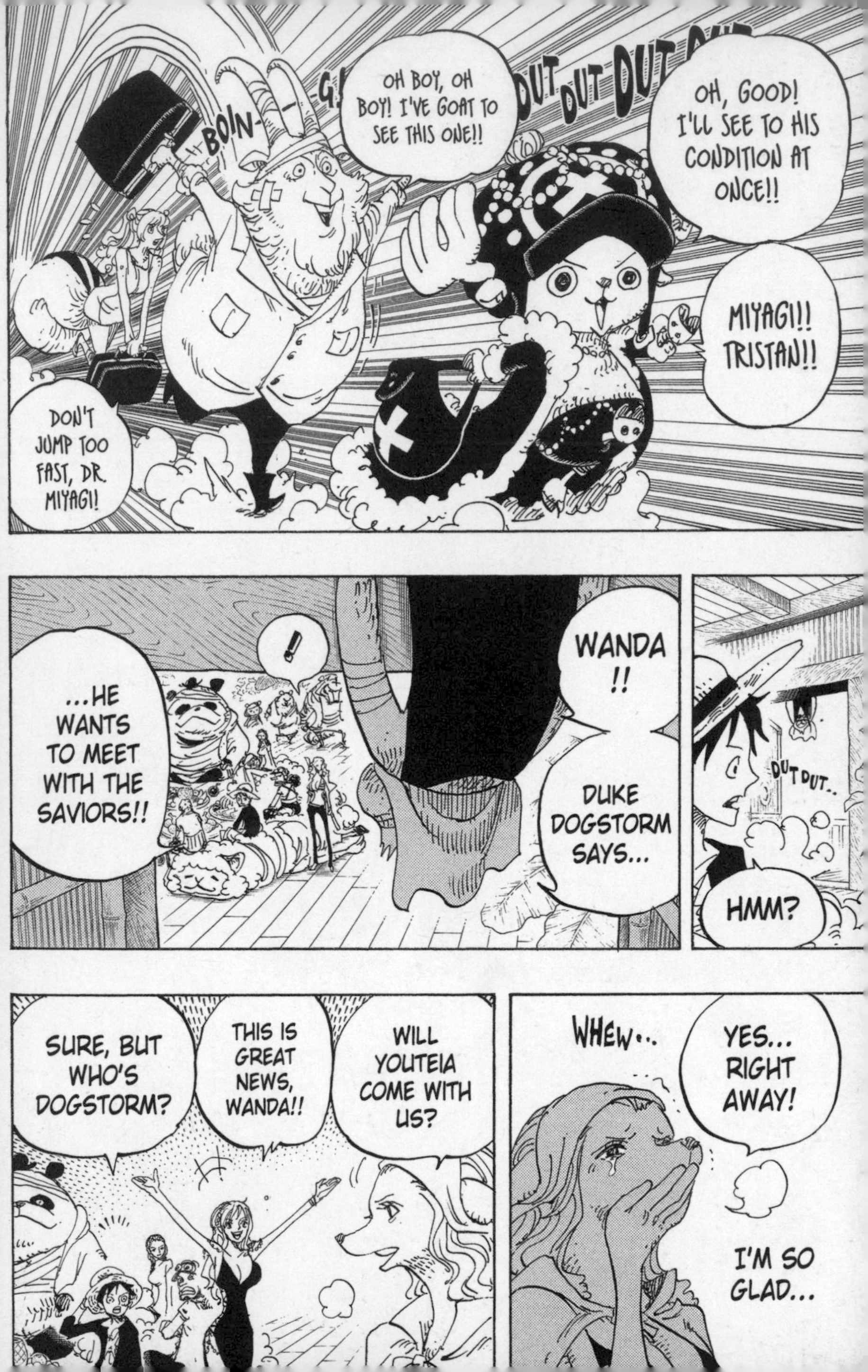
OH, GOOD! I'LL SEE TO HIS CONDITION AT ONCE!!
DUT DUT DUT
OH BOY, OH BOY! I'VE GOAT TO SEE THIS ONE!!
BOIN--G!
MIYAGI!! TRISTAN!!
DON'T JUMP TOO FAST, DR. MIYAGI!
DUT DUT..
HMM?
WANDA!!
DUKE DOGSTORM SAYS...
!
...HE WANTS TO MEET WITH THE SAVIORS!!
YES... RIGHT AWAY!
WHEW...
I'M SO GLAD...
WILL YOUTEIA COME WITH US?
THIS IS GREAT NEWS, WANDA!!
SURE, BUT WHO'S DOGSTORM?

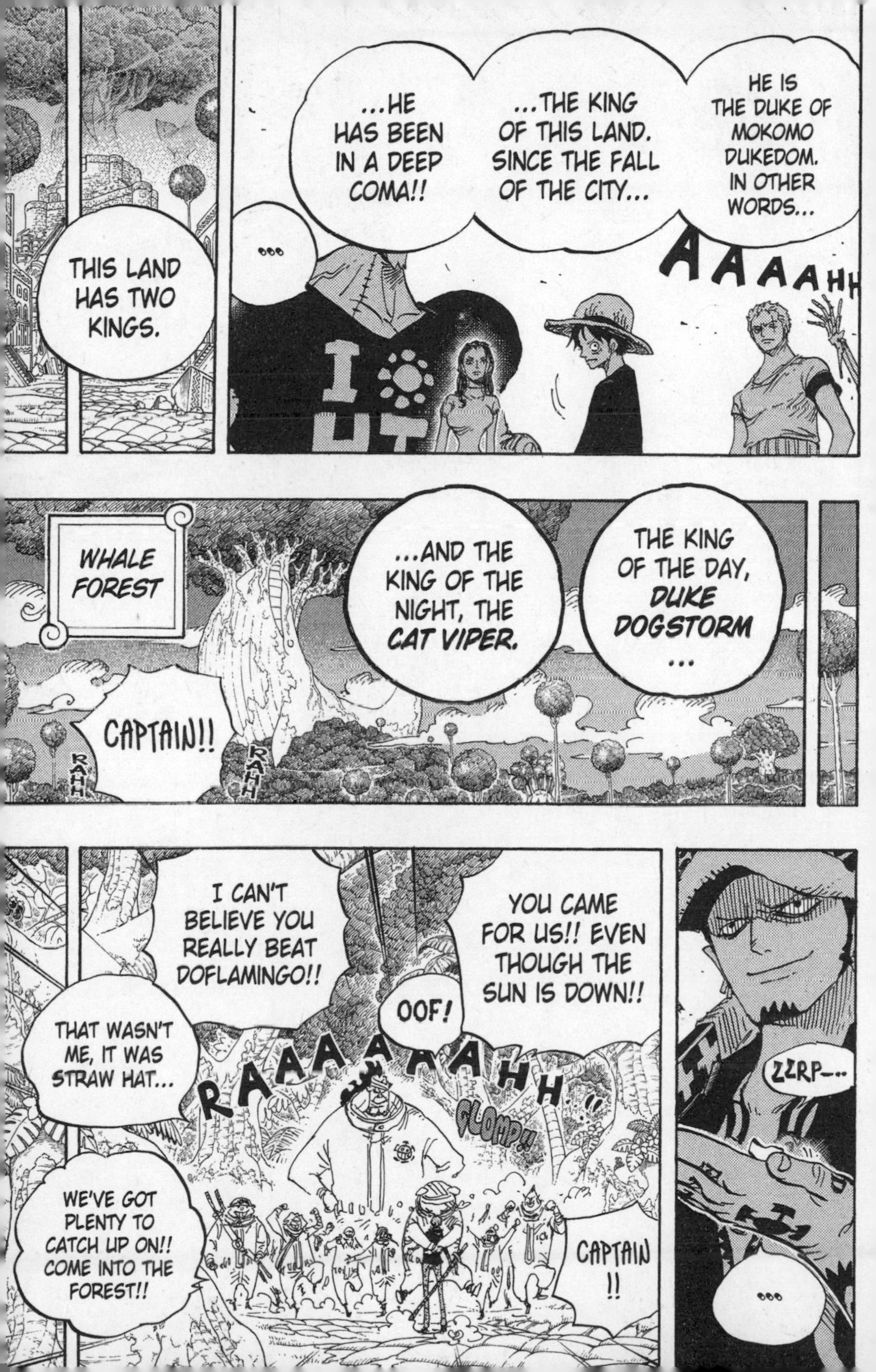
HE IS THE DUKE OF MOKOMO DUKEDOM. IN OTHER WORDS...
...THE KING OF THIS LAND. SINCE THE FALL OF THE CITY...
...HE HAS BEEN IN A DEEP COMA!!
AAAAHH
...
THIS LAND HAS TWO KINGS.
THE KING OF THE DAY, DUKE DOGSTORM ...
...AND THE KING OF THE NIGHT, THE CAT VIPER.
WHALE FOREST
CAPTAIN!!
RAHH
RAHH
ZZRP-...
...
YOU CAME FOR US!! EVEN THOUGH THE SUN IS DOWN!!
I CAN'T BELIEVE YOU REALLY BEAT DOFLAMINGO!!
OOF!
RAAAAAAAHH
FLOMP!!
THAT WASN'T ME, IT WAS STRAW HAT...
CAPTAIN !!
WE'VE GOT PLENTY TO CATCH UP ON!! COME INTO THE FOREST!!

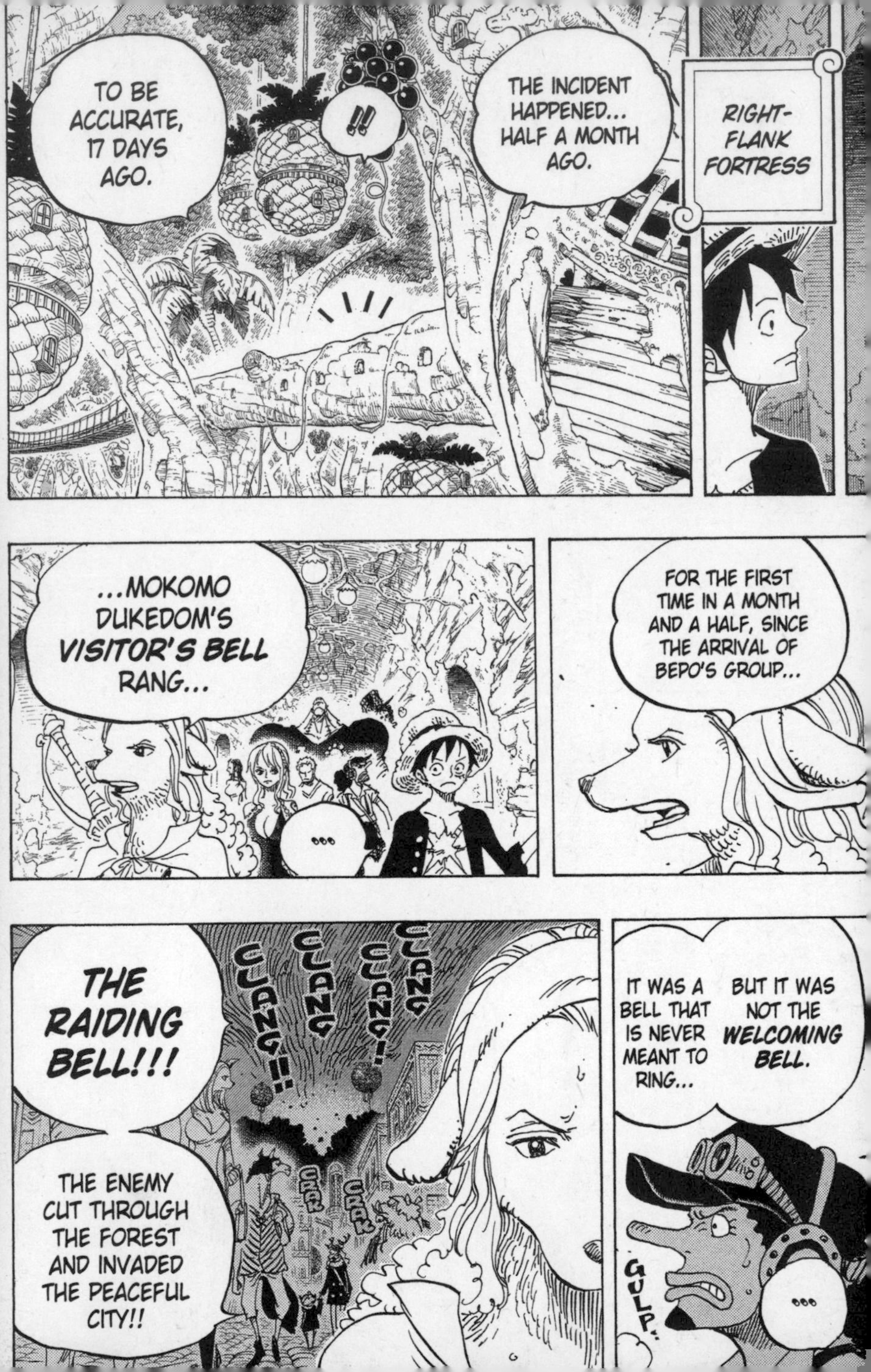
RIGHT-FLANK FORTRESS
THE INCIDENT HAPPENED... HALF A MONTH AGO.
!!
TO BE ACCURATE, 17 DAYS AGO.
FOR THE FIRST TIME IN A MONTH AND A HALF, SINCE THE ARRIVAL OF BEPO'S GROUP...
...MOKOMO DUKEDOM'S VISITOR'S BELL RANG...
...
BUT IT WAS NOT THE WELCOMING BELL.
IT WAS A BELL THAT IS NEVER MEANT TO RING...
GULP.
...
CLANG CLANG
CLANG CLANG!
CLANG CLANG!!
THE RAIDING BELL!!!
CRAK CRAK
THE ENEMY CUT THROUGH THE FOREST AND INVADED THE PEACEFUL CITY!!

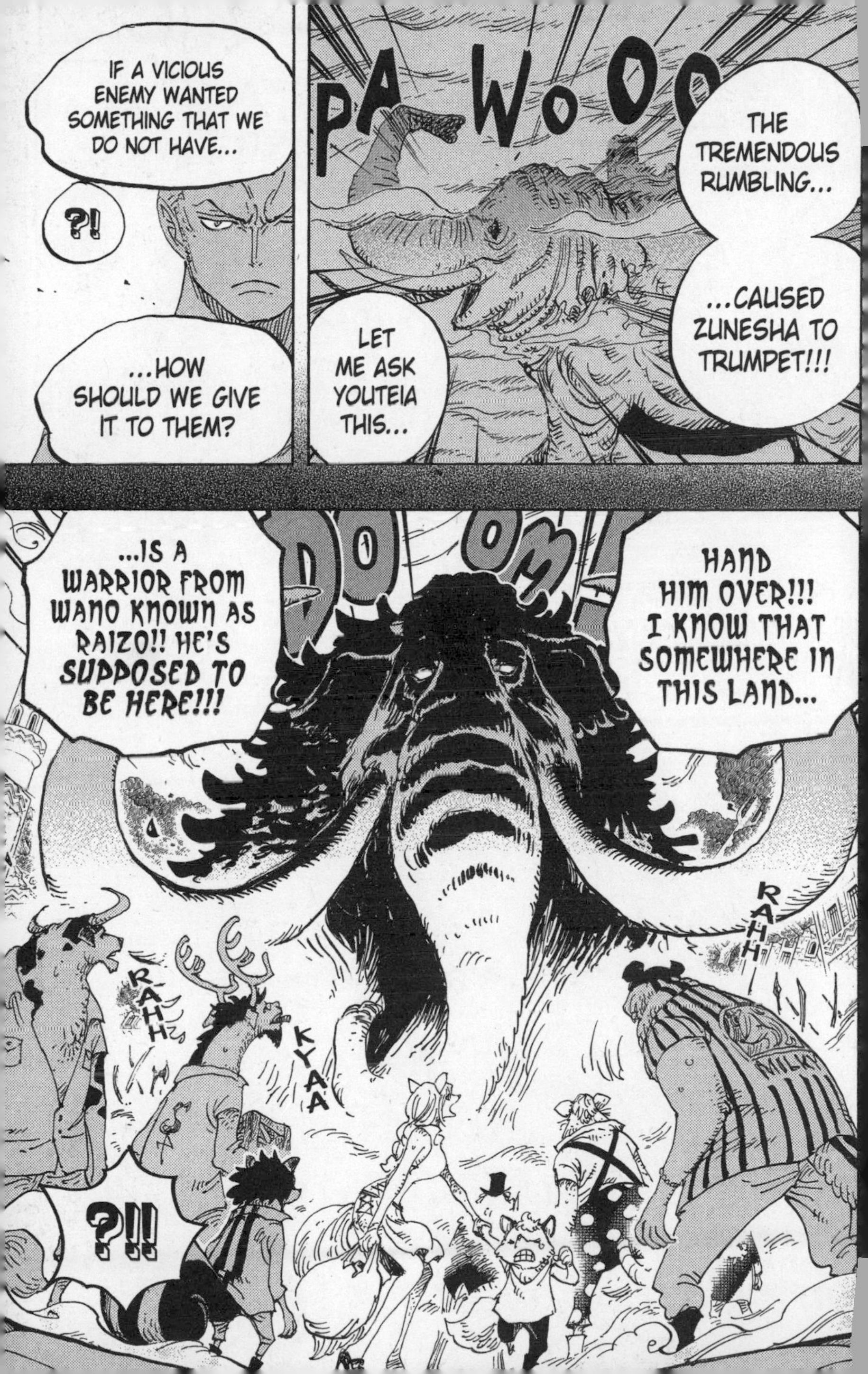
PAWOO
THE TREMENDOUS RUMBLING...
...CAUSED ZUNESHA TO TRUMPET!!!
LET ME ASK YOUTEIA THIS...
IF A VICIOUS ENEMY WANTED SOMETHING THAT WE DO NOT HAVE...
?!
...HOW SHOULD WE GIVE IT TO THEM?
DOOM!
HAND HIM OVER!!! I KNOW THAT SOMEWHERE IN THIS LAND...
...IS A WARRIOR FROM WANO KNOWN AS RAIZO!! HE'S SUPPOSED TO BE HERE!!!
RAHH
KYAA
RAHH
?!!
MILKY

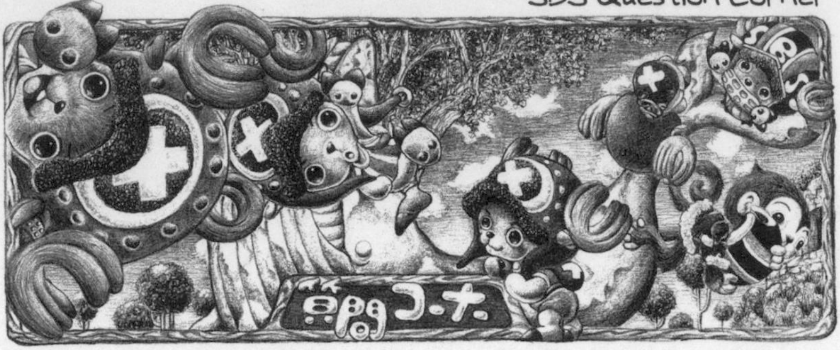

(Takahisa Fujimoto, Nara)

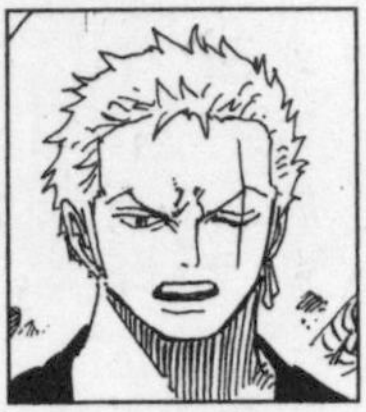

Q: Greetings! Odattsu! Since all ya do is tell dirty jokes on this here SBS, we students are going to do this without you!!

Start on up that SBS!!

Odacchi, Odacchi! I want to see Zolo with a shaved head. Show me!!

--Zolo-loving Misaki (age 15)

A:

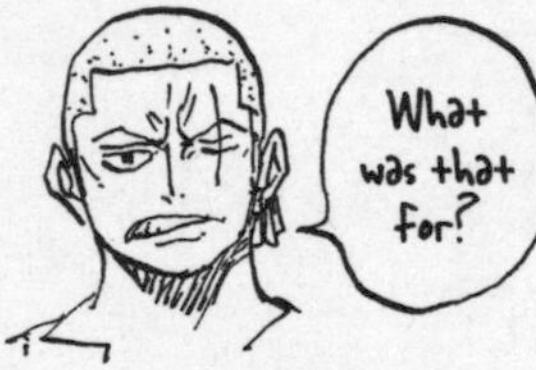
What was that for?

What's the big idea?! The Q&A's starting without me, Zolo's got no hair...none of this makes any sense!

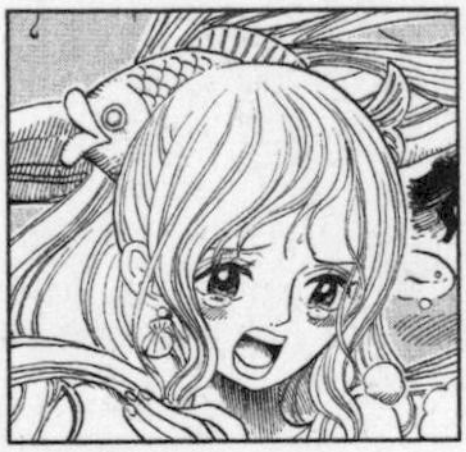

Q: Hello, Odacchi! What is that thing resting on Shirahoshi's head?

--Witch Girl Takkun

A: It's a taiyaki pastry full of sweet red bean paste.

Q: Please draw what Fujitora sees when he envisions Luffy's "kindly" face!!

--Peko

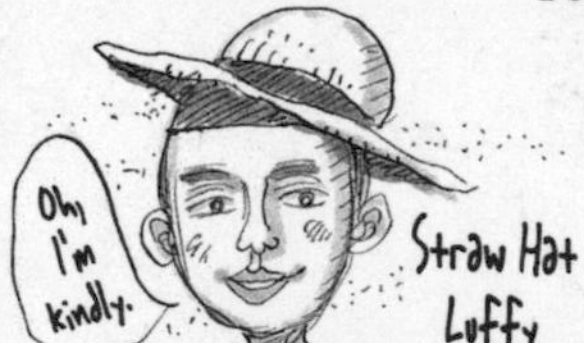
Oh I'm kindly.
Straw Hat Luffy

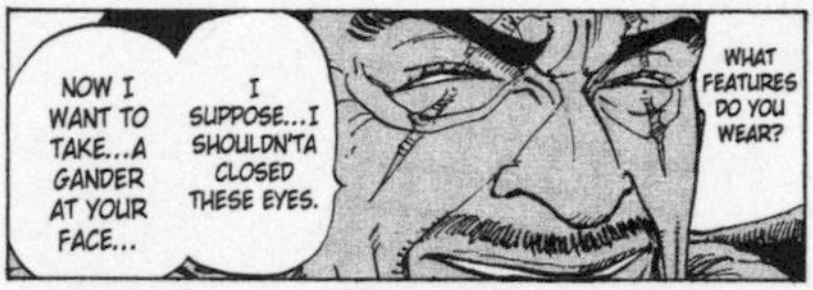
WHAT FEATURES DO YOU WEAR?
I SUPPOSE...I SHOULDN'TA CLOSED THESE EYES.
NOW I WANT TO TAKE...A GANDER AT YOUR FACE...

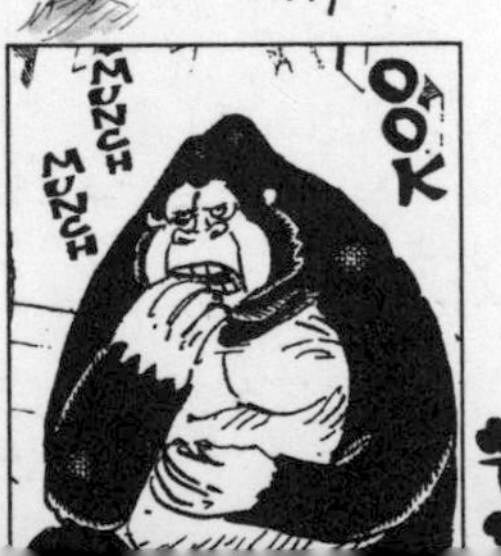
OOK
MUNCH
MUNCH

Q: What's the name of the gorilla hanging out with Sengoku? Is it "Ook-Ook"? Can he be named Ook-Ook? Does Ook-Ook like the Navy-brand crackers?

--Hijiki

A: Um...okay... He's the Navy-cracker-loving gorilla...Ook-Ook...

Chapter 808:

DUKE DOGSTORM

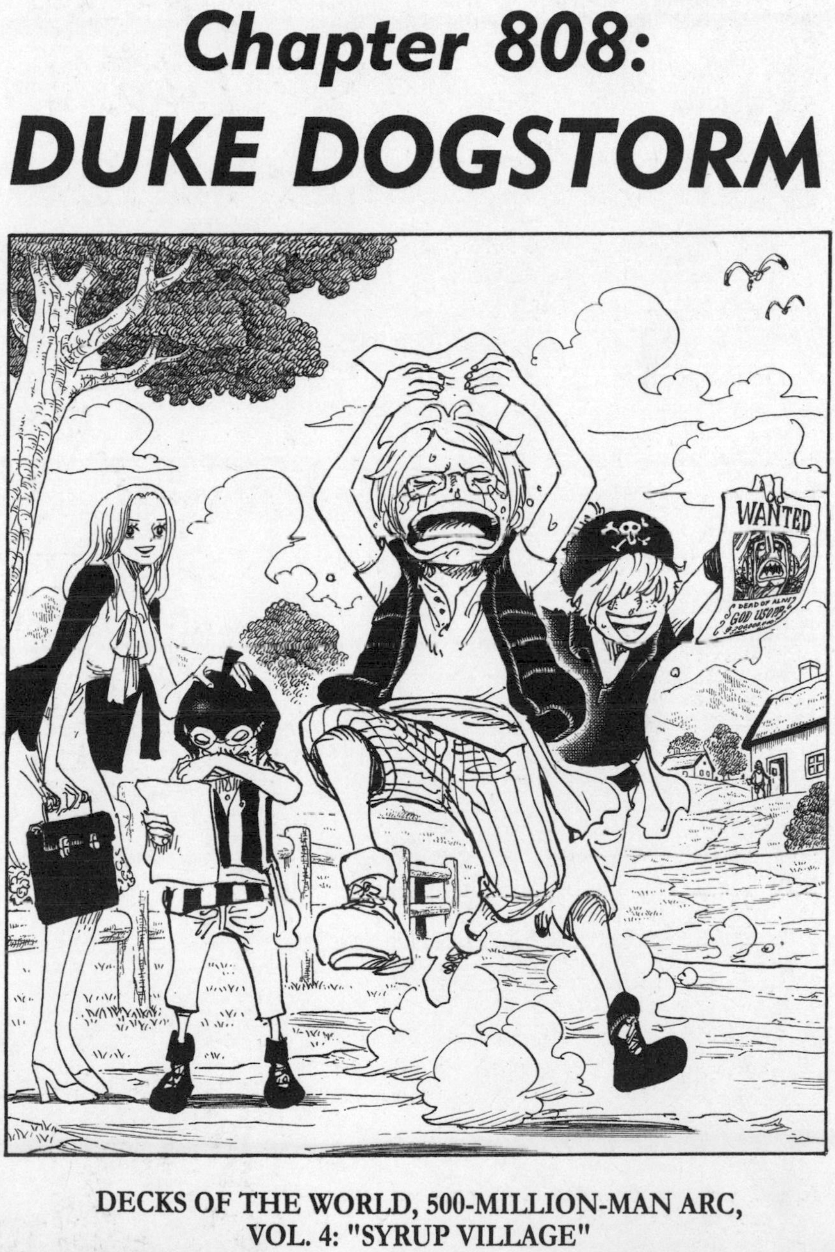
WANTED

DECKS OF THE WORLD, 500-MILLION-MAN ARC,
VOL. 4: "SYRUP VILLAGE"

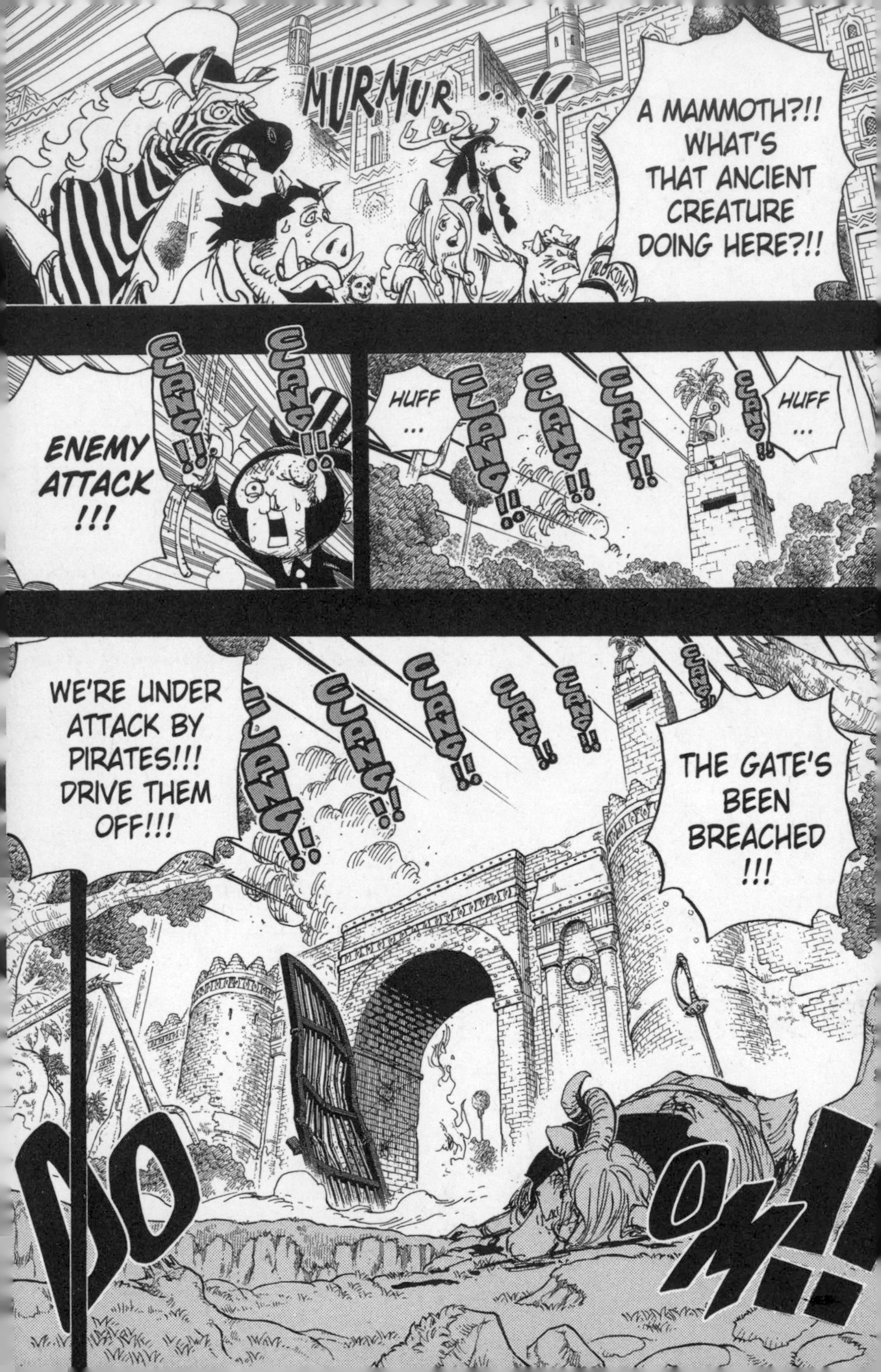
A MAMMOTH?!! WHAT'S THAT ANCIENT CREATURE DOING HERE?!!
MURMUR...!!
HUFF...
CLANG!!
CLANG!!
CLANG!!
CLANG!!
HUFF...
CLANG!!
CLANG!!
ENEMY ATTACK!!!
THE GATE'S BEEN BREACHED!!!
CLANG!!
CLANG!!
CLANG!!
CLANG!!
CLANG!!
CLANG!!
WE'RE UNDER ATTACK BY PIRATES!!! DRIVE THEM OFF!!!
DO
OM!!

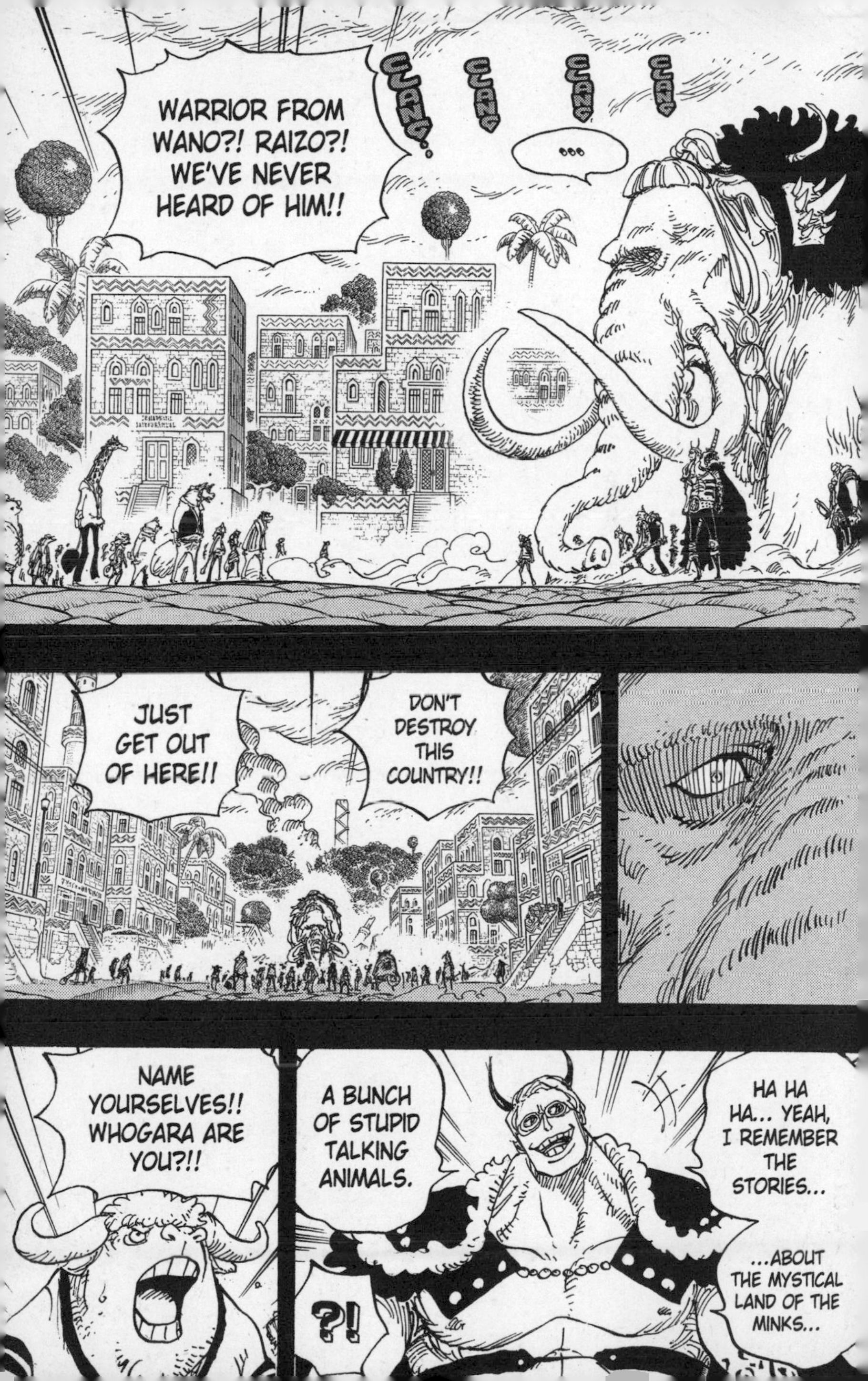
CLANG
CLANG
CLANG
CLANG
...
WARRIOR FROM WANO?! RAIZO?! WE'VE NEVER HEARD OF HIM!!
DON'T DESTROY THIS COUNTRY!!
JUST GET OUT OF HERE!!
HA HA HA... YEAH, I REMEMBER THE STORIES...
...ABOUT THE MYSTICAL LAND OF THE MINKS...
A BUNCH OF STUPID TALKING ANIMALS.
?!
NAME YOURSELVES!! WHOGARA ARE YOU?!!

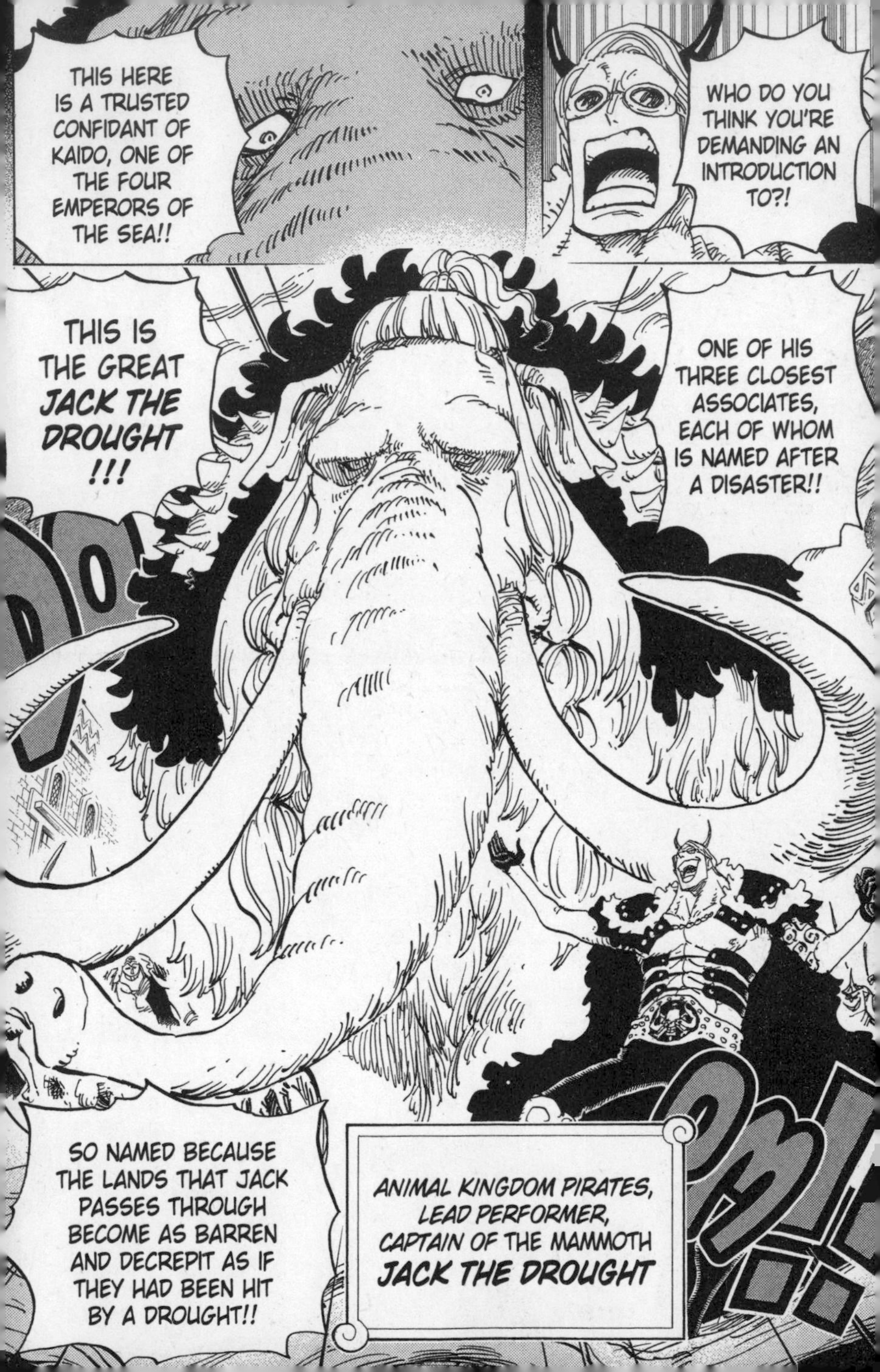
WHO DO YOU THINK YOU'RE DEMANDING AN INTRODUCTION TO?!
THIS HERE IS A TRUSTED CONFIDANT OF KAIDO, ONE OF THE FOUR EMPERORS OF THE SEA!!
ONE OF HIS THREE CLOSEST ASSOCIATES, EACH OF WHOM IS NAMED AFTER A DISASTER!!
THIS IS THE GREAT JACK THE DROUGHT!!!
ANIMAL KINGDOM PIRATES, LEAD PERFORMER, CAPTAIN OF THE MAMMOTH JACK THE DROUGHT
SO NAMED BECAUSE THE LANDS THAT JACK PASSES THROUGH BECOME AS BARREN AND DECREPIT AS IF THEY HAD BEEN HIT BY A DROUGHT!!

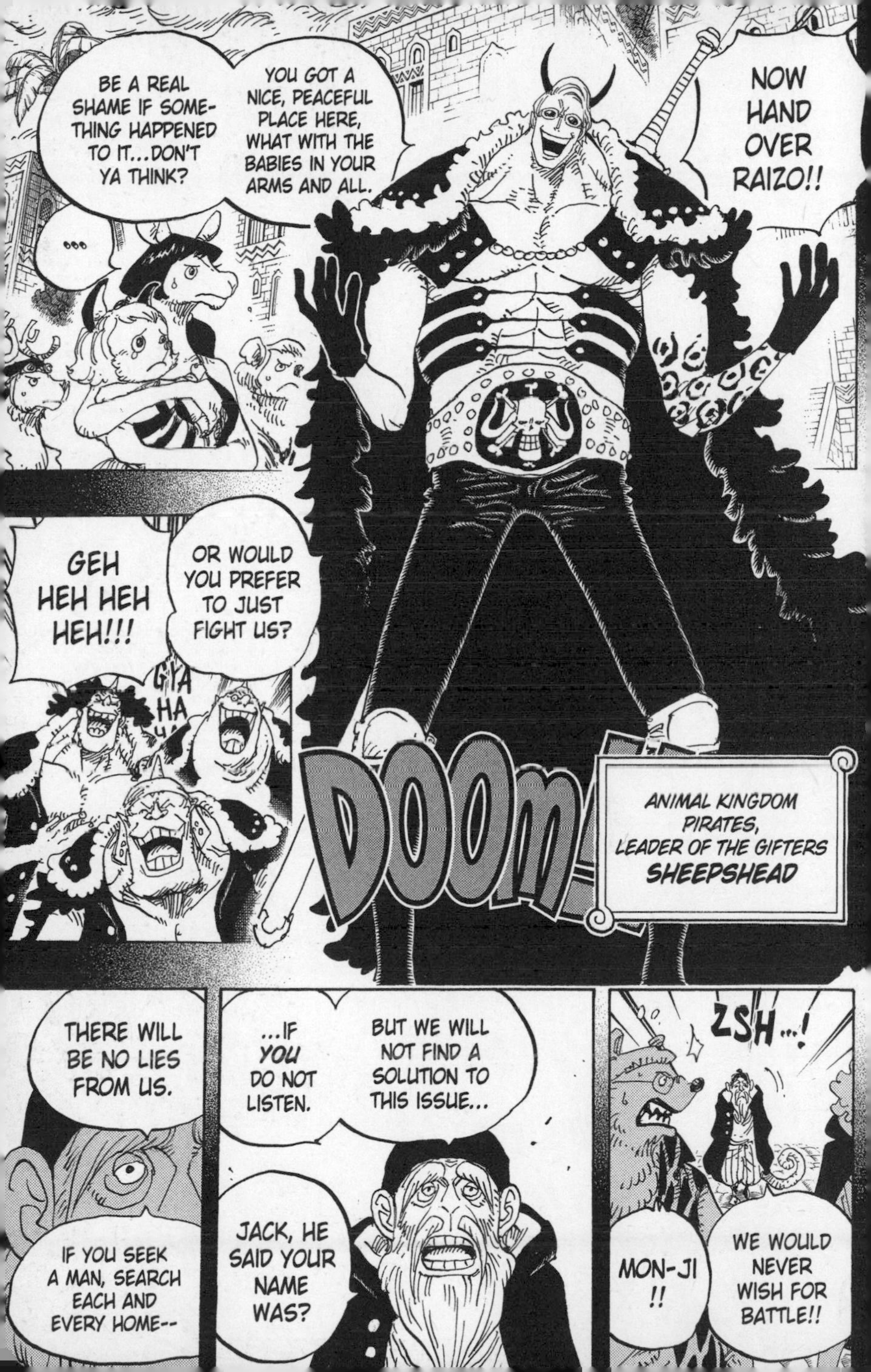
NOW HAND OVER RAIZO!!
YOU GOT A NICE, PEACEFUL PLACE HERE, WHAT WITH THE BABIES IN YOUR ARMS AND ALL.
BE A REAL SHAME IF SOME-THING HAPPENED TO IT...DON'T YA THINK?
...
DOOM
ANIMAL KINGDOM PIRATES, LEADER OF THE GIFTERS SHEEPSHEAD
OR WOULD YOU PREFER TO JUST FIGHT US?
GEH HEH HEH HEH!!!
GYA HA
ZSH...!
WE WOULD NEVER WISH FOR BATTLE!!
MON-JI !!
BUT WE WILL NOT FIND A SOLUTION TO THIS ISSUE...
...IF *YOU* DO NOT LISTEN.
JACK, HE SAID YOUR NAME WAS?
THERE WILL BE NO LIES FROM US.
IF YOU SEEK A MAN, SEARCH EACH AND EVERY HOME--

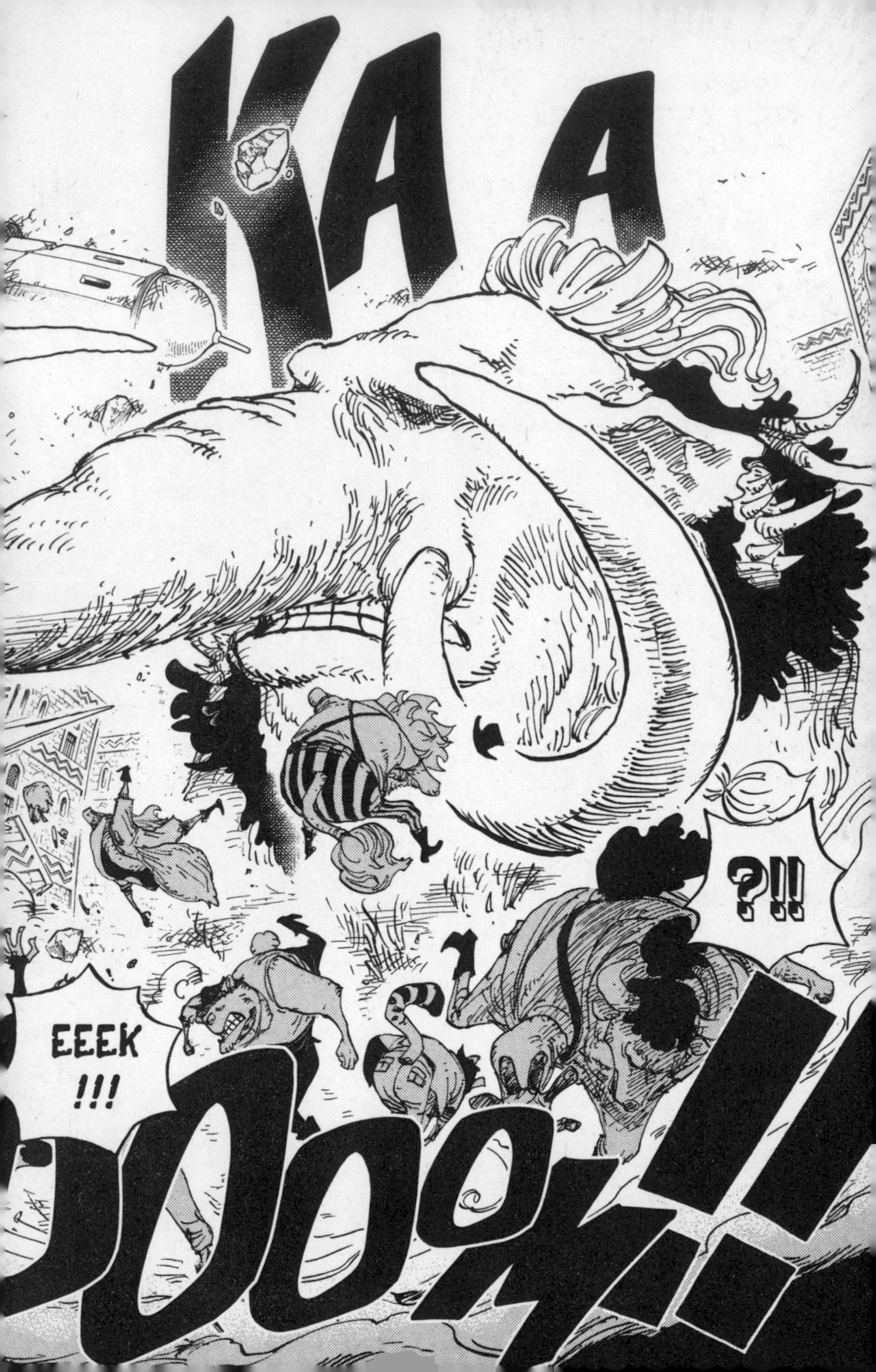
KAA
?!!
EEEK !!!

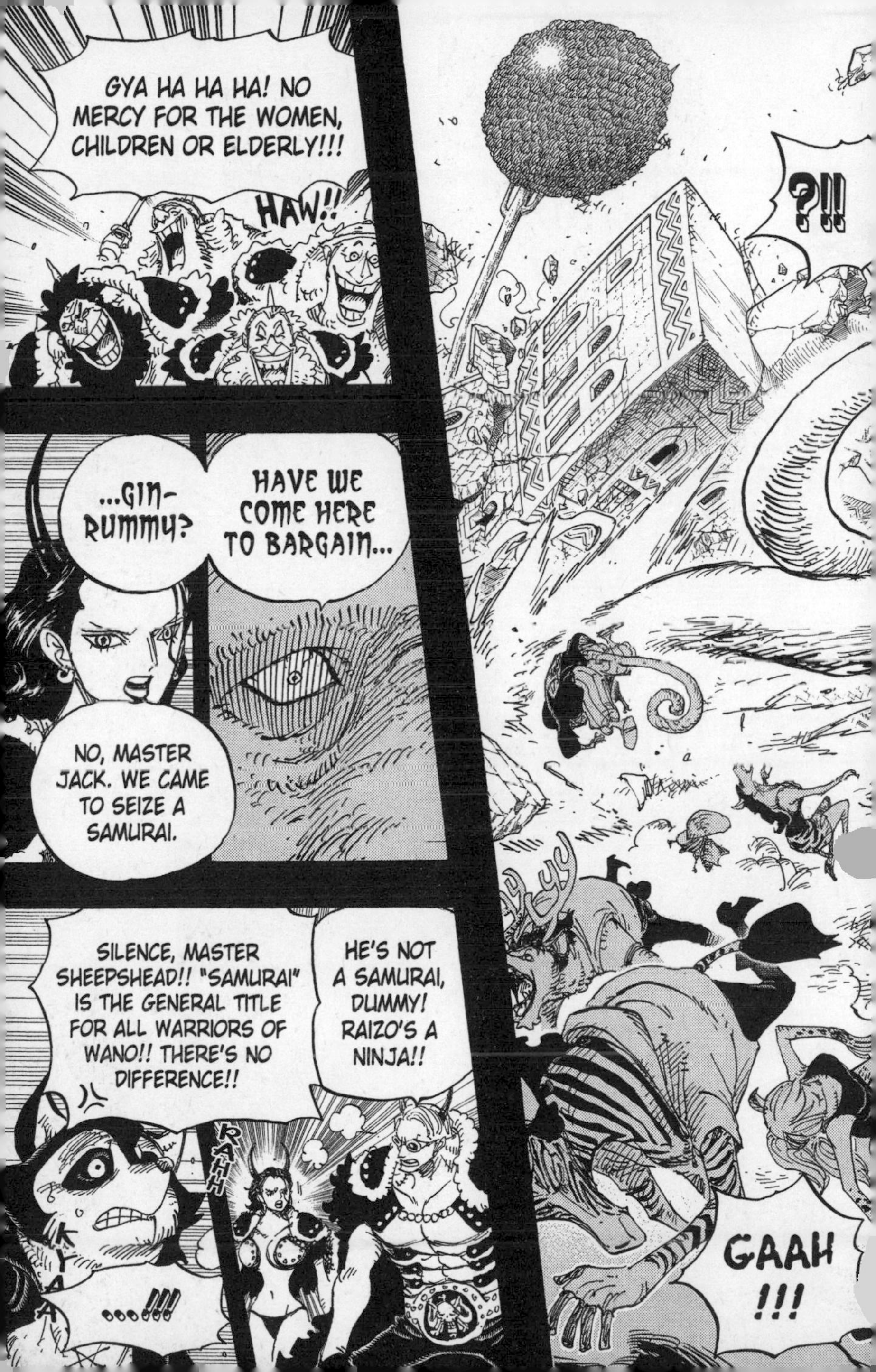
?!!
GAAH !!!
GYA HA HA HA! NO MERCY FOR THE WOMEN, CHILDREN OR ELDERLY!!!
HAW!!
HAVE WE COME HERE TO BARGAIN...
...GIN-RUMMY?
NO, MASTER JACK. WE CAME TO SEIZE A SAMURAI.
HE'S NOT A SAMURAI, DUMMY! RAIZO'S A NINJA!!
RAHHH
...!!!
SILENCE, MASTER SHEEPSHEAD!! "SAMURAI" IS THE GENERAL TITLE FOR ALL WARRIORS OF WANO!! THERE'S NO DIFFERENCE!!
KYAA

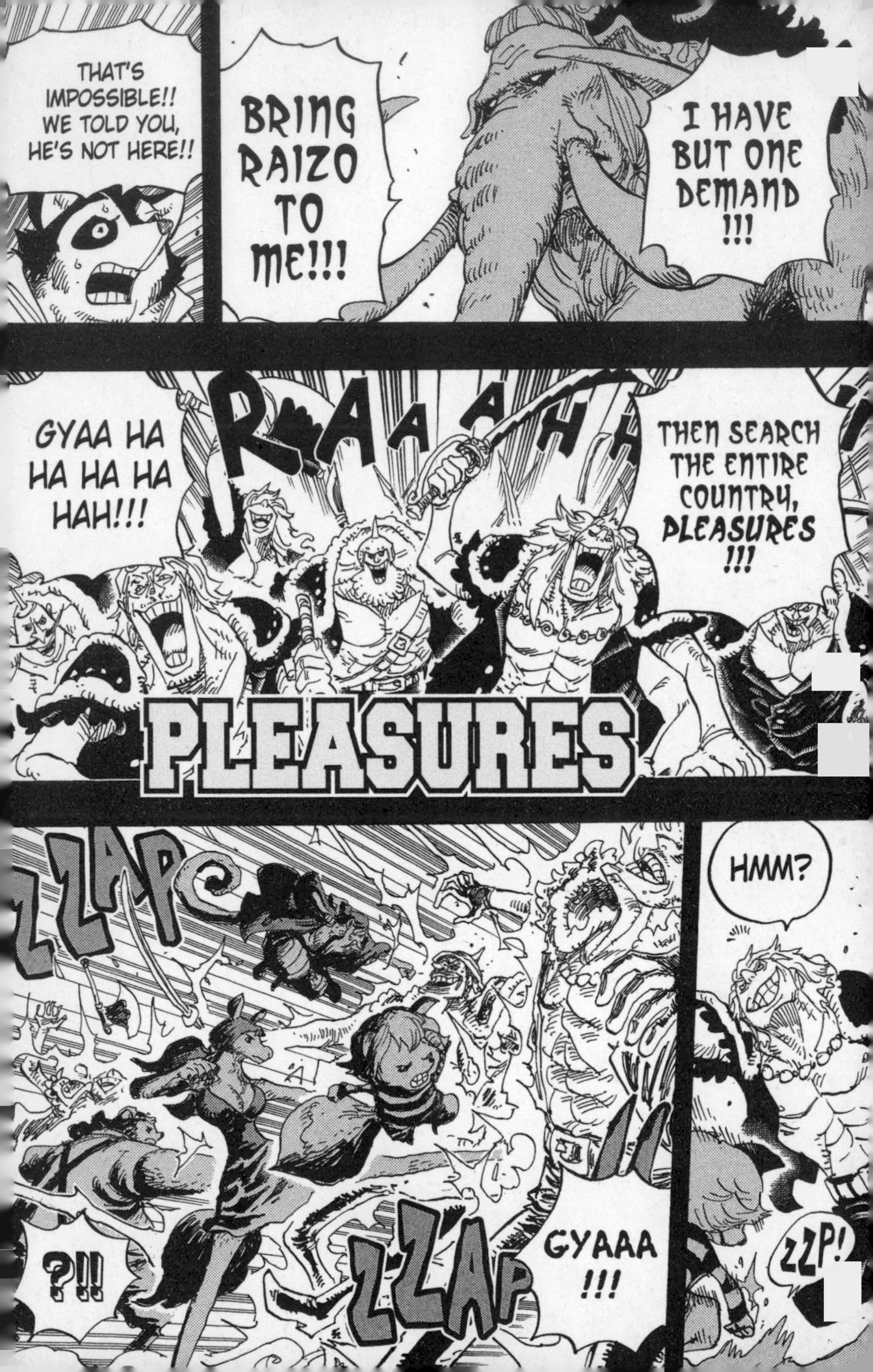
I HAVE BUT ONE DEMAND!!!
BRING RAIZO TO ME!!!
THAT'S IMPOSSIBLE!! WE TOLD YOU, HE'S NOT HERE!!
THEN SEARCH THE ENTIRE COUNTRY, PLEASURES!!!
RAAAHH
GYAA HA HA HA HA HAH!!!
PLEASURES
HMM?
ZZP!
ZZAP
GYAAA!!!
ZZAP
?!!

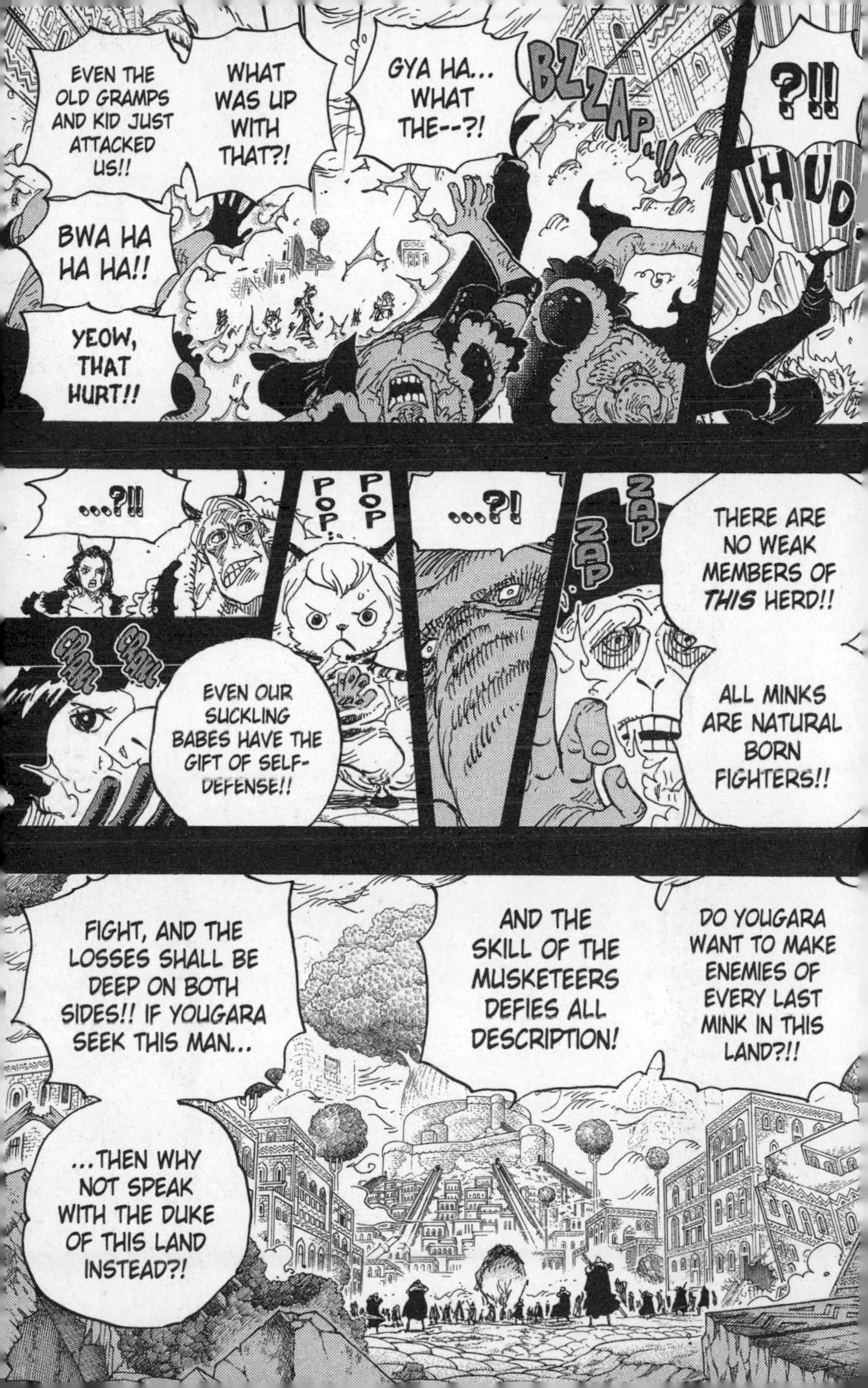
?!!
THUD
BZZAP!!
GYA HA... WHAT THE--?!
WHAT WAS UP WITH THAT?!
EVEN THE OLD GRAMPS AND KID JUST ATTACKED US!!
BWA HA HA HA!!
YEOW, THAT HURT!!
ZAP
ZAP
THERE ARE NO WEAK MEMBERS OF *THIS* HERD!!
ALL MINKS ARE NATURAL BORN FIGHTERS!!
...?!
POP
POP
EVEN OUR SUCKLING BABES HAVE THE GIFT OF SELF-DEFENSE!!
...?!!
DO YOUGARA WANT TO MAKE ENEMIES OF EVERY LAST MINK IN THIS LAND?!!
AND THE SKILL OF THE MUSKETEERS DEFIES ALL DESCRIPTION!
FIGHT, AND THE LOSSES SHALL BE DEEP ON BOTH SIDES!! IF YOUGARA SEEK THIS MAN...
...THEN WHY NOT SPEAK WITH THE DUKE OF THIS LAND INSTEAD?!

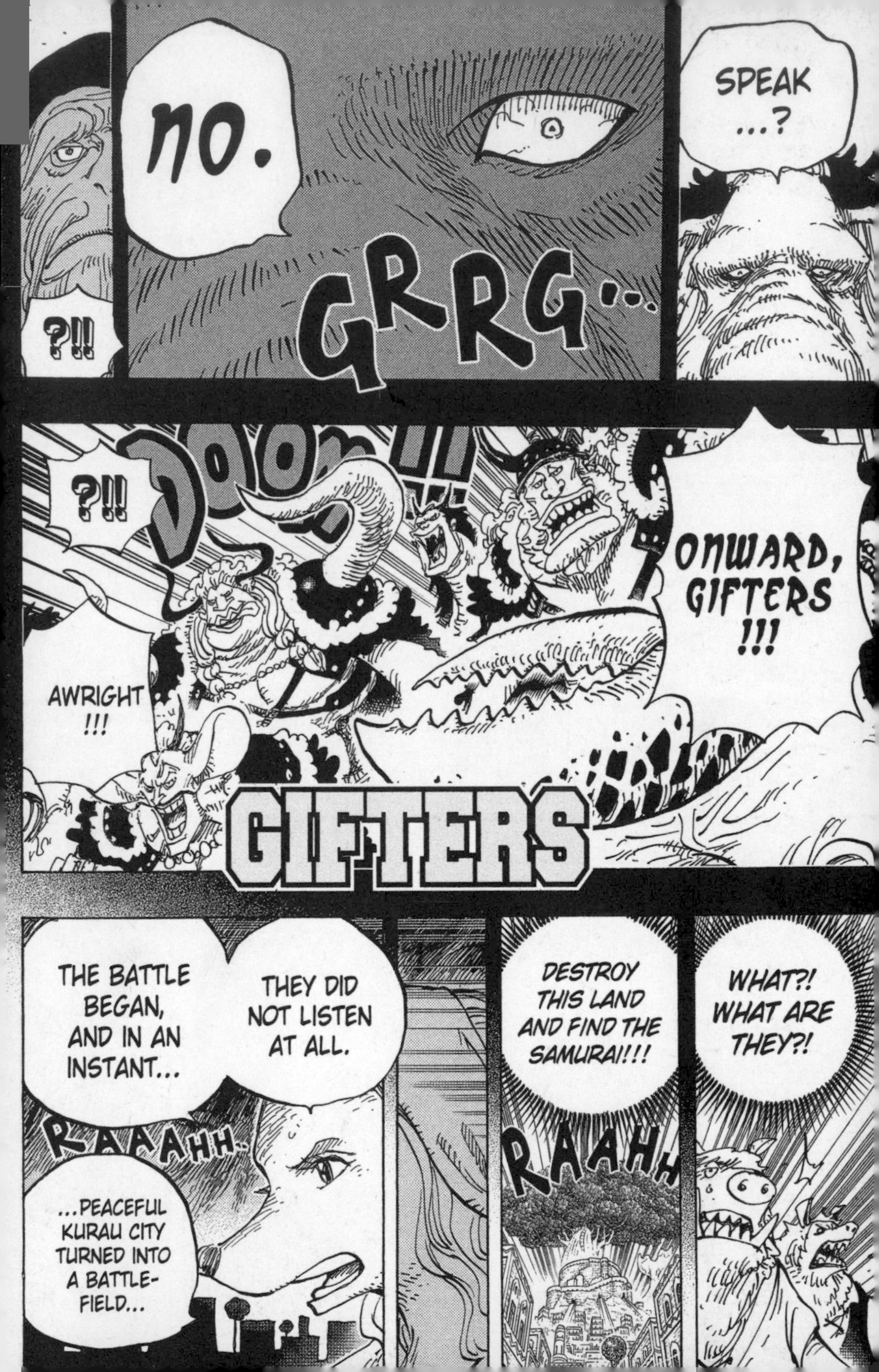
SPEAK ...?
no.
GRRG..
?!!
ONWARD, GIFTERS !!!
DOOM!!
?!!
AWRIGHT !!!
GIFTERS
WHAT?! WHAT ARE THEY?!
DESTROY THIS LAND AND FIND THE SAMURAI!!!
RAAHH
THEY DID NOT LISTEN AT ALL.
THE BATTLE BEGAN, AND IN AN INSTANT...
RAAAHH
...PEACEFUL KURAU CITY TURNED INTO A BATTLE-FIELD...

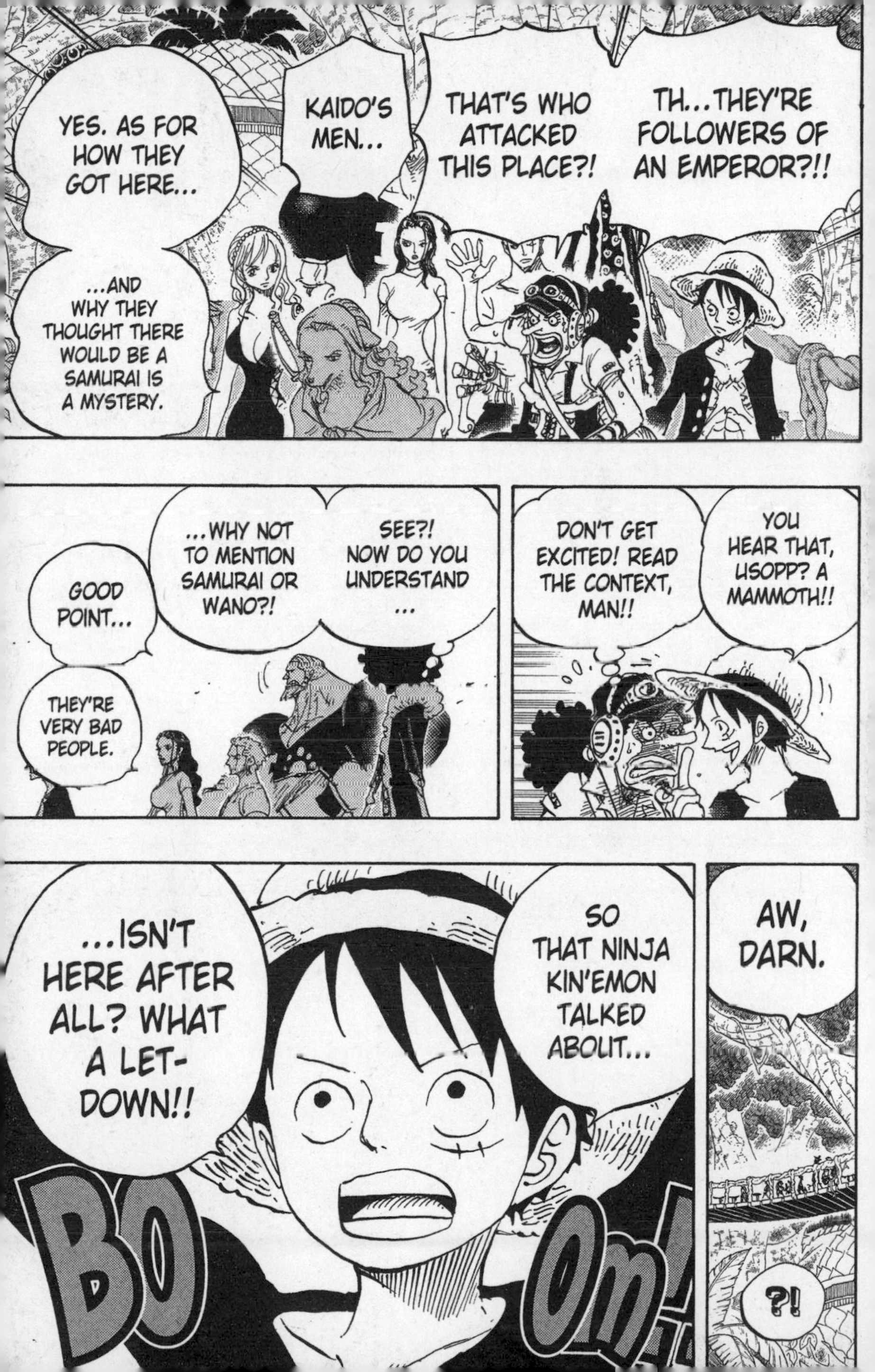

TH...THEY'RE FOLLOWERS OF AN EMPEROR?!!
THAT'S WHO ATTACKED THIS PLACE?!
KAIDO'S MEN...
YES. AS FOR HOW THEY GOT HERE...
...AND WHY THEY THOUGHT THERE WOULD BE A SAMURAI IS A MYSTERY.
YOU HEAR THAT, USOPP? A MAMMOTH!!
DON'T GET EXCITED! READ THE CONTEXT, MAN!!
SEE?! NOW DO YOU UNDERSTAND ...
...WHY NOT TO MENTION SAMURAI OR WANO?!
GOOD POINT...
THEY'RE VERY BAD PEOPLE.
AW, DARN.
?!
SO THAT NINJA KIN'EMON TALKED ABOUT...
...ISN'T HERE AFTER ALL? WHAT A LET-DOWN!!
BOOM!

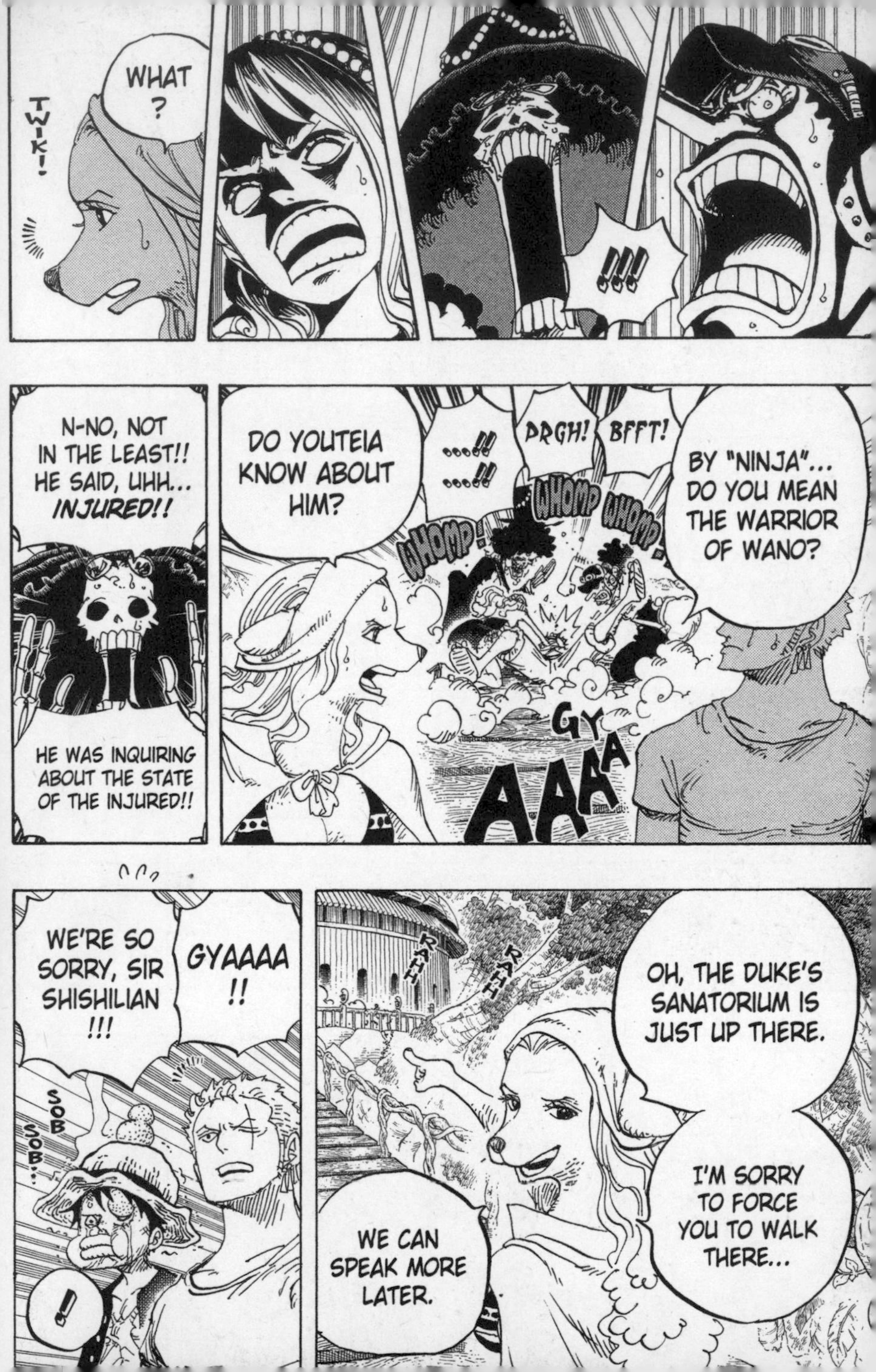
!!!
TWIK!
WHAT?
BY "NINJA"... DO YOU MEAN THE WARRIOR OF WANO?
BFFT!
DRGH!
...!!
...!!
WHOMP WHOMP
WHOMP!
DO YOUTEIA KNOW ABOUT HIM?
GYAAAA
N-NO, NOT IN THE LEAST!! HE SAID, UHH... *INJURED!!*
HE WAS INQUIRING ABOUT THE STATE OF THE INJURED!!
OH, THE DUKE'S SANATORIUM IS JUST UP THERE.
RAHH
RAHH
I'M SORRY TO FORCE YOU TO WALK THERE...
WE CAN SPEAK MORE LATER.
GYAAAA !!
WE'RE SO SORRY, SIR SHISHILIAN !!!
SOB SOB...
!

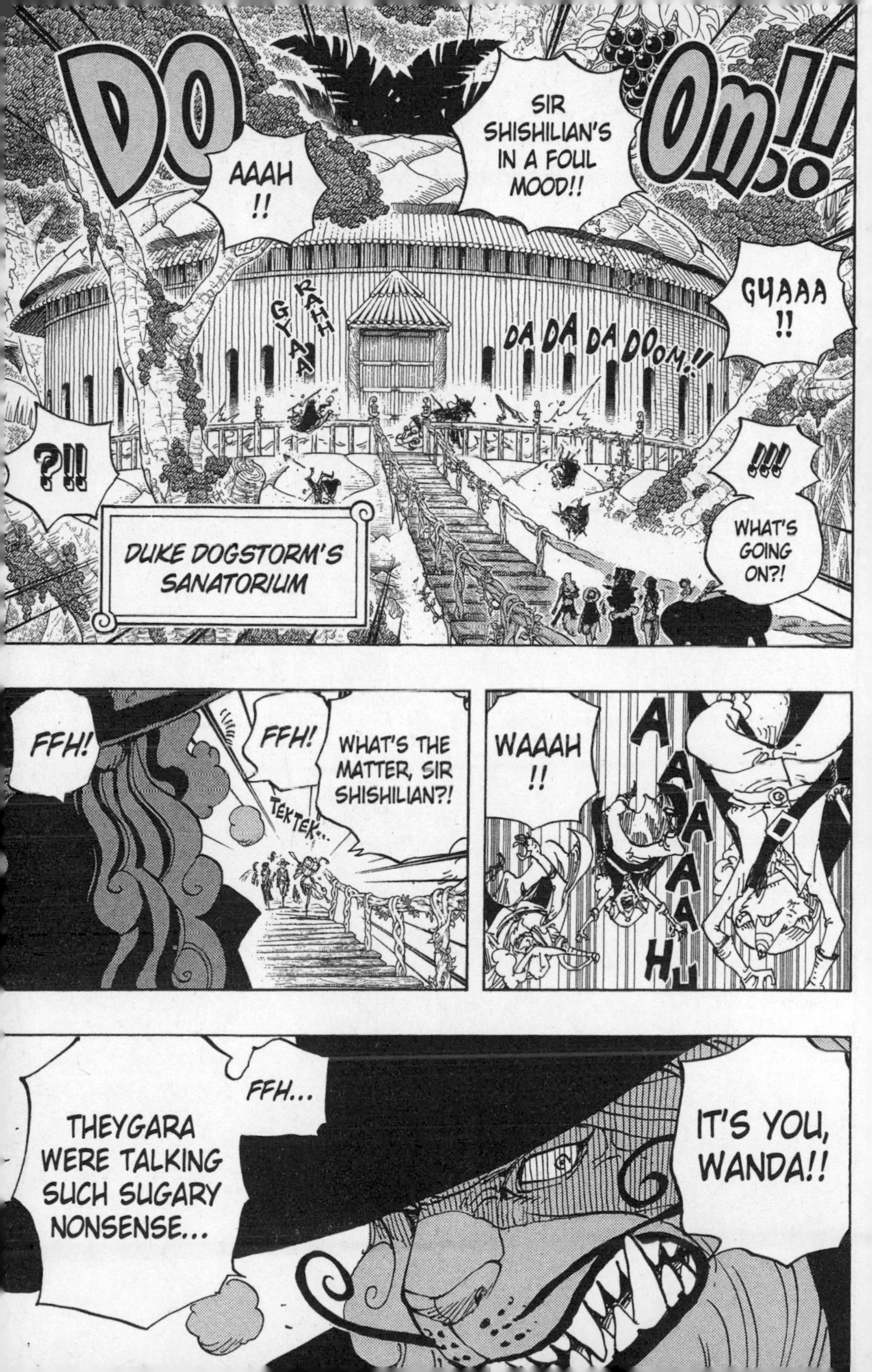
DO OM!!
SIR SHISHILIAN'S IN A FOUL MOOD!!
AAAH !!
GYAAA !!
DA DA DA DOOM!!
GYAA RAHH
!!!
WHAT'S GOING ON?!
?!!
DUKE DOGSTORM'S SANATORIUM
WAAAH !!
AAAAAAH
WHAT'S THE MATTER, SIR SHISHILIAN?!
FFH!
TEKTEK...
FFH!
IT'S YOU, WANDA!!
FFH...
THEYGARA WERE TALKING SUCH SUGARY NONSENSE...

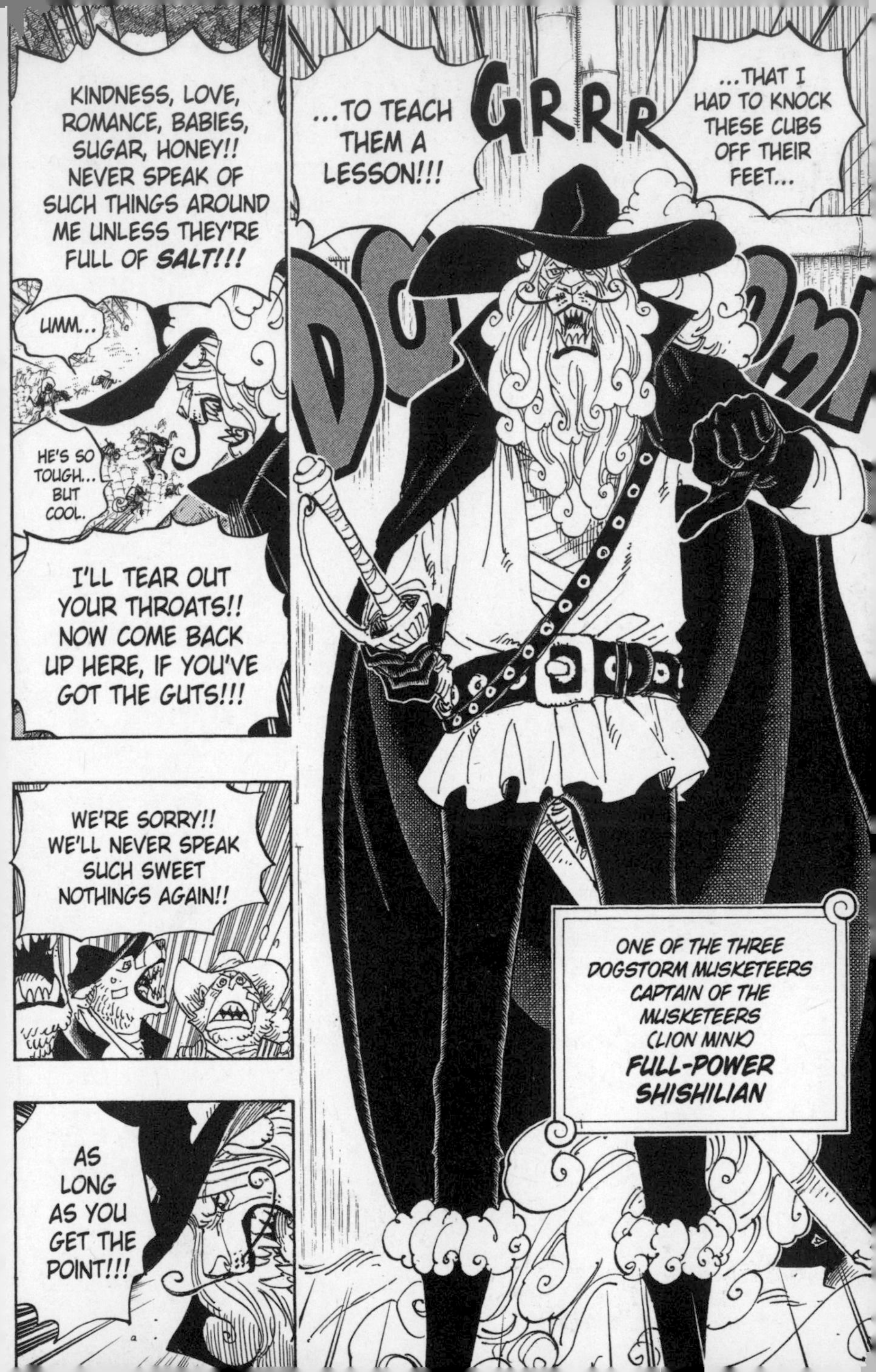
...THAT I HAD TO KNOCK THESE CUBS OFF THEIR FEET...
GRRR
...TO TEACH THEM A LESSON!!!
ONE OF THE THREE DOGSTORM MUSKETEERS CAPTAIN OF THE MUSKETEERS (LION MINK) **FULL-POWER SHISHILIAN**
KINDNESS, LOVE, ROMANCE, BABIES, SUGAR, HONEY!! NEVER SPEAK OF SUCH THINGS AROUND ME UNLESS THEY'RE FULL OF ***SALT!!!***
UMM...
HE'S SO TOUGH... BUT COOL.
I'LL TEAR OUT YOUR THROATS!! NOW COME BACK UP HERE, IF YOU'VE GOT THE GUTS!!!
WE'RE SORRY!! WE'LL NEVER SPEAK SUCH SWEET NOTHINGS AGAIN!!
AS LONG AS YOU GET THE POINT!!!

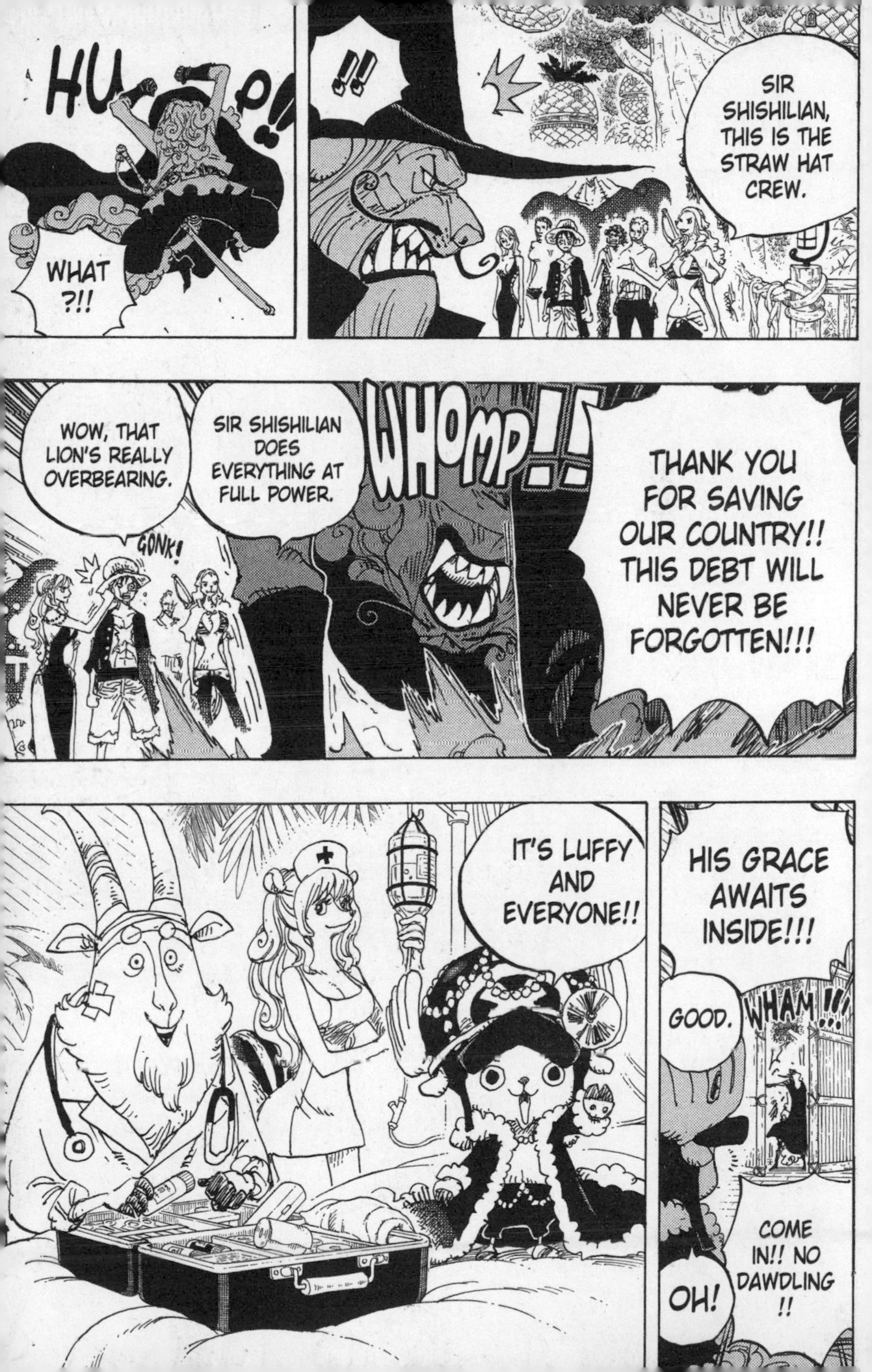
SIR SHISHILIAN, THIS IS THE STRAW HAT CREW.
!!
WHAT ?!!
THANK YOU FOR SAVING OUR COUNTRY!! THIS DEBT WILL NEVER BE FORGOTTEN!!!
WHOMP!!
SIR SHISHILIAN DOES EVERYTHING AT FULL POWER.
WOW, THAT LION'S REALLY OVERBEARING.
GONK!
HIS GRACE AWAITS INSIDE!!!
GOOD.
WHAM!!
COME IN!! NO DAWDLING !!
OH!
IT'S LUFFY AND EVERYONE!!

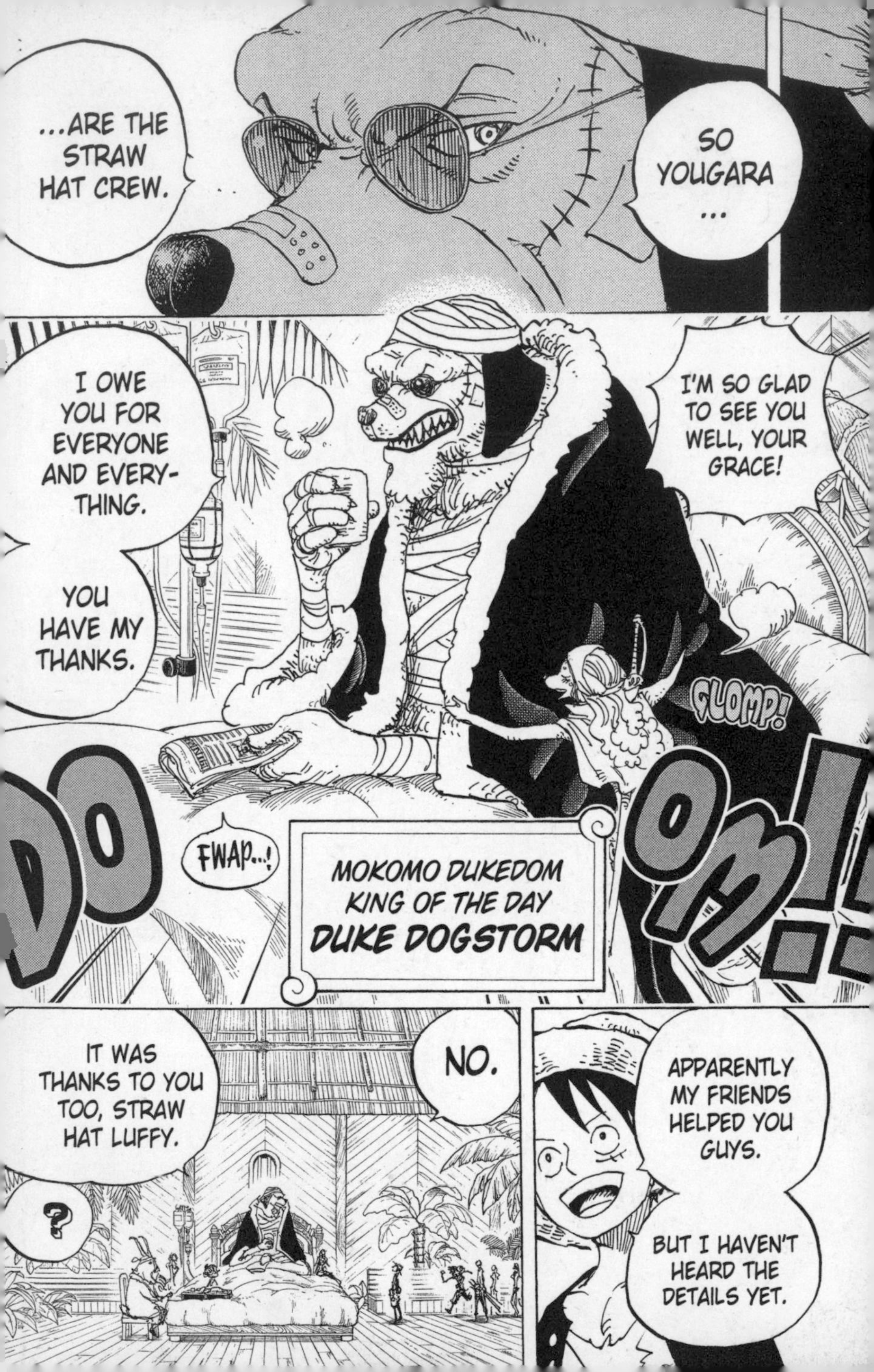
SO YOUGARA ...
...ARE THE STRAW HAT CREW.
I'M SO GLAD TO SEE YOU WELL, YOUR GRACE!
GLOMP!
I OWE YOU FOR EVERYONE AND EVERY-THING.
YOU HAVE MY THANKS.
DOOM!!
FWAP...!
MOKOMO DUKEDOM
KING OF THE DAY
DUKE DOGSTORM
APPARENTLY MY FRIENDS HELPED YOU GUYS.
BUT I HAVEN'T HEARD THE DETAILS YET.
NO.
IT WAS THANKS TO YOU TOO, STRAW HAT LUFFY.
?

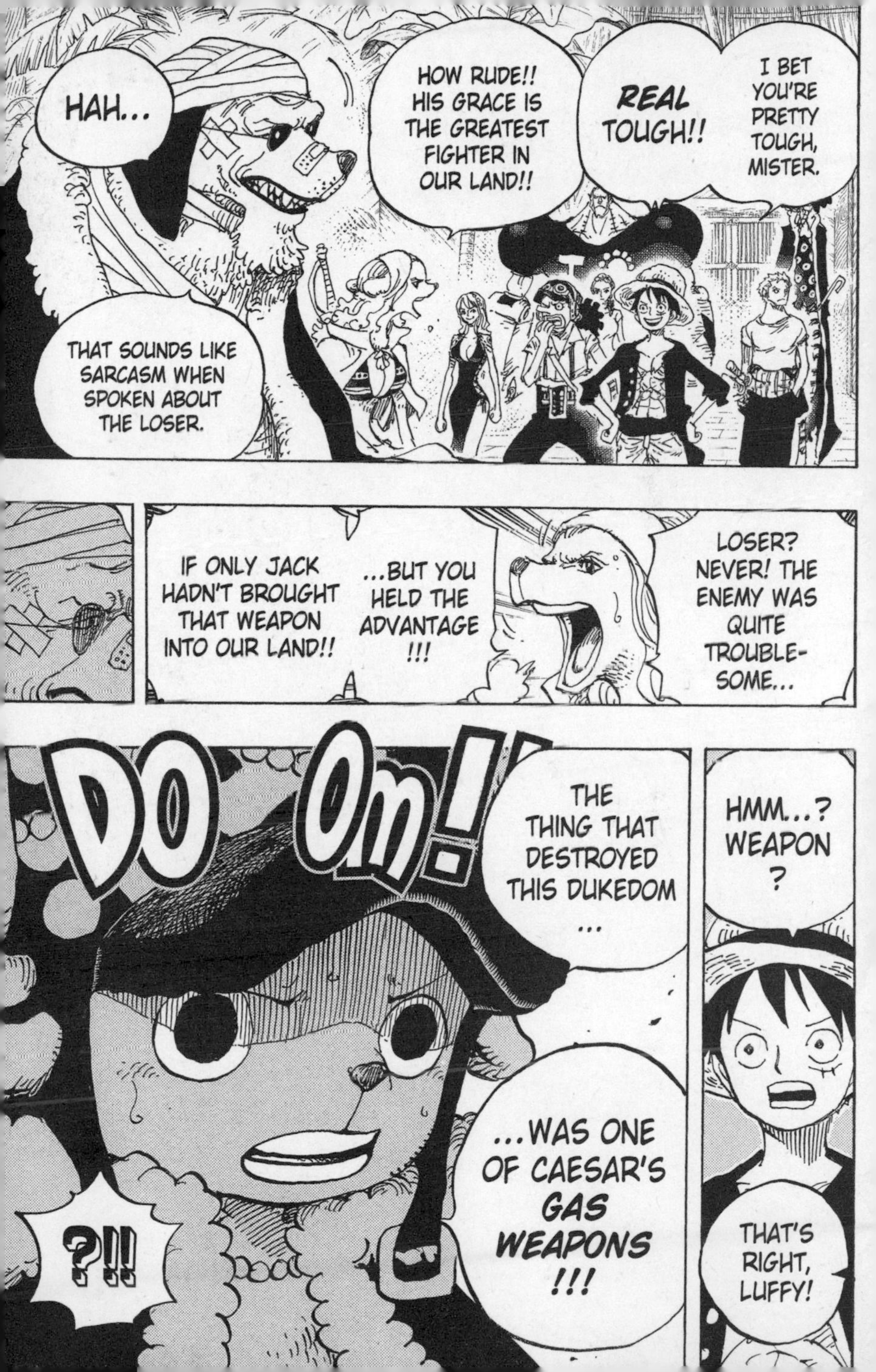
I BET YOU'RE PRETTY TOUGH, MISTER.
REAL TOUGH!!
HOW RUDE!! HIS GRACE IS THE GREATEST FIGHTER IN OUR LAND!!
HAH...
THAT SOUNDS LIKE SARCASM WHEN SPOKEN ABOUT THE LOSER.
LOSER? NEVER! THE ENEMY WAS QUITE TROUBLE-SOME...
...BUT YOU HELD THE ADVANTAGE!!!
IF ONLY JACK HADN'T BROUGHT THAT WEAPON INTO OUR LAND!!
HMM...? WEAPON?
THAT'S RIGHT, LUFFY!
THE THING THAT DESTROYED THIS DUKEDOM...
DO Om!
...WAS ONE OF CAESAR'S GAS WEAPONS!!!
?!!

Chapter 809: THE CAT VIPER

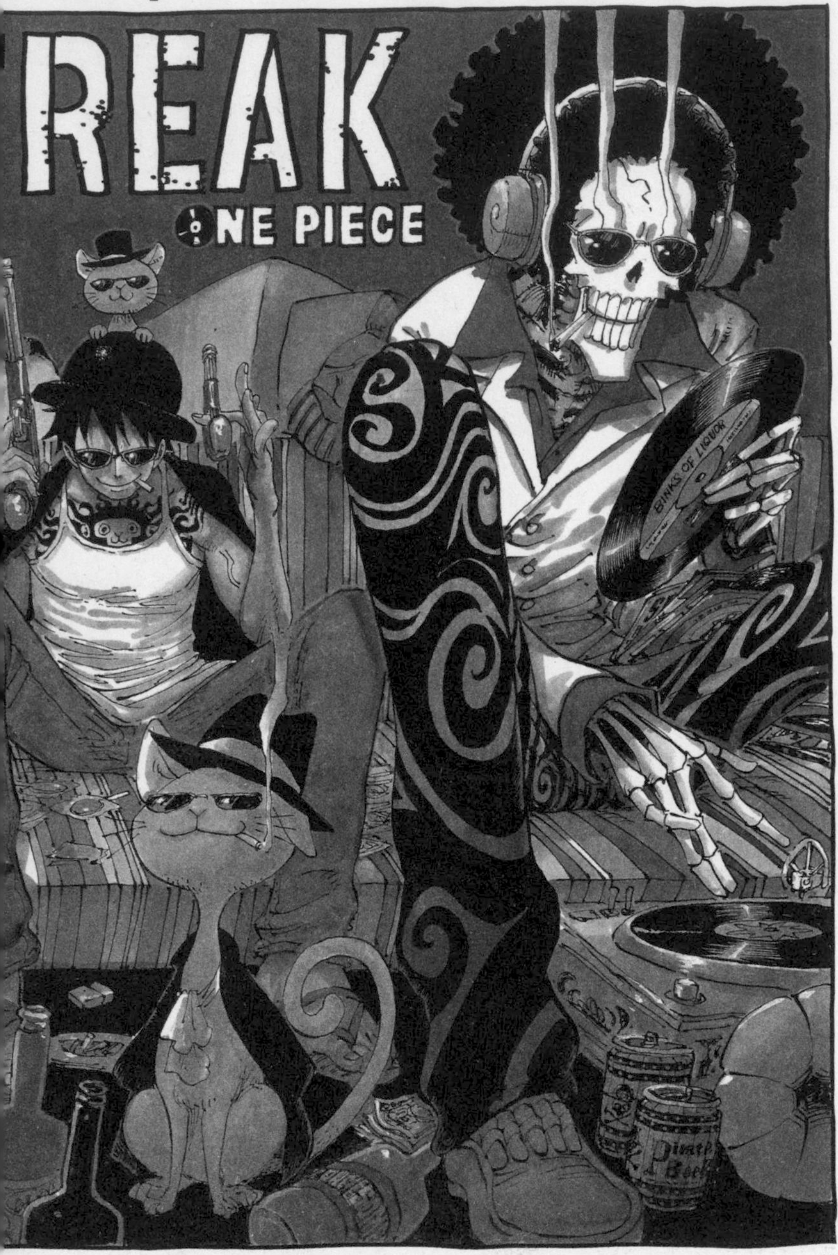
REAK
ONE PIECE
BINKS OF LIQUOR

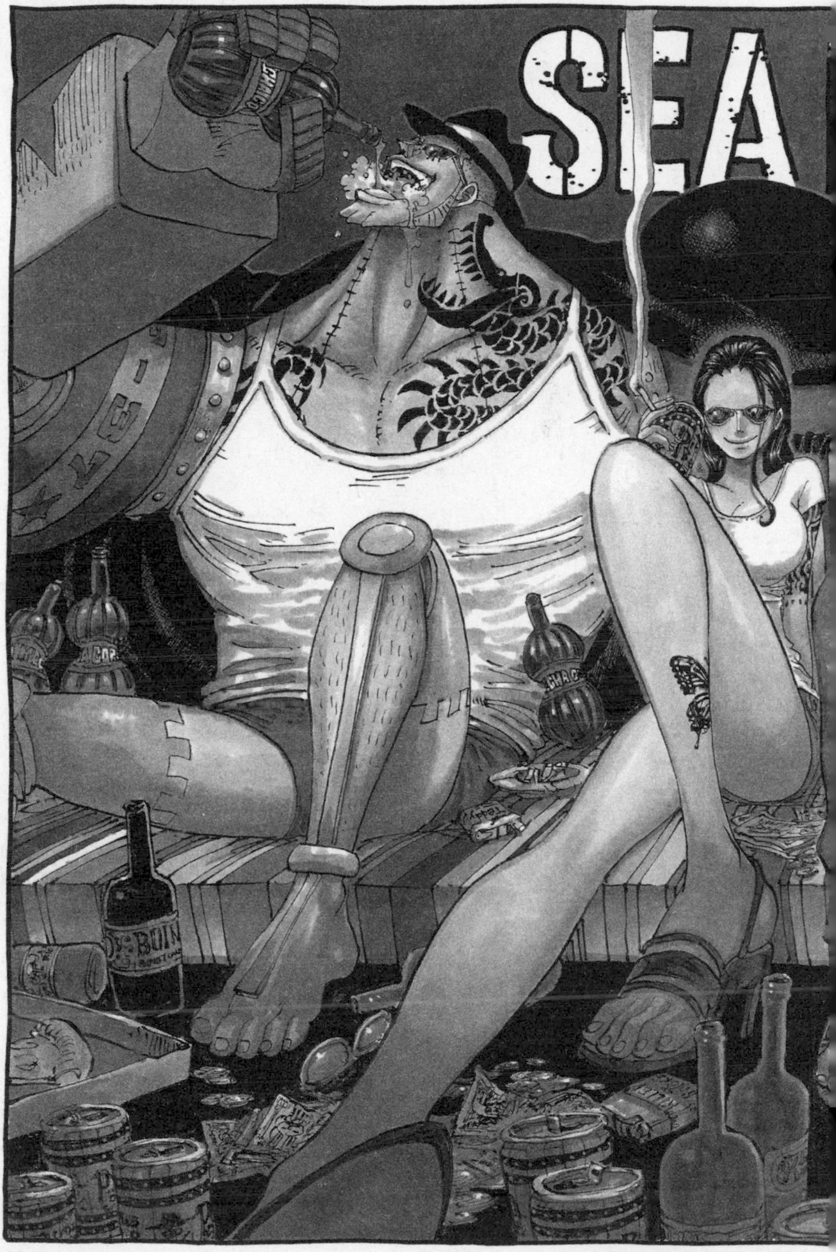
SEA

vol.81

ONE PIECE

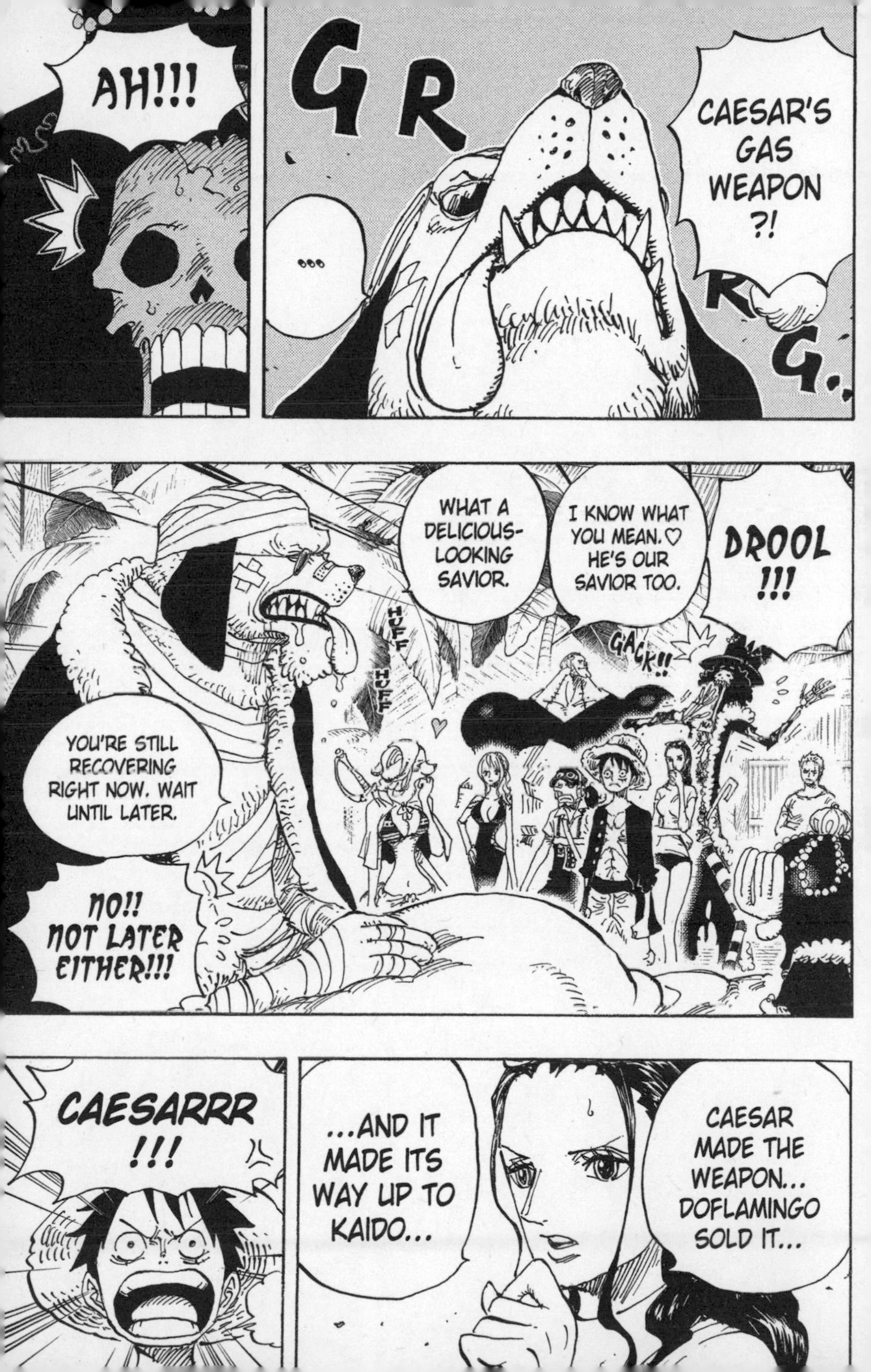
CAESAR'S GAS WEAPON ?!
GR
RG..
...
AH!!!
DROOL!!!
I KNOW WHAT YOU MEAN.♡ HE'S OUR SAVIOR TOO.
WHAT A DELICIOUS-LOOKING SAVIOR.
GACK!!
HUFF HUFF
YOU'RE STILL RECOVERING RIGHT NOW. WAIT UNTIL LATER.
NO!! NOT LATER EITHER!!!
CAESAR MADE THE WEAPON... DOFLAMINGO SOLD IT...
...AND IT MADE ITS WAY UP TO KAIDO...
CAESARRR!!!

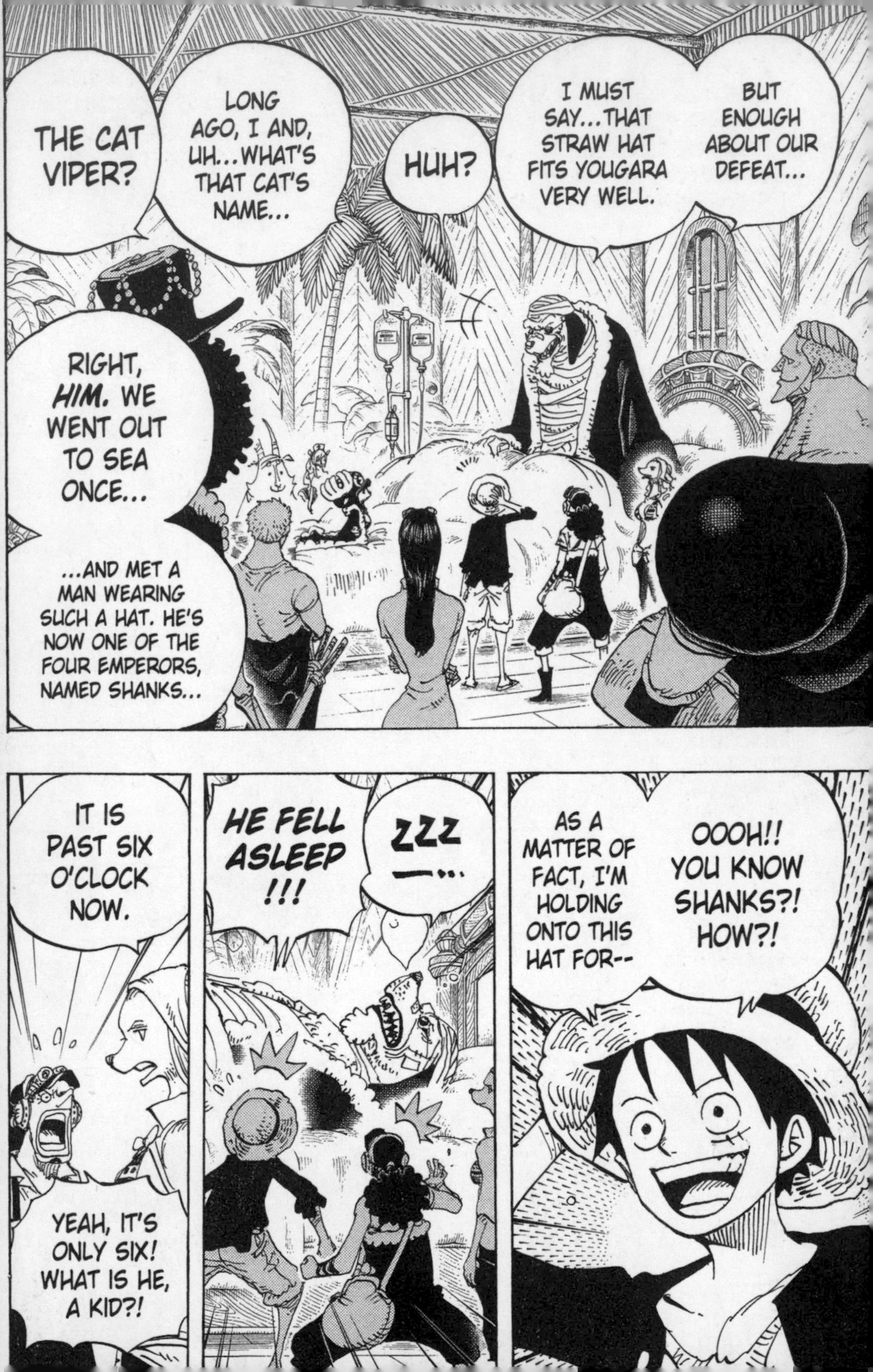
BUT ENOUGH ABOUT OUR DEFEAT...
I MUST SAY...THAT STRAW HAT FITS YOUGARA VERY WELL.
HUH?
LONG AGO, I AND, UH...WHAT'S THAT CAT'S NAME...
THE CAT VIPER?
RIGHT, HIM. WE WENT OUT TO SEA ONCE...
...AND MET A MAN WEARING SUCH A HAT. HE'S NOW ONE OF THE FOUR EMPERORS, NAMED SHANKS...
OOOH!! YOU KNOW SHANKS?! HOW?!
AS A MATTER OF FACT, I'M HOLDING ONTO THIS HAT FOR--
ZZZ —...
HE FELL ASLEEP !!!
IT IS PAST SIX O'CLOCK NOW.
YEAH, IT'S ONLY SIX! WHAT IS HE, A KID?!

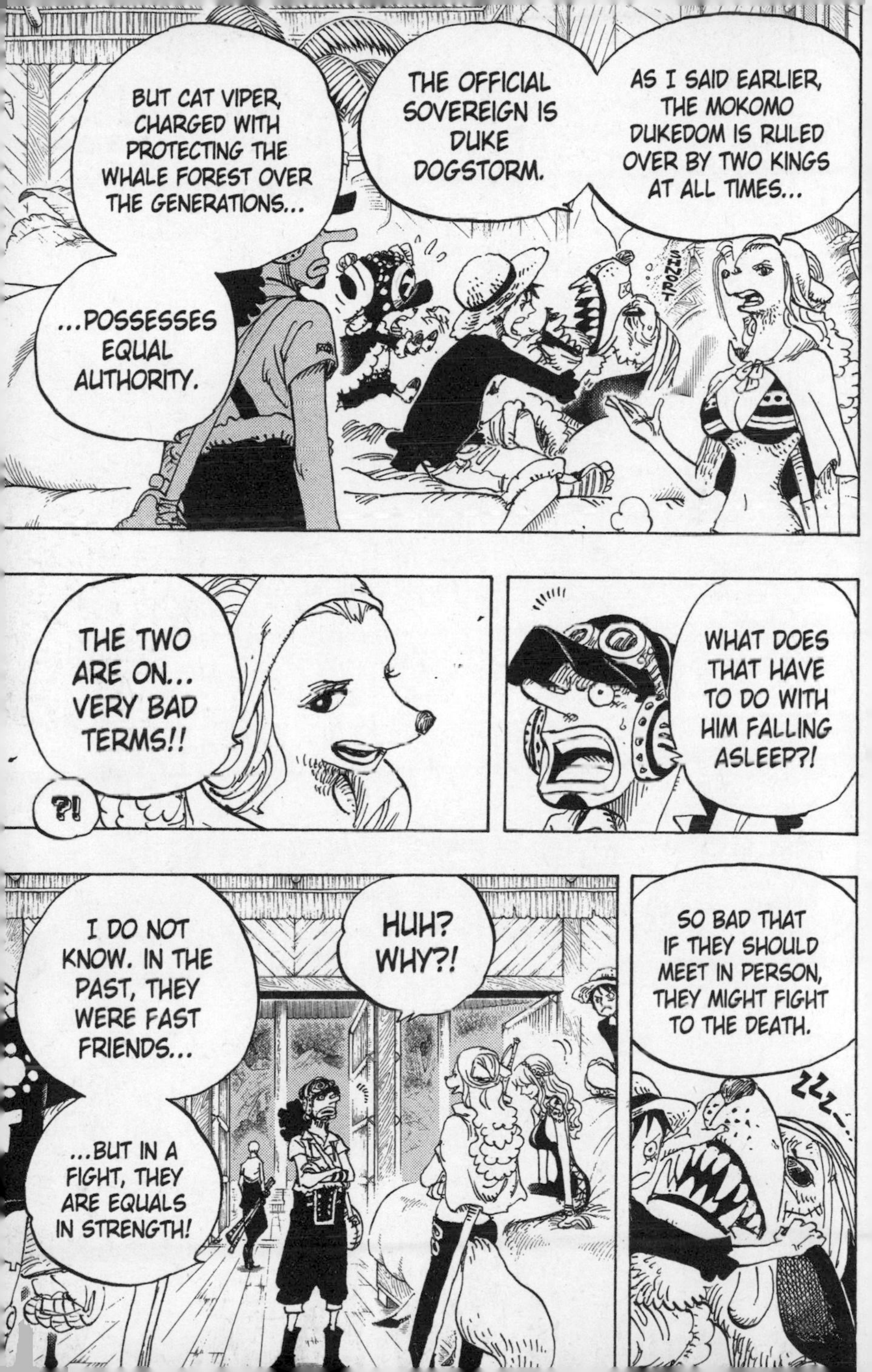
AS I SAID EARLIER, THE MOKOMO DUKEDOM IS RULED OVER BY TWO KINGS AT ALL TIMES...
SNORT
THE OFFICIAL SOVEREIGN IS DUKE DOGSTORM.
BUT CAT VIPER, CHARGED WITH PROTECTING THE WHALE FOREST OVER THE GENERATIONS...
...POSSESSES EQUAL AUTHORITY.
WHAT DOES THAT HAVE TO DO WITH HIM FALLING ASLEEP?!
THE TWO ARE ON... VERY BAD TERMS!!
?!
SO BAD THAT IF THEY SHOULD MEET IN PERSON, THEY MIGHT FIGHT TO THE DEATH.
ZZZ...
HUH? WHY?!
I DO NOT KNOW. IN THE PAST, THEY WERE FAST FRIENDS...
...BUT IN A FIGHT, THEY ARE EQUALS IN STRENGTH!

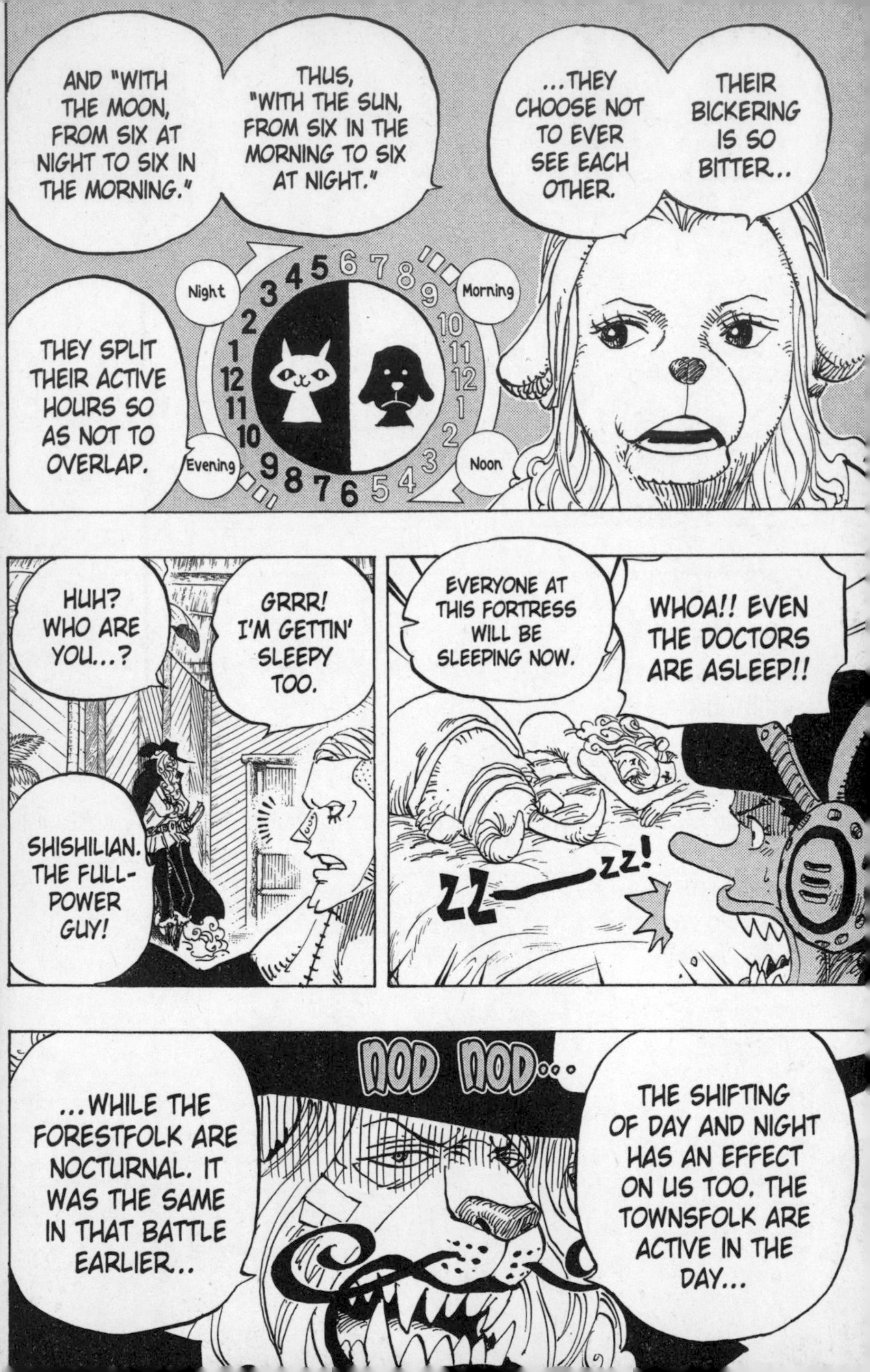
THEIR BICKERING IS SO BITTER...
...THEY CHOOSE NOT TO EVER SEE EACH OTHER.
THUS, "WITH THE SUN, FROM SIX IN THE MORNING TO SIX AT NIGHT."
AND "WITH THE MOON, FROM SIX AT NIGHT TO SIX IN THE MORNING."
Morning
Night
Noon
Evening
THEY SPLIT THEIR ACTIVE HOURS SO AS NOT TO OVERLAP.
WHOA!! EVEN THE DOCTORS ARE ASLEEP!!
EVERYONE AT THIS FORTRESS WILL BE SLEEPING NOW.
ZZ—ZZ!
GRRR! I'M GETTIN' SLEEPY TOO.
HUH? WHO ARE YOU...?
SHISHILIAN. THE FULL-POWER GUY!
THE SHIFTING OF DAY AND NIGHT HAS AN EFFECT ON US TOO. THE TOWNSFOLK ARE ACTIVE IN THE DAY...
NOD NOD...
...WHILE THE FORESTFOLK ARE NOCTURNAL. IT WAS THE SAME IN THAT BATTLE EARLIER...

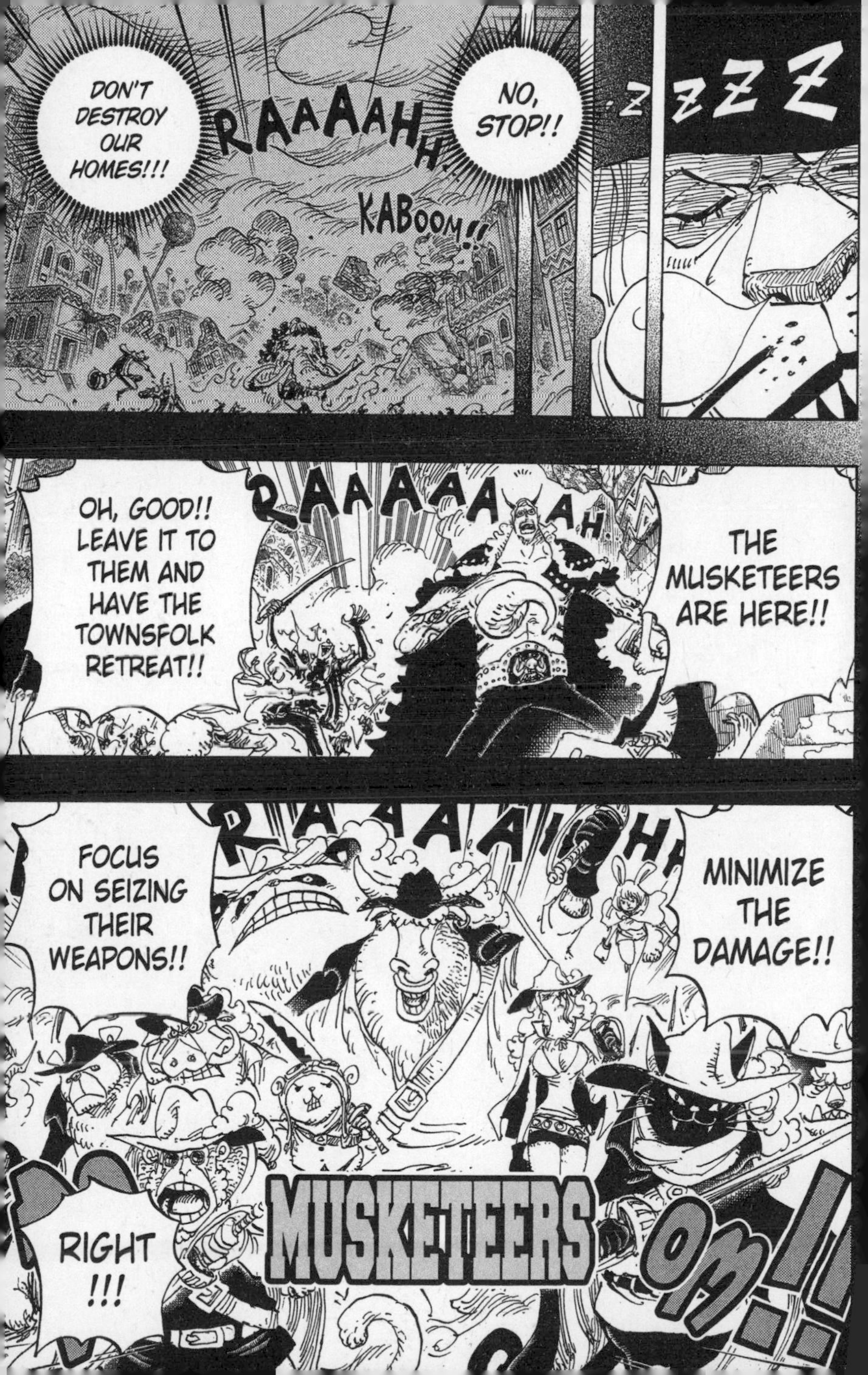
ZZZZ
NO, STOP!!
DON'T DESTROY OUR HOMES!!!
RAAAAHH
KABOOM!!
THE MUSKETEERS ARE HERE!!
RAAAAAAH
OH, GOOD!! LEAVE IT TO THEM AND HAVE THE TOWNSFOLK RETREAT!!
MINIMIZE THE DAMAGE!!
RAAAAAH
FOCUS ON SEIZING THEIR WEAPONS!!
MUSKETEERS ON!!
RIGHT!!!

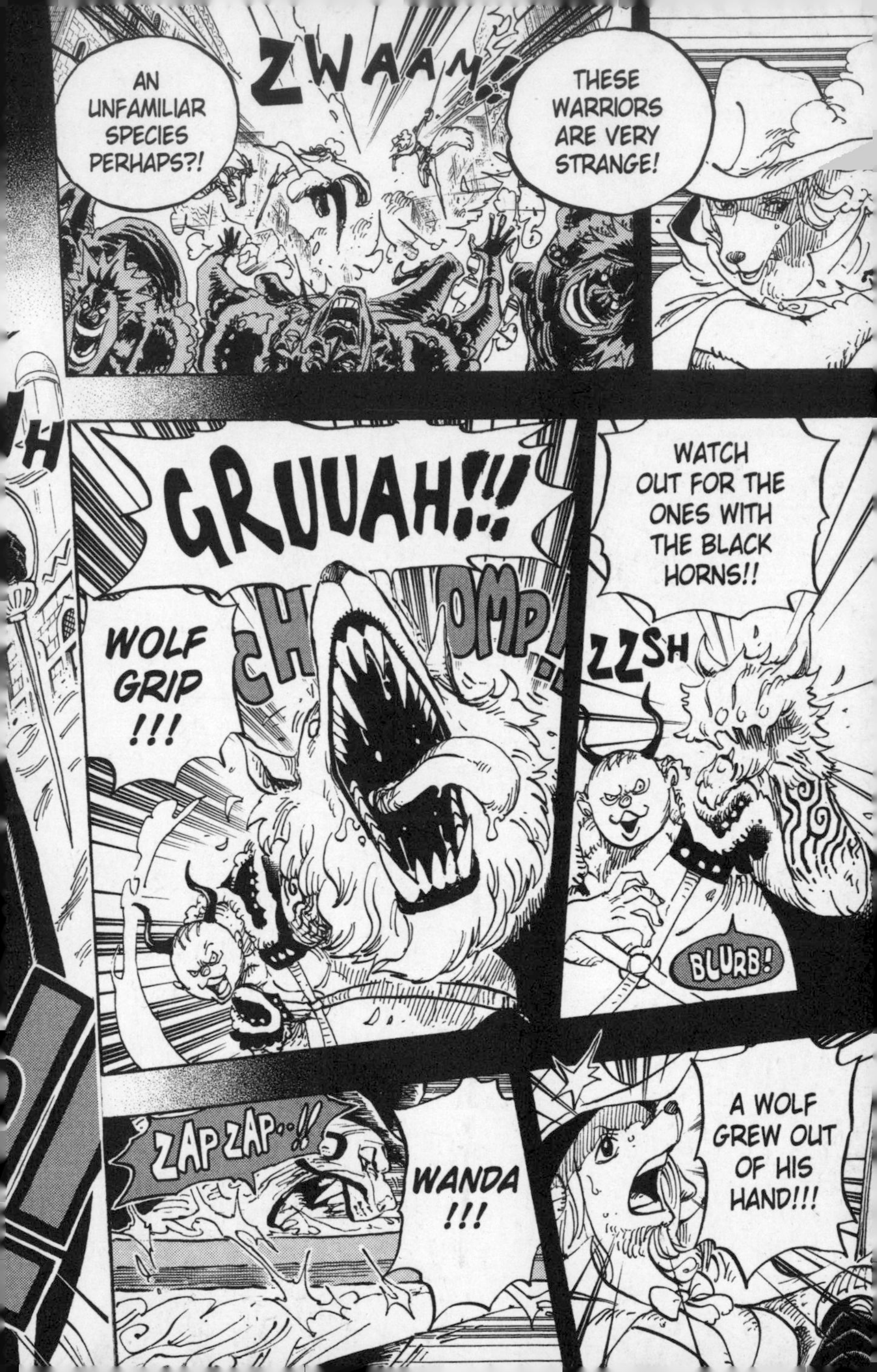
THESE WARRIORS ARE VERY STRANGE!
ZWAAM!!
AN UNFAMILIAR SPECIES PERHAPS?!
WATCH OUT FOR THE ONES WITH THE BLACK HORNS!!
ZZSH
BLURB!
GRUUAH!!!
CHOMP!!
WOLF GRIP !!!
A WOLF GREW OUT OF HIS HAND!!!
WANDA !!!
ZAP ZAP!!

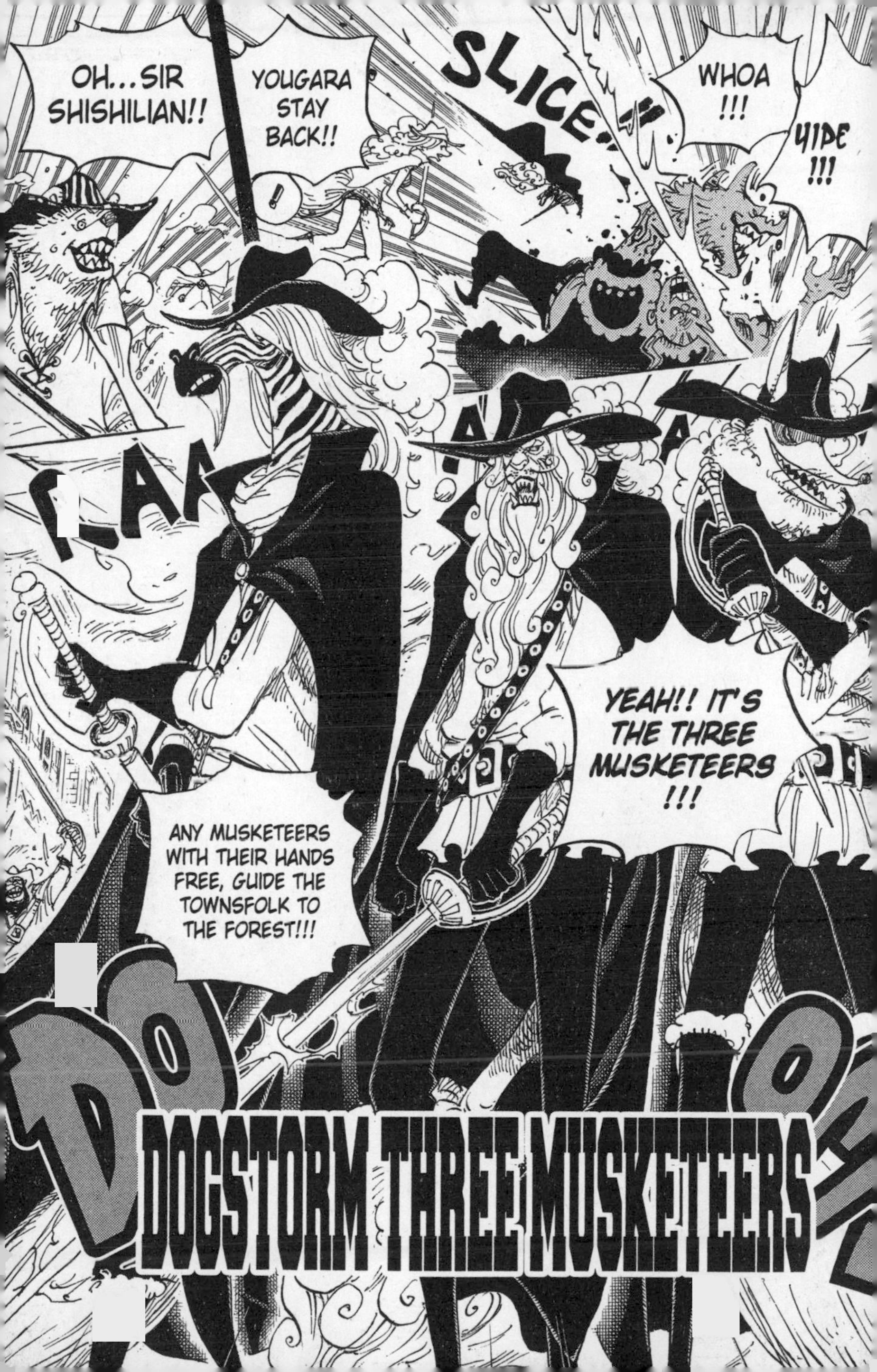
WHOA !!!
YIPE !!!
SLICE
YOUGARA STAY BACK!!
OH...SIR SHISHILIAN!!
!
YEAH!! IT'S THE THREE MUSKETEERS !!!
ANY MUSKETEERS WITH THEIR HANDS FREE, GUIDE THE TOWNSFOLK TO THE FOREST!!!
DOGSTORM THREE MUSKETEERS

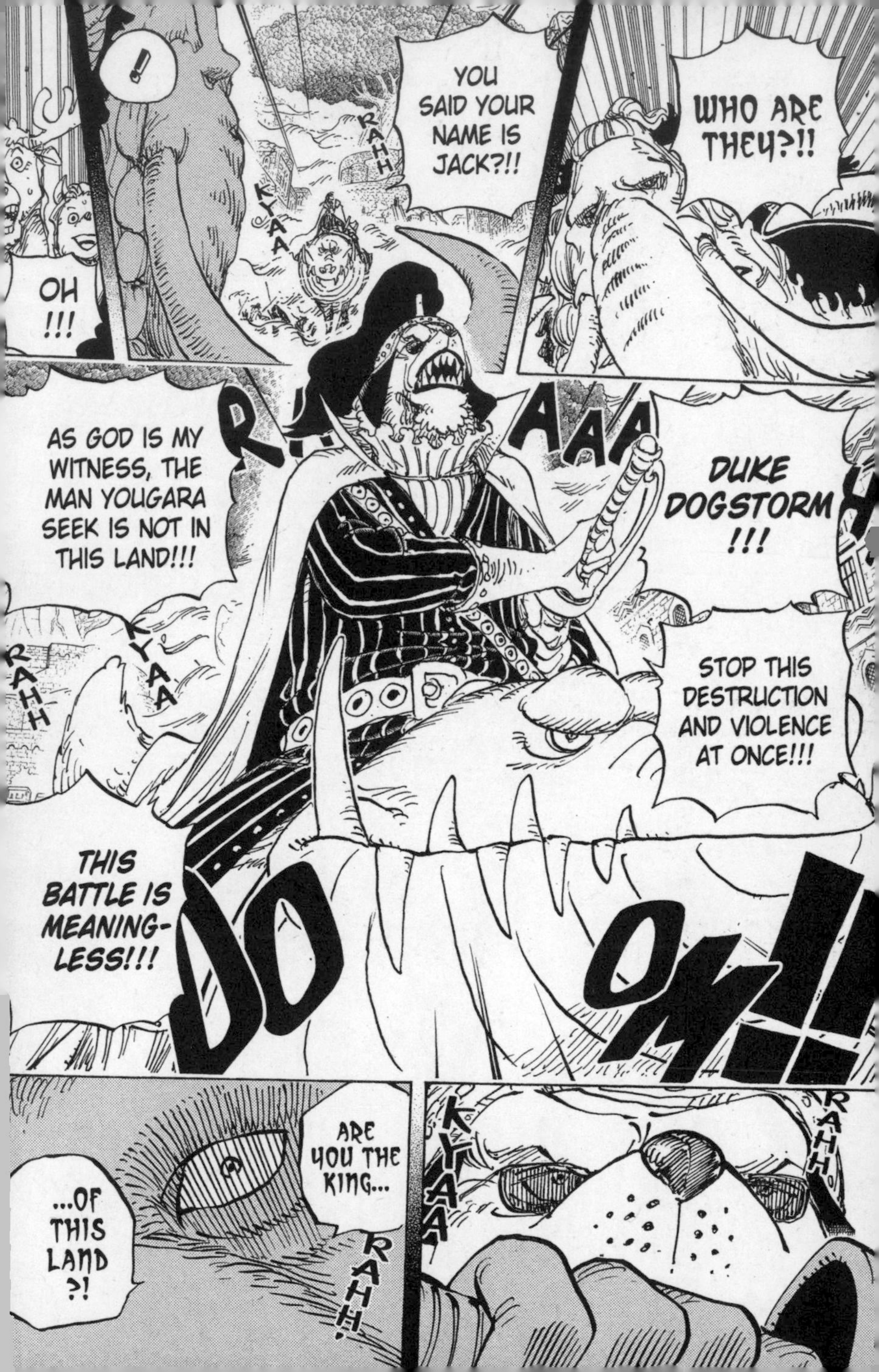
WHO ARE THEY?!!
YOU SAID YOUR NAME IS JACK?!!
RAHH
KYAA
!
OH !!!
DUKE DOGSTORM !!!
STOP THIS DESTRUCTION AND VIOLENCE AT ONCE!!!
AS GOD IS MY WITNESS, THE MAN YOUGARA SEEK IS NOT IN THIS LAND!!!
KYAA
RAHH
THIS BATTLE IS MEANING-LESS!!!
DOOM!!
RAHH
KYAA
ARE YOU THE KING...
...OF THIS LAND ?!
RAHH

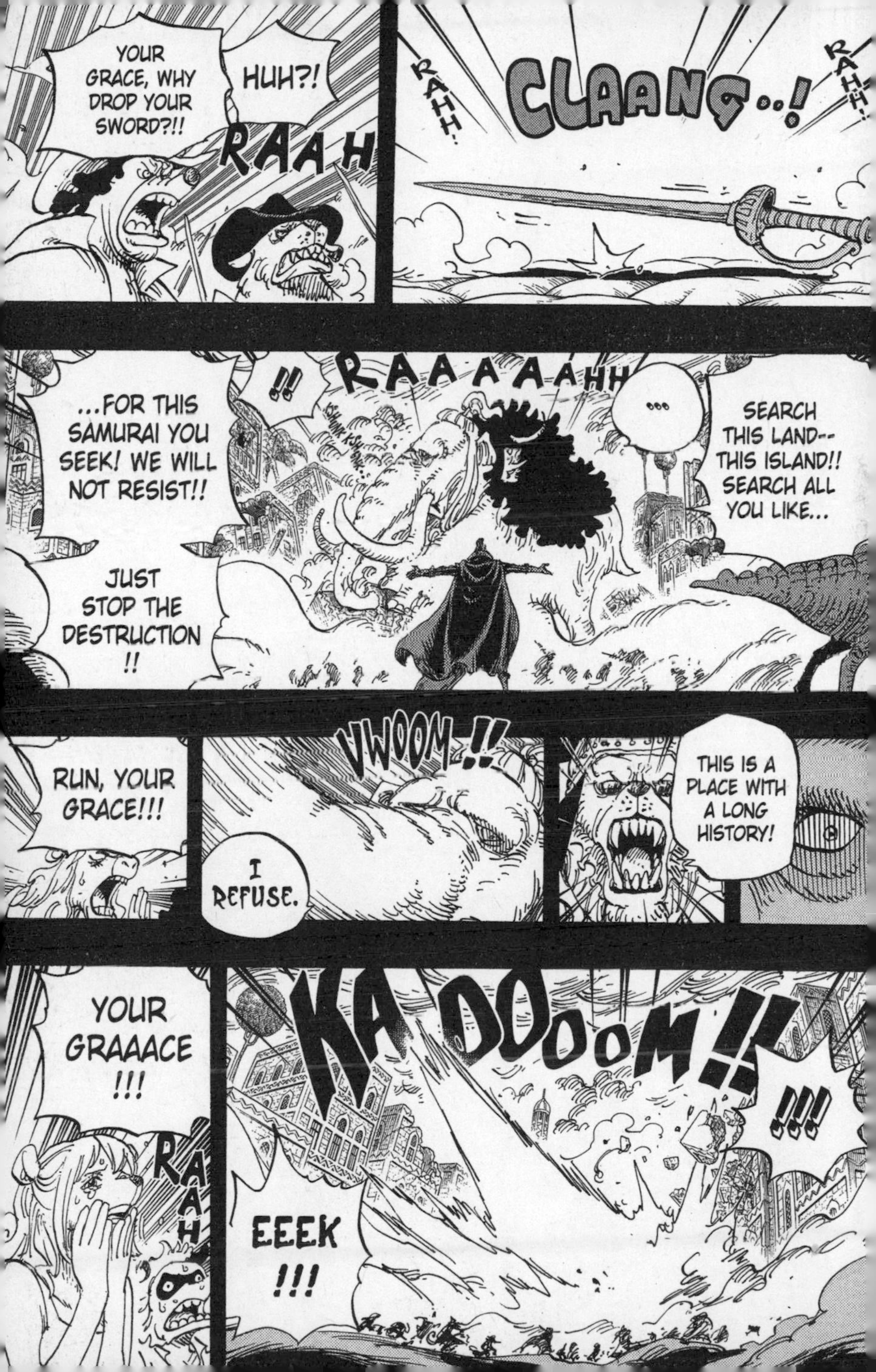
RAHH!
CLAANG..!
RAHH!
HUH?!
YOUR GRACE, WHY DROP YOUR SWORD?!!
RAAH
SEARCH THIS LAND-- THIS ISLAND!! SEARCH ALL YOU LIKE...
...
RAAAAAHH
!!
...FOR THIS SAMURAI YOU SEEK! WE WILL NOT RESIST!!
JUST STOP THE DESTRUCTION !!
THIS IS A PLACE WITH A LONG HISTORY!
VWOOM!!
I REFUSE.
RUN, YOUR GRACE!!!
KADOOOM!!
!!!
EEEK !!!
YOUR GRAAACE !!!
RAAH

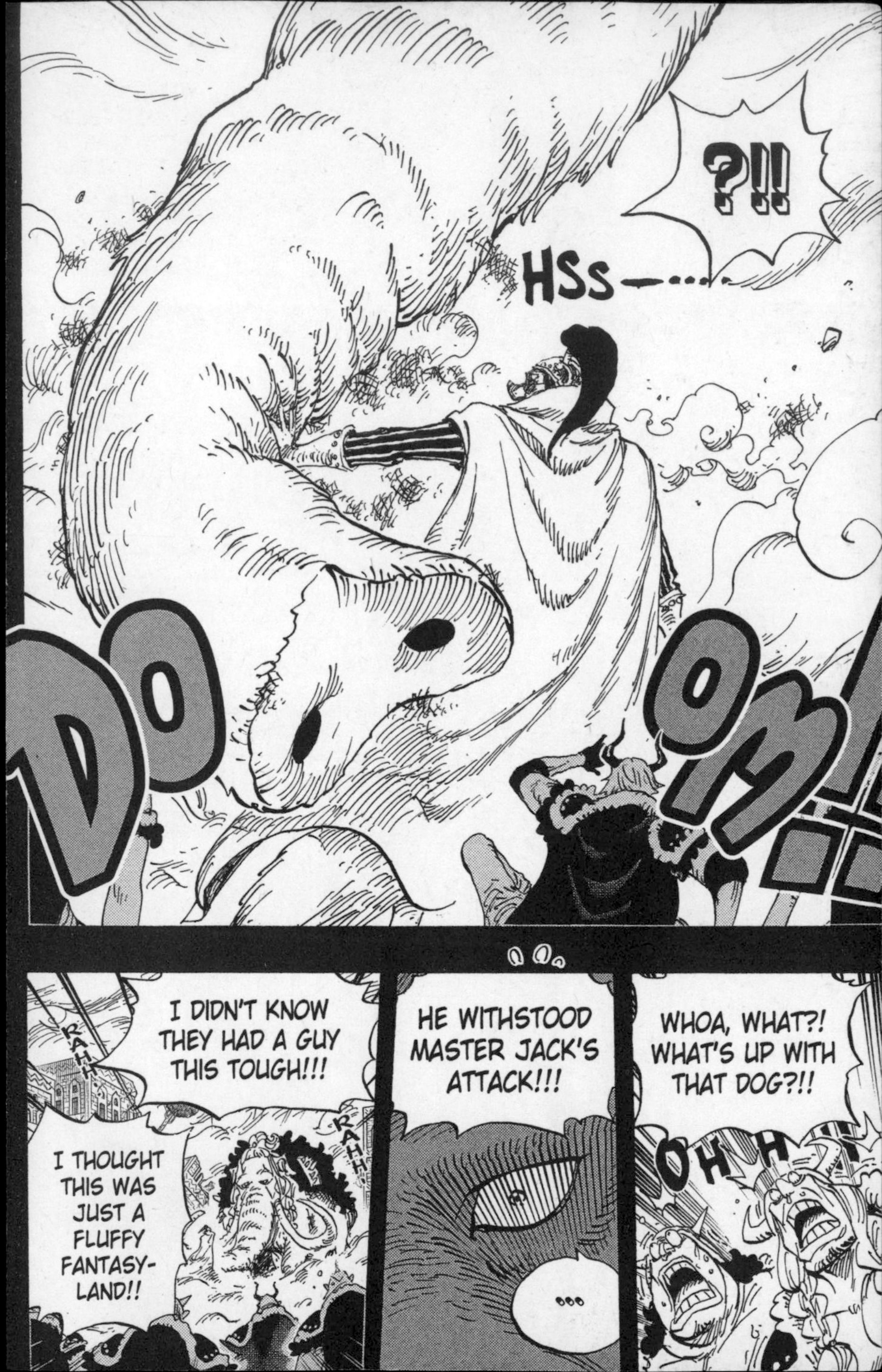
?!!
HSs—...
DOOM!!
WHOA, WHAT?! WHAT'S UP WITH THAT DOG?!!
OHH!!
HE WITHSTOOD MASTER JACK'S ATTACK!!!
...
I DIDN'T KNOW THEY HAD A GUY THIS TOUGH!!!
RAHH
RAHH
I THOUGHT THIS WAS JUST A FLUFFY FANTASY-LAND!!

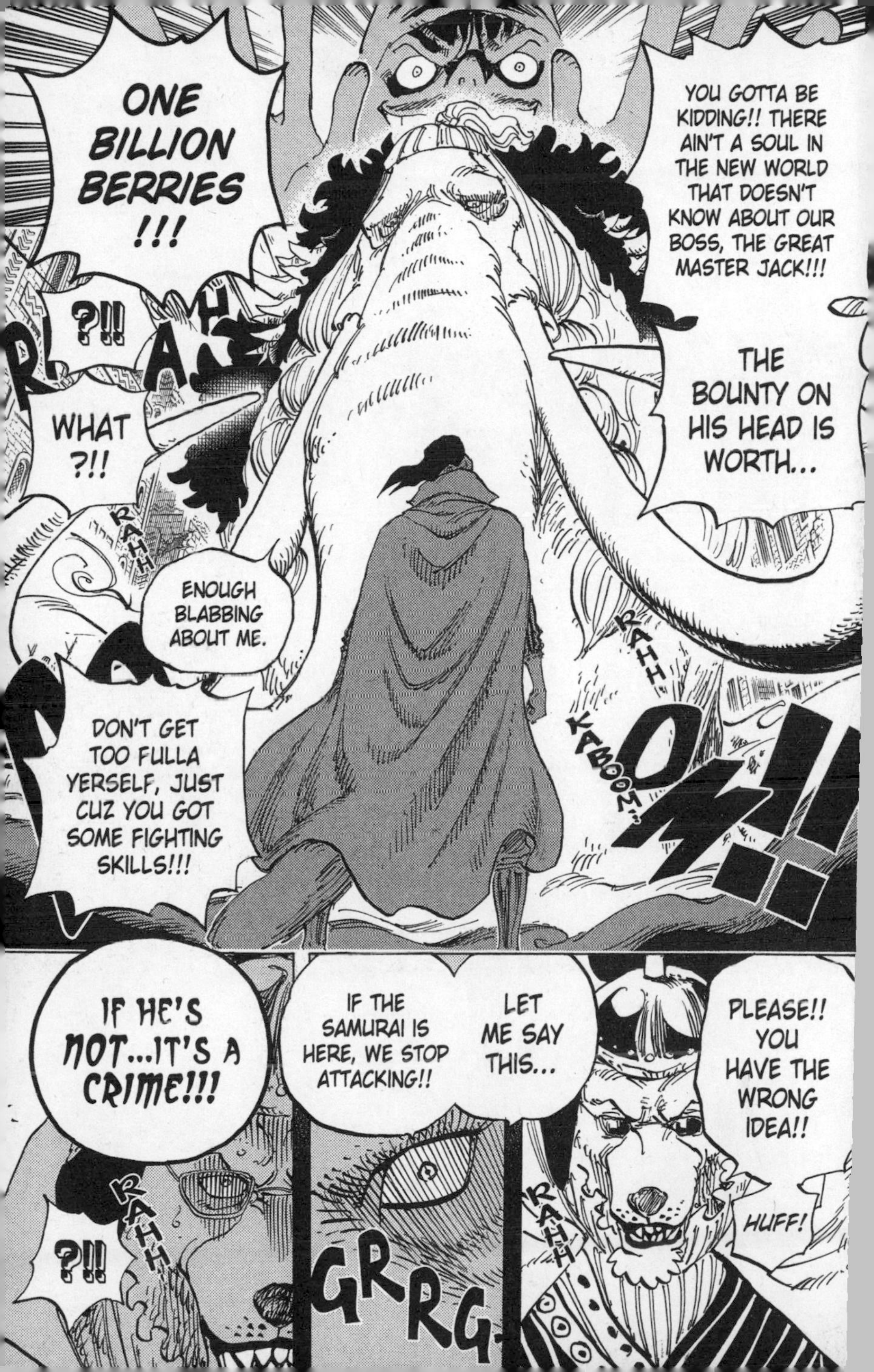
YOU GOTTA BE KIDDING!! THERE AIN'T A SOUL IN THE NEW WORLD THAT DOESN'T KNOW ABOUT OUR BOSS, THE GREAT MASTER JACK!!!
THE BOUNTY ON HIS HEAD IS WORTH...
ONE BILLION BERRIES!!!
?!!
WHAT?!!
RAHH
RAHH
ENOUGH BLABBING ABOUT ME.
KABOOM
DON'T GET TOO FULLA YERSELF, JUST CUZ YOU GOT SOME FIGHTING SKILLS!!!
PLEASE!! YOU HAVE THE WRONG IDEA!!
HUFF!
RAHH
LET ME SAY THIS...
IF THE SAMURAI IS HERE, WE STOP ATTACKING!!
GRRG
IF HE'S NOT...IT'S A CRIME!!!
RAHH
?!!

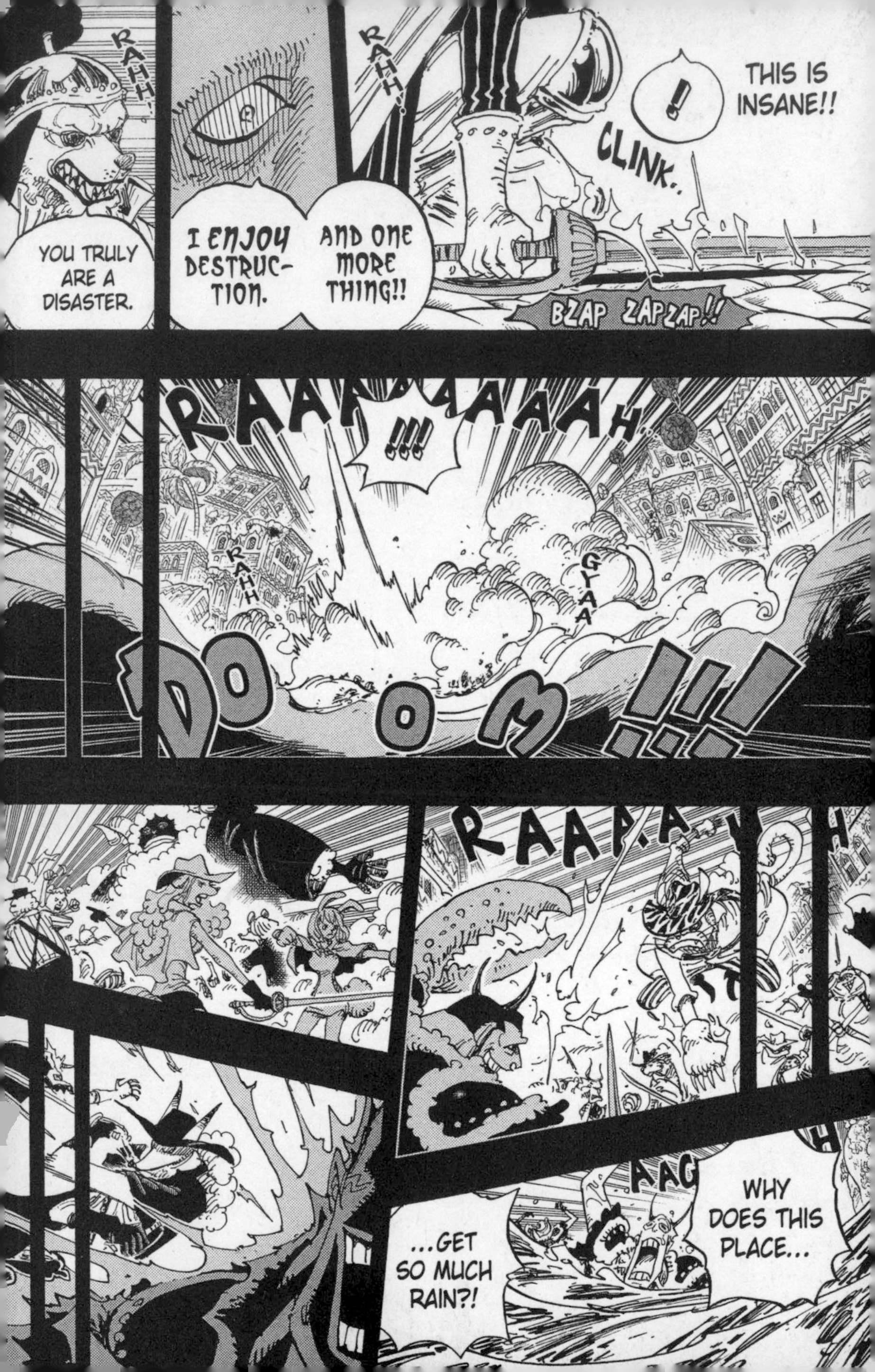
THIS IS INSANE!!
!
RAHH!
CLINK..
BZAP ZAP ZAP!!
AND ONE MORE THING!!
I ENJOY DESTRUCTION.
RAHH!
YOU TRULY ARE A DISASTER.
RAAAAAAAAH
!!!
GYAA
RAHH
DOOM!!!
RAAAAAH
AAG
WHY DOES THIS PLACE...
...GET SO MUCH RAIN?!

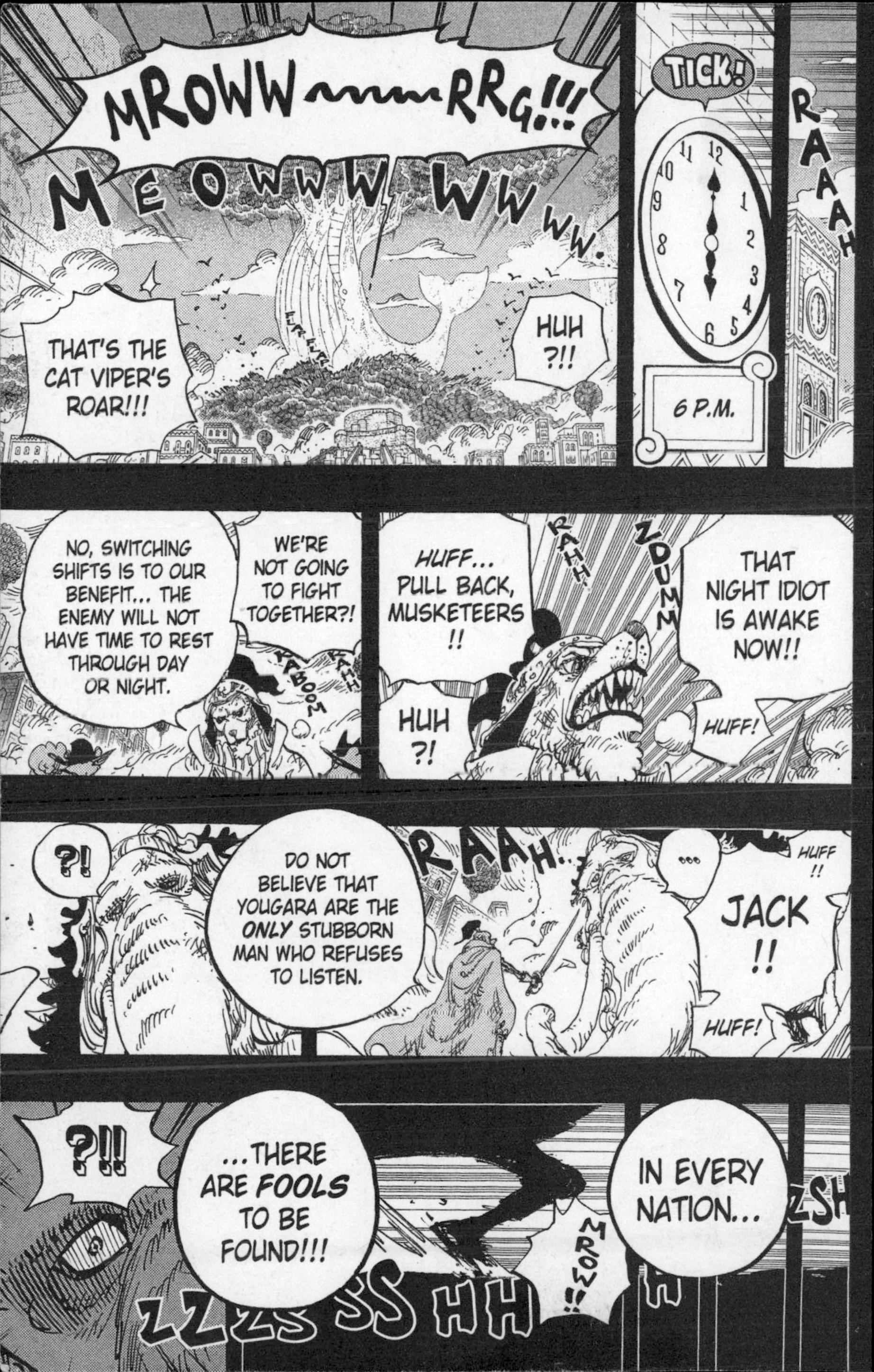
RAAAH
TICK!
6 P.M.
MROWW~~~RRG!!!
MEOWWW WWWWW.
HUH ?!!
THAT'S THE CAT VIPER'S ROAR!!!
THAT NIGHT IDIOT IS AWAKE NOW!!
ZDUMM
RAHH
HUFF!
HUFF... PULL BACK, MUSKETEERS!!
HUH ?!
WE'RE NOT GOING TO FIGHT TOGETHER?!
KAHH
KABOOM
NO, SWITCHING SHIFTS IS TO OUR BENEFIT... THE ENEMY WILL NOT HAVE TIME TO REST THROUGH DAY OR NIGHT.
HUFF !!
JACK !!
...
HUFF!
RAAH..
DO NOT BELIEVE THAT YOUGARA ARE THE *ONLY* STUBBORN MAN WHO REFUSES TO LISTEN.
?!
ZSH
IN EVERY NATION...
MROW!!
...THERE ARE *FOOLS* TO BE FOUND!!!
ZZZSSSHH
?!!

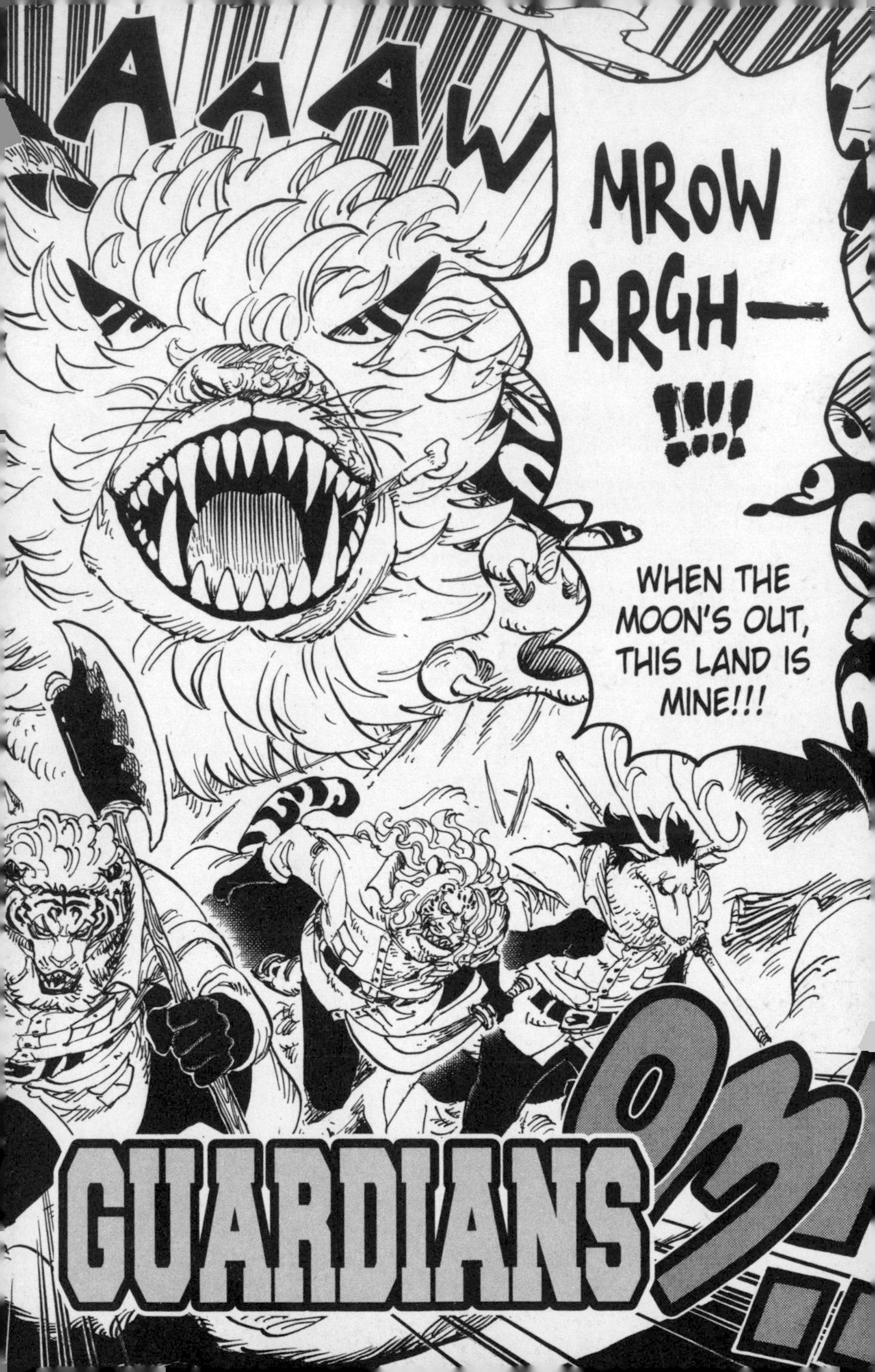
AAAAW
MROW RRGH—!!!!
WHEN THE MOON'S OUT, THIS LAND IS MINE!!!
GUARDIANS

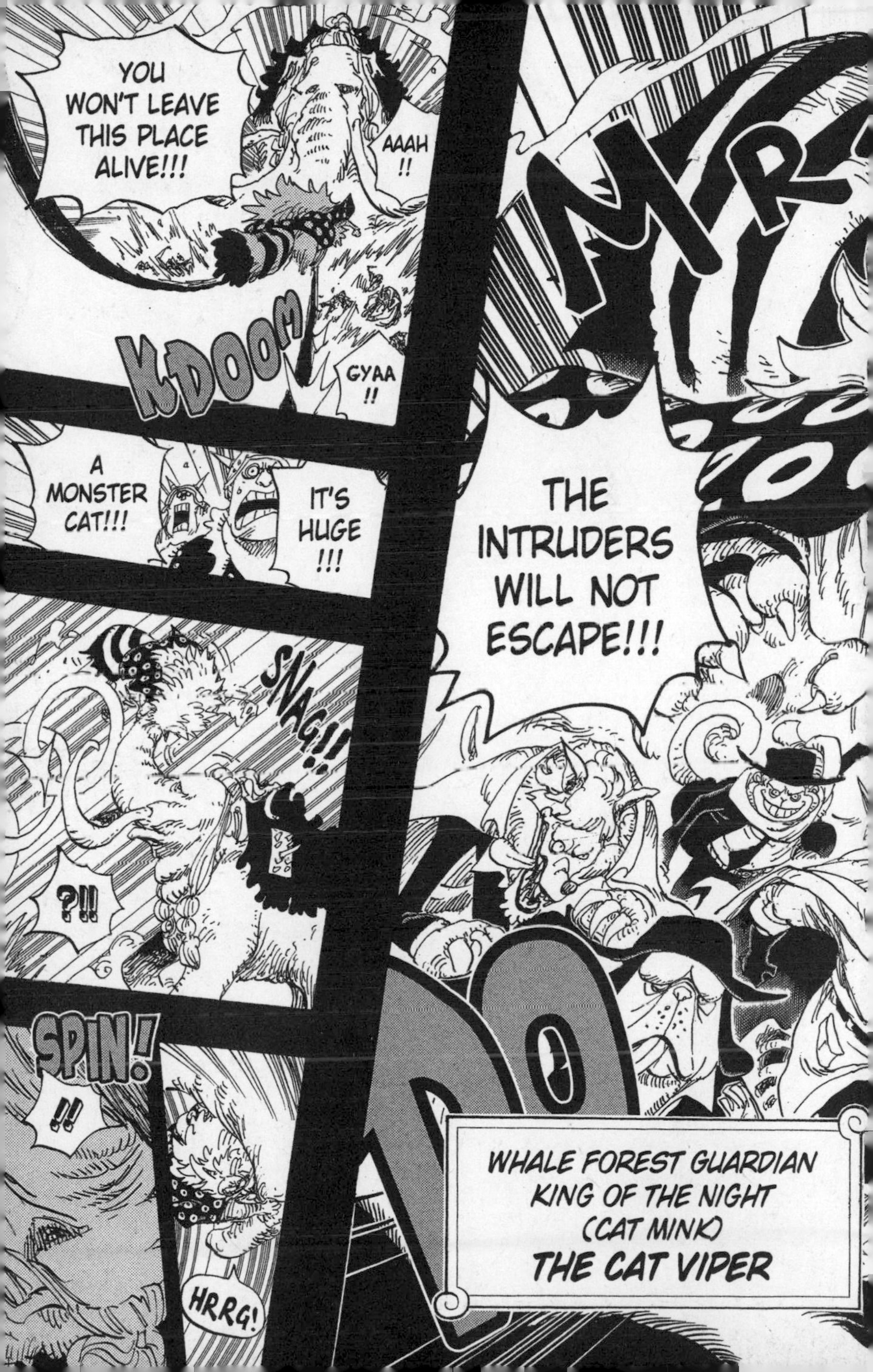
THE INTRUDERS WILL NOT ESCAPE!!!
WHALE FOREST GUARDIAN
KING OF THE NIGHT
(CAT MINK)
THE CAT VIPER
AAAH !!
YOU WON'T LEAVE THIS PLACE ALIVE!!!
KDOOM
GYAA !!
IT'S HUGE !!!
A MONSTER CAT!!!
SNAG!!
?!!
SPIN!
!!
HRRG!

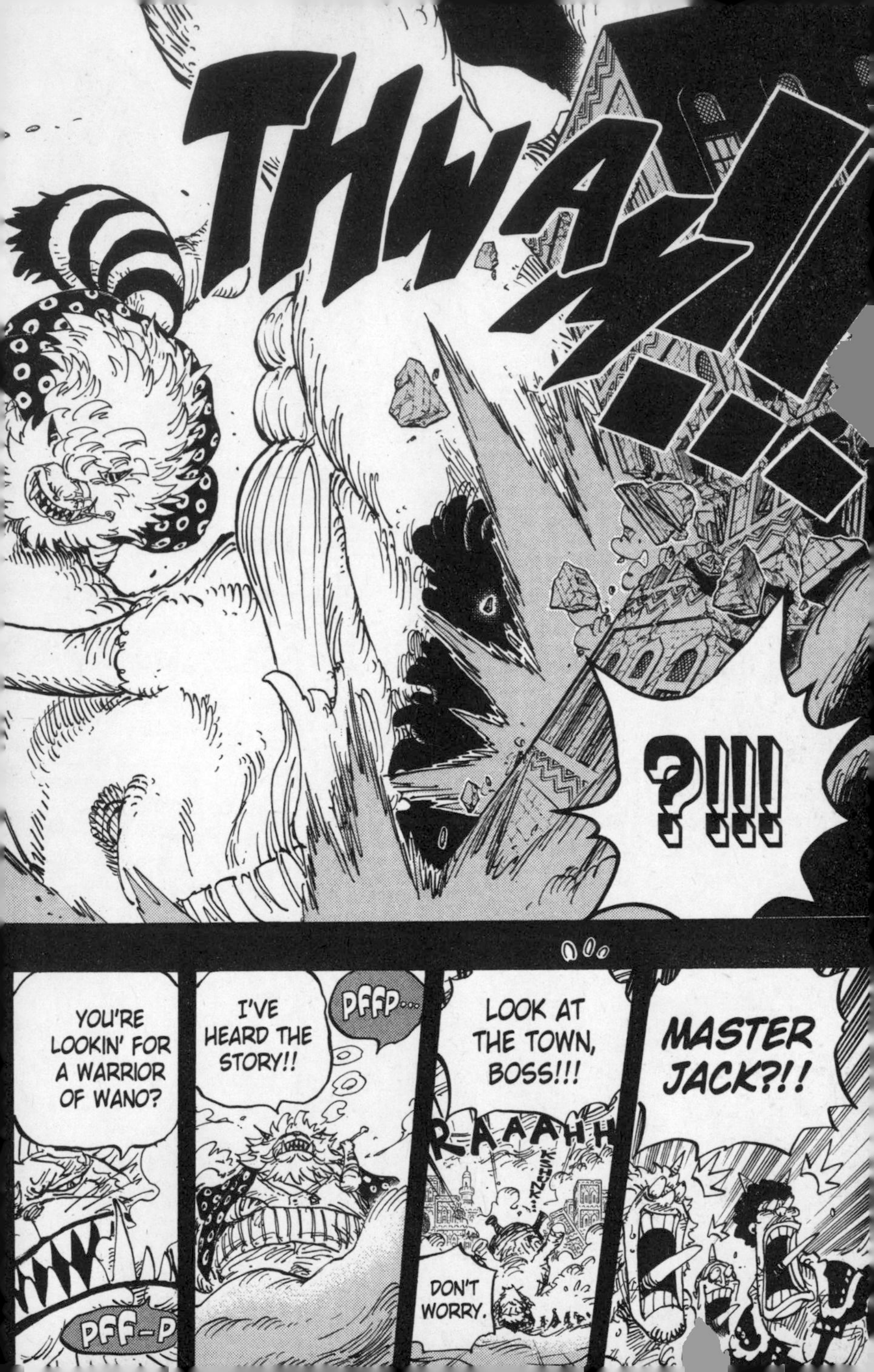
THWAK!!!
?!!!
MASTER JACK?!!
LOOK AT THE TOWN, BOSS!!!
RAAAHH
KSHUNK...
DON'T WORRY.
PFFP...
I'VE HEARD THE STORY!!
YOU'RE LOOKIN' FOR A WARRIOR OF WANO?
PFF-P

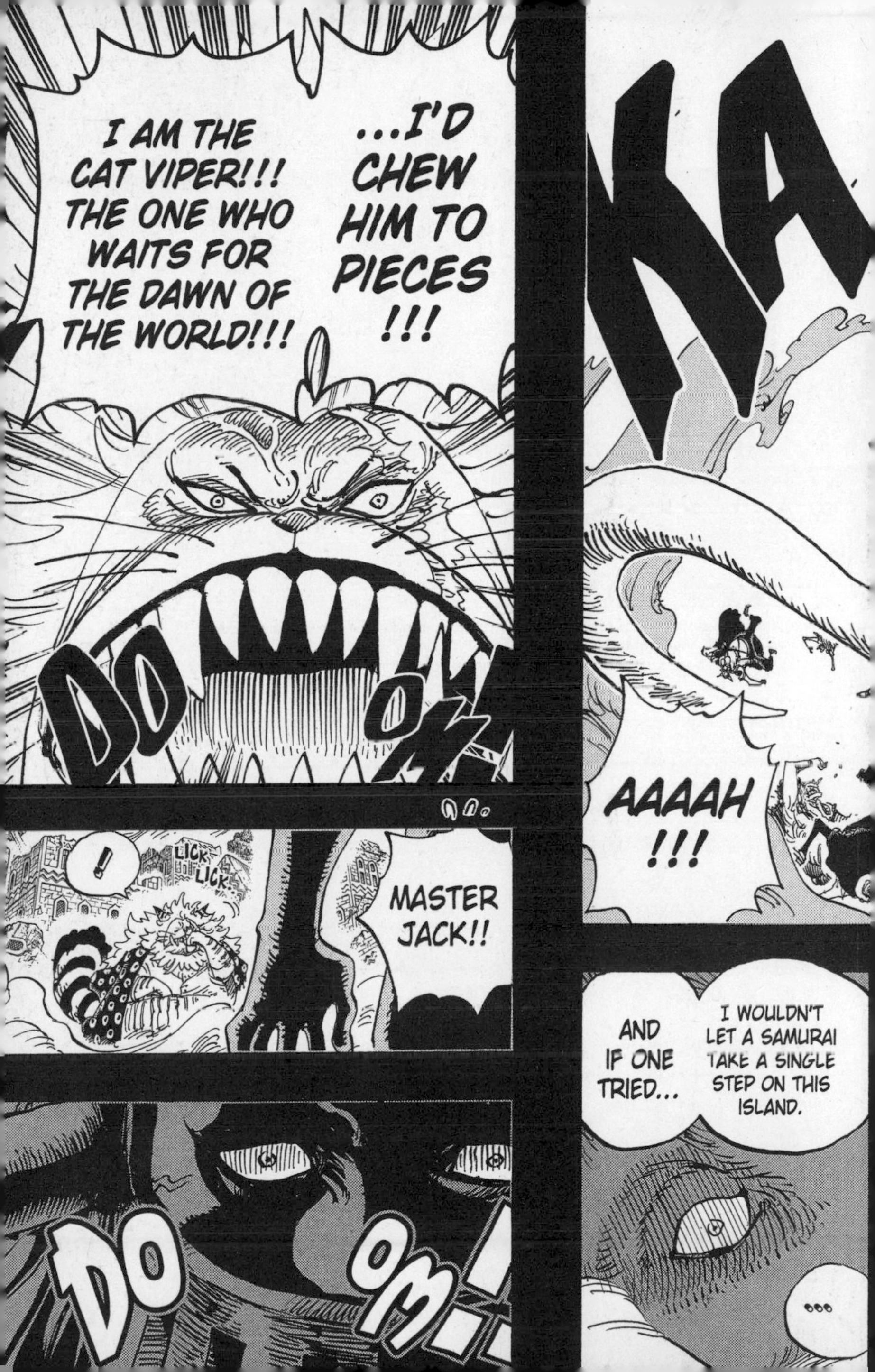
KA
AAAAH!!!
I AM THE CAT VIPER!!! THE ONE WHO WAITS FOR THE DAWN OF THE WORLD!!!
...I'D CHEW HIM TO PIECES!!!
DOOM
I WOULDN'T LET A SAMURAI TAKE A SINGLE STEP ON THIS ISLAND.
AND IF ONE TRIED...
...
!
LICK LICK
MASTER JACK!!
DOOM...

SBS Question Corner

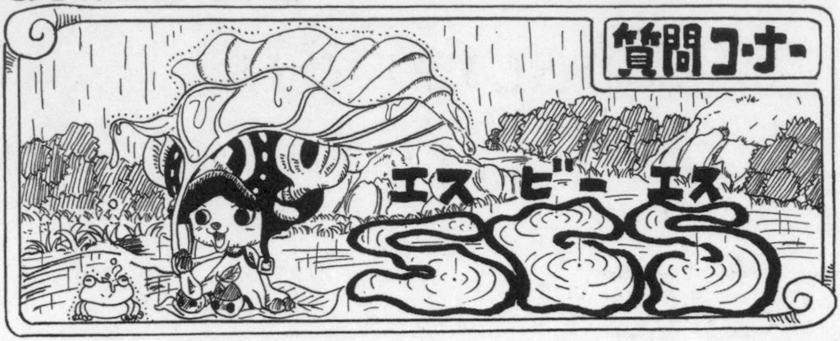

質問コーナー
エスビーエス
SBS

(Michi Nakahara, Tottori)

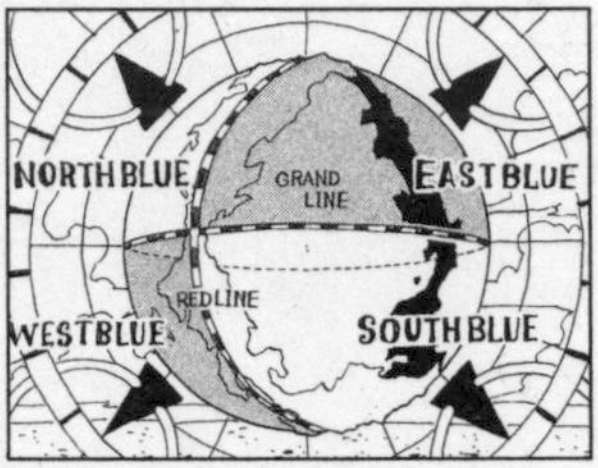

NORTH BLUE
GRAND LINE
EAST BLUE
RED LINE
WEST BLUE
SOUTH BLUE

Q: Hello. I'm having trouble understanding the general world layout of *One Piece*. New World, East Blue, Red Line--I don't get where the heck these things are in relation to each other. Can you explain this in an easy-to-understand way, like with a globe or something?

--Caterpillar

A: Wow...talk about a fresh question!! Yes, I suppose it doesn't add up much, does it? I'm sorry for drawing such an unhelpful manga. So for new readers, we put together a guide to the **World of One Piece** at the end of the book! Check it out, if you want!!

Q: Hi, Mr. Oda. I'm curious about the names of some new characters from Volume 78. Please introduce us to the doctor begging for help, the little granddaughter, and the grandma who told her to run ahead and leave her behind.

--Person

A: Here they are.

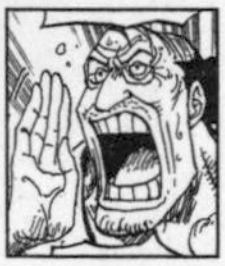

Doctor
Needa Hand
(Hobby: Guitar)

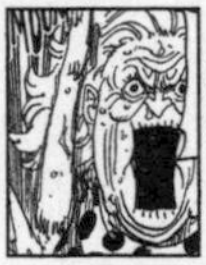

Elderly Woman
Stella Live
(Former Dancer)

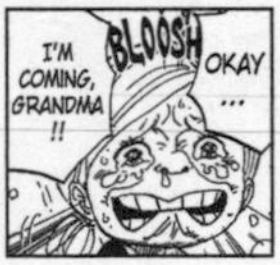

I'M COMING, GRANDMA!!
BLOOSH
OKAY...

Grandkid
Staya Live
(Future Dancer)

Q: I can make out most of them, but can you give us a rundown of who wrote each autograph on page 115 of Volume 80?

--Also, Who Were They For?

A: The five crew members made these autographs for Bartolomeo, of course.

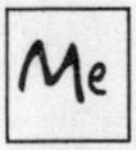

Me

Luffy

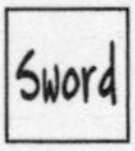

Sword

Zolo

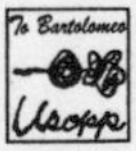

To Bartolomeo
Usopp

Usopp ("To Bartolomeo," a profile of his own head, "Usopp")

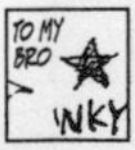

TO MY BRO
NKY

Franky ("To my bro," star symbol, "Franky")

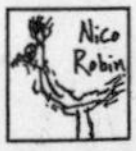

Nico Robin

Robin ("Nico Robin," drawing of a rooster)

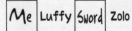

Chapter 810:
THE TWIRLY HAT CREW ARRIVES

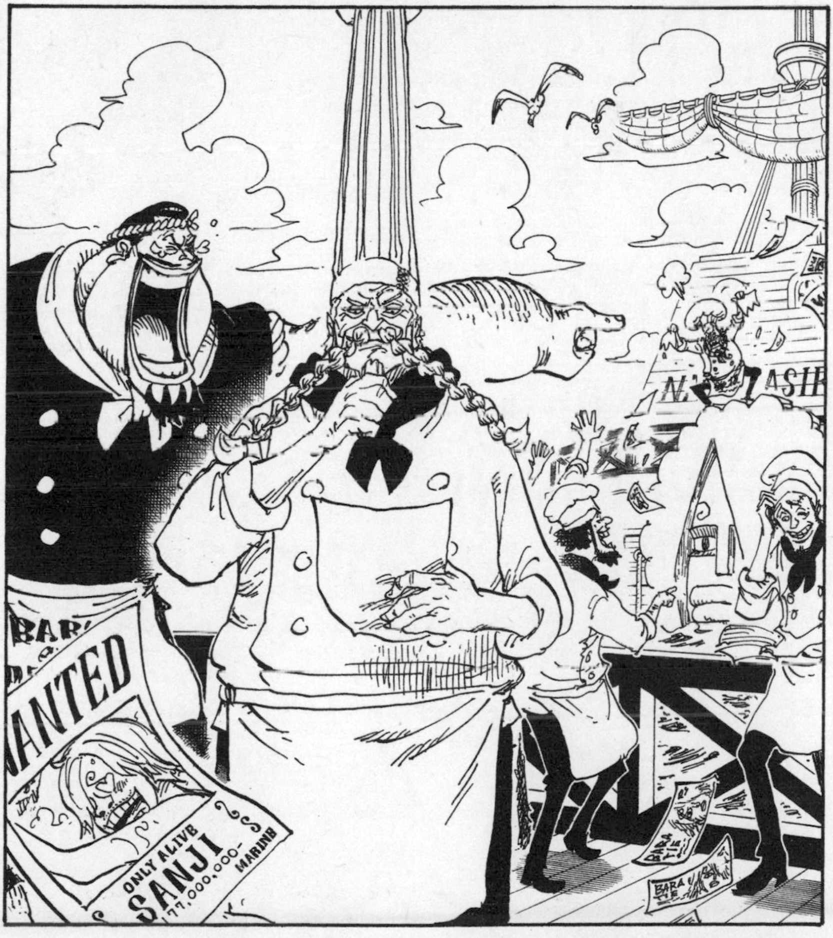
WANTED
SANJI
ONLY ALIVE
77,000,000-
MARINE

DECKS OF THE WORLD, 500-MILLION-MAN ARC, VOL. 5:
"BARATIE--LOTS OF QUESTIONS, BUT AT LEAST HE'S HEALTHY"

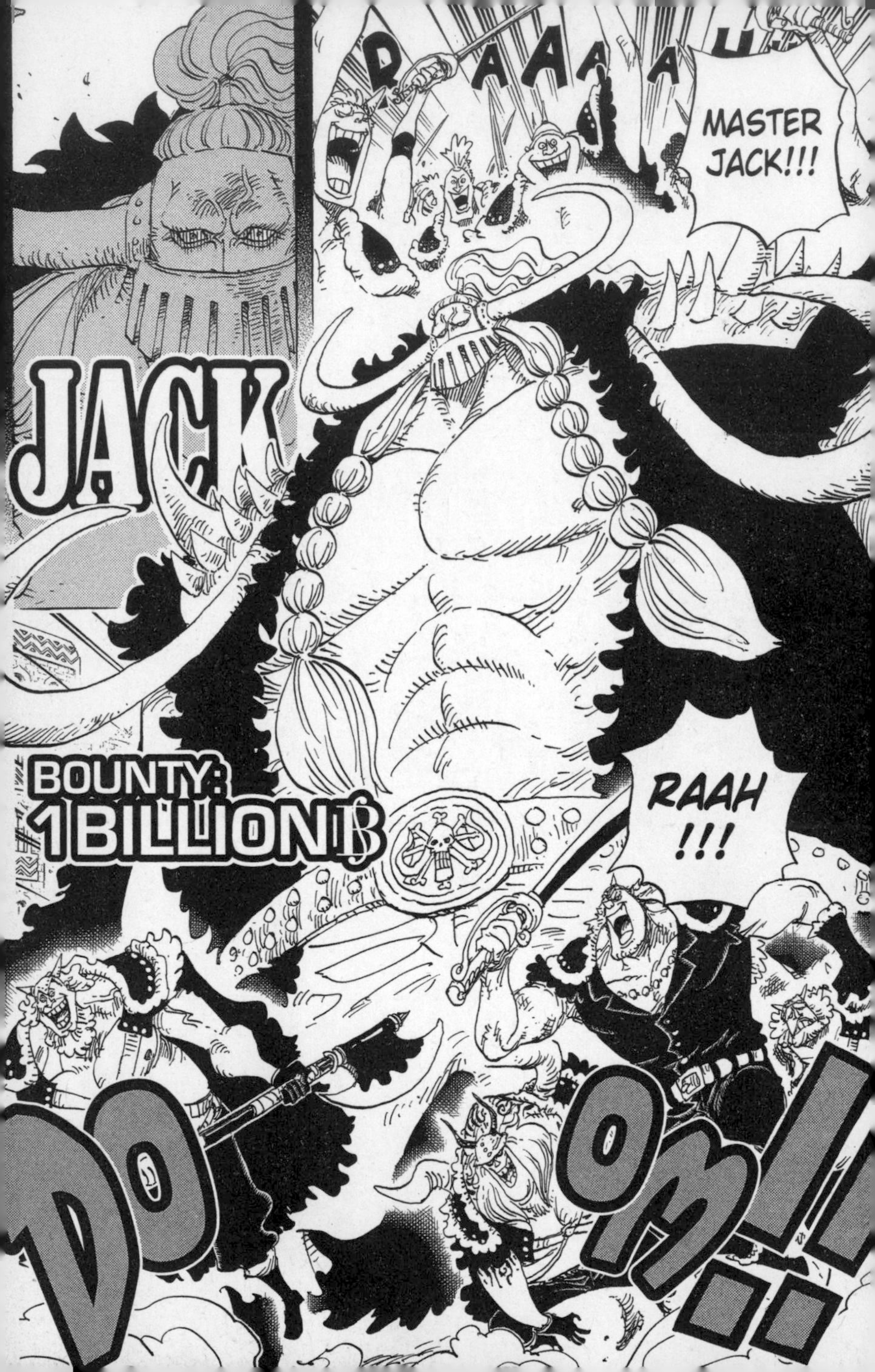
DAAAAA...!!
MASTER JACK!!!
JACK
BOUNTY:
1 BILLION ฿
RAAH !!!
DOOSH..!!

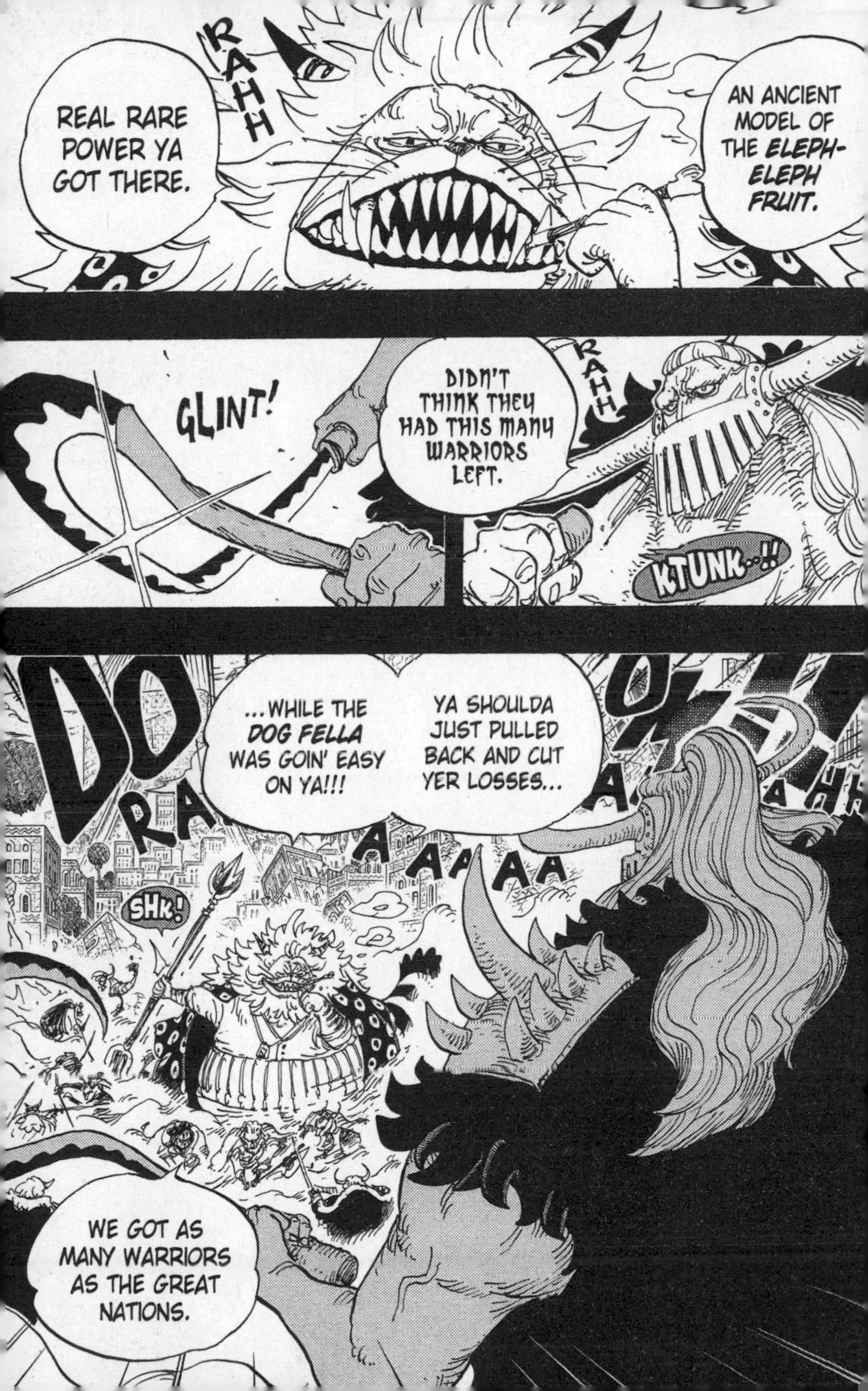
AN ANCIENT MODEL OF THE *ELEPH-ELEPH FRUIT.*
RAHH
REAL RARE POWER YA GOT THERE.
RAHH
KTUNK..!!
DIDN'T THINK THEY HAD THIS MANY WARRIORS LEFT.
GLINT!
YA SHOULDA JUST PULLED BACK AND CUT YER LOSSES...
...WHILE THE *DOG FELLA* WAS GOIN' EASY ON YA!!!
DORAAAAA
SHK!
WE GOT AS MANY WARRIORS AS THE GREAT NATIONS.

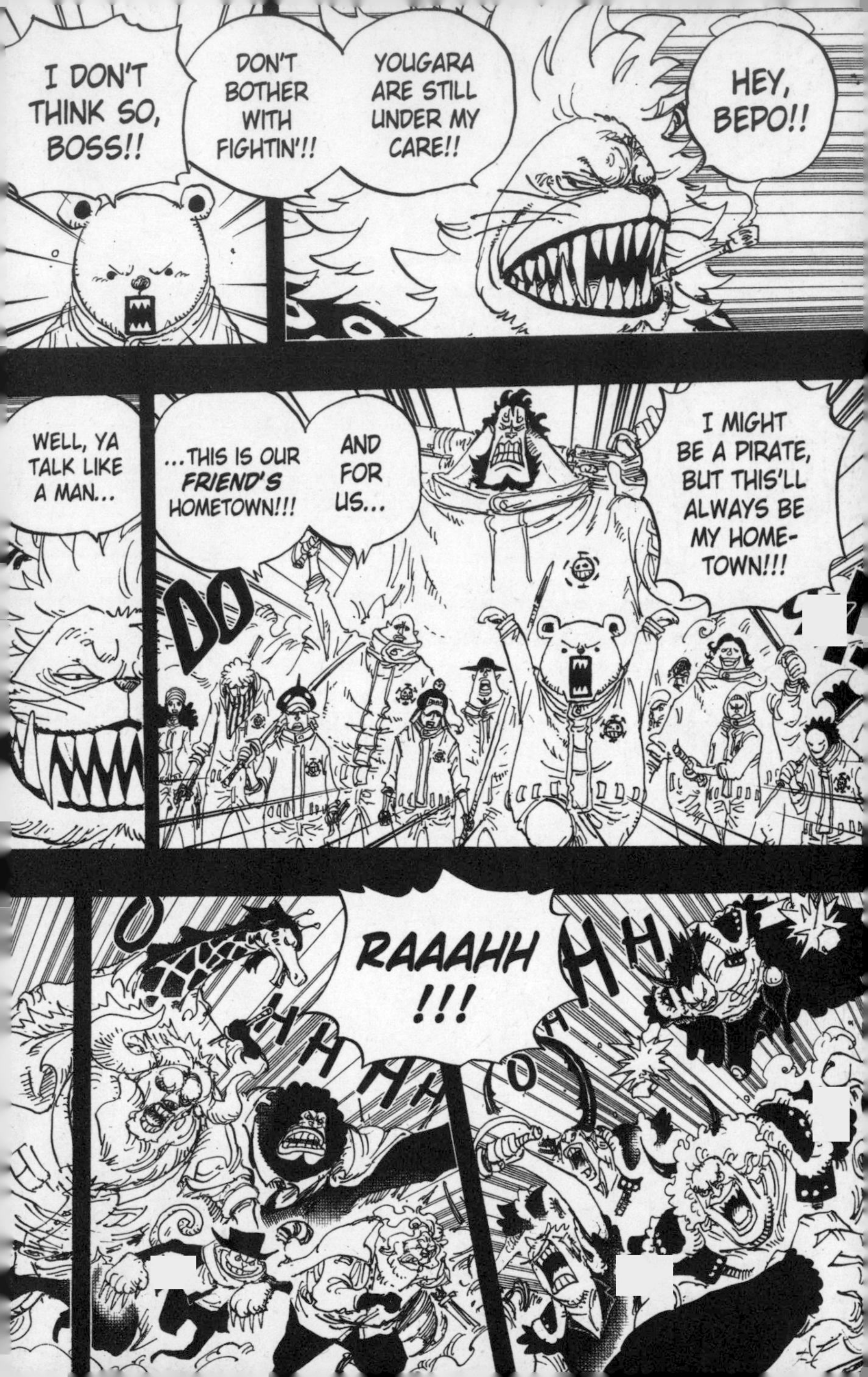
HEY, BEPO!!
YOUGARA ARE STILL UNDER MY CARE!!
DON'T BOTHER WITH FIGHTIN'!!
I DON'T THINK SO, BOSS!!
I MIGHT BE A PIRATE, BUT THIS'LL ALWAYS BE MY HOMETOWN!!!
AND FOR US...
...THIS IS OUR *FRIEND'S* HOMETOWN!!!
DO
WELL, YA TALK LIKE A MAN...
RAAAHH!!!

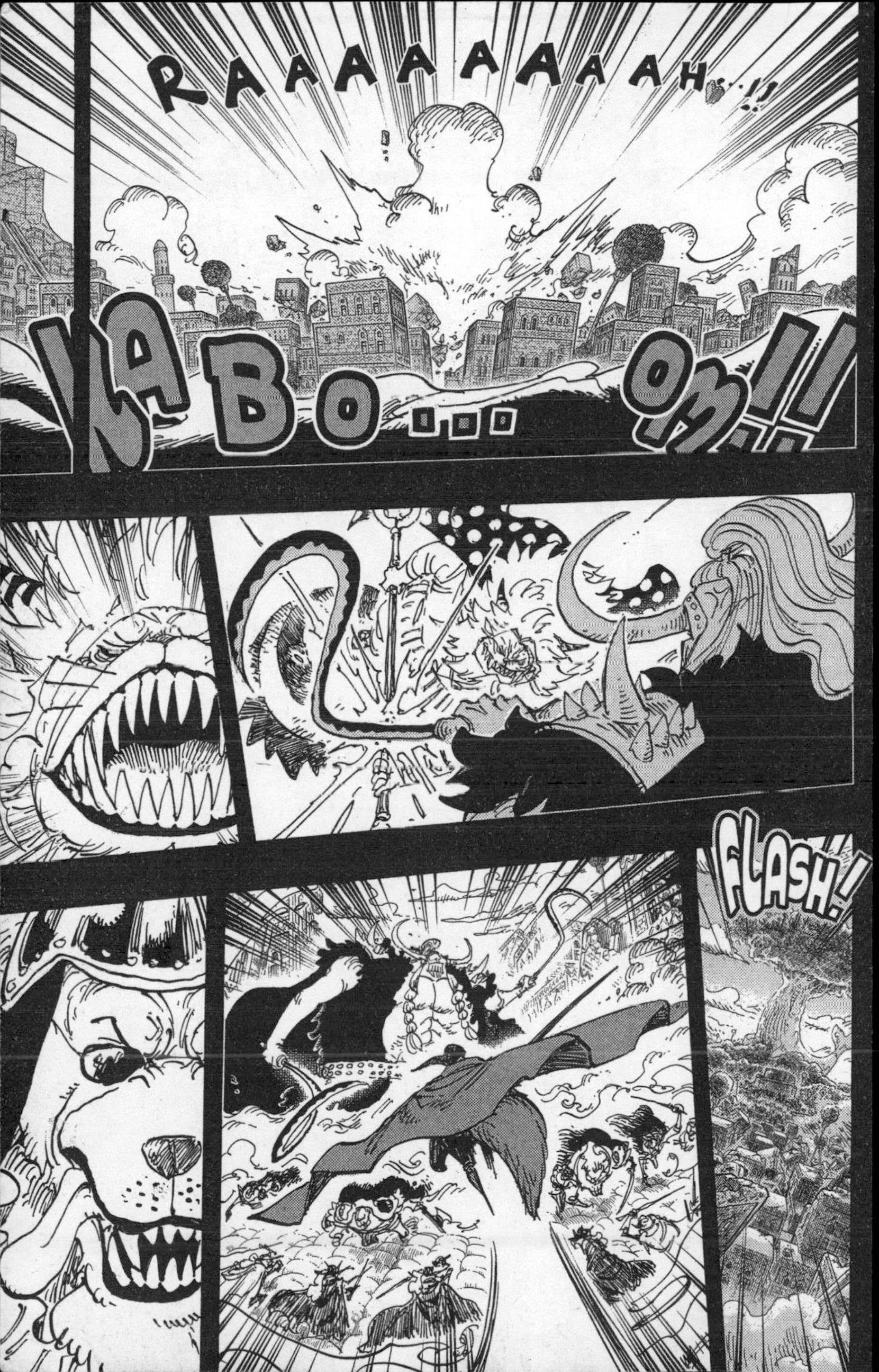
RAAAAAAAAAH!!
KA BO... OM!!
FLASH!

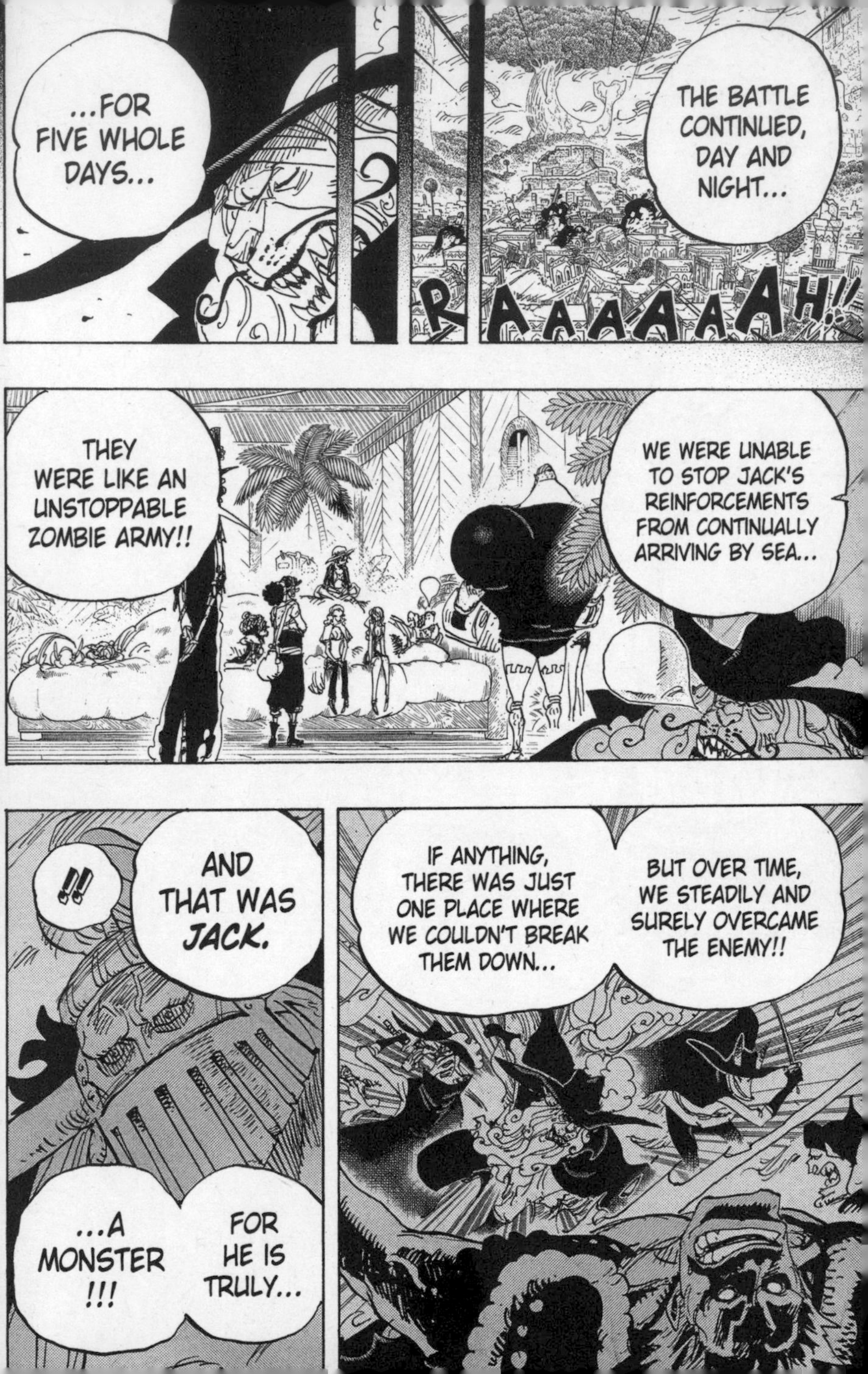
THE BATTLE CONTINUED, DAY AND NIGHT...
RAAAAAH!!
...FOR FIVE WHOLE DAYS...
WE WERE UNABLE TO STOP JACK'S REINFORCEMENTS FROM CONTINUALLY ARRIVING BY SEA...
THEY WERE LIKE AN UNSTOPPABLE ZOMBIE ARMY!!
BUT OVER TIME, WE STEADILY AND SURELY OVERCAME THE ENEMY!!
IF ANYTHING, THERE WAS JUST ONE PLACE WHERE WE COULDN'T BREAK THEM DOWN...
AND THAT WAS JACK.
!!
FOR HE IS TRULY...
...A MONSTER!!!

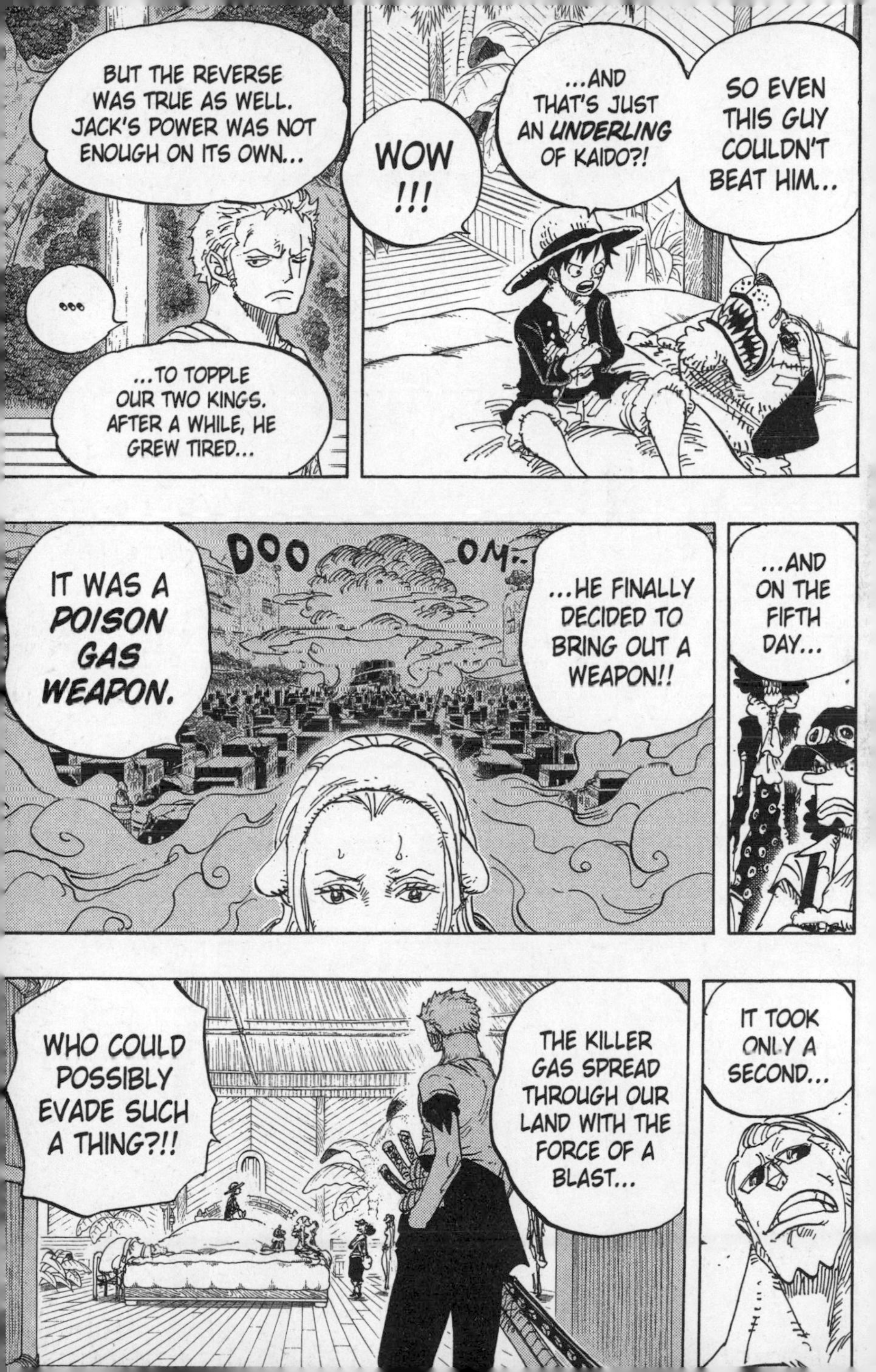
SO EVEN THIS GUY COULDN'T BEAT HIM...
...AND THAT'S JUST AN UNDERLING OF KAIDO?!
WOW !!!
BUT THE REVERSE WAS TRUE AS WELL. JACK'S POWER WAS NOT ENOUGH ON ITS OWN...
...
...TO TOPPLE OUR TWO KINGS. AFTER A WHILE, HE GREW TIRED...
...AND ON THE FIFTH DAY...
...HE FINALLY DECIDED TO BRING OUT A WEAPON!!
DOO OM
IT WAS A POISON GAS WEAPON.
IT TOOK ONLY A SECOND...
THE KILLER GAS SPREAD THROUGH OUR LAND WITH THE FORCE OF A BLAST...
WHO COULD POSSIBLY EVADE SUCH A THING?!!

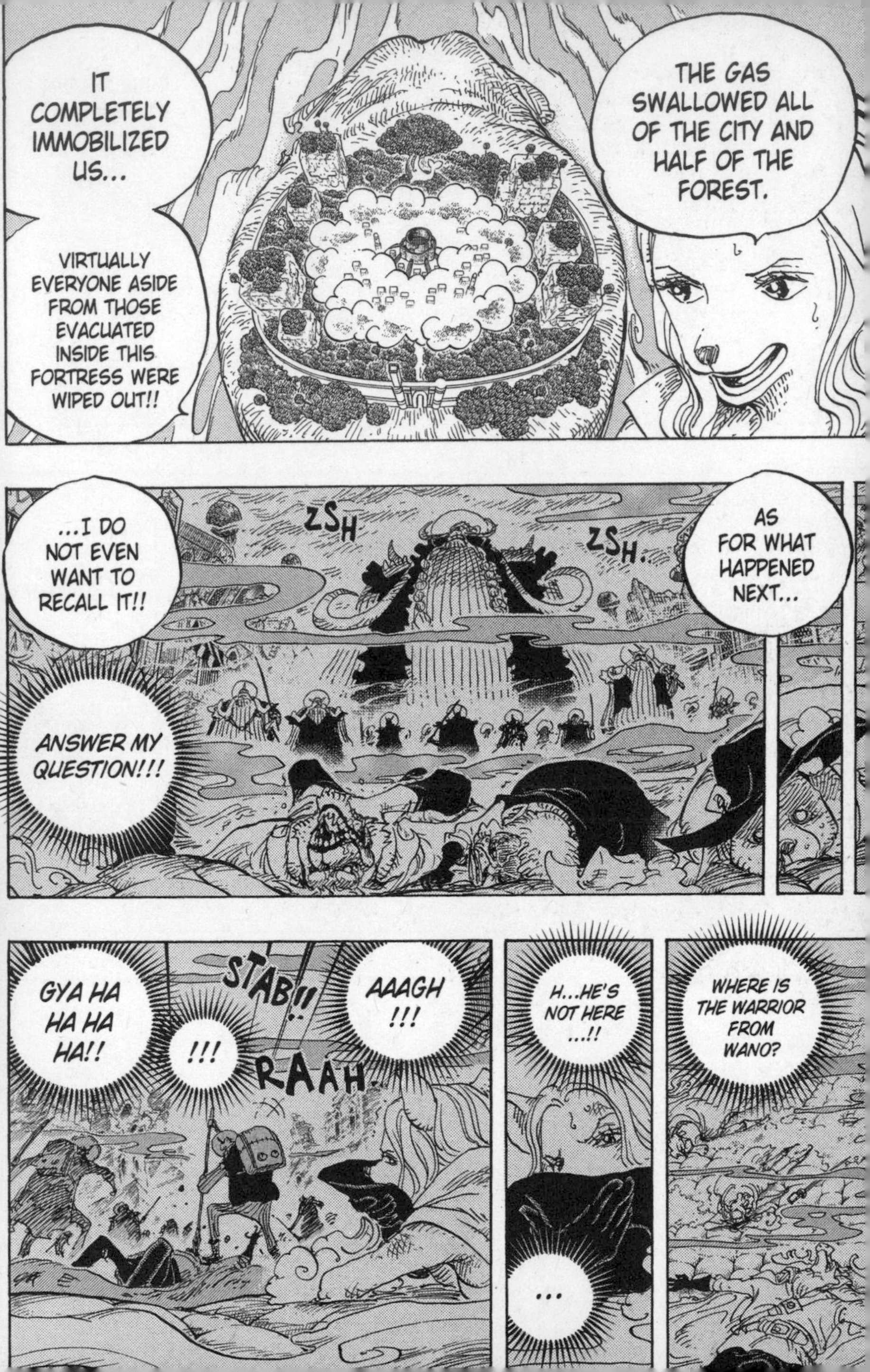
THE GAS SWALLOWED ALL OF THE CITY AND HALF OF THE FOREST.
IT COMPLETELY IMMOBILIZED US...
VIRTUALLY EVERYONE ASIDE FROM THOSE EVACUATED INSIDE THIS FORTRESS WERE WIPED OUT!!
AS FOR WHAT HAPPENED NEXT...
ZSH
ZSH...
...I DO NOT EVEN WANT TO RECALL IT!!
ANSWER MY QUESTION!!!
WHERE IS THE WARRIOR FROM WANO?
H...HE'S NOT HERE ...!!
...
AAAGH !!!
STAB!!
RAAH
!!!
GYA HA HA HA HA!!

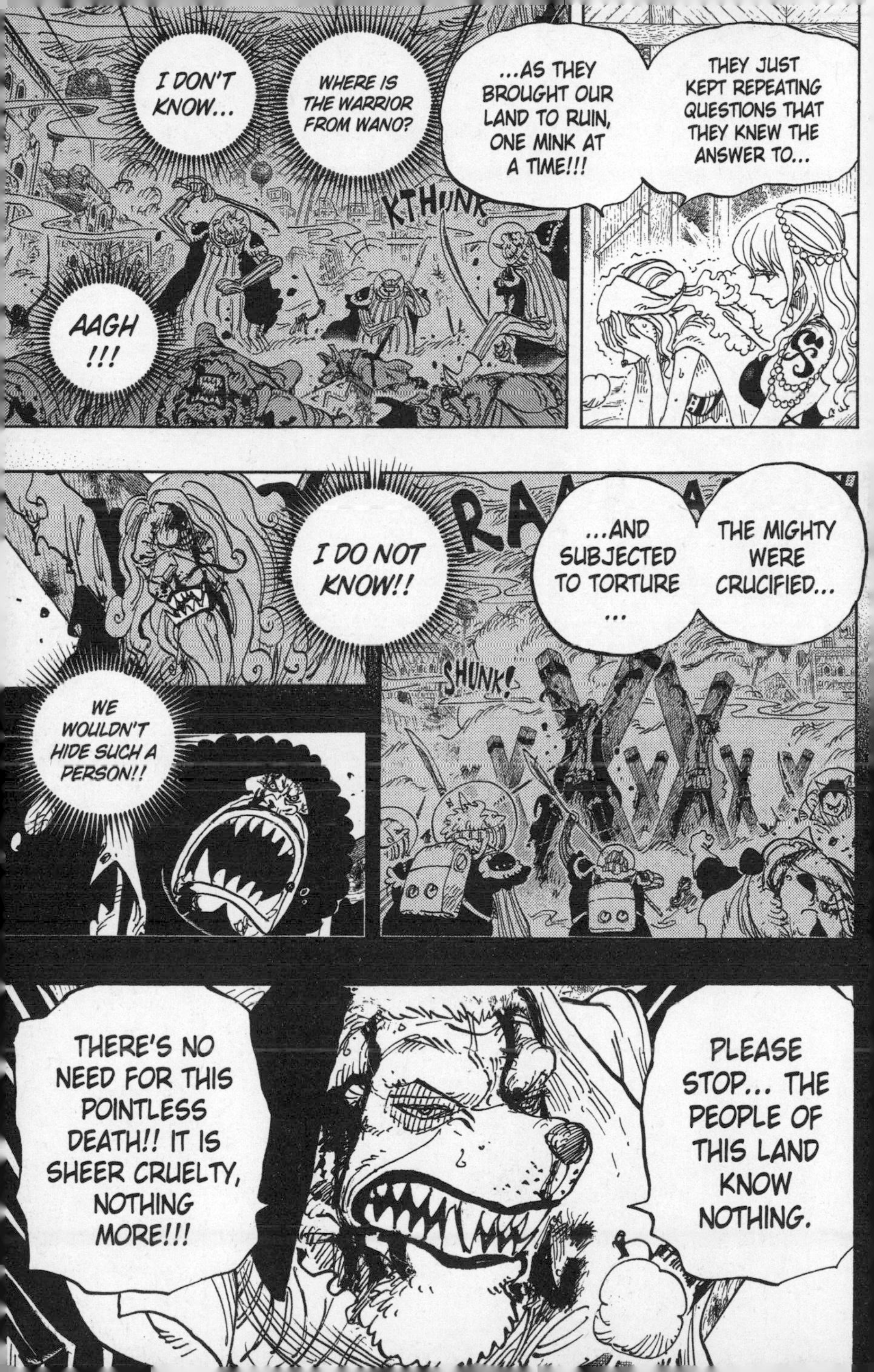
THEY JUST KEPT REPEATING QUESTIONS THAT THEY KNEW THE ANSWER TO...
...AS THEY BROUGHT OUR LAND TO RUIN, ONE MINK AT A TIME!!!
WHERE IS THE WARRIOR FROM WANO?
I DON'T KNOW...
KTHUNK
AAGH!!!
THE MIGHTY WERE CRUCIFIED...
...AND SUBJECTED TO TORTURE ...
SHUNK!
I DO NOT KNOW!!
WE WOULDN'T HIDE SUCH A PERSON!!
PLEASE STOP... THE PEOPLE OF THIS LAND KNOW NOTHING.
THERE'S NO NEED FOR THIS POINTLESS DEATH!! IT IS SHEER CRUELTY, NOTHING MORE!!!

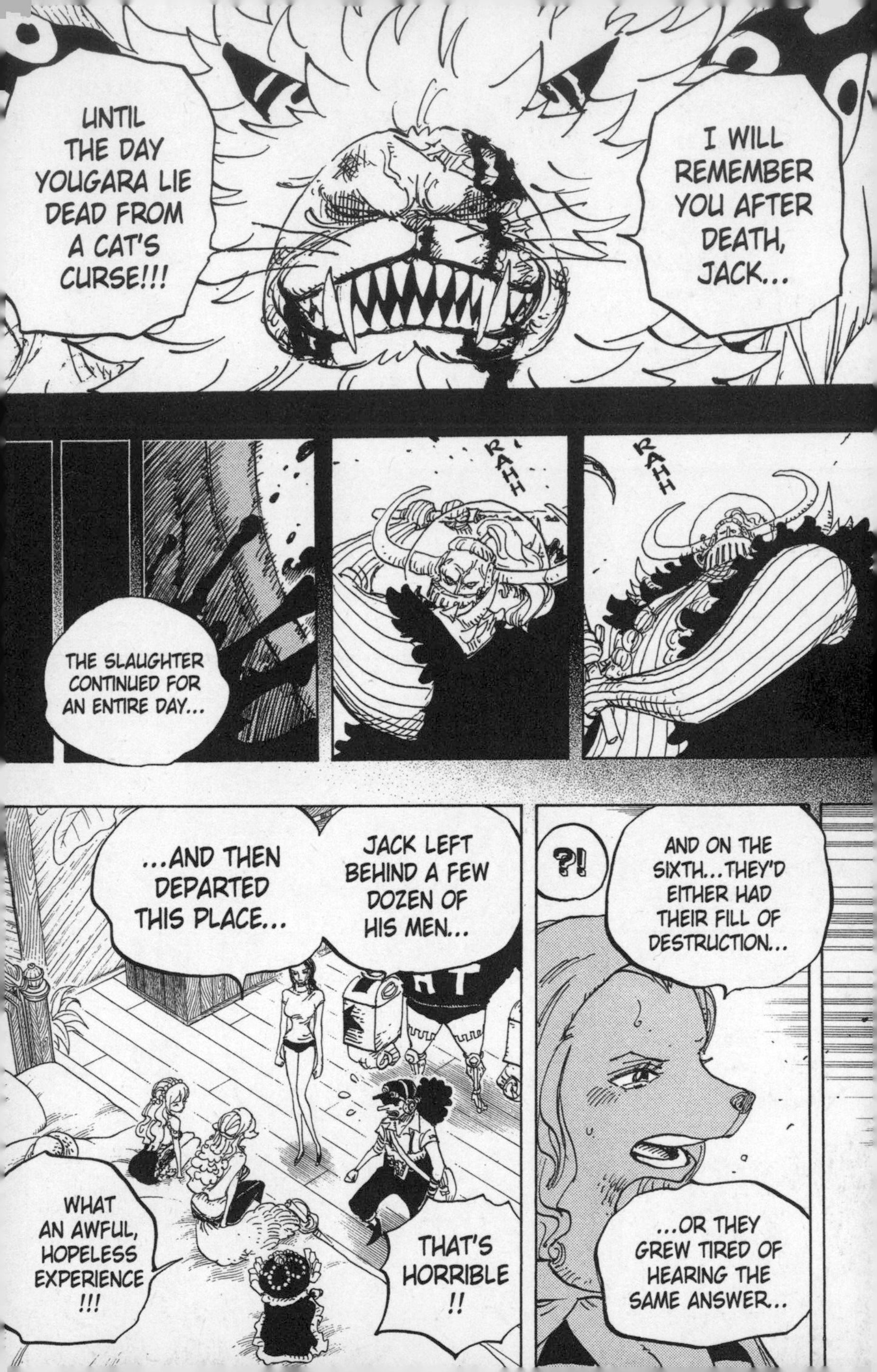
I WILL REMEMBER YOU AFTER DEATH, JACK...
UNTIL THE DAY YOUGARA LIE DEAD FROM A CAT'S CURSE!!!
RAHH
RAHH
THE SLAUGHTER CONTINUED FOR AN ENTIRE DAY...
AND ON THE SIXTH...THEY'D EITHER HAD THEIR FILL OF DESTRUCTION...
?!
...OR THEY GREW TIRED OF HEARING THE SAME ANSWER...
JACK LEFT BEHIND A FEW DOZEN OF HIS MEN...
...AND THEN DEPARTED THIS PLACE...
THAT'S HORRIBLE !!
WHAT AN AWFUL, HOPELESS EXPERIENCE !!!

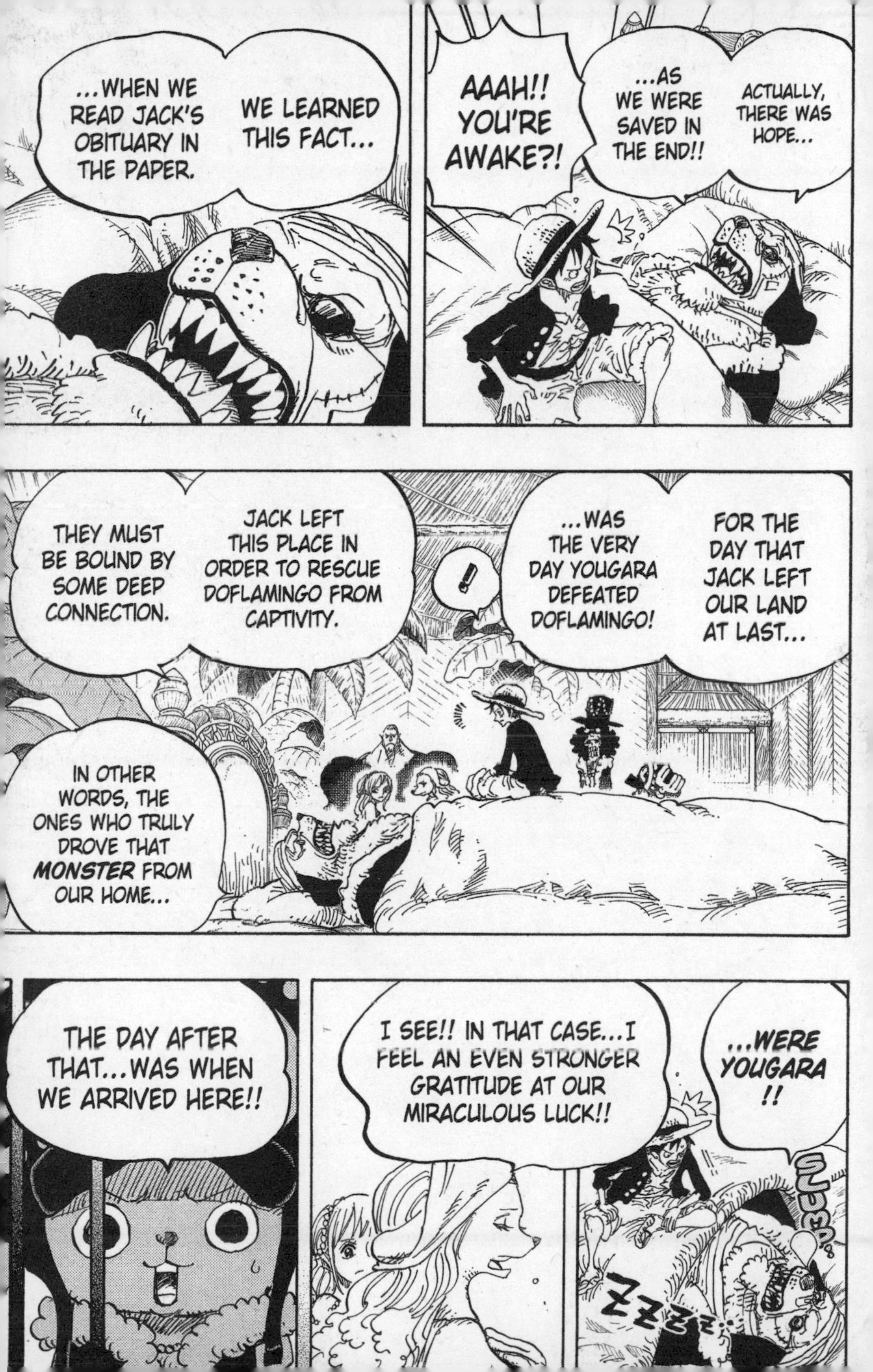
ACTUALLY, THERE WAS HOPE...
...AS WE WERE SAVED IN THE END!!
AAAH!! YOU'RE AWAKE?!
WE LEARNED THIS FACT...
...WHEN WE READ JACK'S OBITUARY IN THE PAPER.
FOR THE DAY THAT JACK LEFT OUR LAND AT LAST...
...WAS THE VERY DAY YOUGARA DEFEATED DOFLAMINGO!
!
JACK LEFT THIS PLACE IN ORDER TO RESCUE DOFLAMINGO FROM CAPTIVITY.
THEY MUST BE BOUND BY SOME DEEP CONNECTION.
IN OTHER WORDS, THE ONES WHO TRULY DROVE THAT *MONSTER* FROM OUR HOME...
...WERE YOUGARA !!
SLUMP
I SEE!! IN THAT CASE...I FEEL AN EVEN STRONGER GRATITUDE AT OUR MIRACULOUS LUCK!!
THE DAY AFTER THAT...WAS WHEN WE ARRIVED HERE!!

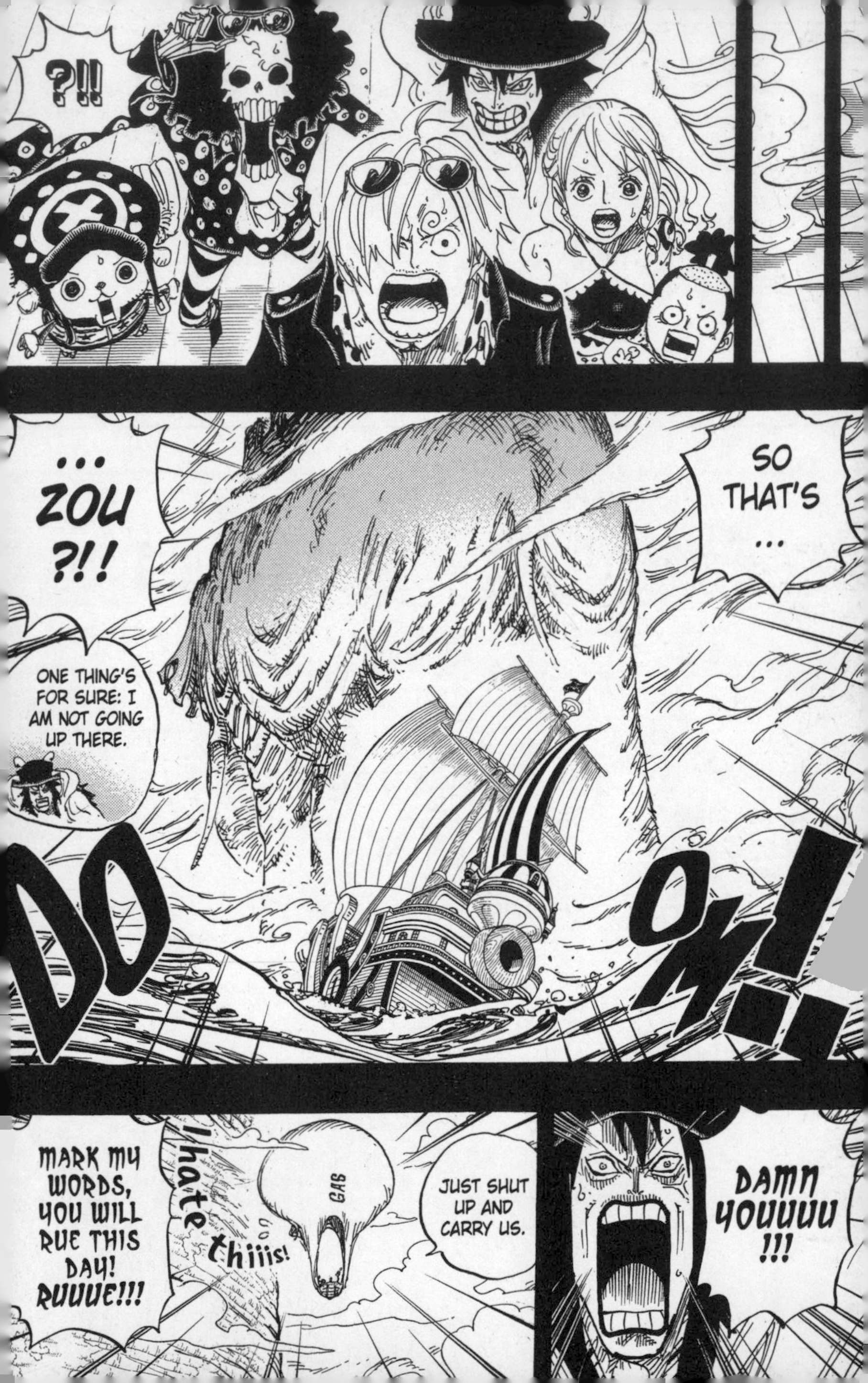
?!!
SO THAT'S ...
... ZOU ?!!
ONE THING'S FOR SURE: I AM NOT GOING UP THERE.
DOON!!
DAMN YOUUUU !!!
JUST SHUT UP AND CARRY US.
GAS
I hate thiiis!
MARK MY WORDS, YOU WILL RUE THIS DAY! RUUUE!!!

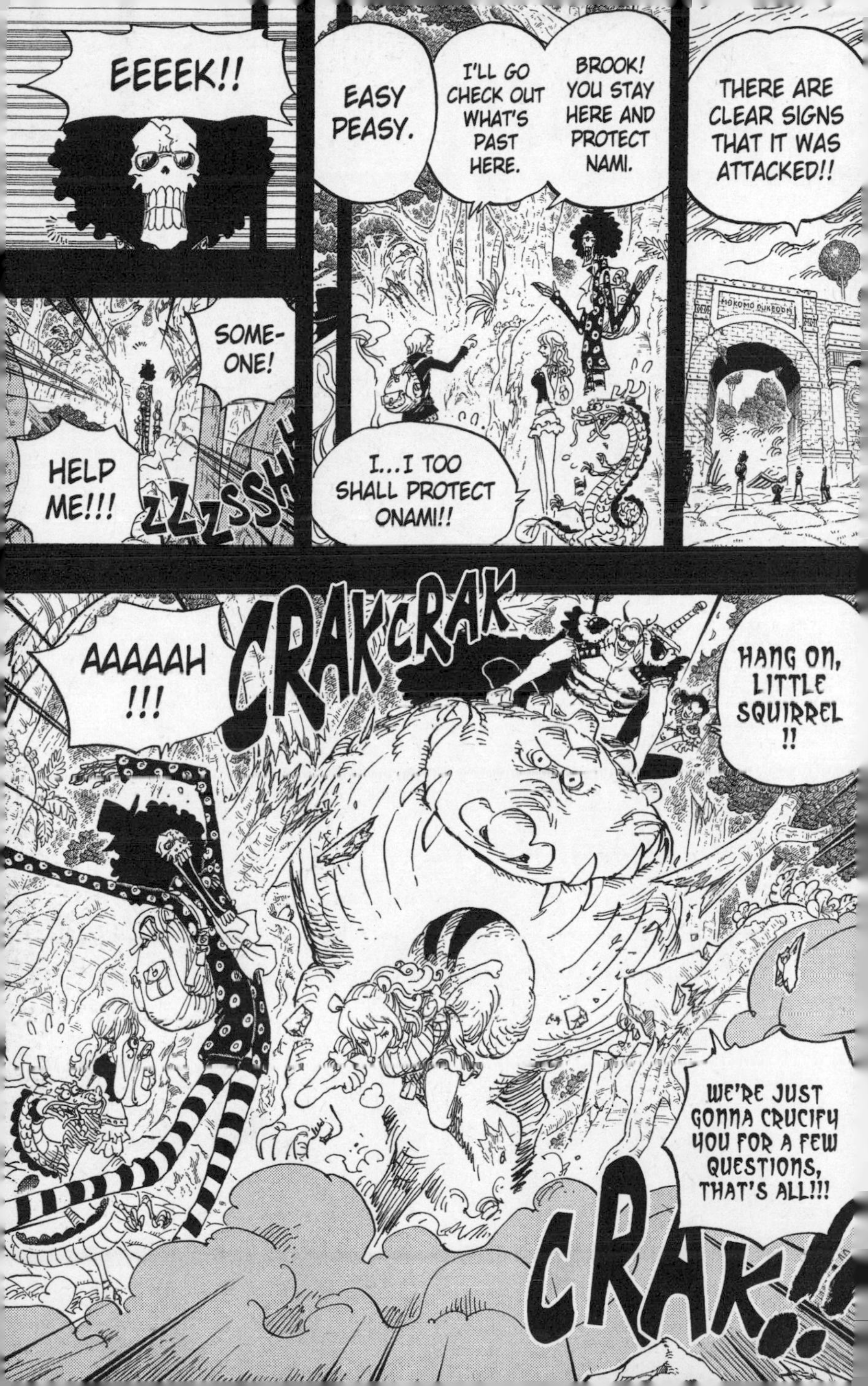
THERE ARE CLEAR SIGNS THAT IT WAS ATTACKED!!
MOKOMO DUKEDOM
BROOK! YOU STAY HERE AND PROTECT NAMI.
I'LL GO CHECK OUT WHAT'S PAST HERE.
EASY PEASY.
I...I TOO SHALL PROTECT ONAMI!!
EEEEK!!
SOME-ONE!
HELP ME!!!
ZZZSSH
HANG ON, LITTLE SQUIRREL!!
CRAKCRAK
AAAAAH!!!
WE'RE JUST GONNA CRUCIFY YOU FOR A FEW QUESTIONS, THAT'S ALL!!!
CRAK!!

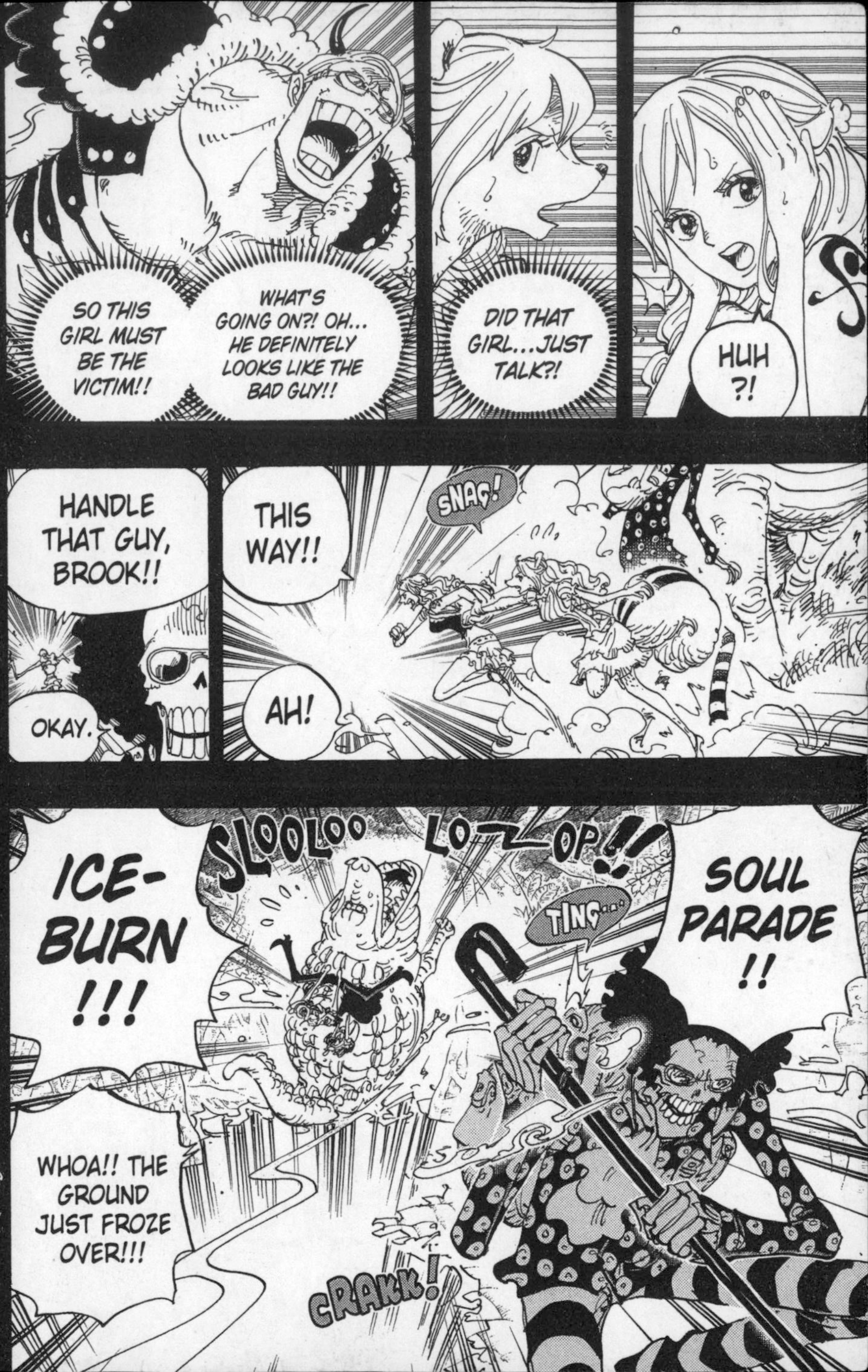
HUH ?!
DID THAT GIRL...JUST TALK?!
WHAT'S GOING ON?! OH... HE DEFINITELY LOOKS LIKE THE BAD GUY!!
SO THIS GIRL MUST BE THE VICTIM!!
SNAG!
THIS WAY!!
AH!
HANDLE THAT GUY, BROOK!!
OKAY.
SOUL PARADE !!
TING...
SLOOLOO LOZOP!!
ICE-BURN !!!
WHOA!! THE GROUND JUST FROZE OVER!!!
CRAKK!

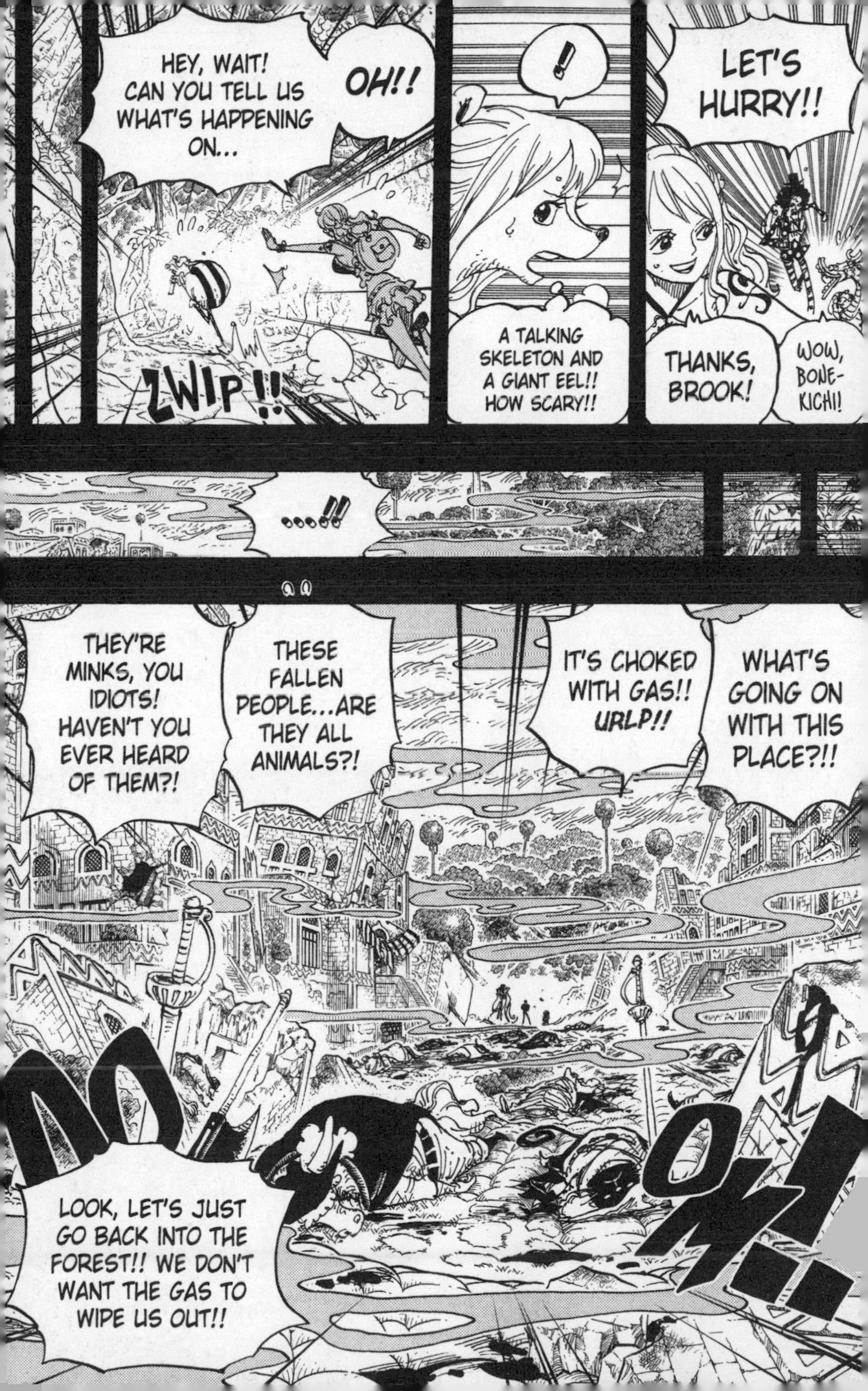
LET'S HURRY!!
WOW, BONE-KICHI!
THANKS, BROOK!
!
A TALKING SKELETON AND A GIANT EEL!! HOW SCARY!!
OH!!
HEY, WAIT! CAN YOU TELL US WHAT'S HAPPENING ON...
ZWIP!!
...!!
WHAT'S GOING ON WITH THIS PLACE?!!
IT'S CHOKED WITH GAS!! URLP!!
THESE FALLEN PEOPLE...ARE THEY ALL ANIMALS?!
THEY'RE MINKS, YOU IDIOTS! HAVEN'T YOU EVER HEARD OF THEM?!
LOOK, LET'S JUST GO BACK INTO THE FOREST!! WE DON'T WANT THE GAS TO WIPE US OUT!!

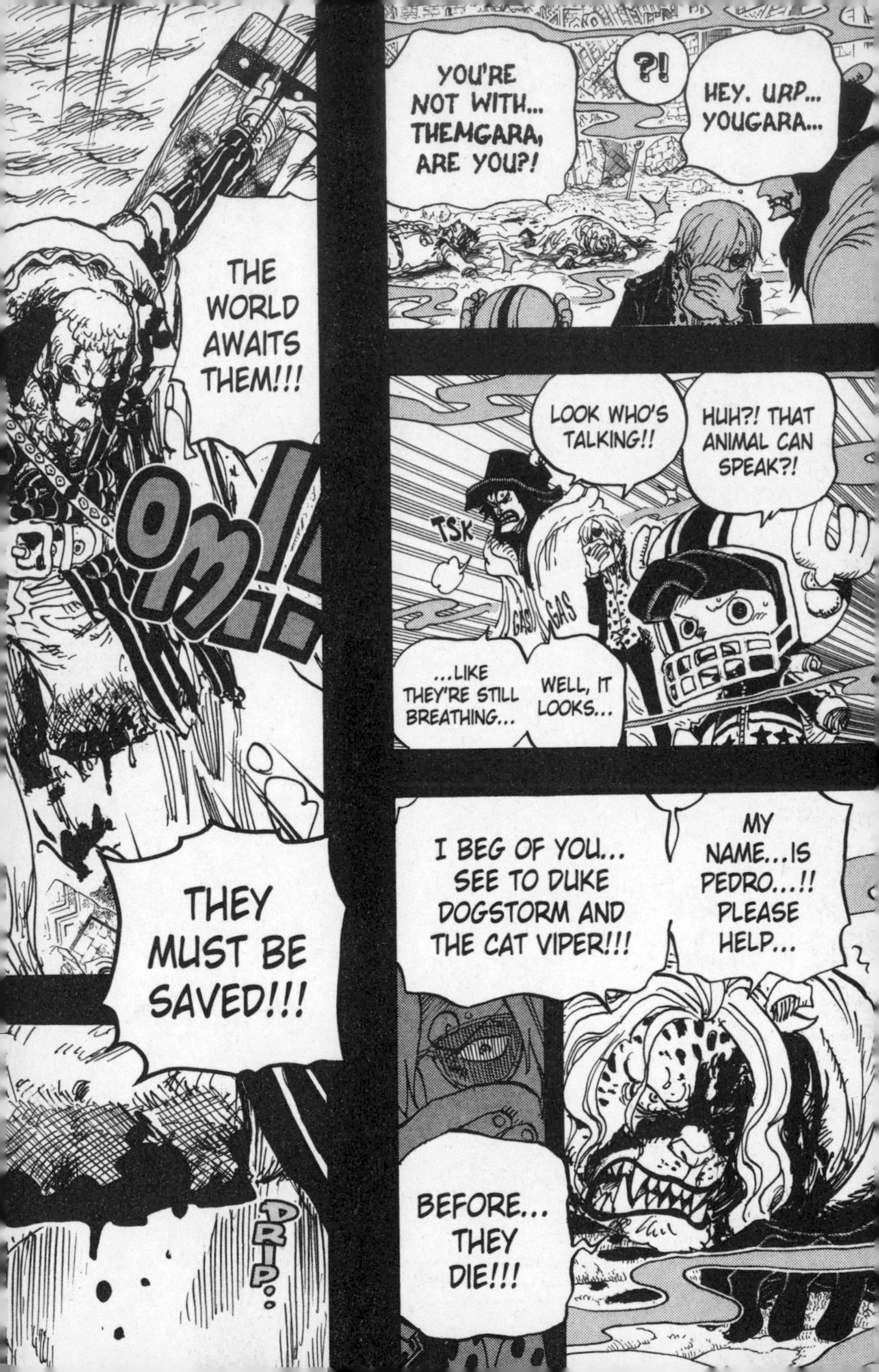

HEY. URP... YOUGARA...
?!
YOU'RE NOT WITH... THEMGARA, ARE YOU?!
HUH?! THAT ANIMAL CAN SPEAK?!
LOOK WHO'S TALKING!!
TSK
GAS GAS
WELL, IT LOOKS...
...LIKE THEY'RE STILL BREATHING...
MY NAME...IS PEDRO...!! PLEASE HELP...
I BEG OF YOU... SEE TO DUKE DOGSTORM AND THE CAT VIPER!!!
BEFORE... THEY DIE!!!
THE WORLD AWAITS THEM!!!
THEY MUST BE SAVED!!!
DRIP..

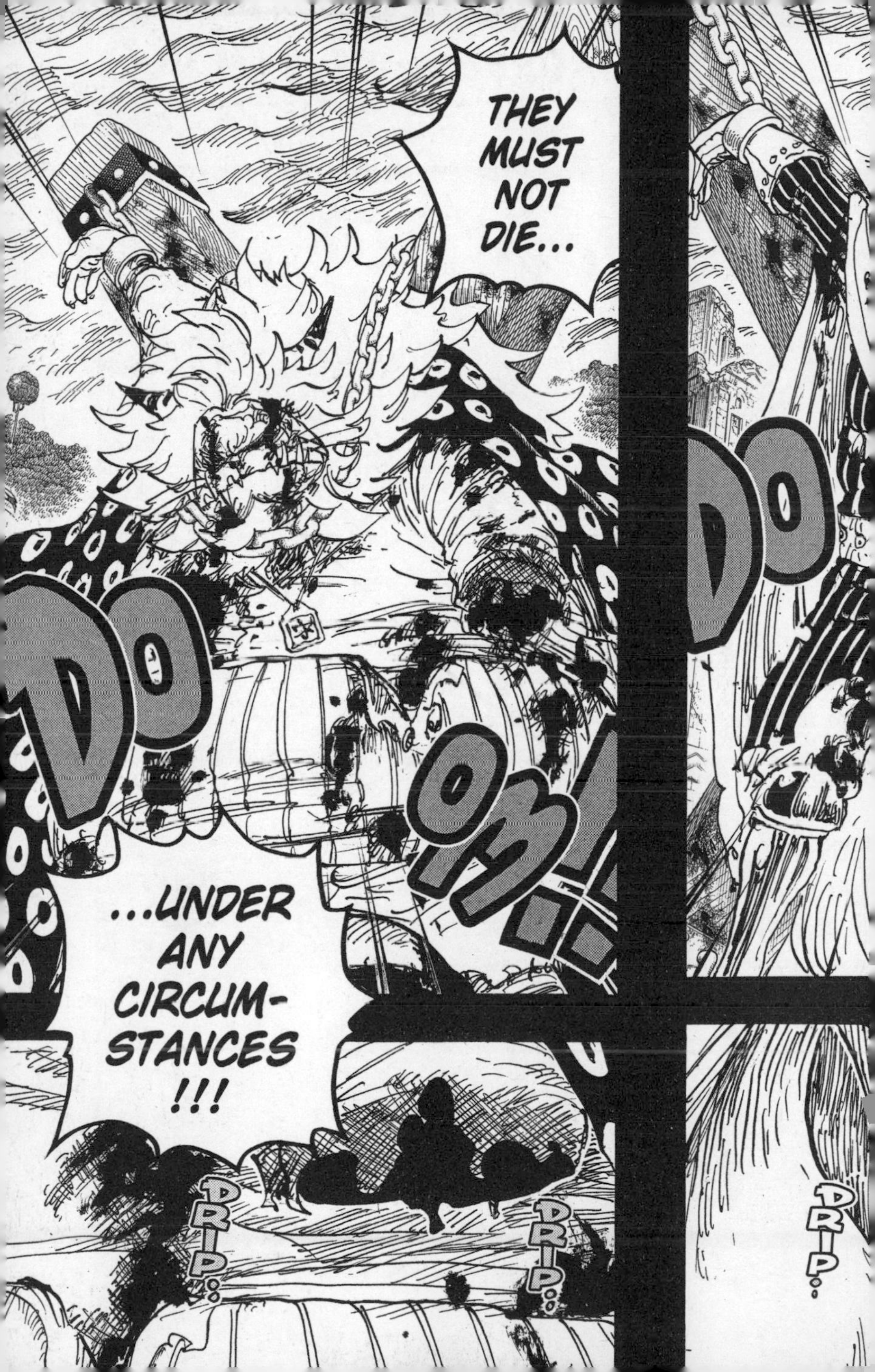
THEY MUST NOT DIE...
...UNDER ANY CIRCUM-STANCES!!!
DOOM!!
DO
DRIP..
DRIP..
DRIP..

Chapter 811: ROKO

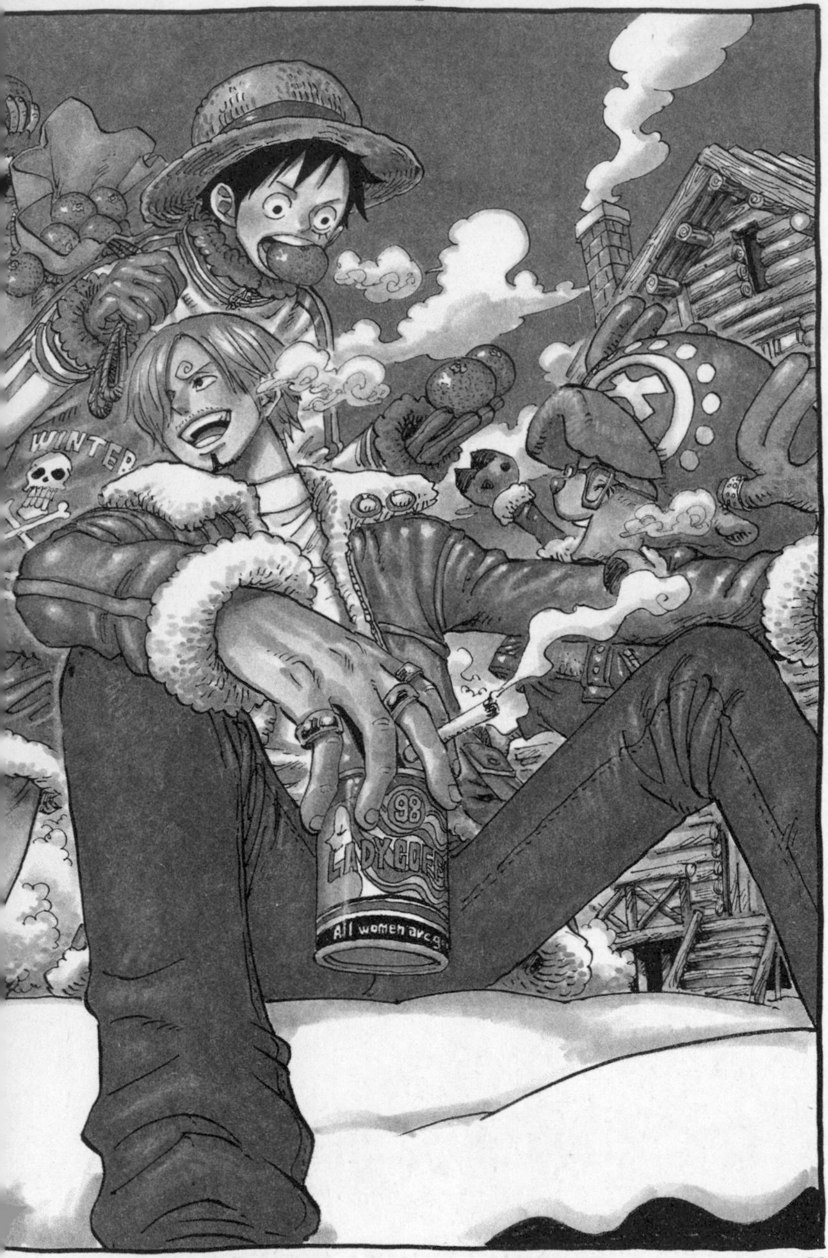
WINTER
98
LADY COFFE
All women are g

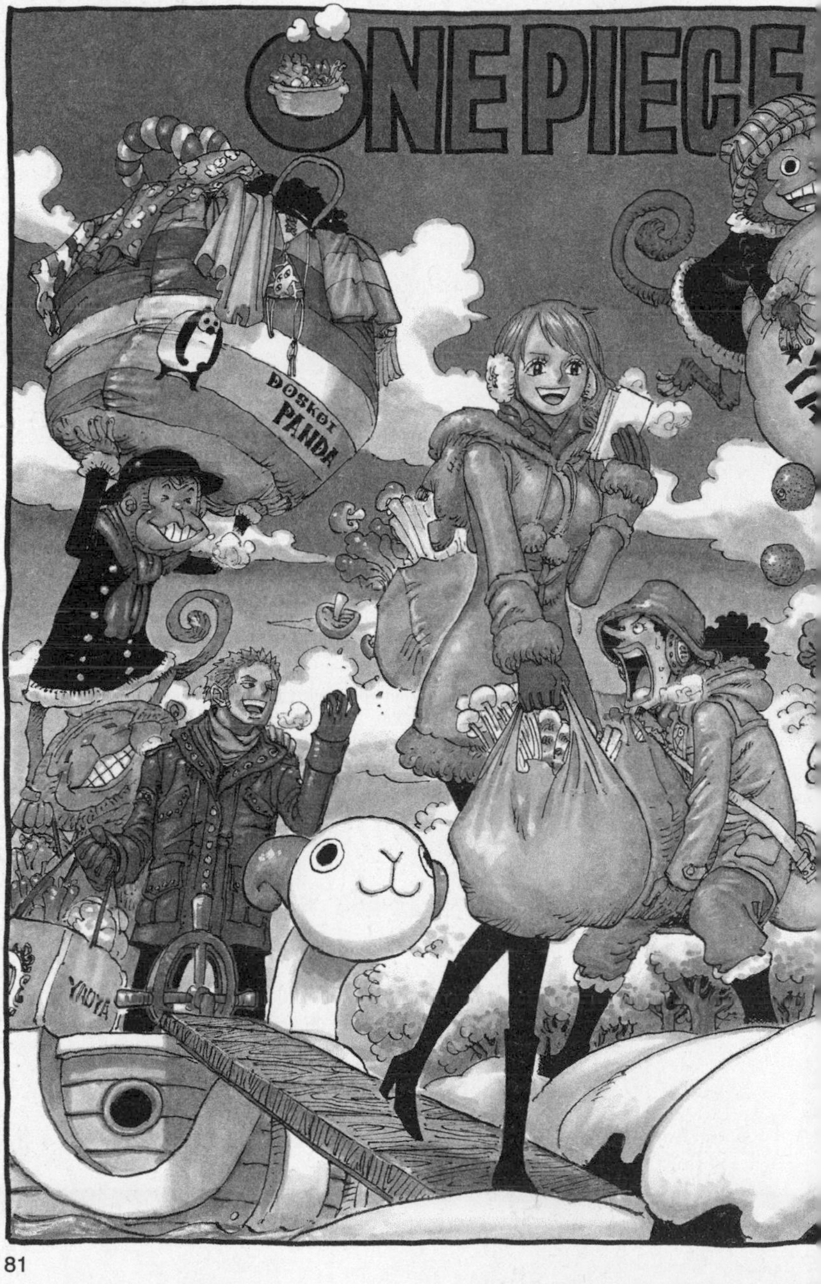
ONE PIECE
DOSKOI PANDA
YAOYA

vol.81
ONE PIECE

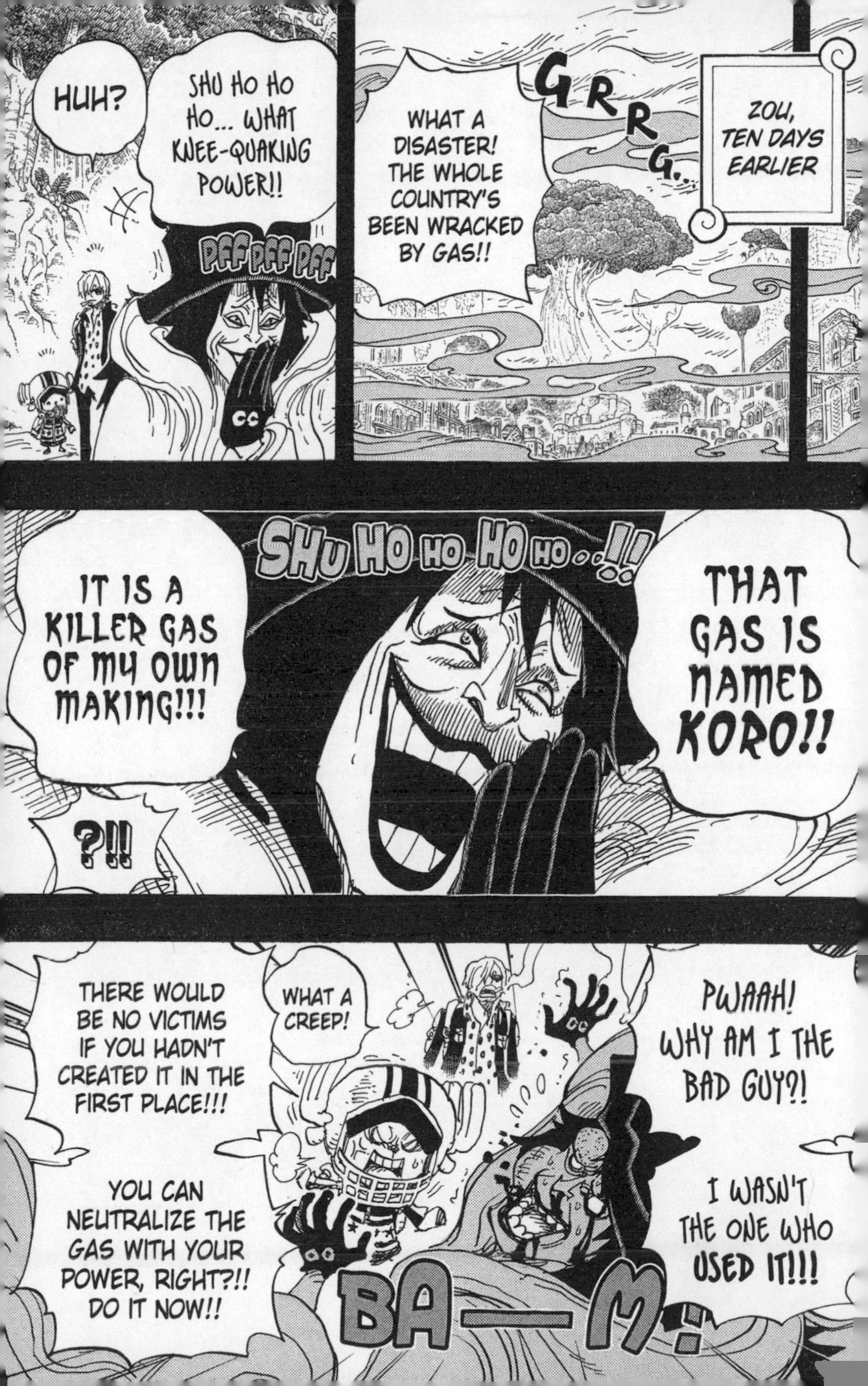
ZOU, TEN DAYS EARLIER
GRRRG..
WHAT A DISASTER! THE WHOLE COUNTRY'S BEEN WRACKED BY GAS!!
SHU HO HO HO... WHAT KNEE-QUAKING POWER!!
HUH?
PFF PFF PFF
THAT GAS IS NAMED KORO!!
SHU HO HO HO HO..!!
IT IS A KILLER GAS OF MY OWN MAKING!!!
?!!
PWAAH! WHY AM I THE BAD GUY?!
WHAT A CREEP!
THERE WOULD BE NO VICTIMS IF YOU HADN'T CREATED IT IN THE FIRST PLACE!!!
I WASN'T THE ONE WHO USED IT!!!
YOU CAN NEUTRALIZE THE GAS WITH YOUR POWER, RIGHT?!! DO IT NOW!!
BA—M!

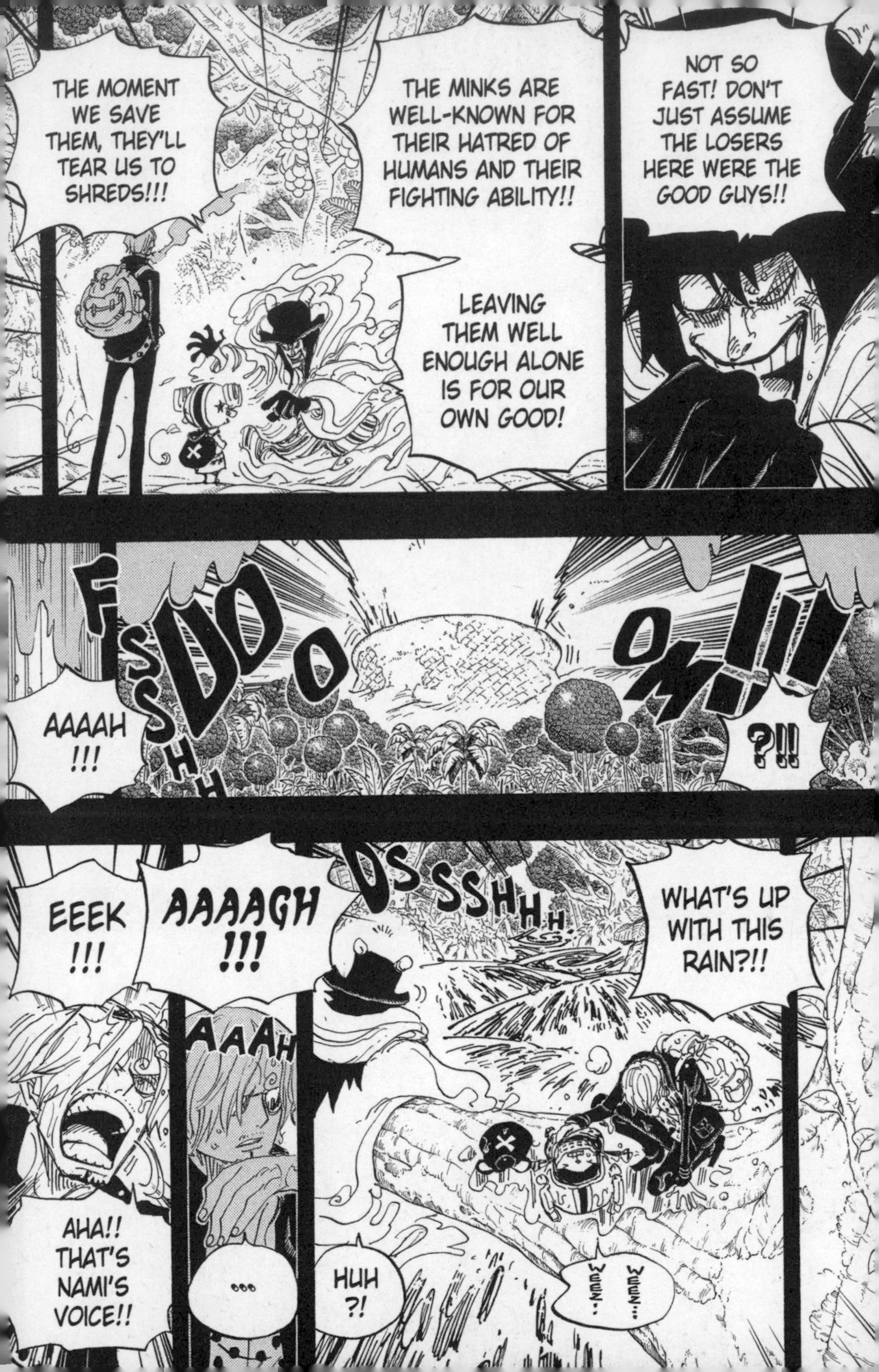
NOT SO FAST! DON'T JUST ASSUME THE LOSERS HERE WERE THE GOOD GUYS!!
THE MINKS ARE WELL-KNOWN FOR THEIR HATRED OF HUMANS AND THEIR FIGHTING ABILITY!!
THE MOMENT WE SAVE THEM, THEY'LL TEAR US TO SHREDS!!!
LEAVING THEM WELL ENOUGH ALONE IS FOR OUR OWN GOOD!
?!!
AAAAH !!!
FSSHH
DOOOM!!!
WHAT'S UP WITH THIS RAIN?!!
DSSSHHH
AAAAGH !!!
EEEK !!!
AAAAH
WEEZ.. WEEZ...
HUH ?!
...
AHA!! THAT'S NAMI'S VOICE!!

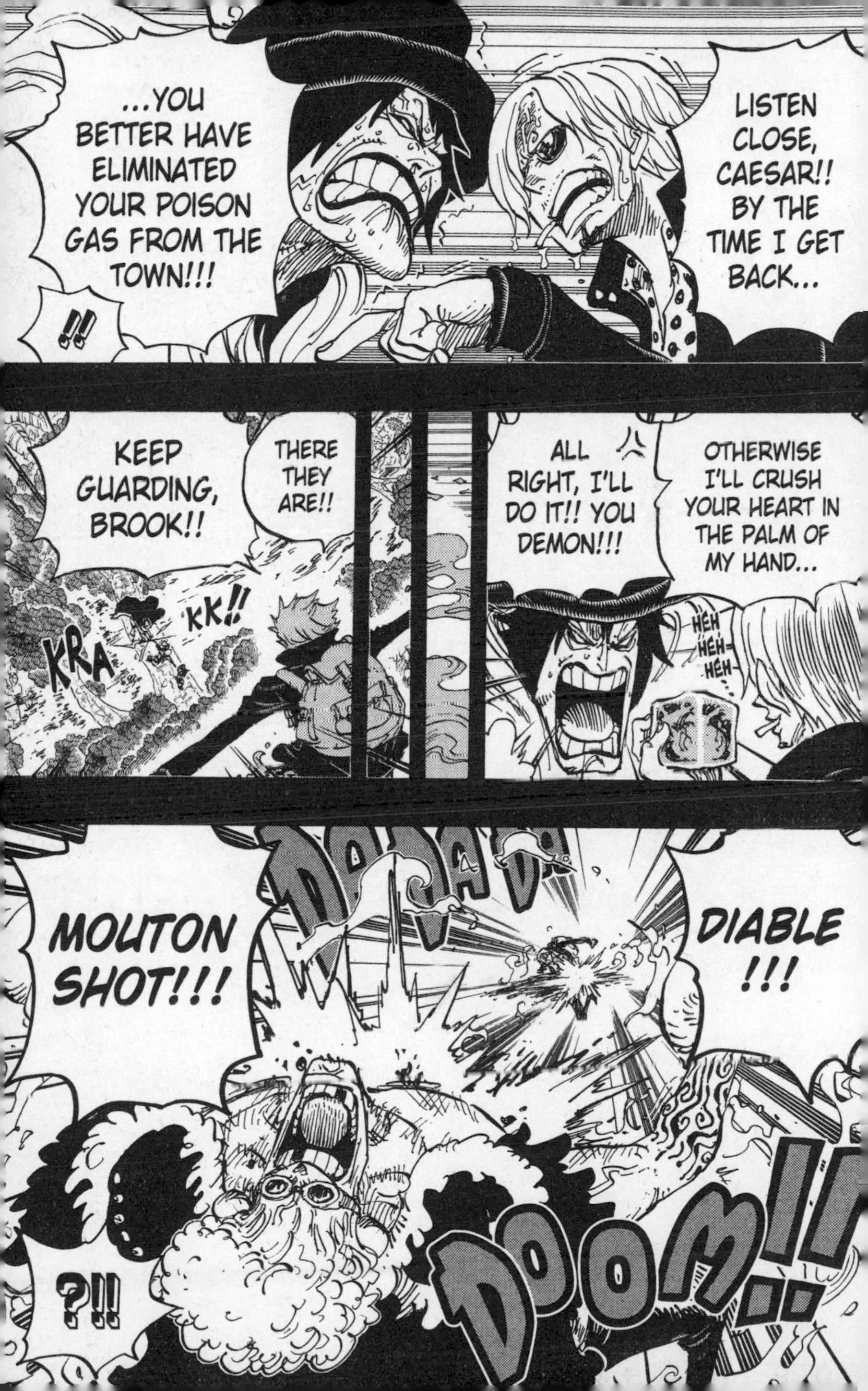
LISTEN CLOSE, CAESAR!! BY THE TIME I GET BACK...
...YOU BETTER HAVE ELIMINATED YOUR POISON GAS FROM THE TOWN!!!
!!
OTHERWISE I'LL CRUSH YOUR HEART IN THE PALM OF MY HAND...
HEH HEH HEH
ALL RIGHT, I'LL DO IT!! YOU DEMON!!!
THERE THEY ARE!!
KEEP GUARDING, BROOK!!
KRA KK!!
DIABLE !!!
MOUTON SHOT!!!
DOOM!!
?!!

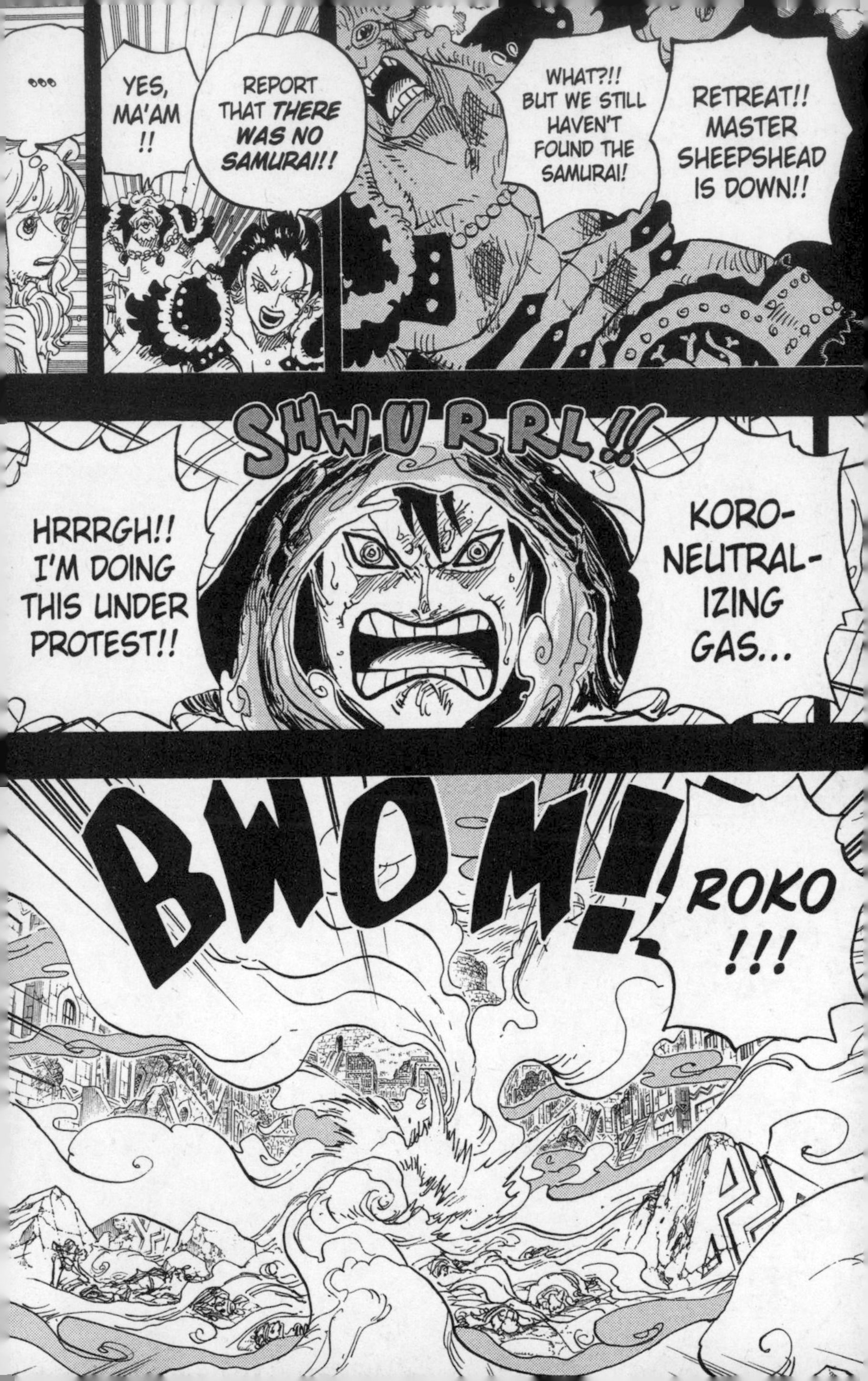

RETREAT!! MASTER SHEEPSHEAD IS DOWN!!
WHAT?!! BUT WE STILL HAVEN'T FOUND THE SAMURAI!
REPORT THAT THERE WAS NO SAMURAI!!
YES, MA'AM !!
...
SHWURRL!!
KORO-NEUTRAL-IZING GAS...
HRRRGH!! I'M DOING THIS UNDER PROTEST!!
BWOM!
ROKO !!!

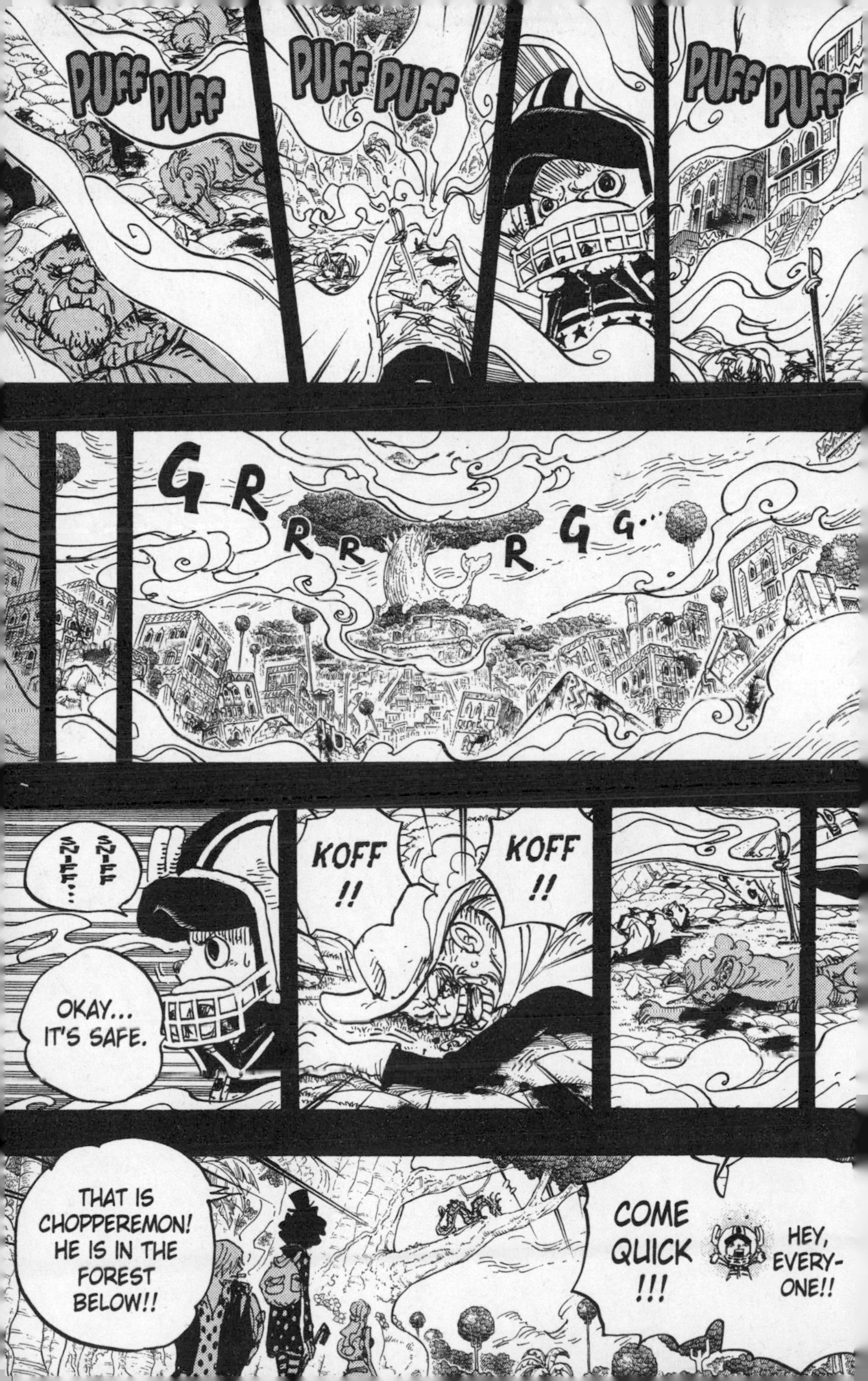
PUFF PUFF
PUFF PUFF
PUFF PUFF
GRRRRGG...
KOFF!!
KOFF!!
SNIFF SNIFF...
OKAY... IT'S SAFE.
HEY, EVERYONE!!
COME QUICK!!!
THAT IS CHOPPEREMON! HE IS IN THE FOREST BELOW!!

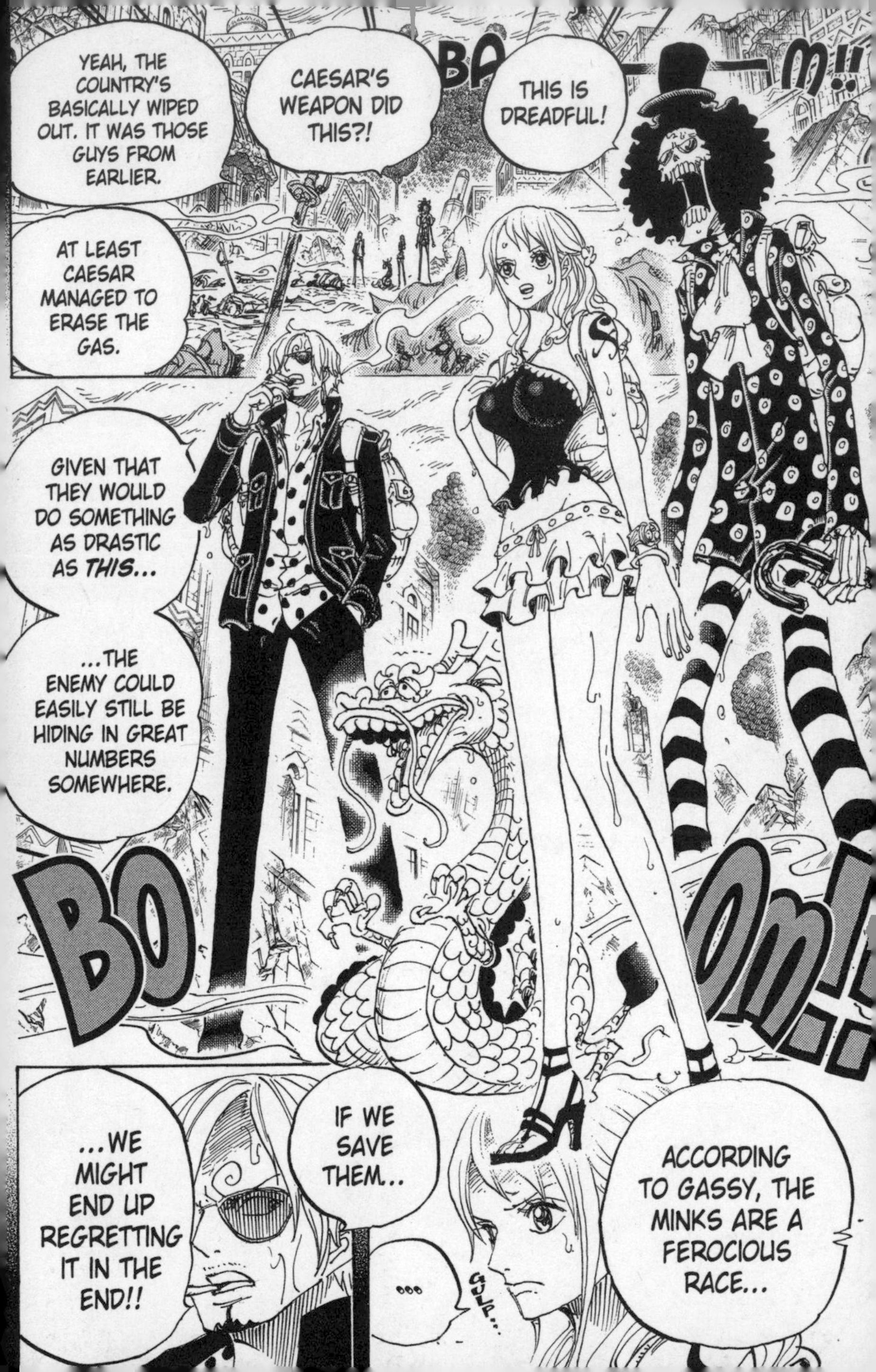
BA—M!!
THIS IS DREADFUL!
CAESAR'S WEAPON DID THIS?!
YEAH, THE COUNTRY'S BASICALLY WIPED OUT. IT WAS THOSE GUYS FROM EARLIER.
AT LEAST CAESAR MANAGED TO ERASE THE GAS.
GIVEN THAT THEY WOULD DO SOMETHING AS DRASTIC AS *THIS*...
...THE ENEMY COULD EASILY STILL BE HIDING IN GREAT NUMBERS SOMEWHERE.
BOOM!!
ACCORDING TO GASSY, THE MINKS ARE A FEROCIOUS RACE...
GULP...
...
IF WE SAVE THEM...
...WE MIGHT END UP REGRETTING IT IN THE END!!

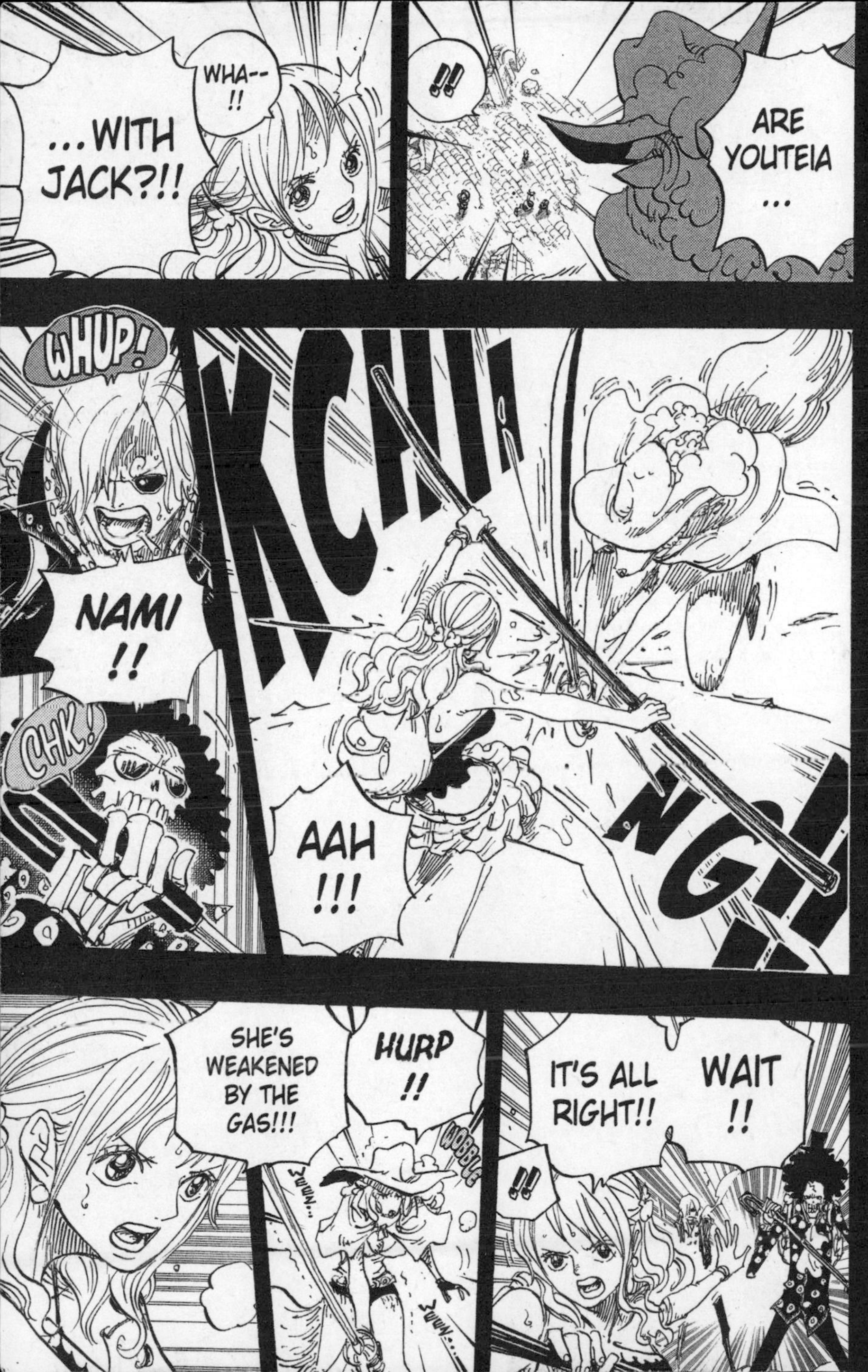
ARE YOUTEIA ...
!!
WHA-- !!
...WITH JACK?!!
NGH!!
AAH !!!
WHUP!
NAMI !!
CHK!
WAIT !!
IT'S ALL RIGHT!!
!!
HURP !!
WOBBLE
SHE'S WEAKENED BY THE GAS!!!

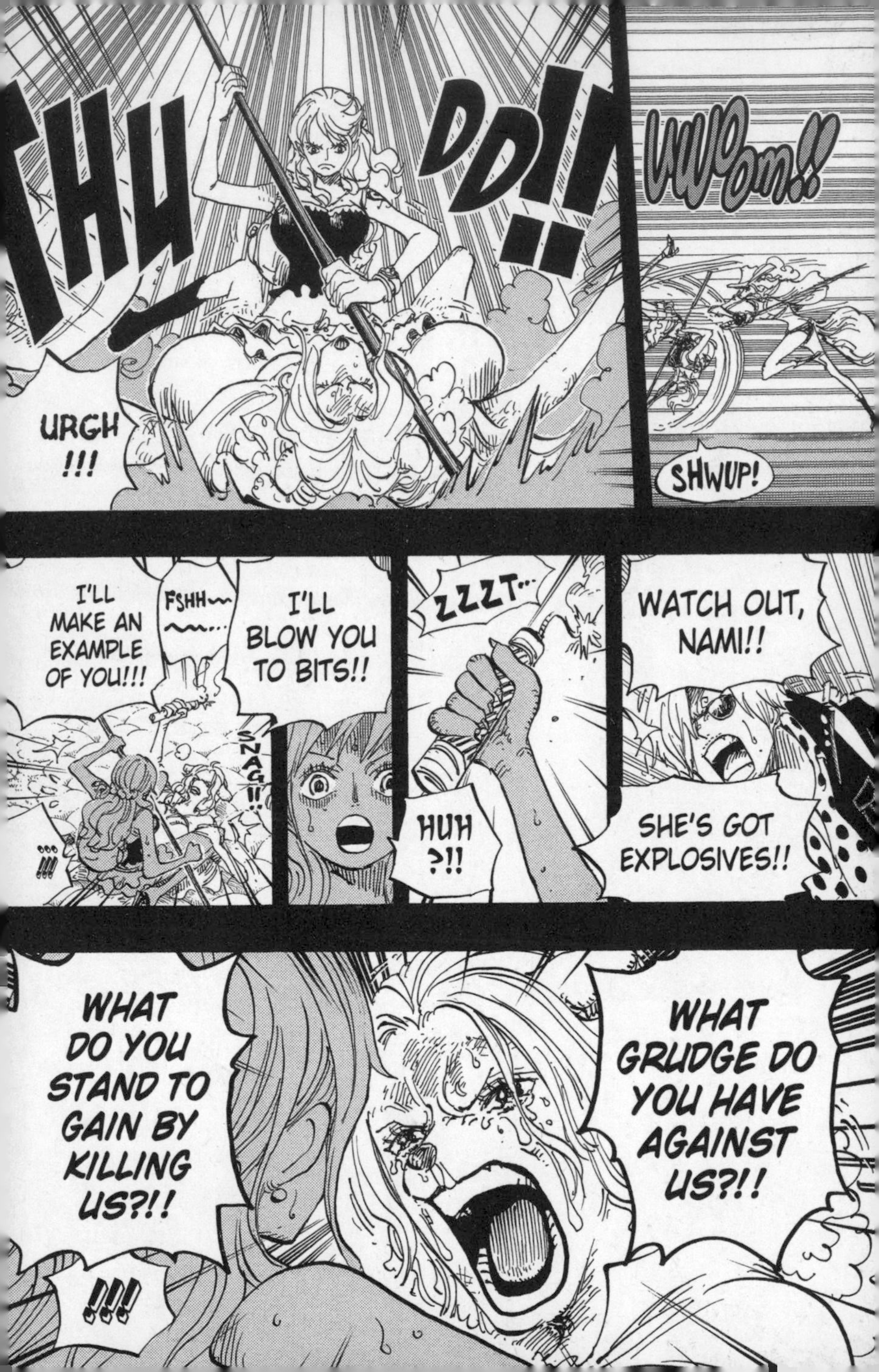
VWOOM!!
SHWUP!
CHUDD!!
URGH!!!
WATCH OUT, NAMI!!
SHE'S GOT EXPLOSIVES!!
ZZZT...
HUH?!!
I'LL BLOW YOU TO BITS!!
FSHH~~~...
I'LL MAKE AN EXAMPLE OF YOU!!!
SNAG!!
...!!!
WHAT GRUDGE DO YOU HAVE AGAINST US?!!
WHAT DO YOU STAND TO GAIN BY KILLING US?!!
!!!

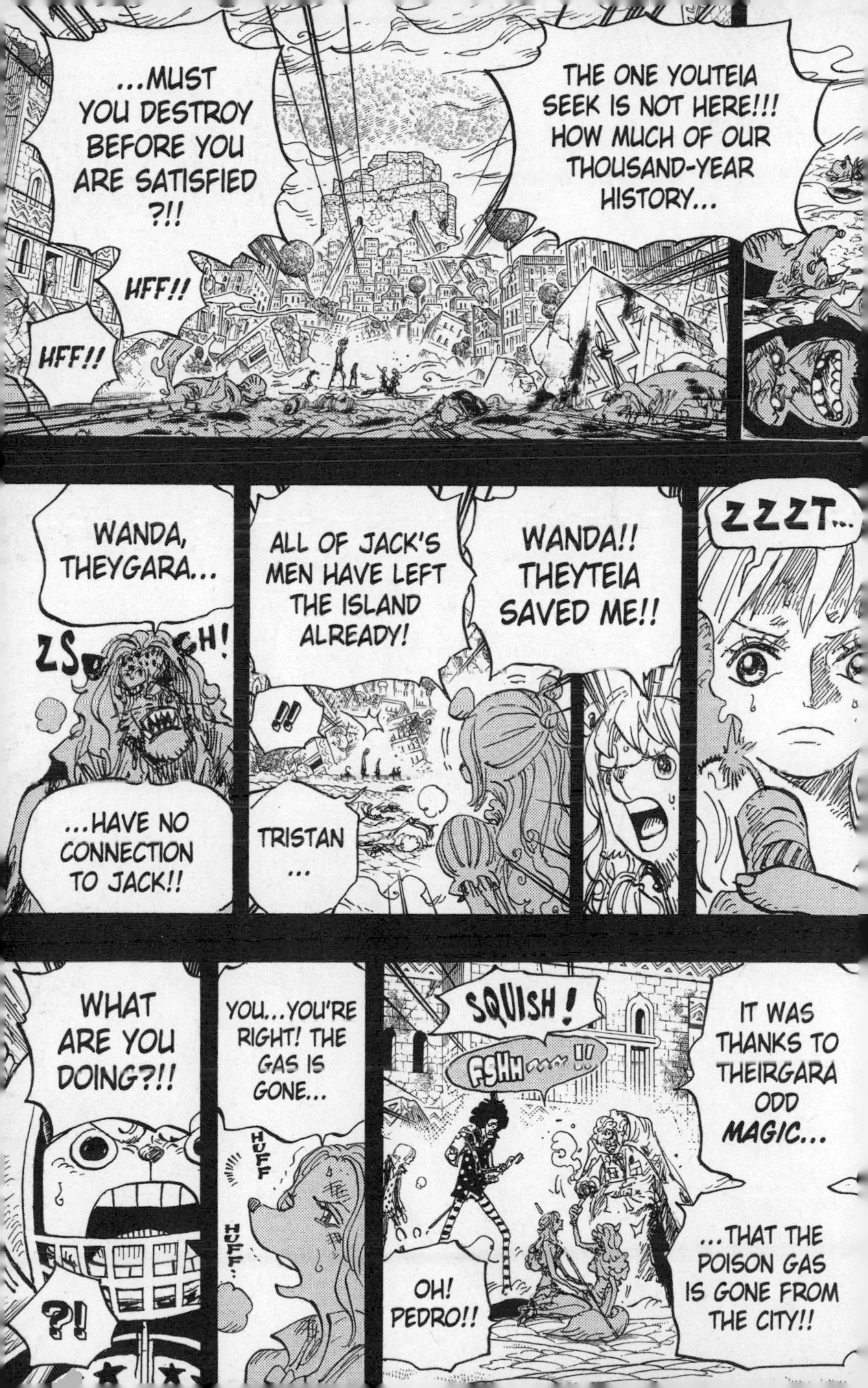
THE ONE YOUTEIA SEEK IS NOT HERE!!! HOW MUCH OF OUR THOUSAND-YEAR HISTORY...
...MUST YOU DESTROY BEFORE YOU ARE SATISFIED ?!!
HFF!!
HFF!!
ZZZT...
WANDA!! THEYTEIA SAVED ME!!
ALL OF JACK'S MEN HAVE LEFT THE ISLAND ALREADY!
!!
TRISTAN ...
WANDA, THEYGARA...
...HAVE NO CONNECTION TO JACK!!
IT WAS THANKS TO THEIRGARA ODD *MAGIC*...
SQUISH!
...THAT THE POISON GAS IS GONE FROM THE CITY!!
OH! PEDRO!!
YOU...YOU'RE RIGHT! THE GAS IS GONE...
HUFF
HUFF..
WHAT ARE YOU DOING?!!
?!

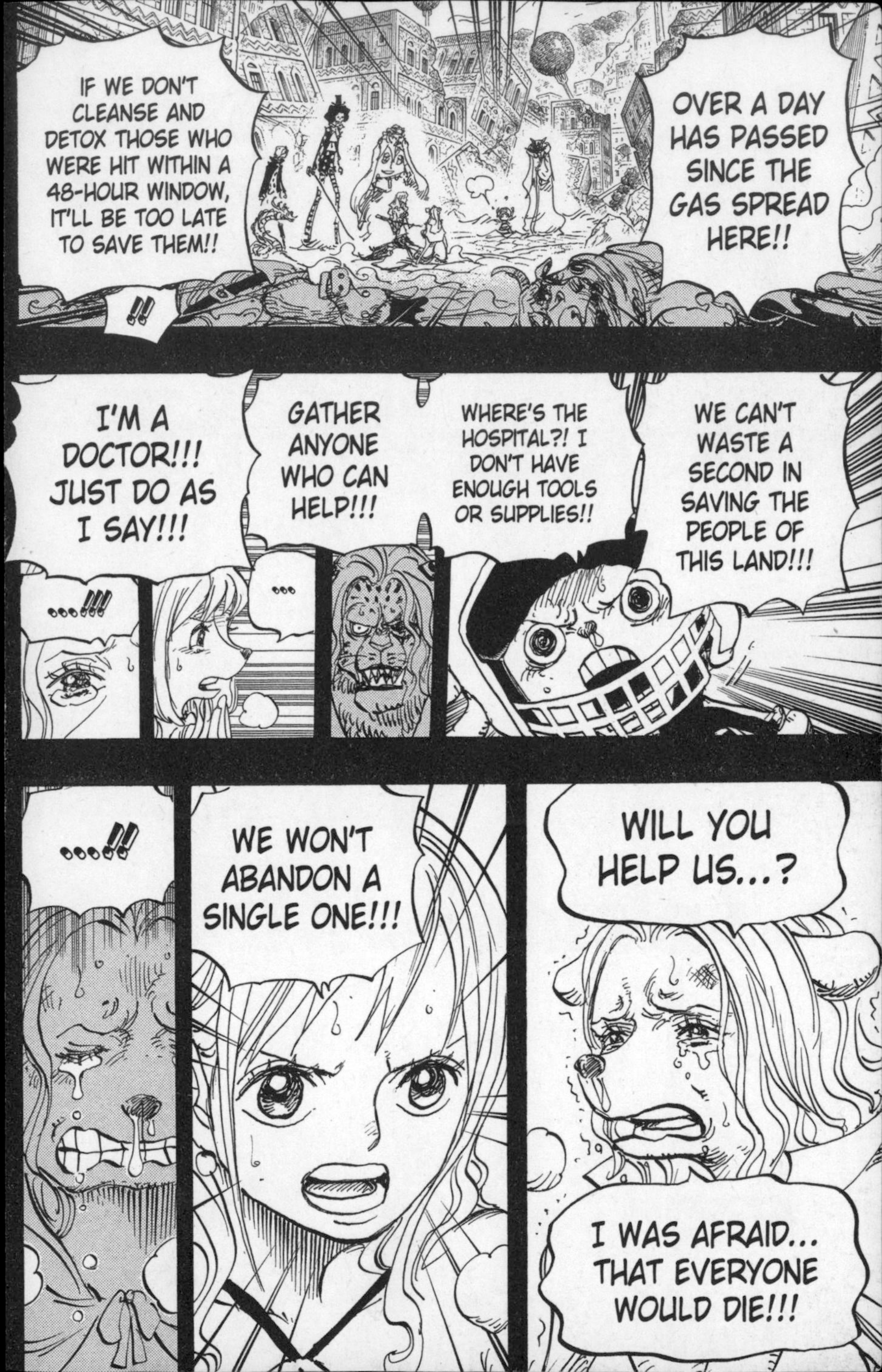
OVER A DAY HAS PASSED SINCE THE GAS SPREAD HERE!!
IF WE DON'T CLEANSE AND DETOX THOSE WHO WERE HIT WITHIN A 48-HOUR WINDOW, IT'LL BE TOO LATE TO SAVE THEM!!
!!
WE CAN'T WASTE A SECOND IN SAVING THE PEOPLE OF THIS LAND!!!
WHERE'S THE HOSPITAL?! I DON'T HAVE ENOUGH TOOLS OR SUPPLIES!!
GATHER ANYONE WHO CAN HELP!!!
I'M A DOCTOR!!! JUST DO AS I SAY!!!
...
...!!!
WILL YOU HELP US...?
I WAS AFRAID... THAT EVERYONE WOULD DIE!!!
WE WON'T ABANDON A SINGLE ONE!!!
...!!

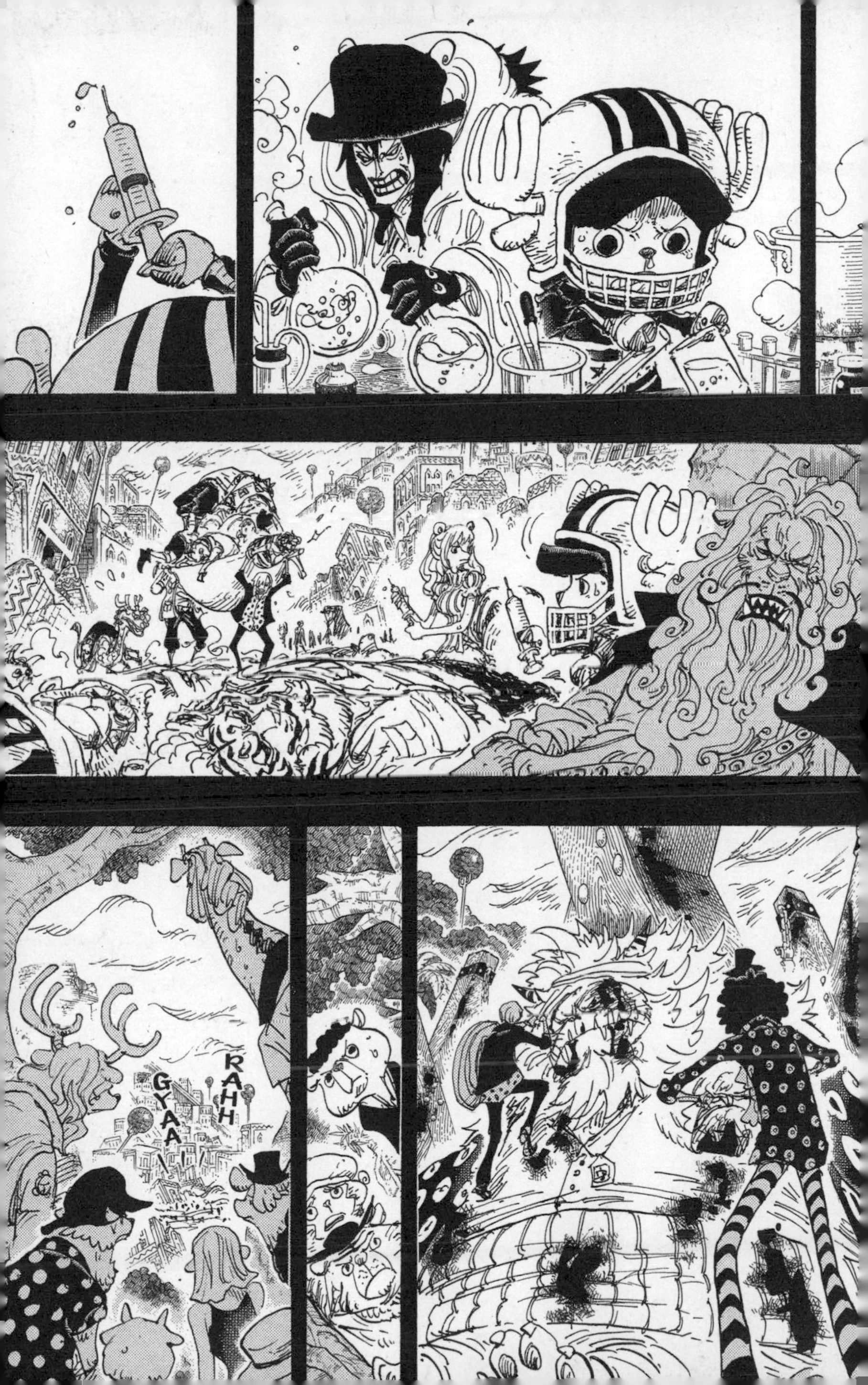
RAHH
GYAA!

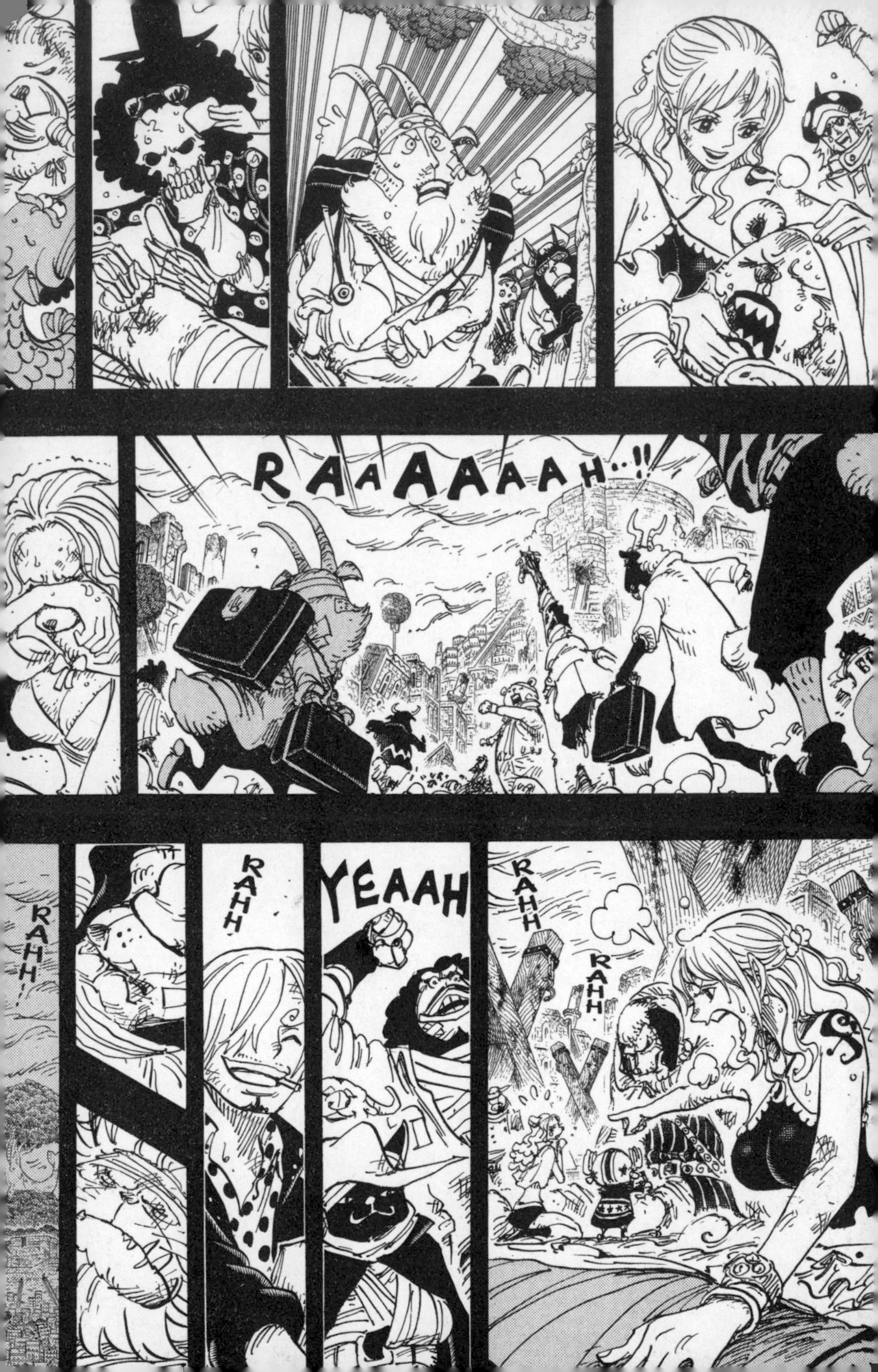
RAAAAAAH..!!
RAHH
RAHH
YEAAH
RAHH
RAHH!

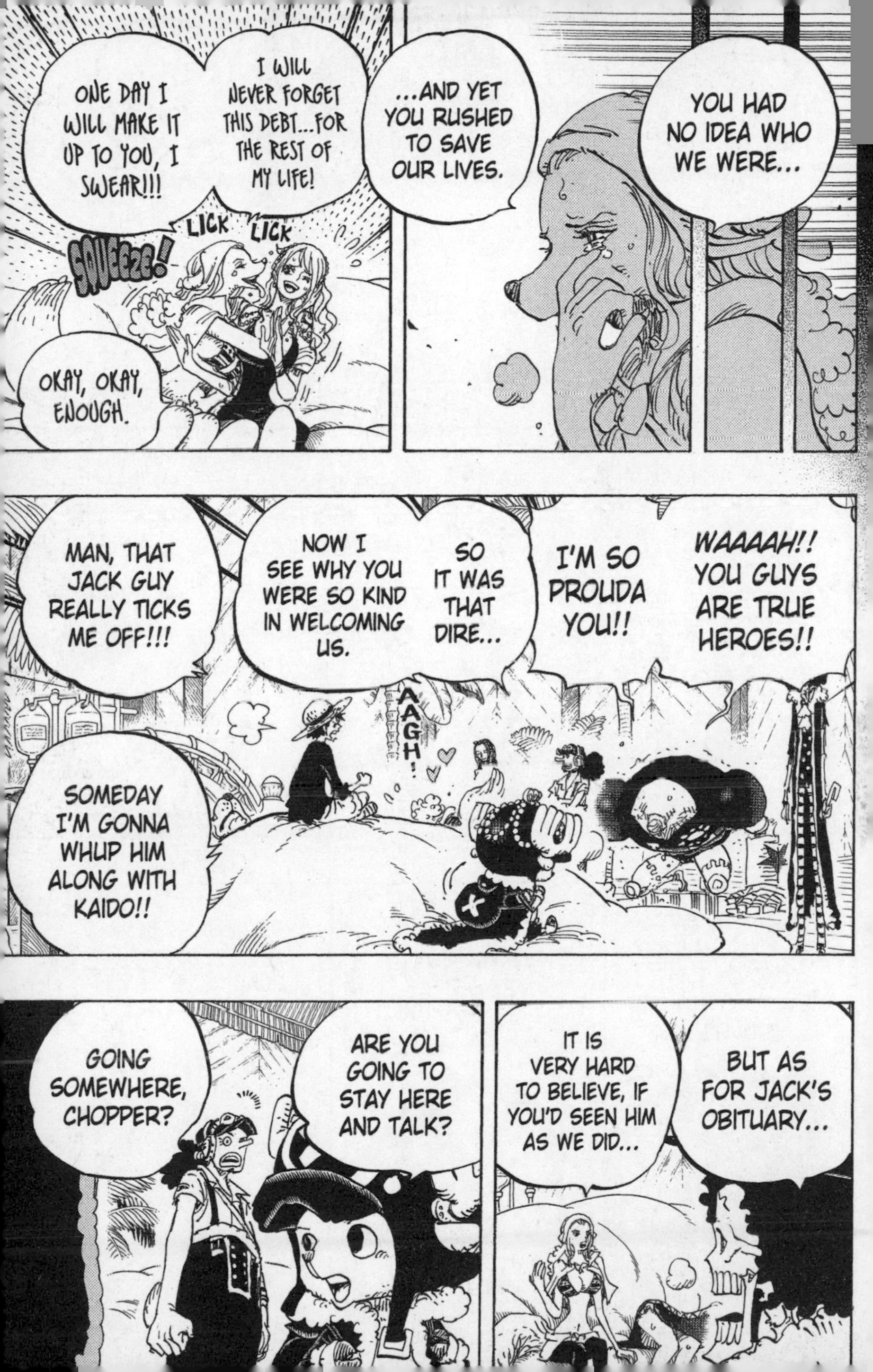
YOU HAD NO IDEA WHO WE WERE...
...AND YET YOU RUSHED TO SAVE OUR LIVES.
I WILL NEVER FORGET THIS DEBT...FOR THE REST OF MY LIFE!
ONE DAY I WILL MAKE IT UP TO YOU, I SWEAR!!!
LICK
LICK
SQUEEZE!
OKAY, OKAY, ENOUGH.
WAAAAH!! YOU GUYS ARE TRUE HEROES!!
I'M SO PROUDA YOU!!
SO IT WAS THAT DIRE...
NOW I SEE WHY YOU WERE SO KIND IN WELCOMING US.
MAN, THAT JACK GUY REALLY TICKS ME OFF!!!
AAGH!
SOMEDAY I'M GONNA WHUP HIM ALONG WITH KAIDO!!
BUT AS FOR JACK'S OBITUARY...
IT IS VERY HARD TO BELIEVE, IF YOU'D SEEN HIM AS WE DID...
ARE YOU GOING TO STAY HERE AND TALK?
GOING SOMEWHERE, CHOPPER?

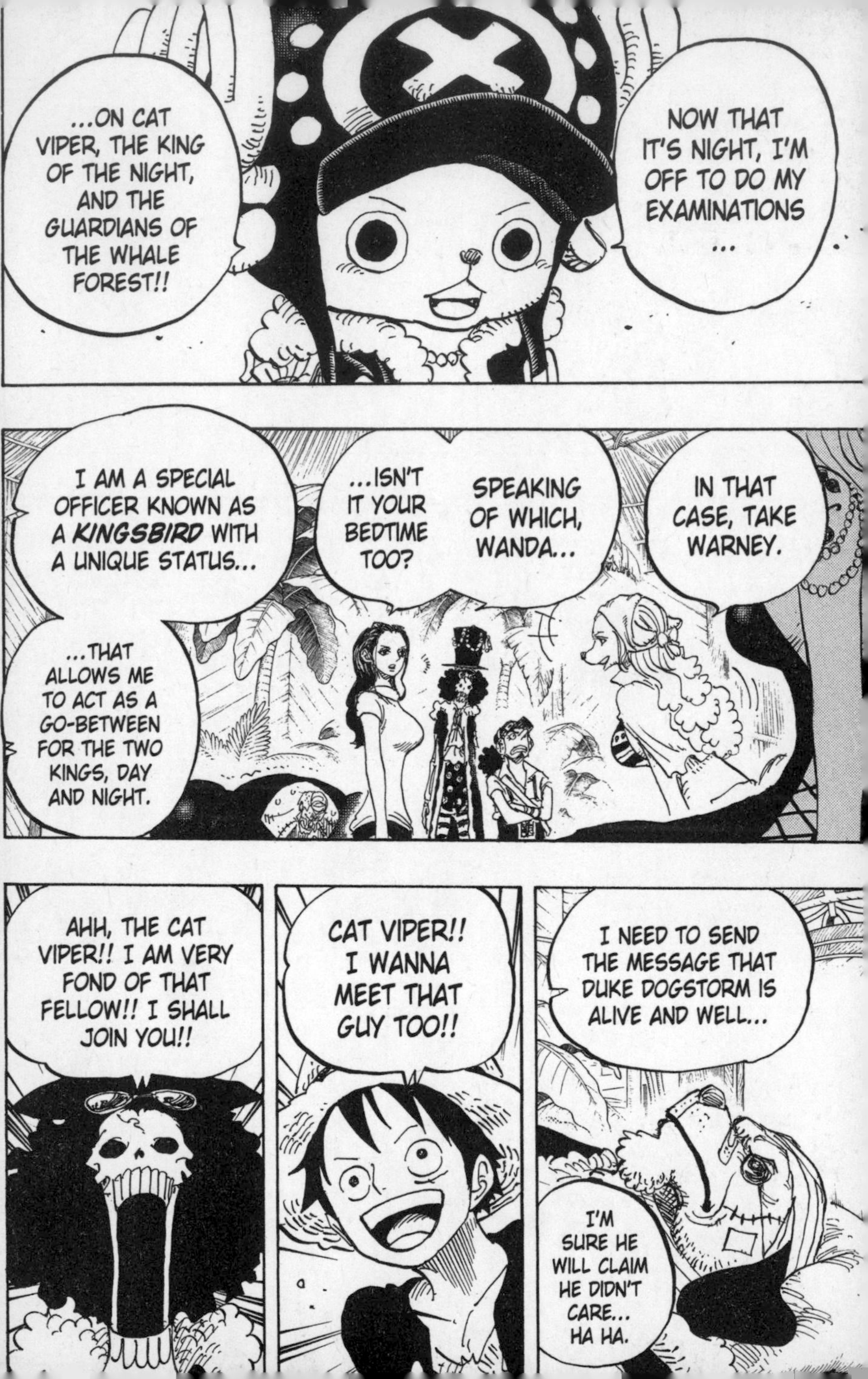
NOW THAT IT'S NIGHT, I'M OFF TO DO MY EXAMINATIONS ...
...ON CAT VIPER, THE KING OF THE NIGHT, AND THE GUARDIANS OF THE WHALE FOREST!!
IN THAT CASE, TAKE WARNEY.
SPEAKING OF WHICH, WANDA...
...ISN'T IT YOUR BEDTIME TOO?
I AM A SPECIAL OFFICER KNOWN AS A KINGSBIRD WITH A UNIQUE STATUS...
...THAT ALLOWS ME TO ACT AS A GO-BETWEEN FOR THE TWO KINGS, DAY AND NIGHT.
I NEED TO SEND THE MESSAGE THAT DUKE DOGSTORM IS ALIVE AND WELL...
I'M SURE HE WILL CLAIM HE DIDN'T CARE... HA HA.
CAT VIPER!! I WANNA MEET THAT GUY TOO!!
AHH, THE CAT VIPER!! I AM VERY FOND OF THAT FELLOW!! I SHALL JOIN YOU!!

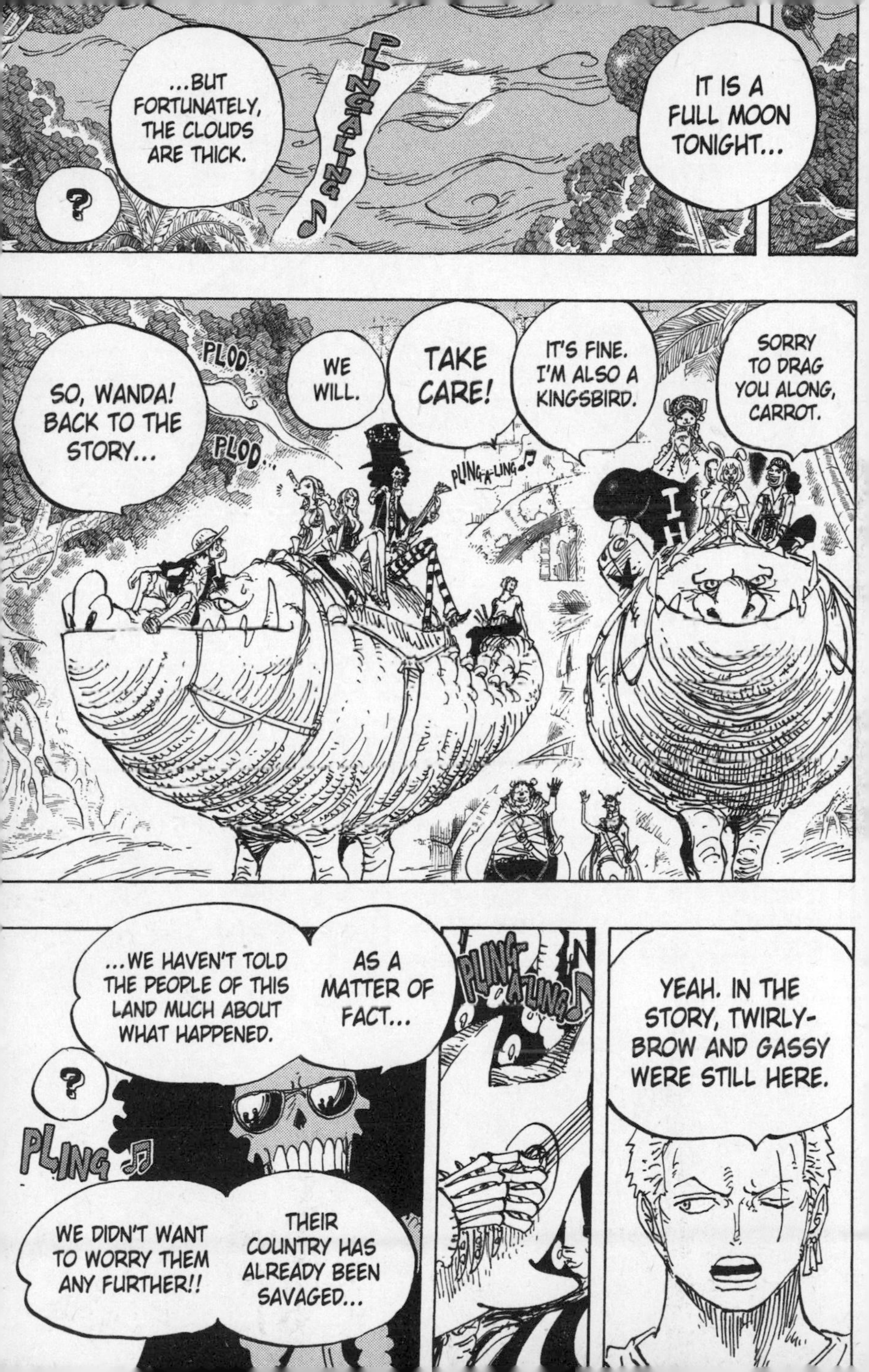
IT IS A FULL MOON TONIGHT...
PLINGALING
...BUT FORTUNATELY, THE CLOUDS ARE THICK.
?
SORRY TO DRAG YOU ALONG, CARROT.
IT'S FINE. I'M ALSO A KINGSBIRD.
TAKE CARE!
WE WILL.
PLING-A-LING
PLOD...
SO, WANDA! BACK TO THE STORY...
PLOD...
YEAH. IN THE STORY, TWIRLY-BROW AND GASSY WERE STILL HERE.
PLING-A-LING
AS A MATTER OF FACT...
...WE HAVEN'T TOLD THE PEOPLE OF THIS LAND MUCH ABOUT WHAT HAPPENED.
?
PLING
THEIR COUNTRY HAS ALREADY BEEN SAVAGED...
WE DIDN'T WANT TO WORRY THEM ANY FURTHER!!

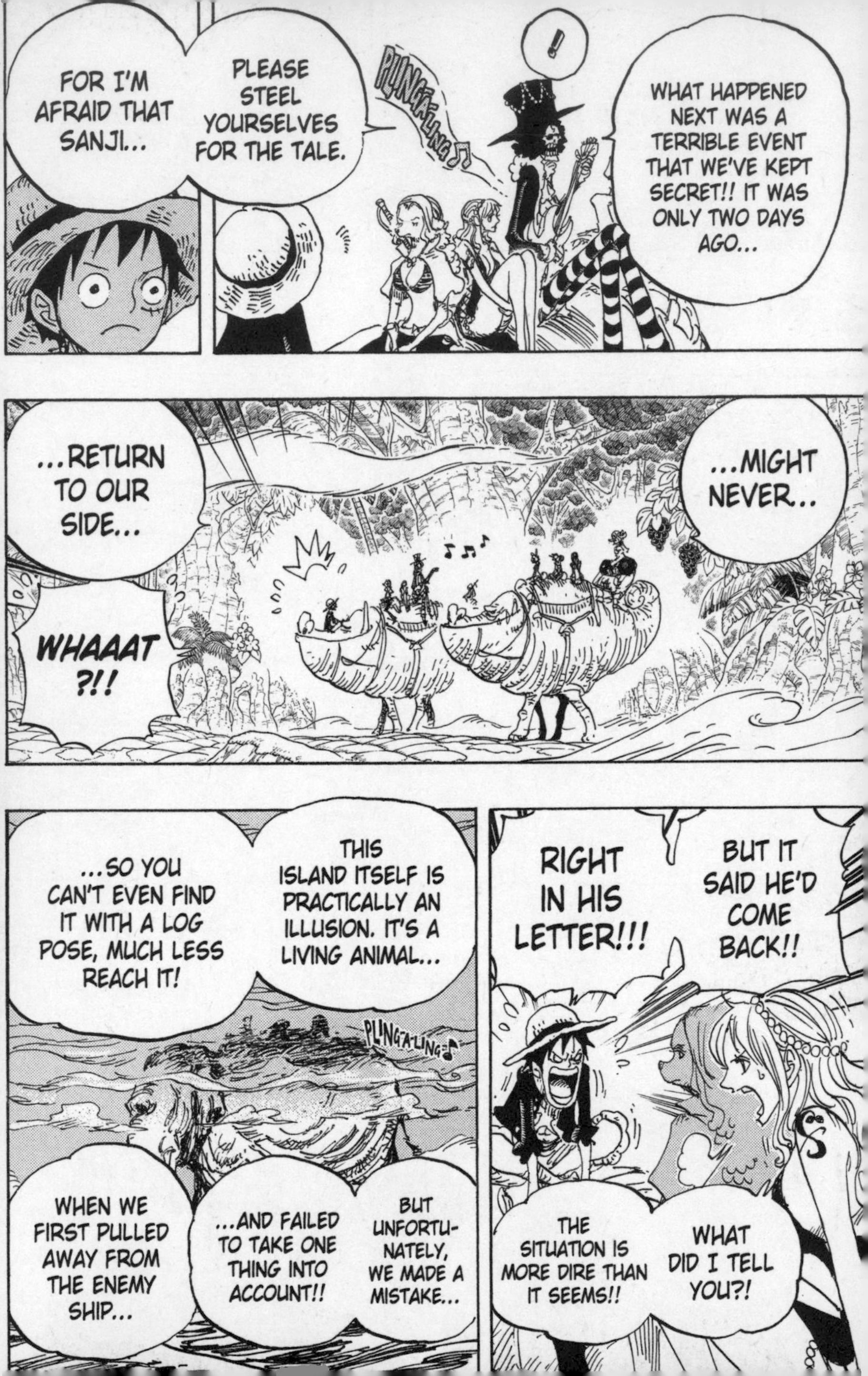
!
WHAT HAPPENED NEXT WAS A TERRIBLE EVENT THAT WE'VE KEPT SECRET!! IT WAS ONLY TWO DAYS AGO...
PLING-A-LING♫
PLEASE STEEL YOURSELVES FOR THE TALE.
FOR I'M AFRAID THAT SANJI...
...MIGHT NEVER...
...RETURN TO OUR SIDE...
WHAAAT ?!!
BUT IT SAID HE'D COME BACK!!
RIGHT IN HIS LETTER!!!
WHAT DID I TELL YOU?!
THE SITUATION IS MORE DIRE THAN IT SEEMS!!
THIS ISLAND ITSELF IS PRACTICALLY AN ILLUSION. IT'S A LIVING ANIMAL...
...SO YOU CAN'T EVEN FIND IT WITH A LOG POSE, MUCH LESS REACH IT!
PLING-A-LING♪
BUT UNFORTUNATELY, WE MADE A MISTAKE...
...AND FAILED TO TAKE ONE THING INTO ACCOUNT!!
WHEN WE FIRST PULLED AWAY FROM THE ENEMY SHIP...

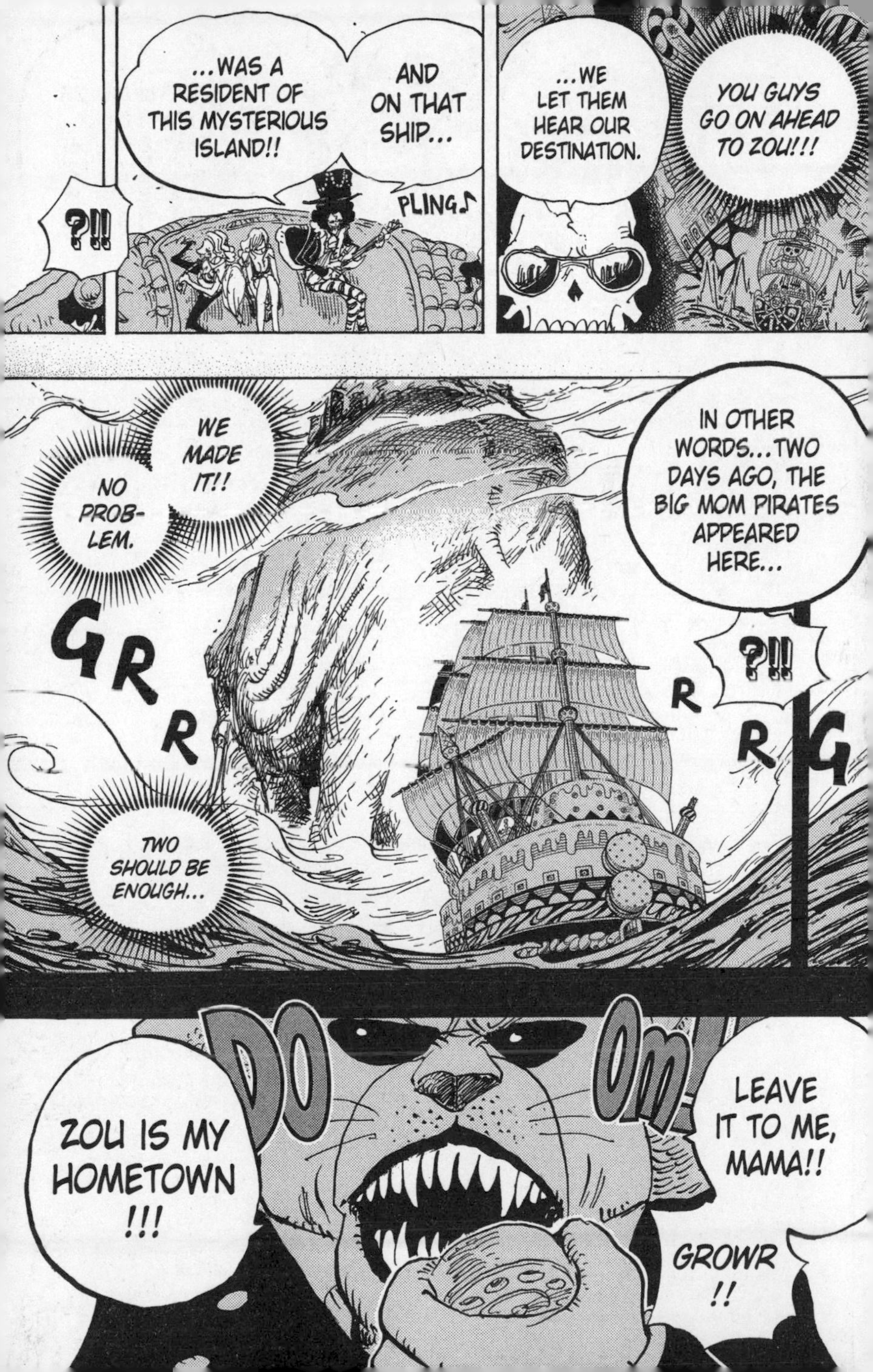
YOU GUYS GO ON AHEAD TO ZOU!!!
...WE LET THEM HEAR OUR DESTINATION.
AND ON THAT SHIP...
...WAS A RESIDENT OF THIS MYSTERIOUS ISLAND!!
PLING♪
?!!
IN OTHER WORDS...TWO DAYS AGO, THE BIG MOM PIRATES APPEARED HERE...
?!!
RRG
WE MADE IT!!
NO PROB-LEM.
GRR R
TWO SHOULD BE ENOUGH...
LEAVE IT TO ME, MAMA!!
DOOM
GROWR !!
ZOU IS MY HOMETOWN !!!

質問コーナー
SBS Question Corner
エス ビー エス
SBS

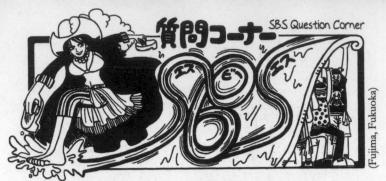

(Fujima, Fukuoka)

Q: Hello, Odacchi. I've thought up some birthdays for those people who haven't got any characters on their birthday yet. How are these?
--Masao, Born December 14th (Someone come up with a character for me!!)

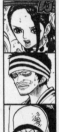

Violet (April 30)
The violet flower is "sumire," and "su" is 4 in Chinese

Gin (April 7)
47 is the atomic number for silver, or "gin"

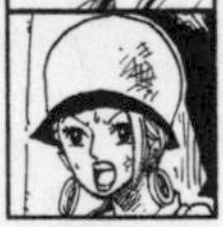

Miss Valentine
(February 14)
Valentine's Day

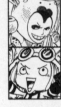

Miss Father's Day (June 21)
Father's Day

Leo (July 24)
The first day of the Leo zodiac range

A: Very nice. You went for the days that hadn't been taken! And yet there's no one listed on your own birthday yet. That's very kind of you. They're all accepted.

Q: Can Kuina's birthday be 9/17 for "ku" (nine) "i-chi" (one) "na-na" (seven)? What? What-what-what was that?! Huh? Oh yeah, yeah, yeah, yeah, yeah-yeah-yeah! (Trebol-style)
--God, Punya, Inazuma

Q: Odacchi! Hello!! So, for Penguin and Shachi, the duo from the Heart Pirates, I came up with these dates to fill in the empty spots in the calendar!
--Sami

PENGUIN

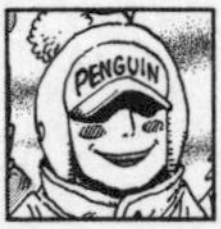

Penguin (April 25)
World Penguin Day

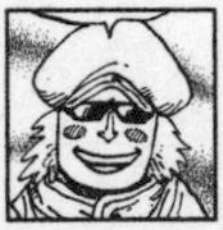

Shachi (April 7)
Shi and chi makes "four" and "seven"

Q: Oda Sensei! How about Rebecca's father Kyros (*ku* for nine) holding up the peace sign with both hands for 22--September 22nd!
Please recognize my hard effort on this.
--Chibimaru

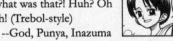

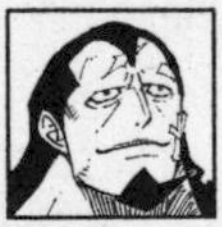

A: Thanks, guys. You really stretched for some of these. But as long as they fill the calendar, I don't care!! Anything goes! Whoever gets there first, wins!!

Chapter 812:

CAPONE "GANG" BEGE

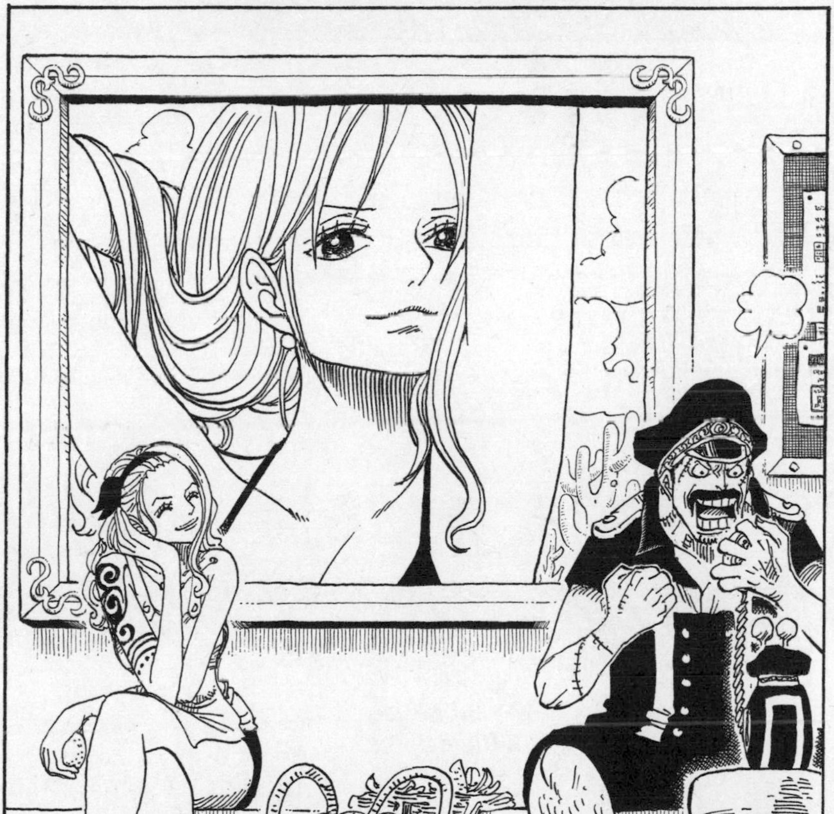

DECKS OF THE WORLD, 500-MILLION-MAN ARC, VOL. 6: "COCOYASHI--HOW DARE YOU USE THIS PROBLEMATIC PHOTO ON HER BOUNTY POSTER!!"

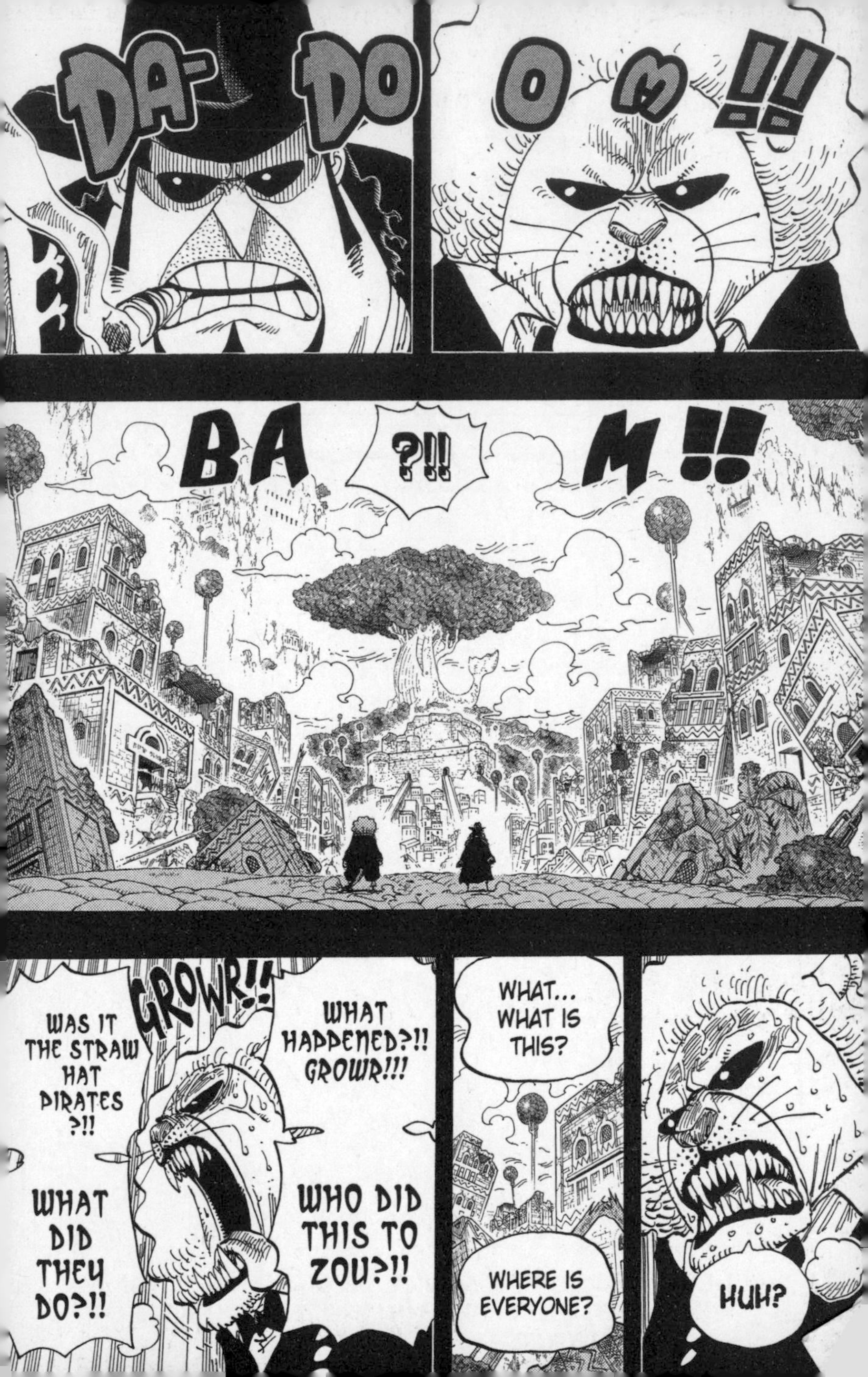
DA-DOOM!!
BAM!!
?!!
HUH?
WHAT... WHAT IS THIS?
WHERE IS EVERYONE?
WHAT HAPPENED?!! GROWR!!!
GROWR!!
WAS IT THE STRAW HAT PIRATES?!!
WHO DID THIS TO ZOU?!!
WHAT DID THEY DO?!!

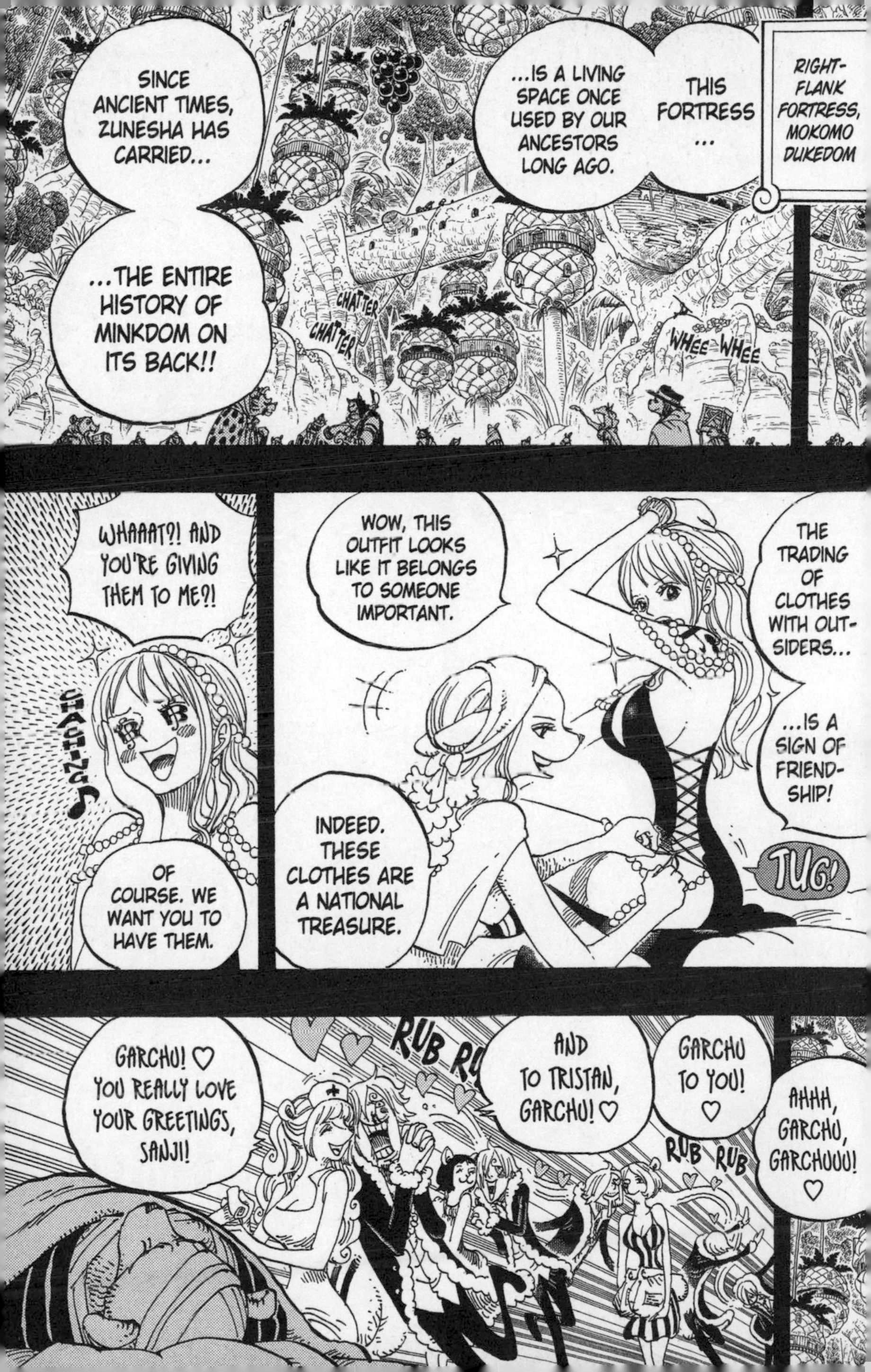
RIGHT-FLANK FORTRESS, MOKOMO DUKEDOM
THIS FORTRESS...
...IS A LIVING SPACE ONCE USED BY OUR ANCESTORS LONG AGO.
SINCE ANCIENT TIMES, ZUNESHA HAS CARRIED...
...THE ENTIRE HISTORY OF MINKDOM ON ITS BACK!!
WHEE WHEE
CHATTER
CHATTER
THE TRADING OF CLOTHES WITH OUTSIDERS...
...IS A SIGN OF FRIENDSHIP!
TUG!
WOW, THIS OUTFIT LOOKS LIKE IT BELONGS TO SOMEONE IMPORTANT.
INDEED. THESE CLOTHES ARE A NATIONAL TREASURE.
WHAAAT?! AND YOU'RE GIVING THEM TO ME?!
CHACHING
OF COURSE. WE WANT YOU TO HAVE THEM.
AHHH, GARCHU, GARCHUUU! ♡
GARCHU TO YOU! ♡
RUB RUB
AND TO TRISTAN, GARCHU! ♡
RUB RU
GARCHU! ♡ YOU REALLY LOVE YOUR GREETINGS, SANJI!

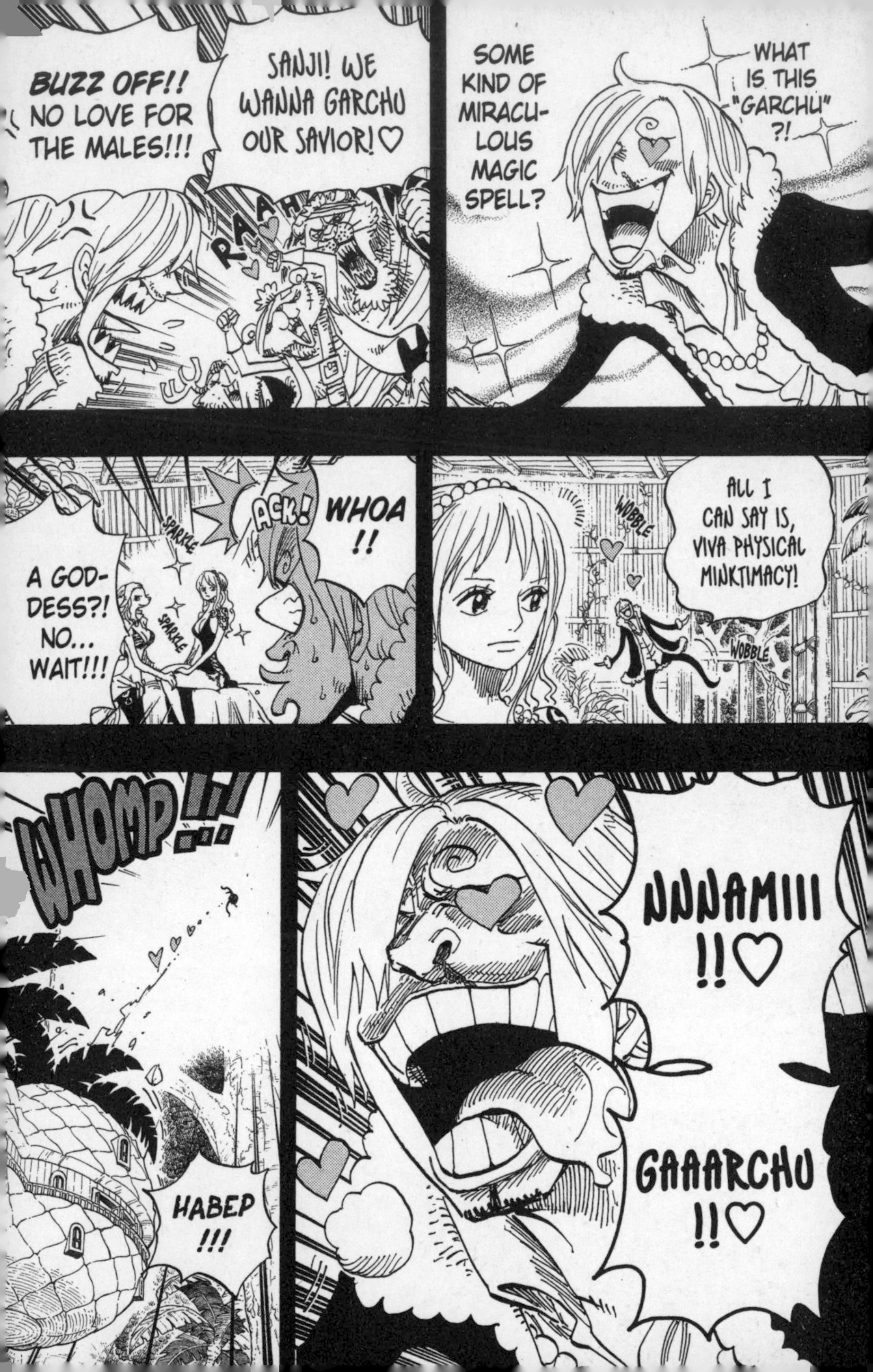
WHAT IS THIS "GARCHU" ?!
SOME KIND OF MIRACULOUS MAGIC SPELL?
SANJI! WE WANNA GARCHU OUR SAVIOR!♡
BUZZ OFF!! NO LOVE FOR THE MALES!!!
RAAH
ALL I CAN SAY IS, VIVA PHYSICAL MINKTIMACY!
WOBBLE
WOBBLE
WHOA !!
ACK!
SPARKLE
A GODDESS?! NO... WAIT!!!
SPARKLE
NNNAMIII !!♡
GAAARCHU !!♡
WHOMP!!
HABEP !!!

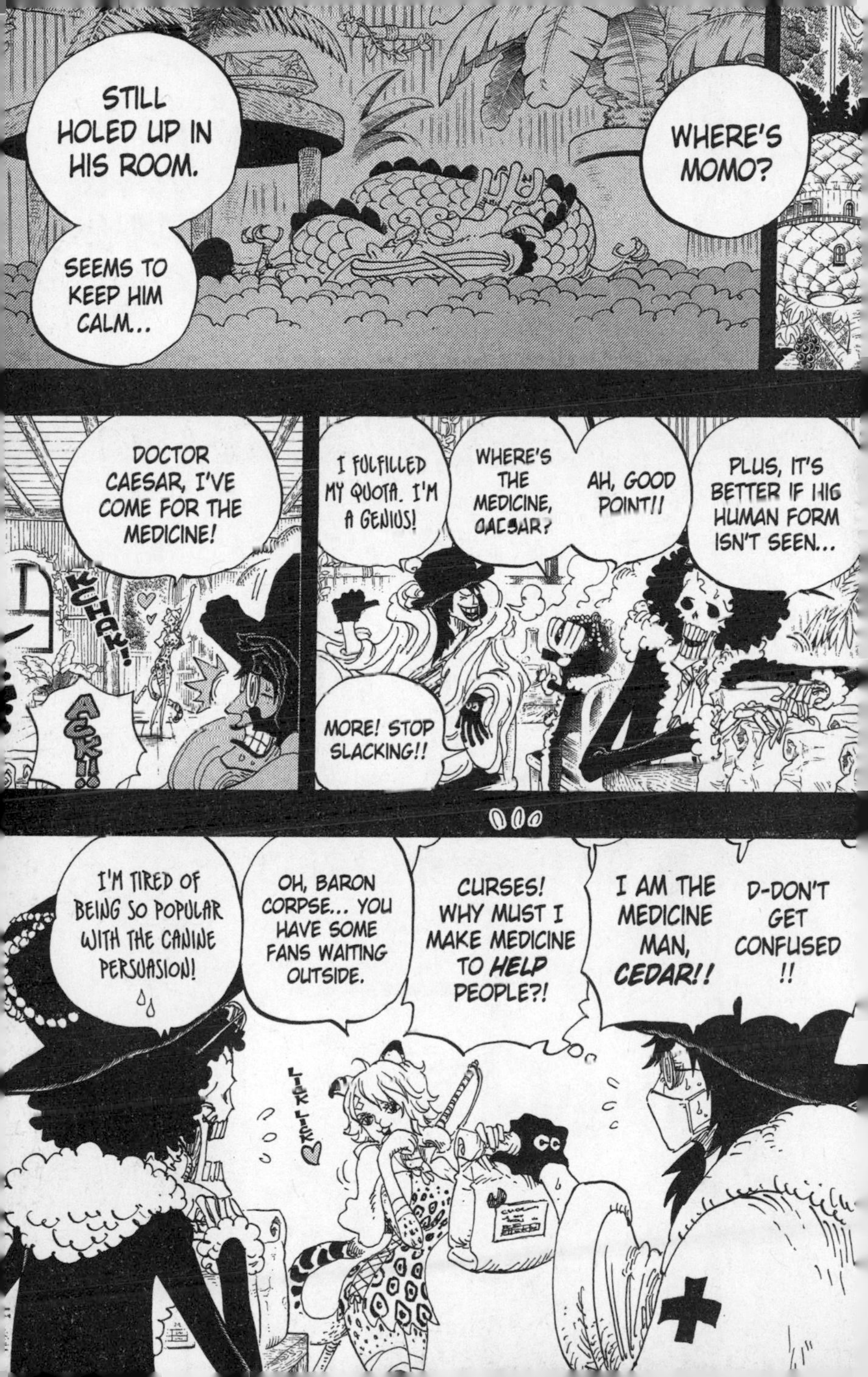
WHERE'S MOMO?
STILL HOLED UP IN HIS ROOM.
SEEMS TO KEEP HIM CALM...
PLUS, IT'S BETTER IF HIS HUMAN FORM ISN'T SEEN...
AH, GOOD POINT!!
WHERE'S THE MEDICINE, CAESAR?
I FULFILLED MY QUOTA. I'M A GENIUS!
MORE! STOP SLACKING!!
DOCTOR CAESAR, I'VE COME FOR THE MEDICINE!
KCHAK!
ACK!!
D-DON'T GET CONFUSED!!
I AM THE MEDICINE MAN, CEDAR!!
CURSES! WHY MUST I MAKE MEDICINE TO HELP PEOPLE?!
OH, BARON CORPSE... YOU HAVE SOME FANS WAITING OUTSIDE.
LICK LICK
I'M TIRED OF BEING SO POPULAR WITH THE CANINE PERSUASION!

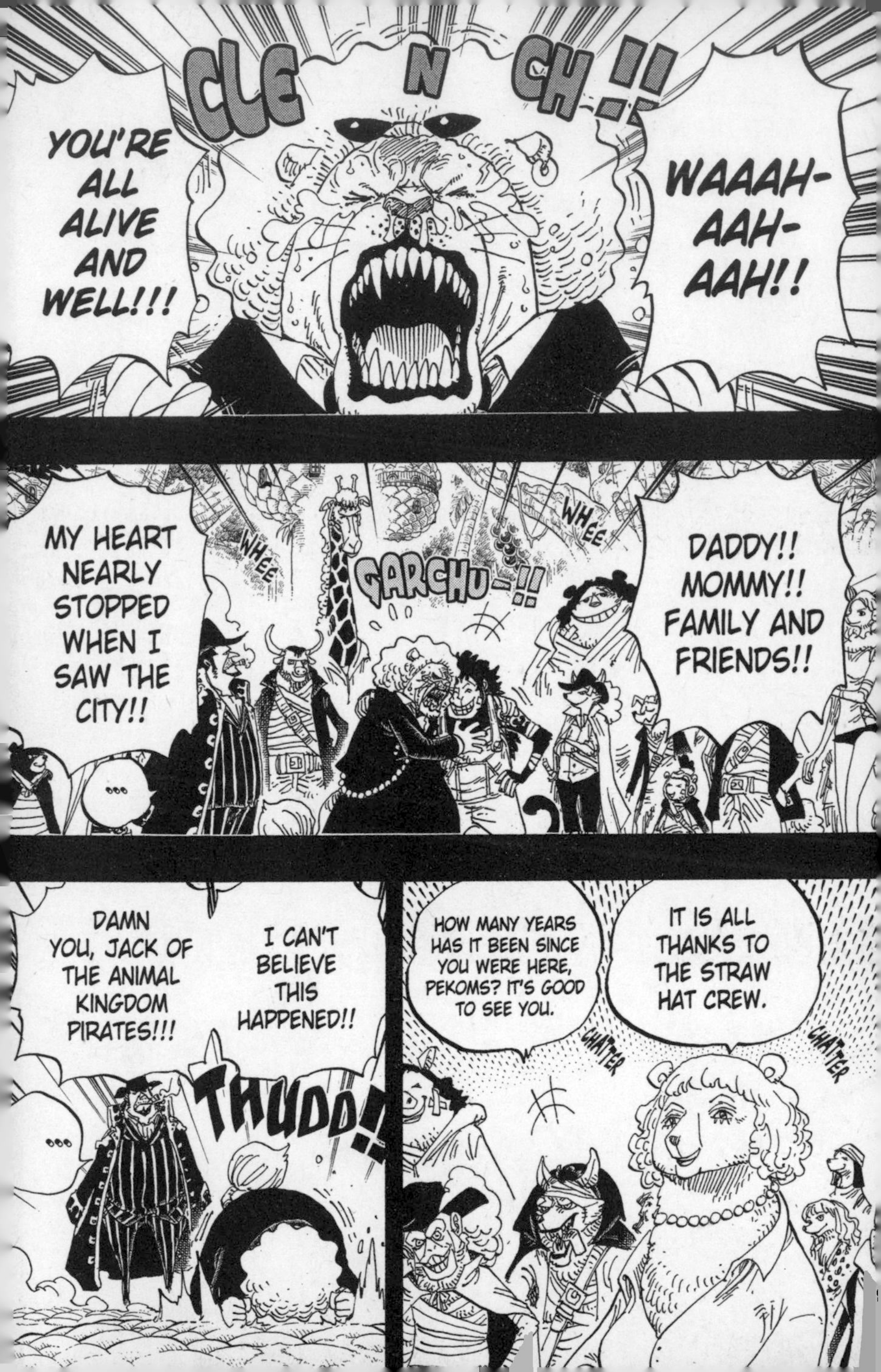
WAAAH-AAH-AAH!!
CLENCH!!
YOU'RE ALL ALIVE AND WELL!!!
DADDY!! MOMMY!! FAMILY AND FRIENDS!!
WHEE
GARCHU-!!
WHEE
MY HEART NEARLY STOPPED WHEN I SAW THE CITY!!
...
IT IS ALL THANKS TO THE STRAW HAT CREW.
CHATTER
HOW MANY YEARS HAS IT BEEN SINCE YOU WERE HERE, PEKOMS? IT'S GOOD TO SEE YOU.
CHATTER
I CAN'T BELIEVE THIS HAPPENED!!
DAMN YOU, JACK OF THE ANIMAL KINGDOM PIRATES!!!
THUDD!!
...

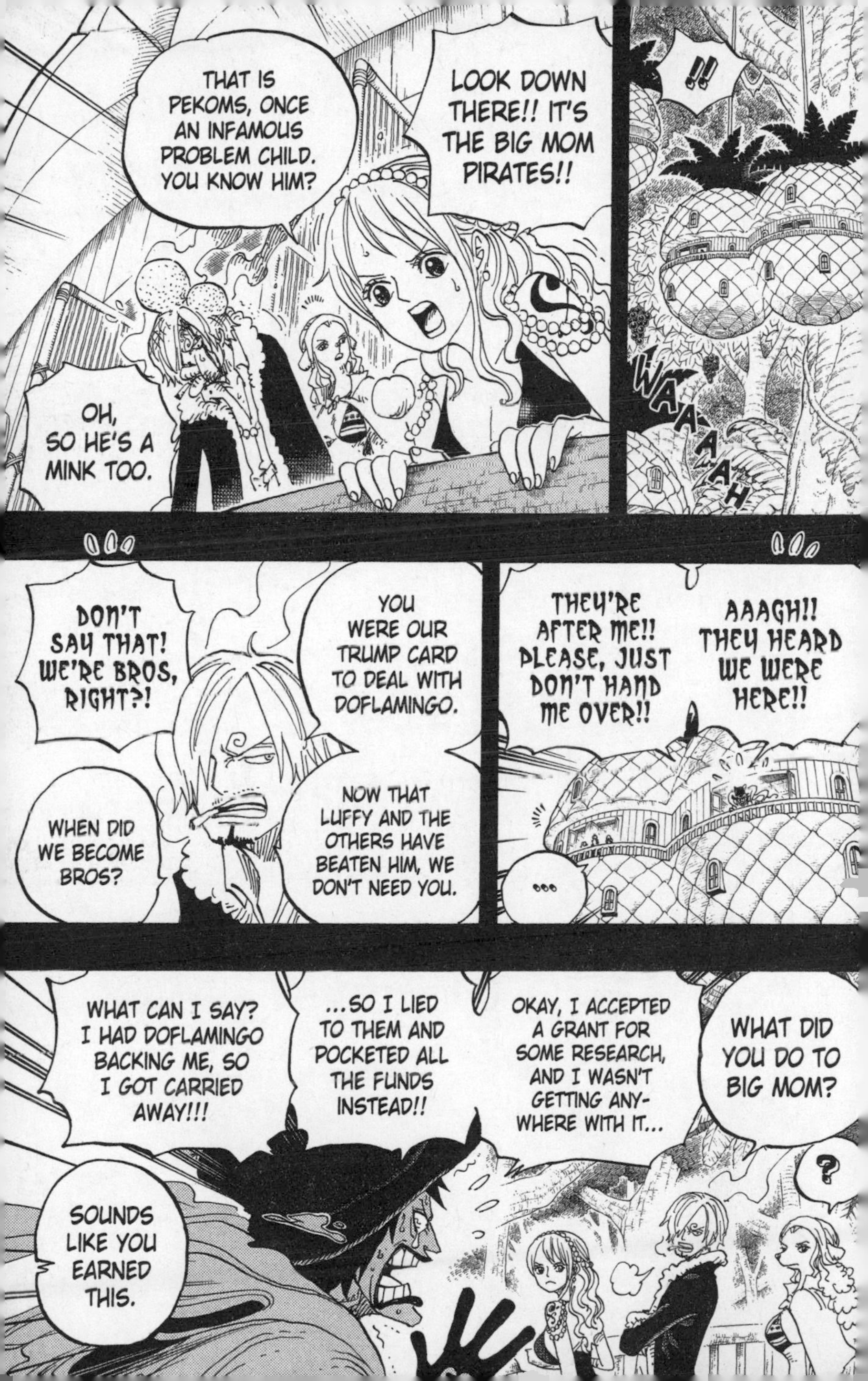
!!
WAAAAAH
LOOK DOWN THERE!! IT'S THE BIG MOM PIRATES!!
THAT IS PEKOMS, ONCE AN INFAMOUS PROBLEM CHILD. YOU KNOW HIM?
OH, SO HE'S A MINK TOO.
AAAGH!! THEY HEARD WE WERE HERE!!
THEY'RE AFTER ME!! PLEASE, JUST DON'T HAND ME OVER!!
...
YOU WERE OUR TRUMP CARD TO DEAL WITH DOFLAMINGO.
DON'T SAY THAT! WE'RE BROS, RIGHT?!
NOW THAT LUFFY AND THE OTHERS HAVE BEATEN HIM, WE DON'T NEED YOU.
WHEN DID WE BECOME BROS?
WHAT DID YOU DO TO BIG MOM?
?
OKAY, I ACCEPTED A GRANT FOR SOME RESEARCH, AND I WASN'T GETTING ANY-WHERE WITH IT...
...SO I LIED TO THEM AND POCKETED ALL THE FUNDS INSTEAD!!
WHAT CAN I SAY? I HAD DOFLAMINGO BACKING ME, SO I GOT CARRIED AWAY!!!
SOUNDS LIKE YOU EARNED THIS.

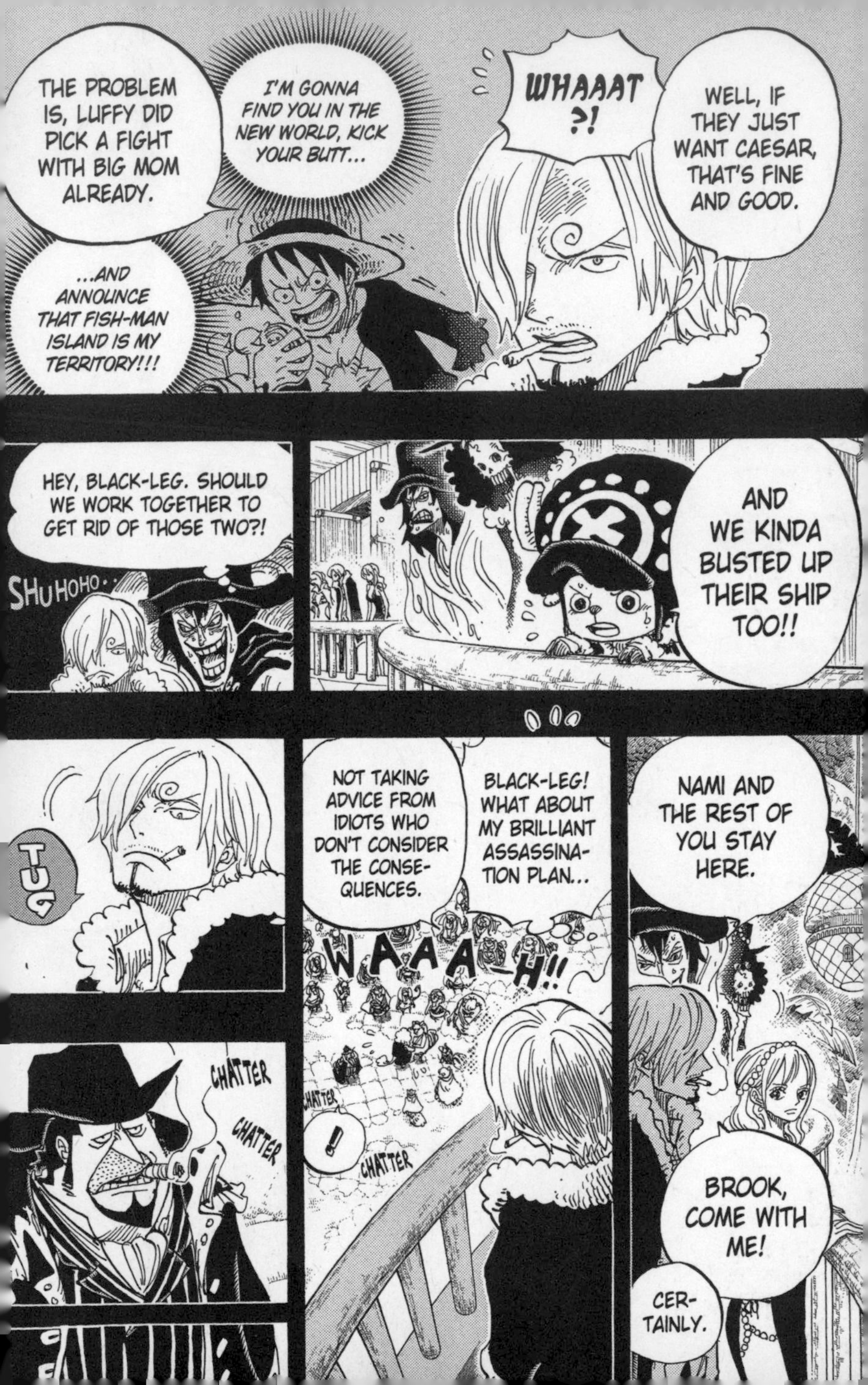
WELL, IF THEY JUST WANT CAESAR, THAT'S FINE AND GOOD.
WHAAAT ?!
THE PROBLEM IS, LUFFY DID PICK A FIGHT WITH BIG MOM ALREADY.
I'M GONNA FIND YOU IN THE NEW WORLD, KICK YOUR BUTT...
...AND ANNOUNCE THAT FISH-MAN ISLAND IS MY TERRITORY!!!
AND WE KINDA BUSTED UP THEIR SHIP TOO!!
HEY, BLACK-LEG. SHOULD WE WORK TOGETHER TO GET RID OF THOSE TWO?!
SHUHOHO..
NAMI AND THE REST OF YOU STAY HERE.
BROOK, COME WITH ME!
CER-TAINLY.
BLACK-LEG! WHAT ABOUT MY BRILLIANT ASSASSINA-TION PLAN...
NOT TAKING ADVICE FROM IDIOTS WHO DON'T CONSIDER THE CONSE-QUENCES.
WAAAA-H!!
CHATTER
!
CHATTER
TUG
CHATTER
CHATTER

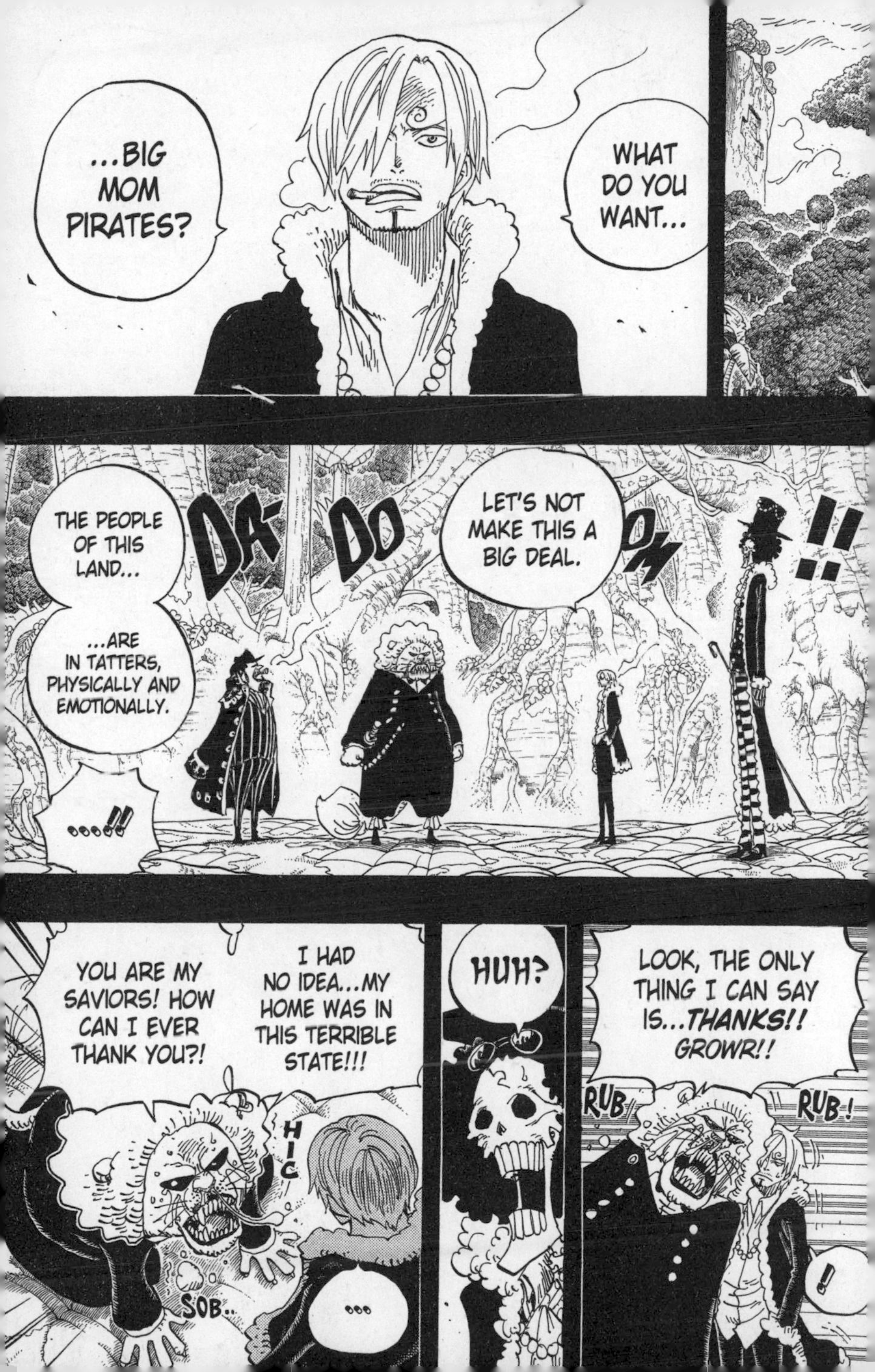
WHAT DO YOU WANT...
...BIG MOM PIRATES?
!!
LET'S NOT MAKE THIS A BIG DEAL.
DA-DO-OM
THE PEOPLE OF THIS LAND...
...ARE IN TATTERS, PHYSICALLY AND EMOTIONALLY.
...!!
RUB!
LOOK, THE ONLY THING I CAN SAY IS...THANKS!! GROWR!!
RUB
!
HUH?
I HAD NO IDEA...MY HOME WAS IN THIS TERRIBLE STATE!!!
HIC
YOU ARE MY SAVIORS! HOW CAN I EVER THANK YOU?!
...
SOB..

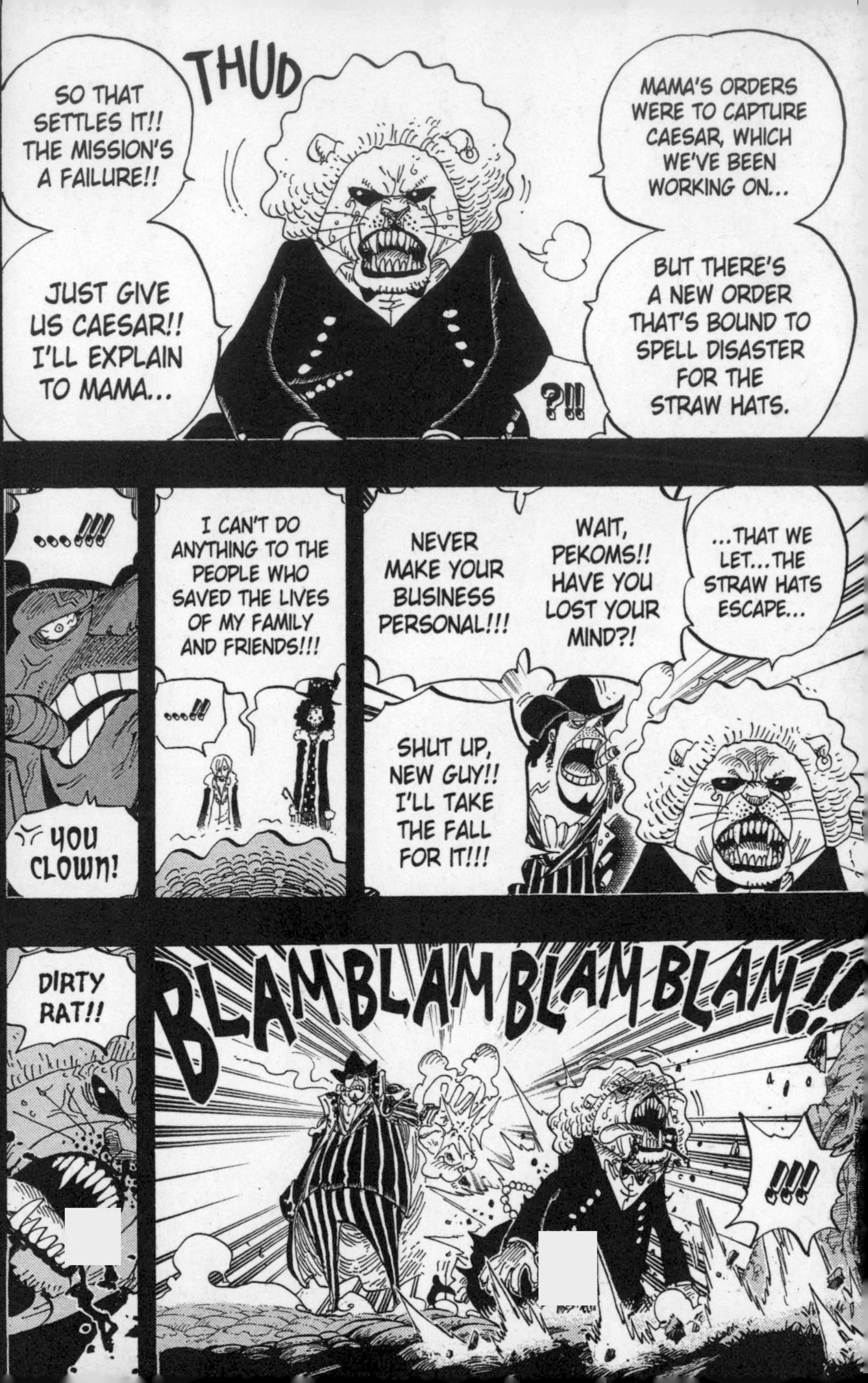
MAMA'S ORDERS WERE TO CAPTURE CAESAR, WHICH WE'VE BEEN WORKING ON...
BUT THERE'S A NEW ORDER THAT'S BOUND TO SPELL DISASTER FOR THE STRAW HATS.
THUD
SO THAT SETTLES IT!! THE MISSION'S A FAILURE!!
JUST GIVE US CAESAR!! I'LL EXPLAIN TO MAMA...
?!!
...THAT WE LET...THE STRAW HATS ESCAPE...
WAIT, PEKOMS!! HAVE YOU LOST YOUR MIND?!
NEVER MAKE YOUR BUSINESS PERSONAL!!!
SHUT UP, NEW GUY!! I'LL TAKE THE FALL FOR IT!!!
I CAN'T DO ANYTHING TO THE PEOPLE WHO SAVED THE LIVES OF MY FAMILY AND FRIENDS!!!
...!!
...!!!
YOU CLOWN!
BLAMBLAMBLAMBLAM!!
!!!
DIRTY RAT!!

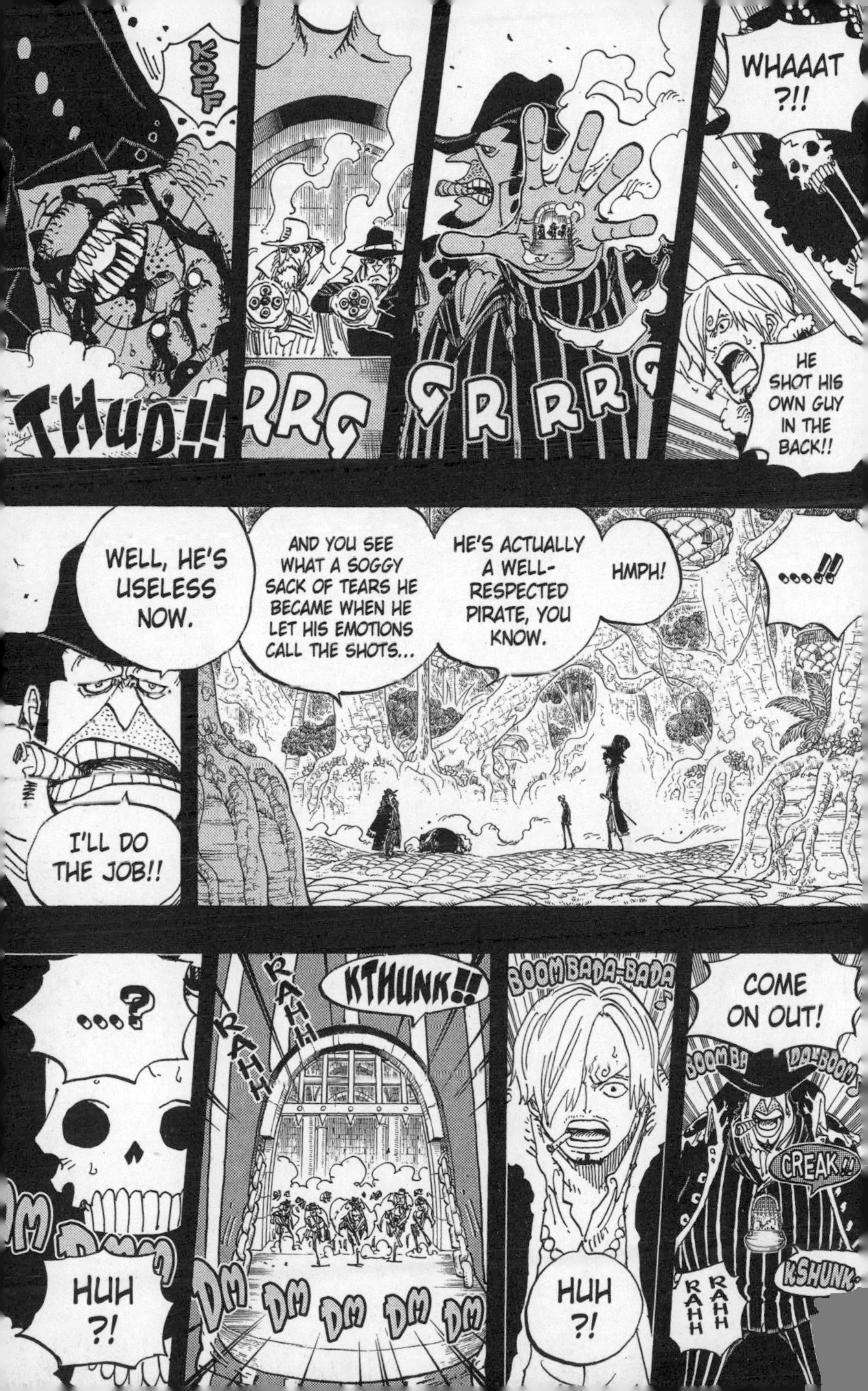
WHAAAT ?!!
HE SHOT HIS OWN GUY IN THE BACK!!
GRRRG
RRRG
KOFF
THUD!!
...!!
HMPH!
HE'S ACTUALLY A WELL-RESPECTED PIRATE, YOU KNOW.
AND YOU SEE WHAT A SOGGY SACK OF TEARS HE BECAME WHEN HE LET HIS EMOTIONS CALL THE SHOTS...
WELL, HE'S USELESS NOW.
I'LL DO THE JOB!!
COME ON OUT!
BOOM BA DA-BOOM
CREAK!!
KSHUNK
RAHH RAHH
BOOM BADA-BADA
HUH ?!
KTHUNK!!
RAHH RAHH
DM DM DM DM DM
...?
HUH ?!

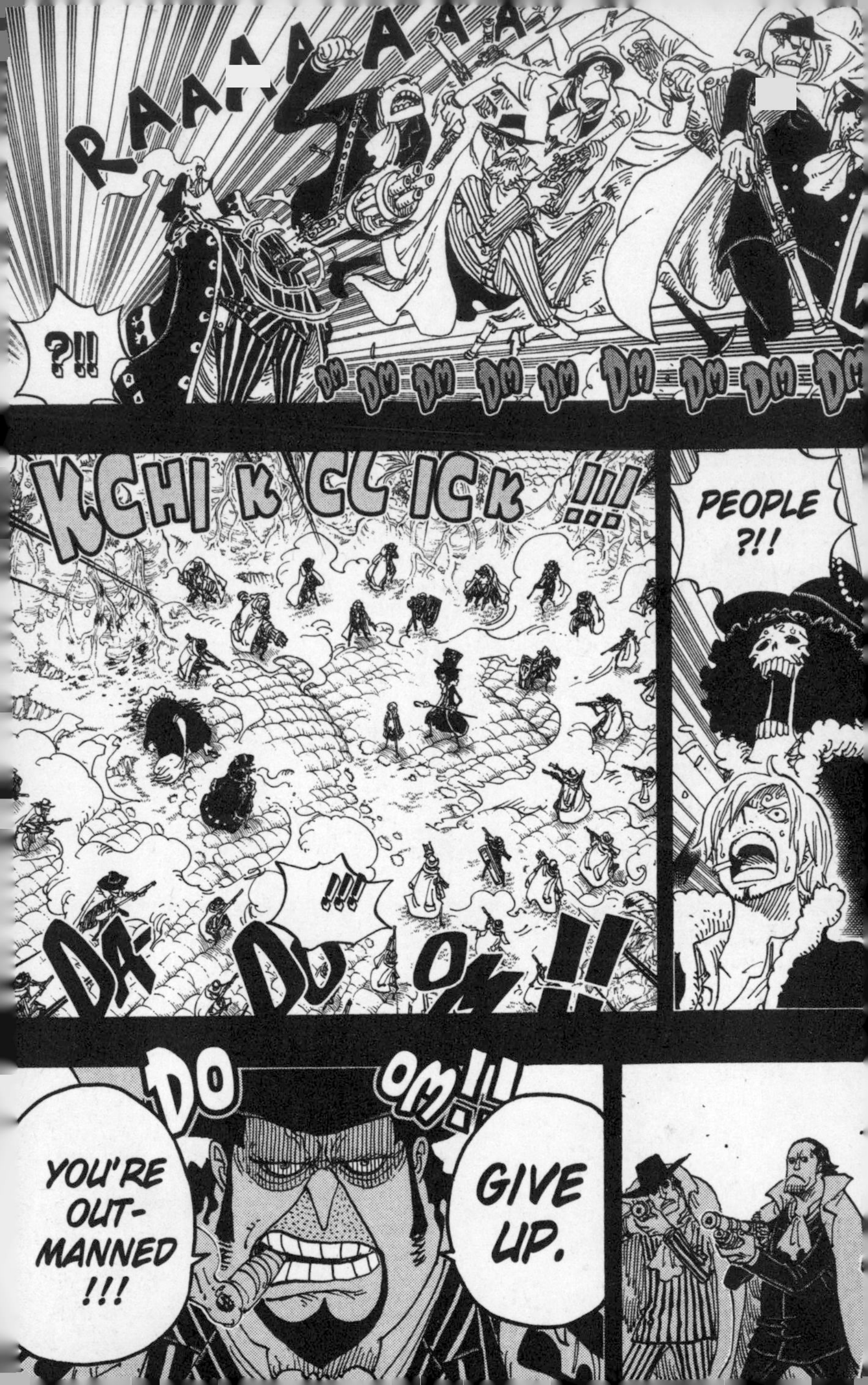
RAAAAAAA
?!!
DM DM DM DM DM DM DM DM DM
PEOPLE ?!!
KCHIK CLICK!!!
!!!
DA-DOOM!!
DOOM!!
GIVE UP.
YOU'RE OUT-MANNED!!!

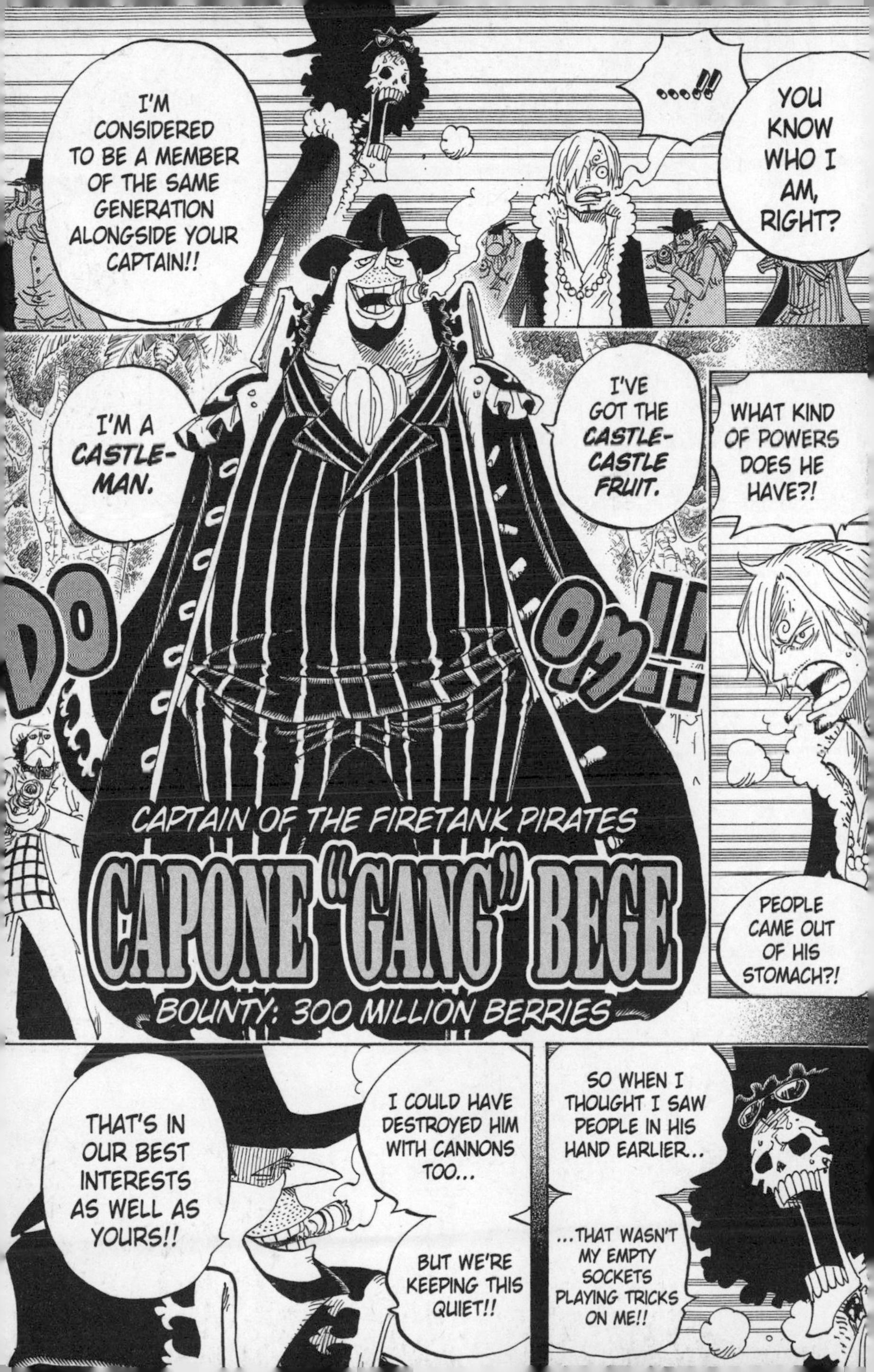
YOU KNOW WHO I AM, RIGHT?
......!!
I'M CONSIDERED TO BE A MEMBER OF THE SAME GENERATION ALONGSIDE YOUR CAPTAIN!!
WHAT KIND OF POWERS DOES HE HAVE?!
PEOPLE CAME OUT OF HIS STOMACH?!
I'VE GOT THE CASTLE-CASTLE FRUIT.
I'M A CASTLE-MAN.
DOOM!!
CAPTAIN OF THE FIRETANK PIRATES
CAPONE "GANG" BEGE
BOUNTY: 300 MILLION BERRIES
SO WHEN I THOUGHT I SAW PEOPLE IN HIS HAND EARLIER...
...THAT WASN'T MY EMPTY SOCKETS PLAYING TRICKS ON ME!!
I COULD HAVE DESTROYED HIM WITH CANNONS TOO...
BUT WE'RE KEEPING THIS QUIET!!
THAT'S IN OUR BEST INTERESTS AS WELL AS YOURS!!

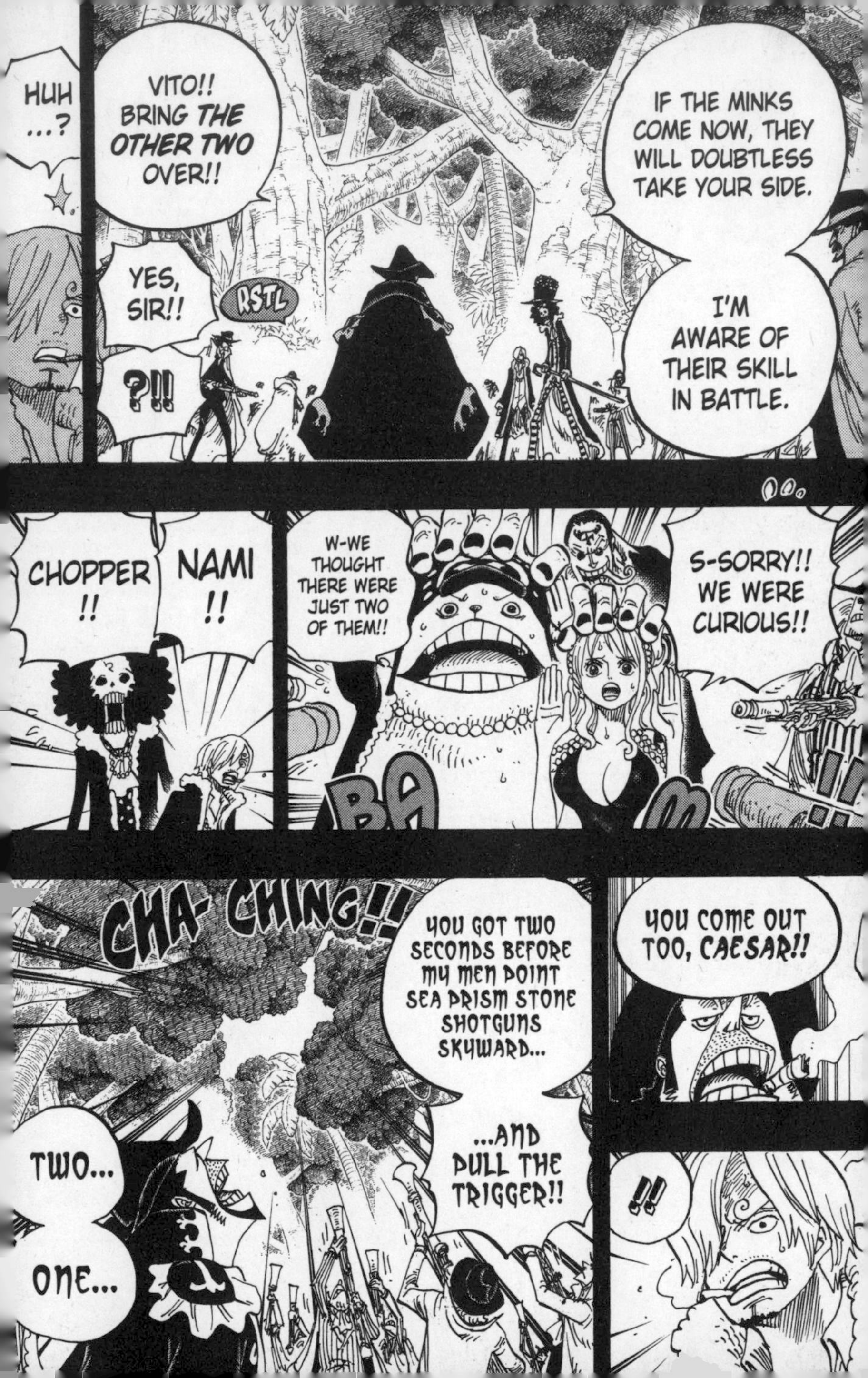
IF THE MINKS COME NOW, THEY WILL DOUBTLESS TAKE YOUR SIDE.
I'M AWARE OF THEIR SKILL IN BATTLE.
VITO!! BRING THE OTHER TWO OVER!!
YES, SIR!!
RSTL
?!!
HUH ...?
S-SORRY!! WE WERE CURIOUS!!
W-WE THOUGHT THERE WERE JUST TWO OF THEM!!
BAM!!
NAMI !!
CHOPPER !!
YOU COME OUT TOO, CAESAR!!
!!
CHA-CHING!!
YOU GOT TWO SECONDS BEFORE MY MEN POINT SEA PRISM STONE SHOTGUNS SKYWARD...
...AND PULL THE TRIGGER!!
TWO...
ONE...

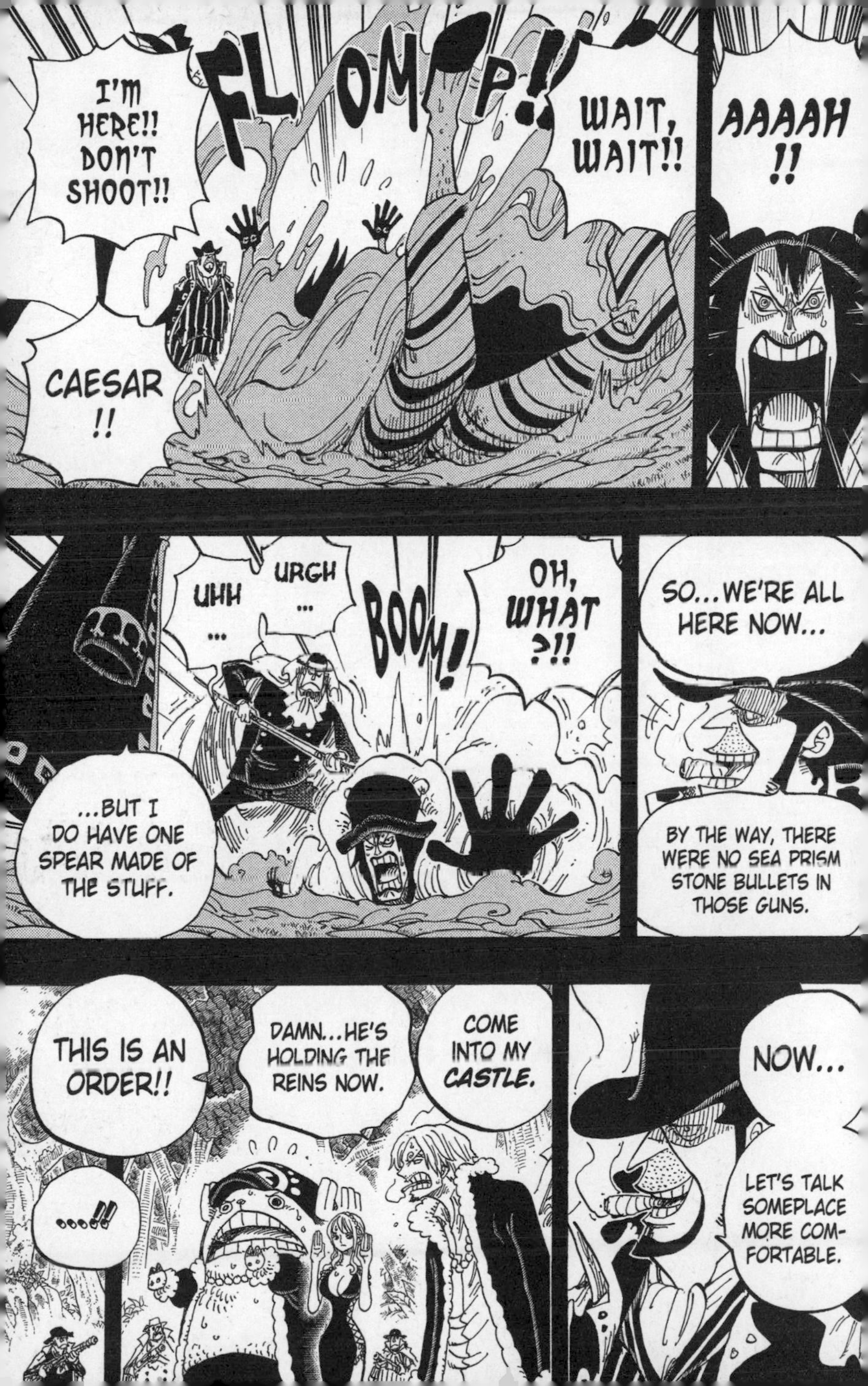
AAAAH !!
WAIT, WAIT!!
FLOMP!!
I'M HERE!! DON'T SHOOT!!
CAESAR !!
SO...WE'RE ALL HERE NOW...
BY THE WAY, THERE WERE NO SEA PRISM STONE BULLETS IN THOSE GUNS.
OH, WHAT ?!!
BOOM!
URGH ...
UHH ...
...BUT I DO HAVE ONE SPEAR MADE OF THE STUFF.
NOW...
LET'S TALK SOMEPLACE MORE COM-FORTABLE.
COME INTO MY *CASTLE.*
DAMN...HE'S HOLDING THE REINS NOW.
THIS IS AN ORDER!!
....!!

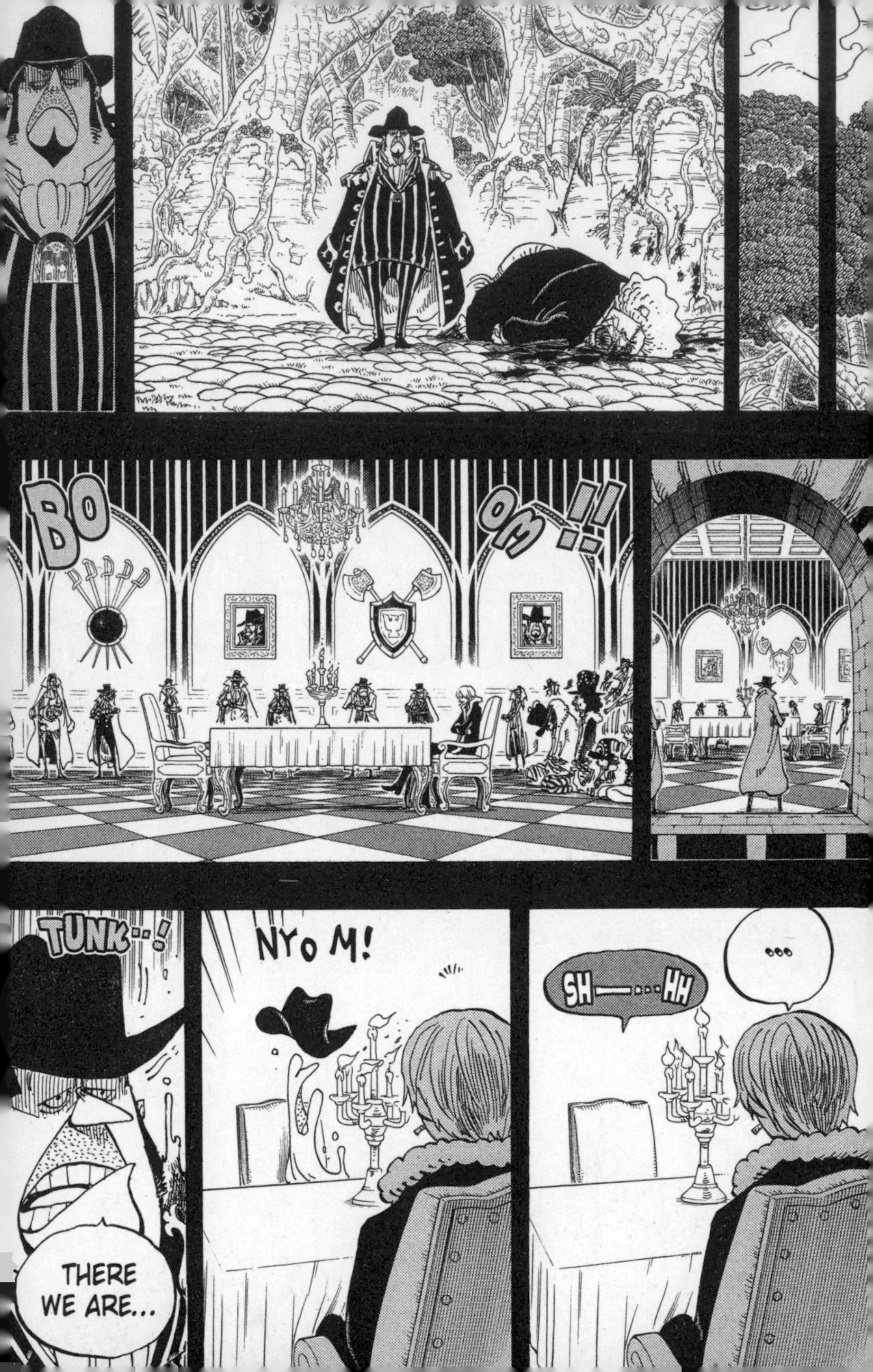
BOOM!!
...
SH—...HH
NYOM!
TUNK..!
THERE WE ARE...

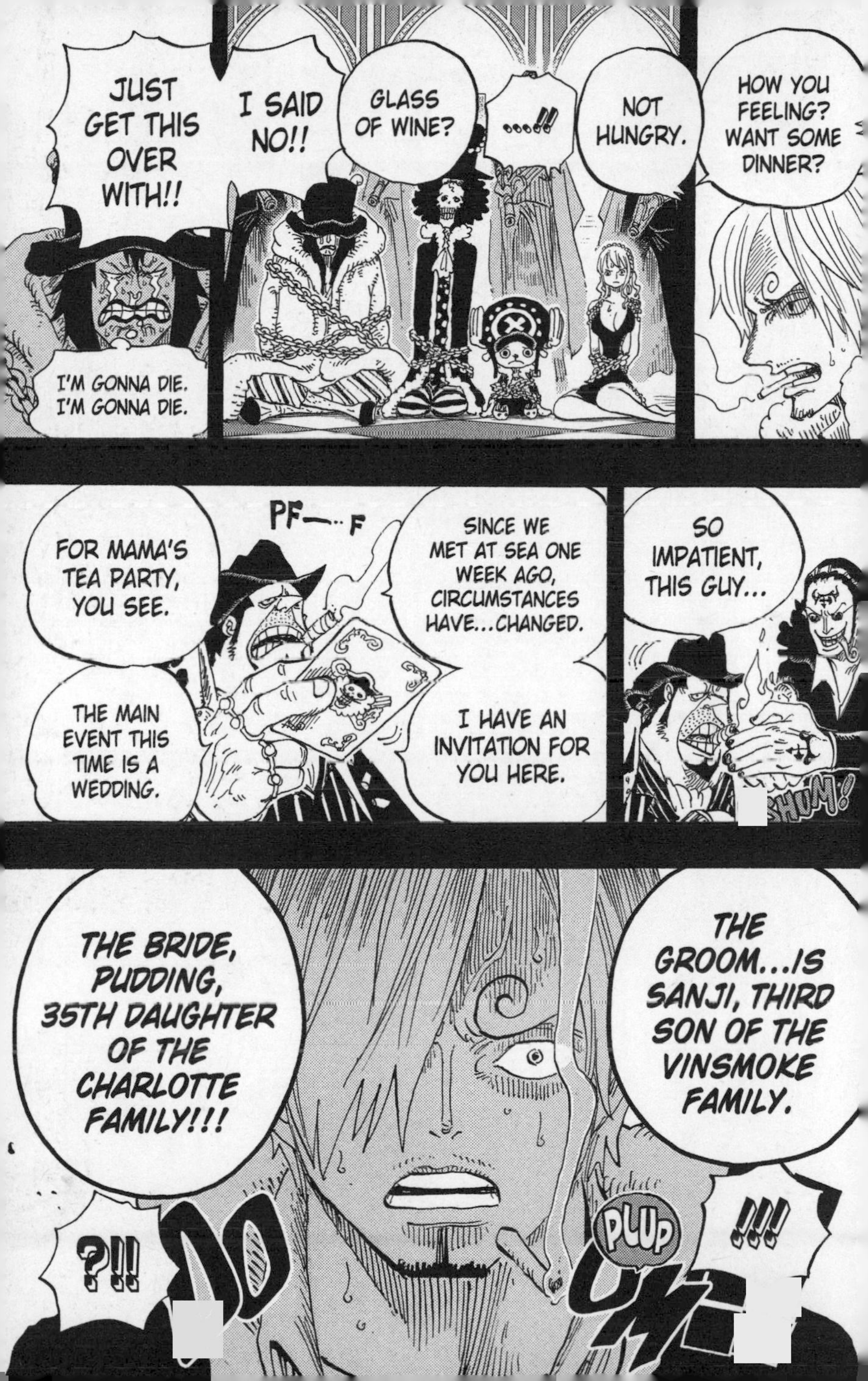
HOW YOU FEELING? WANT SOME DINNER?
NOT HUNGRY.
...!!
GLASS OF WINE?
I SAID NO!!
JUST GET THIS OVER WITH!!
I'M GONNA DIE. I'M GONNA DIE.
SO IMPATIENT, THIS GUY...
SHUM!
SINCE WE MET AT SEA ONE WEEK AGO, CIRCUMSTANCES HAVE...CHANGED.
I HAVE AN INVITATION FOR YOU HERE.
PF—...F
FOR MAMA'S TEA PARTY, YOU SEE.
THE MAIN EVENT THIS TIME IS A WEDDING.
THE GROOM...IS SANJI, THIRD SON OF THE VINSMOKE FAMILY.
THE BRIDE, PUDDING, 35TH DAUGHTER OF THE CHARLOTTE FAMILY!!!
!!!
PLUP
?!!

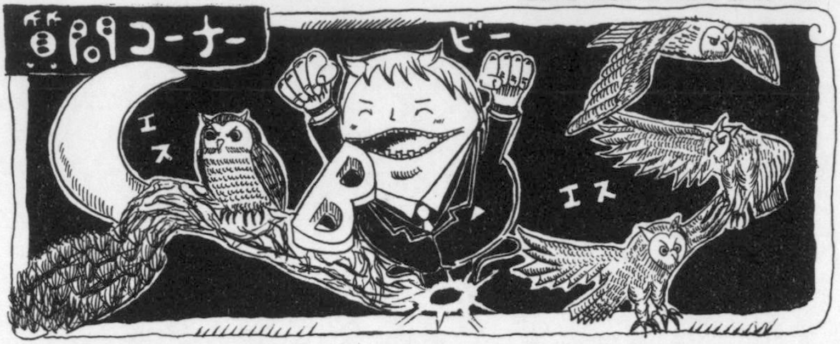

(Yuki Yokohata, Kanagawa)

Q: Greetings, Oda Sensei! In Chapter 800 of Volume 80, I noticed that the sails of some of the Yontamaria ships said *3 Tamaria* (San Tamaria) and *2 Tamaria* (Ni Tamaria). Since *yon* means "four," are these a representation of the rank of the ships? Does Columbus ride on a 3 Tamaria? Also, is the insignia of the egg taken from the concept of the "Egg of Columbus"?

--Samurai Ryota

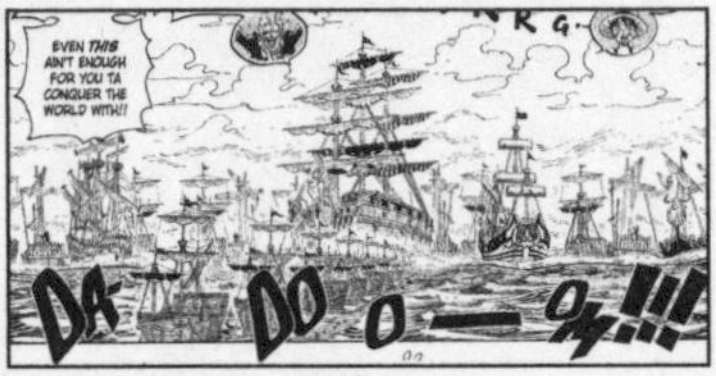
EVEN THIS AIN'T ENOUGH FOR YOU TA CONQUER THE WORLD WITH!!
DA DO O— OM!!!

A: Good call. That's right: there are three ranks of ships in the Yontamaria Fleet. There are 50 Nitamaria ships that take the lead, another five Santamaria ships that are slightly larger, and the biggest one is the mothership, Yontamaria.

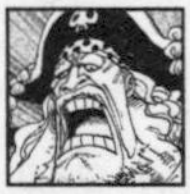

(Nitamaria)

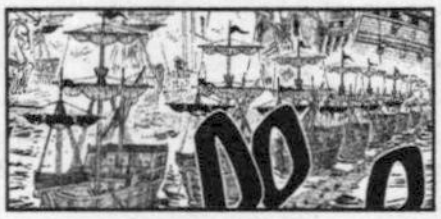
DO O

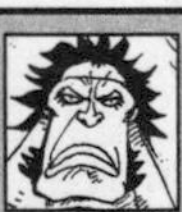

(Happosai)

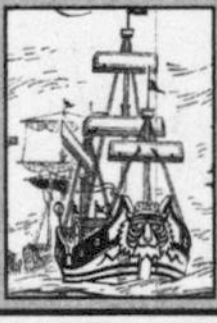

(Ipposai)

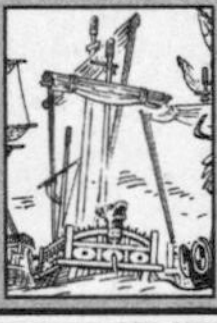

Meanwhile, Sai's Happosui have one big *Happosai* and seven armored *Ipposai* ships.

(Santamaria)

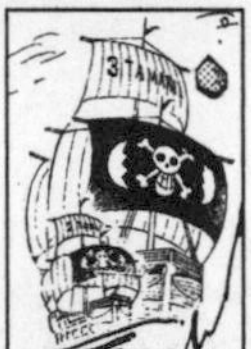

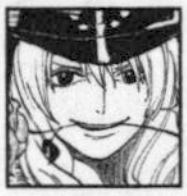

Cavendish leads the *Sleeping Forest White Steed.*

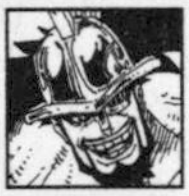

Hajrudin's Viking-style *Naglfar.*

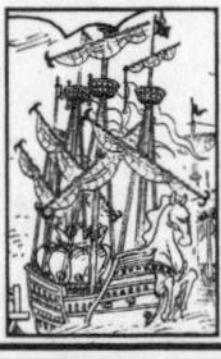

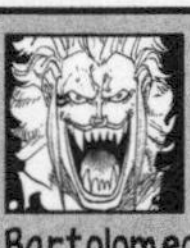

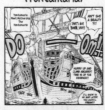

Bartolomeo's weird ship.

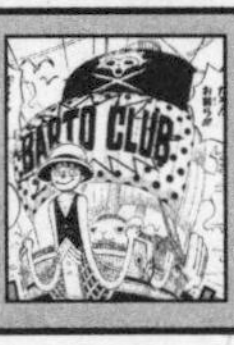
BARTO CLUB

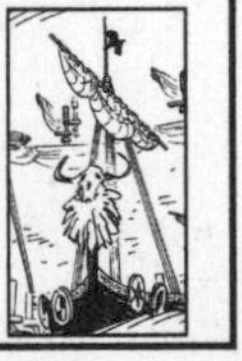

(Yontamaria)

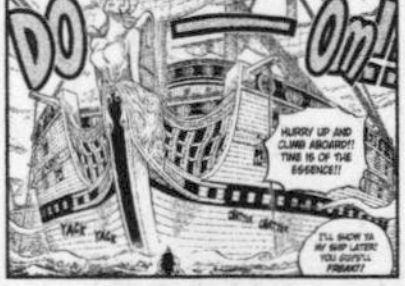
Yontamaria Fleet Mothership The Yontamaria
AIN'T SHE A BEAUTY ?!!
THAT'S NOT YOUR SHIP!!
DO— OM!!
HURRY UP AND CLIMB ABOARD!! TIME IS OF THE ESSENCE!!
YACK YACK
I'LL SHOW YA MY SHIP LATER! YOU GOTTA FREAK!?

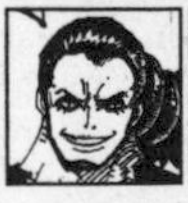

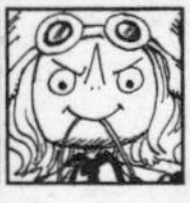

Ideo and Leo don't have ships, so Ideo caught a ride with Orlumbus. Of course, you don't need to remember any of this information!

Chapter 813:
TEA PARTY INVITATION

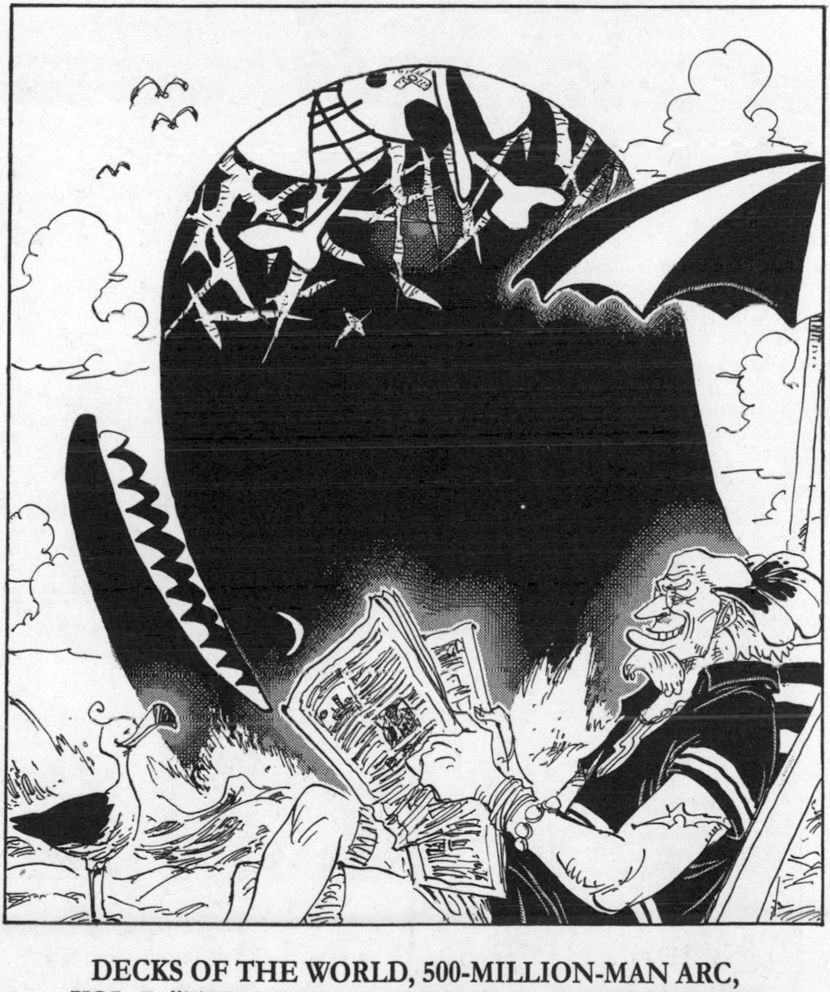

DECKS OF THE WORLD, 500-MILLION-MAN ARC, VOL. 7: "TWIN CAPE--LABOON'S IN GOOD SPIRITS"

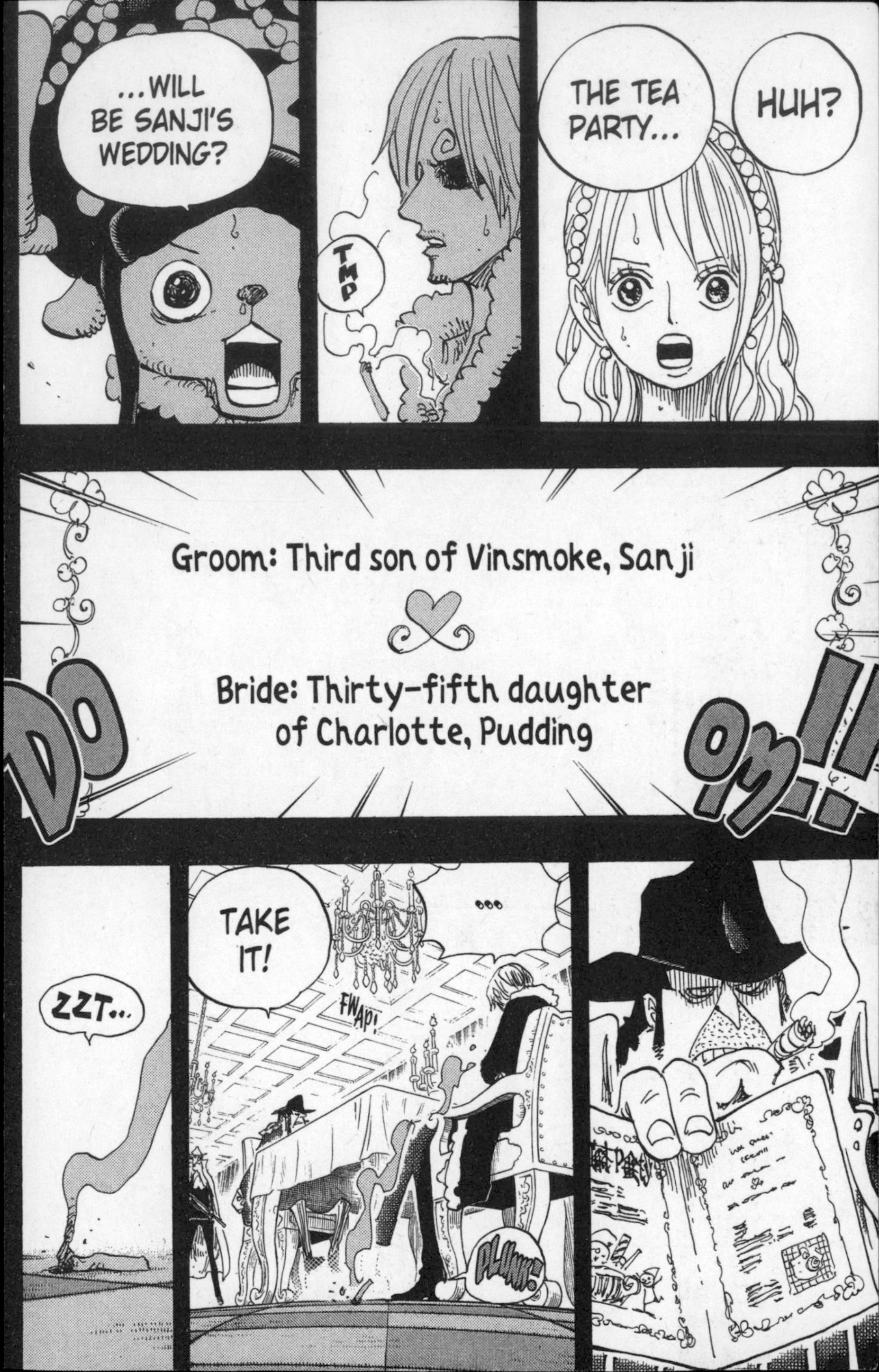
HUH?
THE TEA PARTY...
TMP
...WILL BE SANJI'S WEDDING?
Groom: Third son of Vinsmoke, Sanji
Bride: Thirty-fifth daughter of Charlotte, Pudding
DOOM!!
...
TAKE IT!
FWAP!
PLINK!
ZZT...

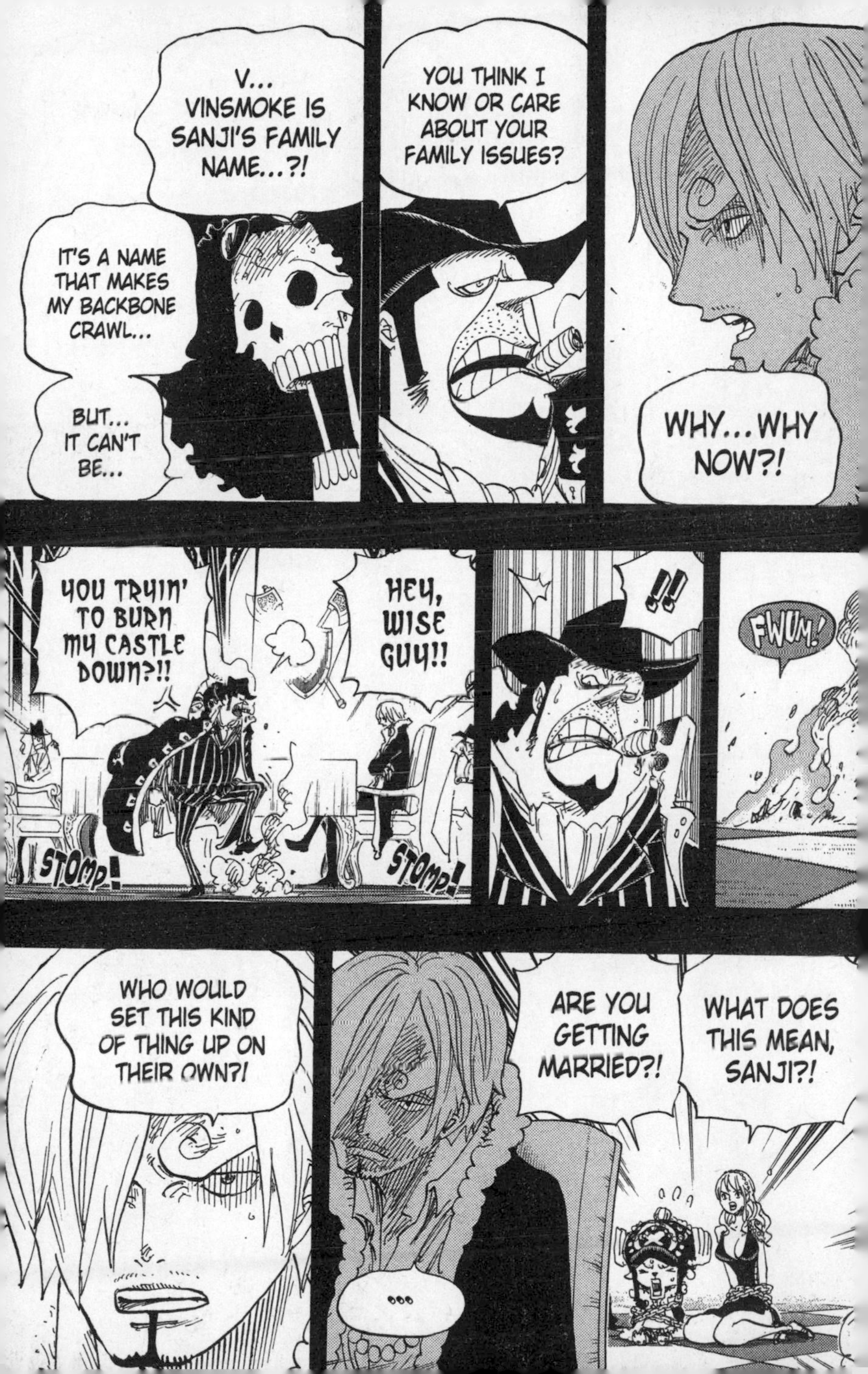
WHY...WHY NOW?!
YOU THINK I KNOW OR CARE ABOUT YOUR FAMILY ISSUES?
V... VINSMOKE IS SANJI'S FAMILY NAME...?!
IT'S A NAME THAT MAKES MY BACKBONE CRAWL...
BUT... IT CAN'T BE...
FWUM!
!!
HEY, WISE GUY!!
YOU TRYIN' TO BURN MY CASTLE DOWN?!!
STOMP!
STOMP!
WHAT DOES THIS MEAN, SANJI?!
ARE YOU GETTING MARRIED?!
...
WHO WOULD SET THIS KIND OF THING UP ON THEIR OWN?!

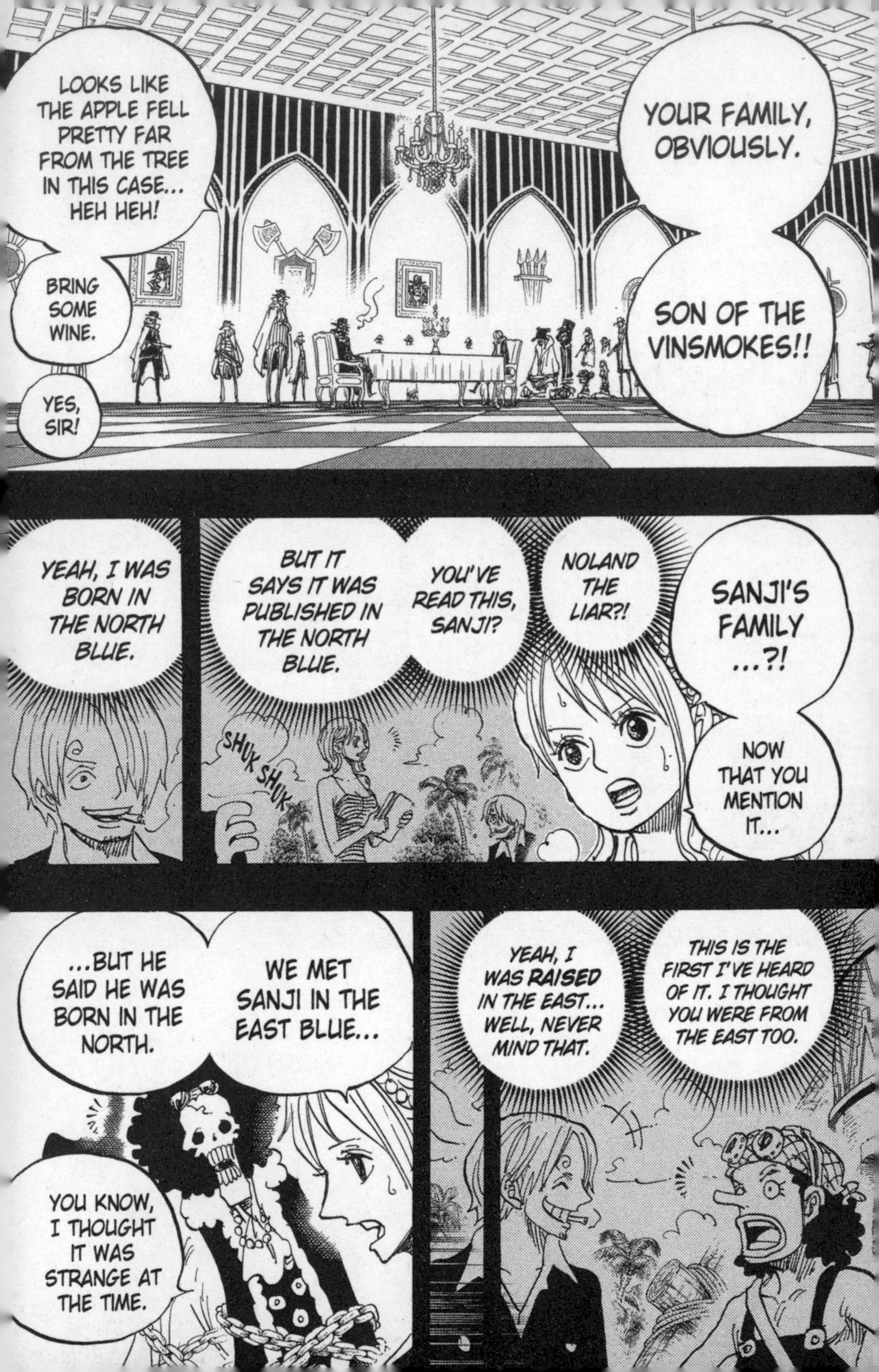
YOUR FAMILY, OBVIOUSLY.
SON OF THE VINSMOKES!!
LOOKS LIKE THE APPLE FELL PRETTY FAR FROM THE TREE IN THIS CASE... HEH HEH!
BRING SOME WINE.
YES, SIR!
SANJI'S FAMILY ...?!
NOW THAT YOU MENTION IT...
NOLAND THE LIAR?!
YOU'VE READ THIS, SANJI?
BUT IT SAYS IT WAS PUBLISHED IN THE NORTH BLUE.
SHUK SHUK
YEAH, I WAS BORN IN THE NORTH BLUE.
THIS IS THE FIRST I'VE HEARD OF IT. I THOUGHT YOU WERE FROM THE EAST TOO.
YEAH, I WAS **RAISED** IN THE EAST... WELL, NEVER MIND THAT.
WE MET SANJI IN THE EAST BLUE...
...BUT HE SAID HE WAS BORN IN THE NORTH.
YOU KNOW, I THOUGHT IT WAS STRANGE AT THE TIME.

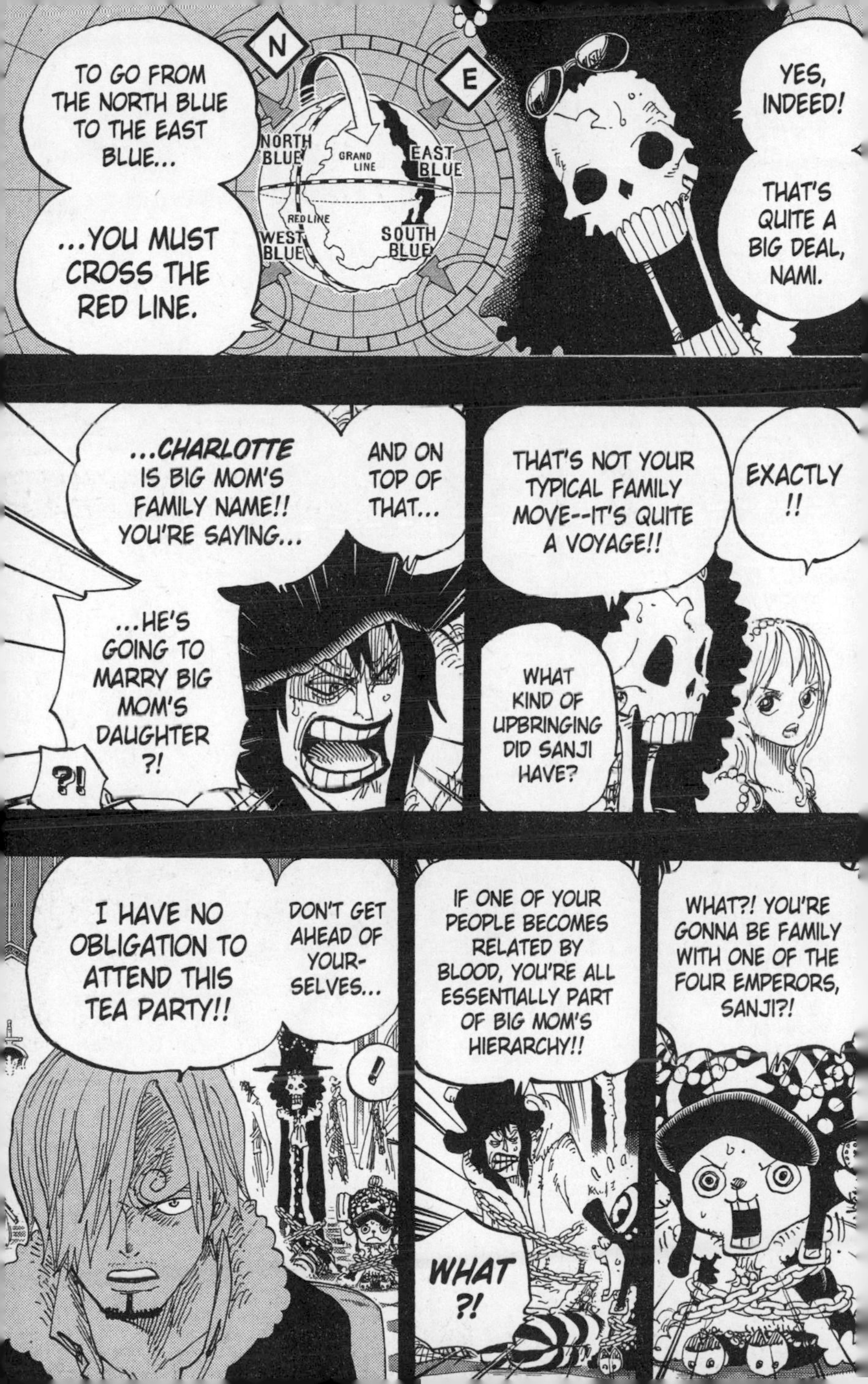
YES, INDEED!
THAT'S QUITE A BIG DEAL, NAMI.
TO GO FROM THE NORTH BLUE TO THE EAST BLUE...
...YOU MUST CROSS THE RED LINE.
N
E
NORTH BLUE
GRAND LINE
EAST BLUE
RED LINE
WEST BLUE
SOUTH BLUE
EXACTLY!!
THAT'S NOT YOUR TYPICAL FAMILY MOVE--IT'S QUITE A VOYAGE!!
WHAT KIND OF UPBRINGING DID SANJI HAVE?
AND ON TOP OF THAT...
...*CHARLOTTE* IS BIG MOM'S FAMILY NAME!! YOU'RE SAYING...
...HE'S GOING TO MARRY BIG MOM'S DAUGHTER?!
?!
WHAT?! YOU'RE GONNA BE FAMILY WITH ONE OF THE FOUR EMPERORS, SANJI?!
IF ONE OF YOUR PEOPLE BECOMES RELATED BY BLOOD, YOU'RE ALL ESSENTIALLY PART OF BIG MOM'S HIERARCHY!!
WHAT?!
DON'T GET AHEAD OF YOURSELVES...
I HAVE NO OBLIGATION TO ATTEND THIS TEA PARTY!!
!

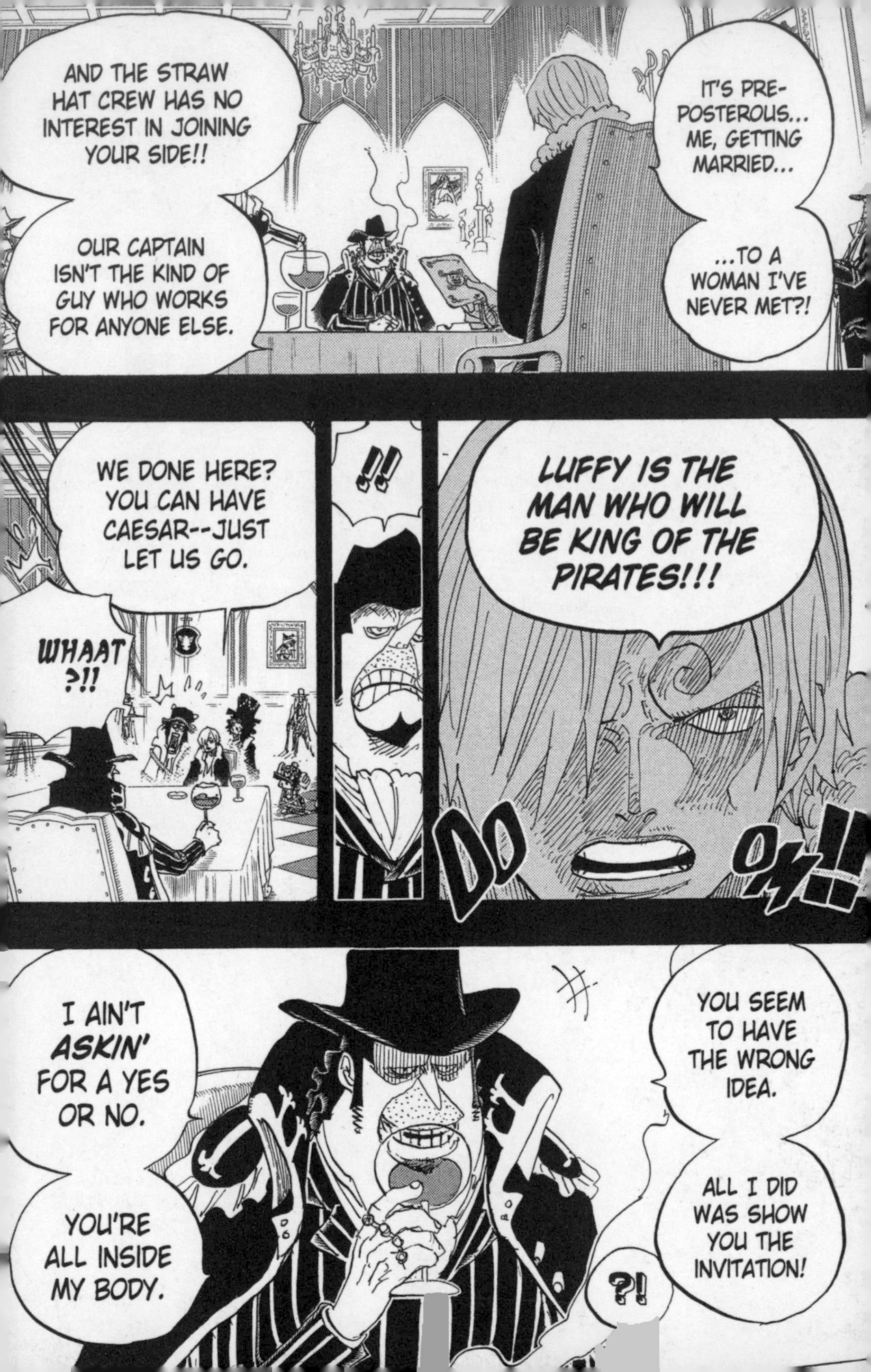
IT'S PRE-POSTEROUS... ME, GETTING MARRIED...
...TO A WOMAN I'VE NEVER MET?!
AND THE STRAW HAT CREW HAS NO INTEREST IN JOINING YOUR SIDE!!
OUR CAPTAIN ISN'T THE KIND OF GUY WHO WORKS FOR ANYONE ELSE.
LUFFY IS THE MAN WHO WILL BE KING OF THE PIRATES!!!
DO
OH!!
!!
WE DONE HERE? YOU CAN HAVE CAESAR--JUST LET US GO.
WHAAT ?!!
YOU SEEM TO HAVE THE WRONG IDEA.
ALL I DID WAS SHOW YOU THE INVITATION!
?!
I AIN'T ASKIN' FOR A YES OR NO.
YOU'RE ALL INSIDE MY BODY.

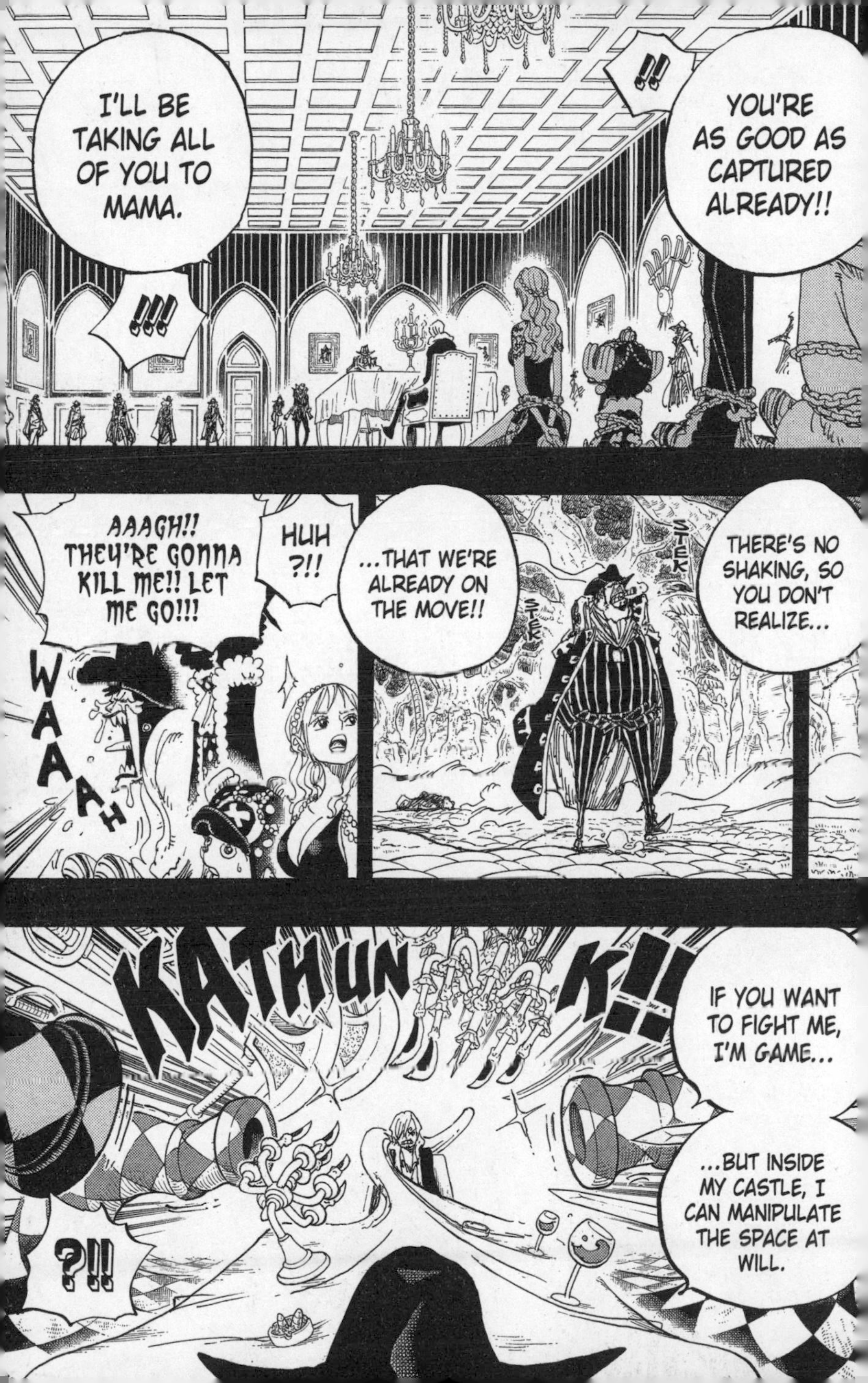
!!
YOU'RE AS GOOD AS CAPTURED ALREADY!!
I'LL BE TAKING ALL OF YOU TO MAMA.
!!!
THERE'S NO SHAKING, SO YOU DON'T REALIZE...
STEK
STEK
...THAT WE'RE ALREADY ON THE MOVE!!
HUH ?!!
AAAGH!! THEY'RE GONNA KILL ME!! LET ME GO!!!
WAAAH
IF YOU WANT TO FIGHT ME, I'M GAME...
KATHUNK!!
...BUT INSIDE MY CASTLE, I CAN MANIPULATE THE SPACE AT WILL.
?!!

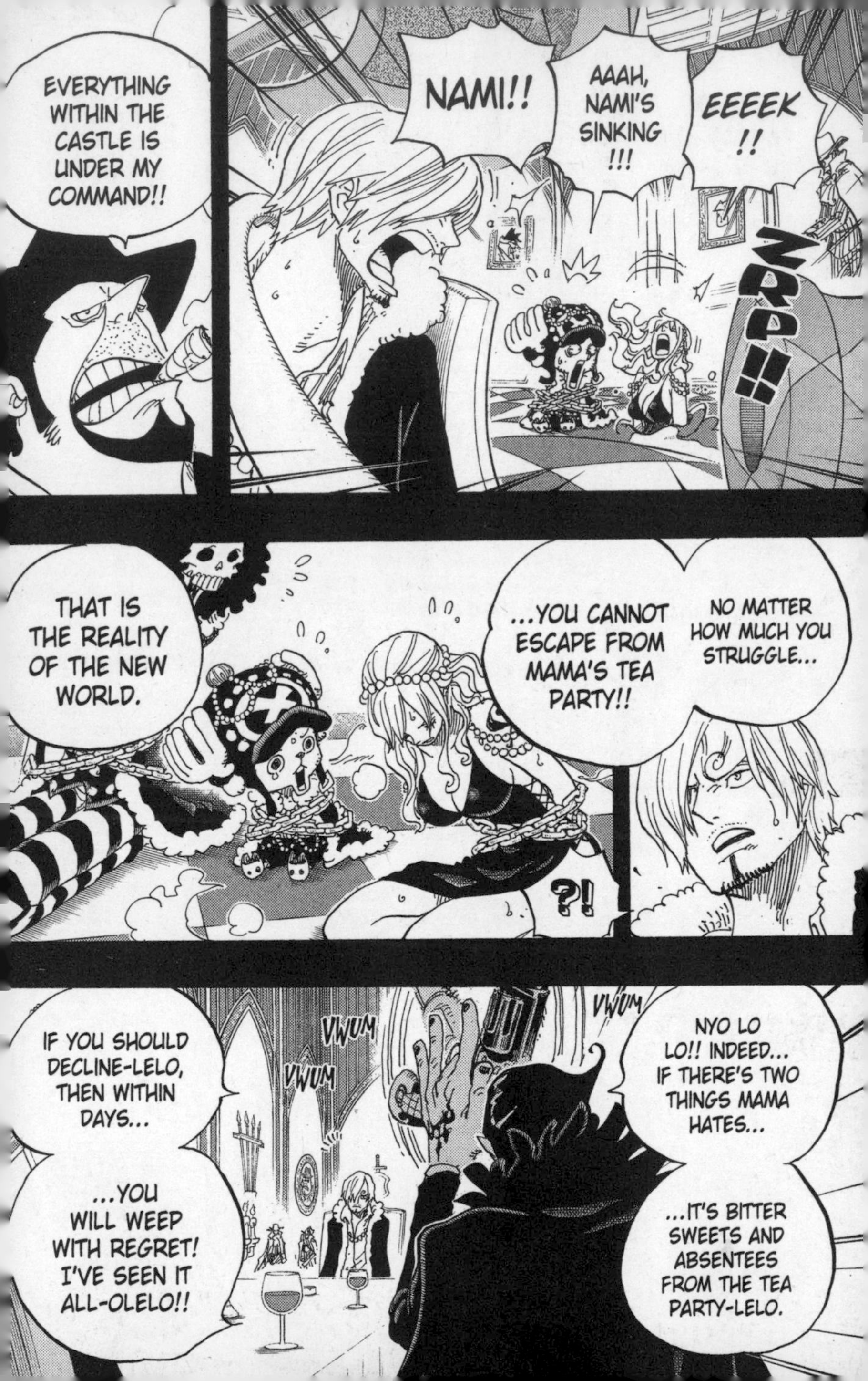
EEEEK !!
AAAH, NAMI'S SINKING !!!
NAMI!!
ZRP!!
EVERYTHING WITHIN THE CASTLE IS UNDER MY COMMAND!!
NO MATTER HOW MUCH YOU STRUGGLE...
...YOU CANNOT ESCAPE FROM MAMA'S TEA PARTY!!
?!
THAT IS THE REALITY OF THE NEW WORLD.
NYO LO LO!! INDEED... IF THERE'S TWO THINGS MAMA HATES...
...IT'S BITTER SWEETS AND ABSENTEES FROM THE TEA PARTY-LELO.
VWUM
VWUM
VWUM
IF YOU SHOULD DECLINE-LELO, THEN WITHIN DAYS...
...YOU WILL WEEP WITH REGRET! I'VE SEEN IT ALL-OLELO!!

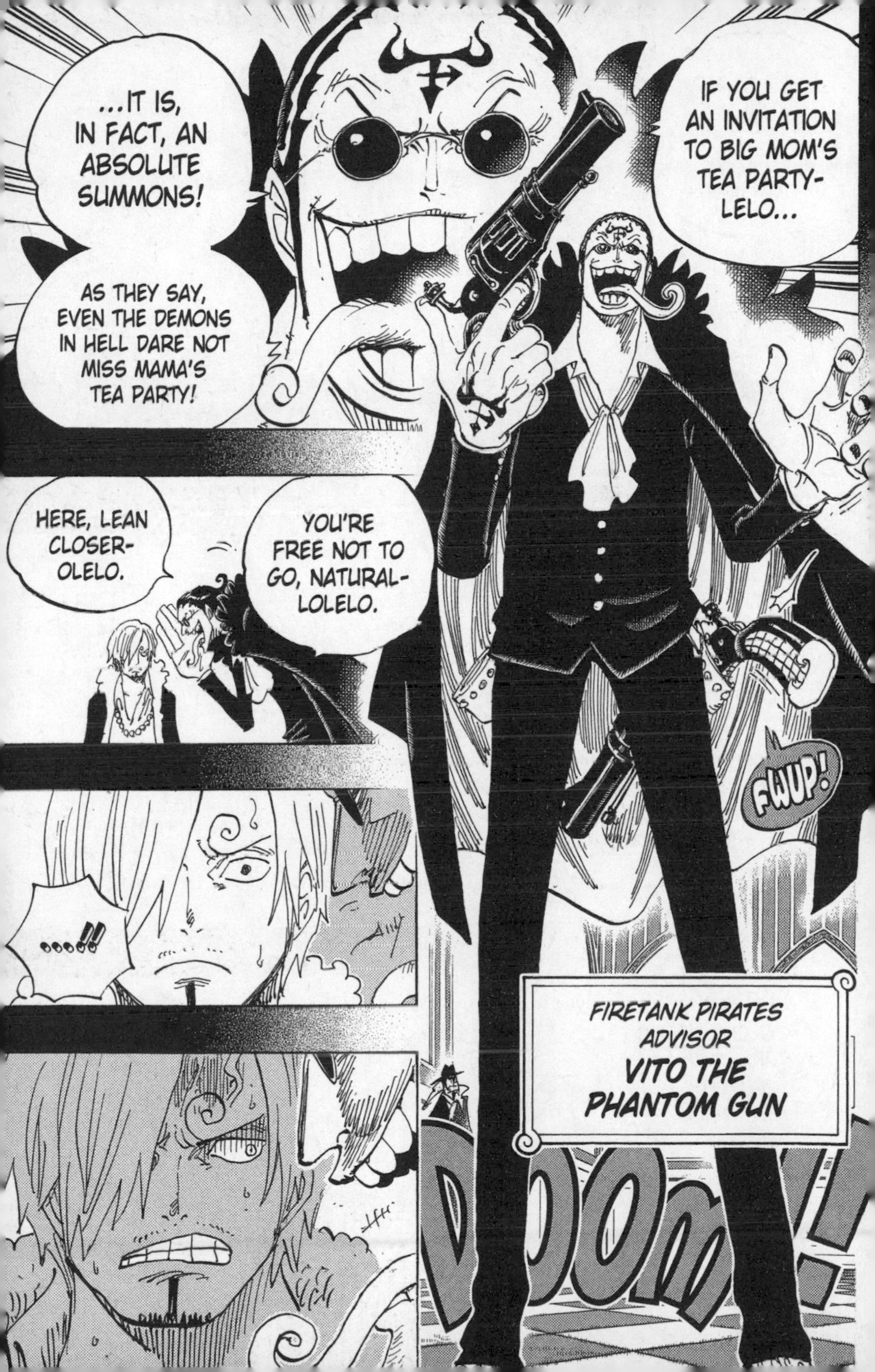
IF YOU GET AN INVITATION TO BIG MOM'S TEA PARTY-LELO...
...IT IS, IN FACT, AN ABSOLUTE SUMMONS!
AS THEY SAY, EVEN THE DEMONS IN HELL DARE NOT MISS MAMA'S TEA PARTY!
FWUP!
FIRETANK PIRATES ADVISOR
VITO THE PHANTOM GUN
DOOM!
YOU'RE FREE NOT TO GO, NATURAL-LOLELO.
HERE, LEAN CLOSER-OLELO.
....!!

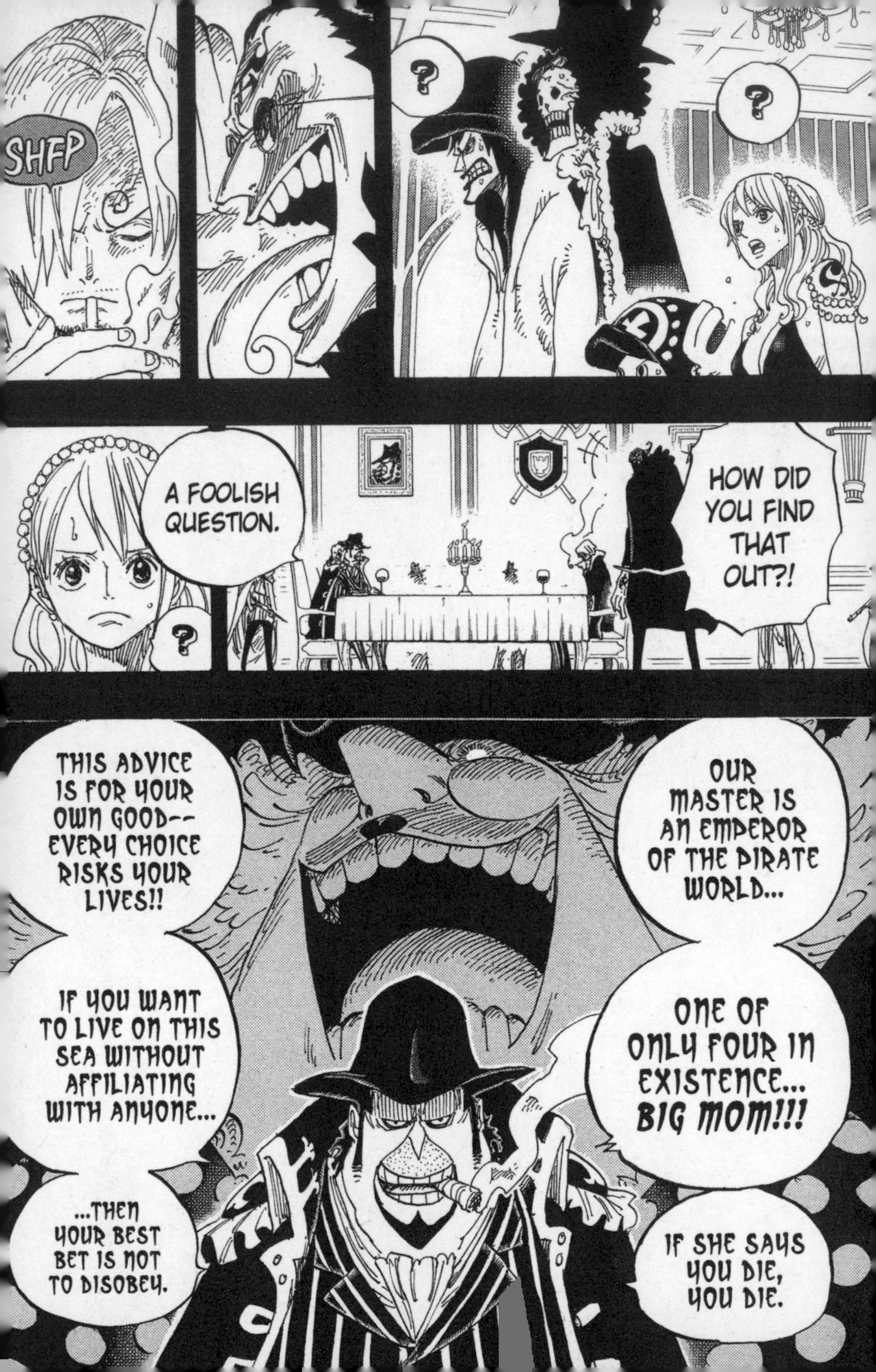
?
?
SHFP
HOW DID YOU FIND THAT OUT?!
A FOOLISH QUESTION.
?
OUR MASTER IS AN EMPEROR OF THE PIRATE WORLD...
ONE OF ONLY FOUR IN EXISTENCE... **BIG MOM!!!**
IF SHE SAYS YOU DIE, YOU DIE.
THIS ADVICE IS FOR YOUR OWN GOOD-- EVERY CHOICE RISKS YOUR LIVES!!
IF YOU WANT TO LIVE ON THIS SEA WITHOUT AFFILIATING WITH ANYONE...
...THEN YOUR BEST BET IS NOT TO DISOBEY.

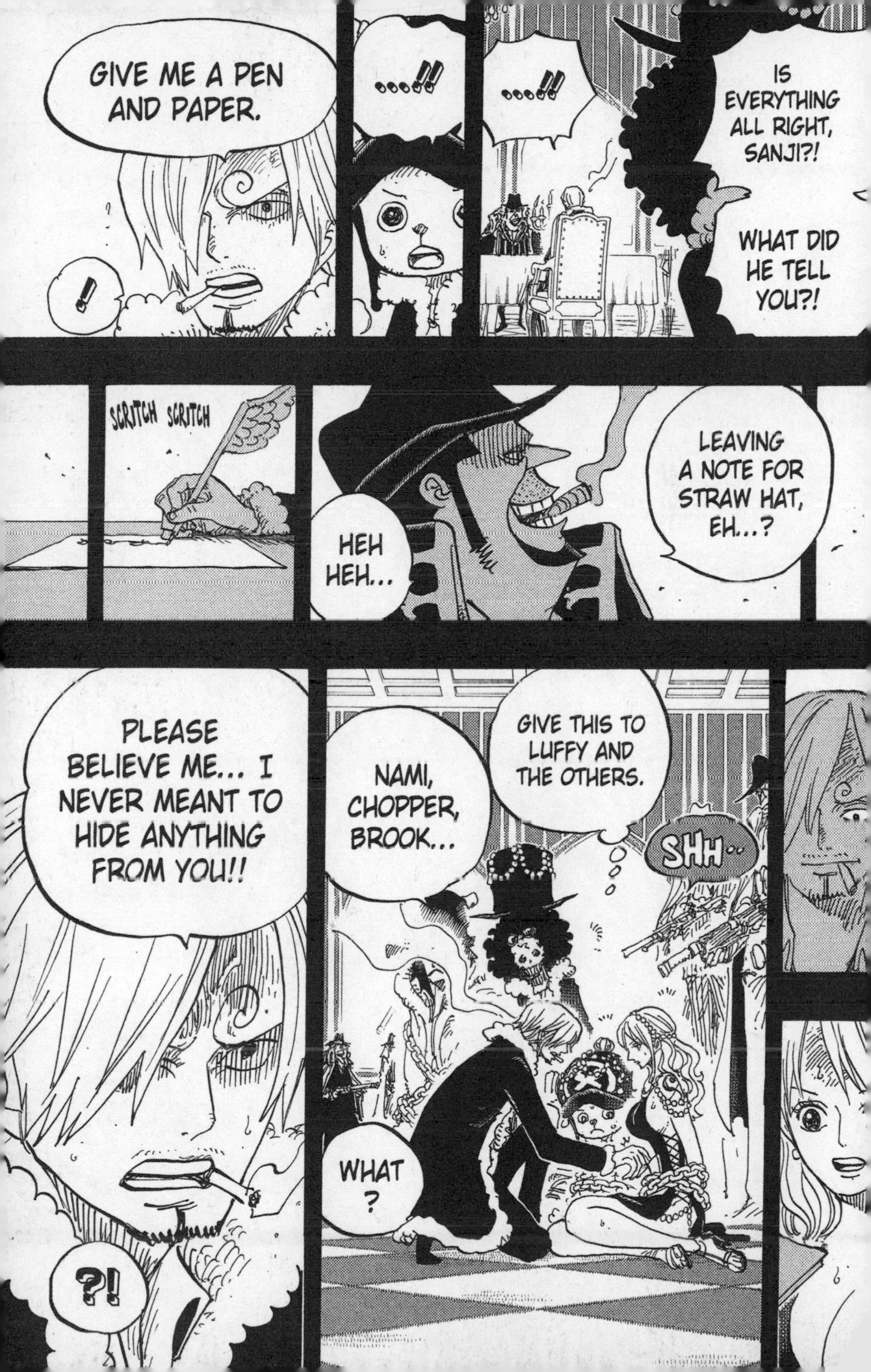
IS EVERYTHING ALL RIGHT, SANJI?!
WHAT DID HE TELL YOU?!
....!!
....!!
GIVE ME A PEN AND PAPER.
!
LEAVING A NOTE FOR STRAW HAT, EH...?
HEH HEH...
SCRITCH SCRITCH
GIVE THIS TO LUFFY AND THE OTHERS.
NAMI, CHOPPER, BROOK...
SHH
WHAT ?
PLEASE BELIEVE ME... I NEVER MEANT TO HIDE ANYTHING FROM YOU!!
?!

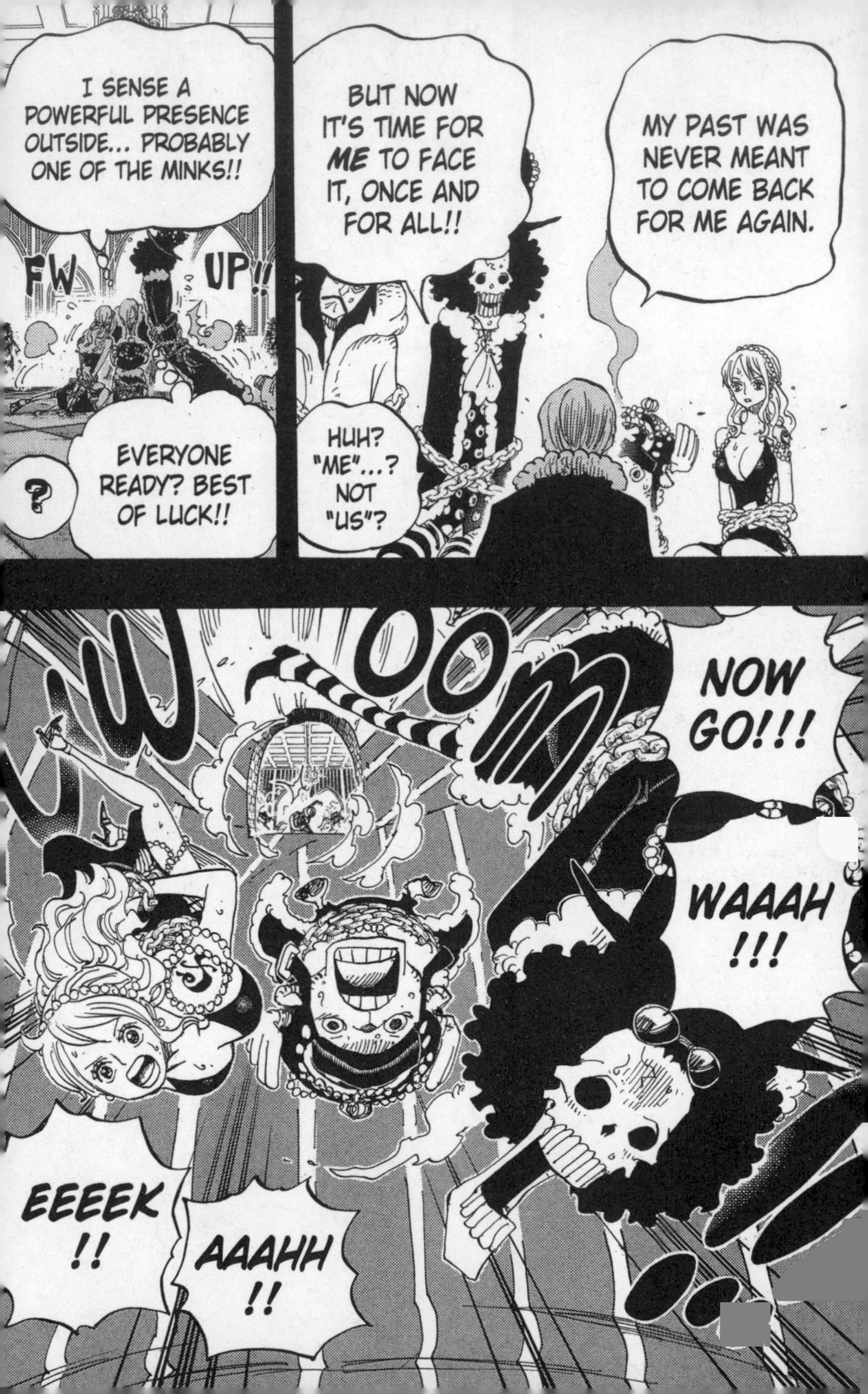
MY PAST WAS NEVER MEANT TO COME BACK FOR ME AGAIN.
BUT NOW IT'S TIME FOR ME TO FACE IT, ONCE AND FOR ALL!!
HUH? "ME"...? NOT "US"?
I SENSE A POWERFUL PRESENCE OUTSIDE... PROBABLY ONE OF THE MINKS!!
FW UP!!
EVERYONE READY? BEST OF LUCK!!
?
WOOM
NOW GO!!!
WAAAH !!!
AAAHH !!
EEEEK !!

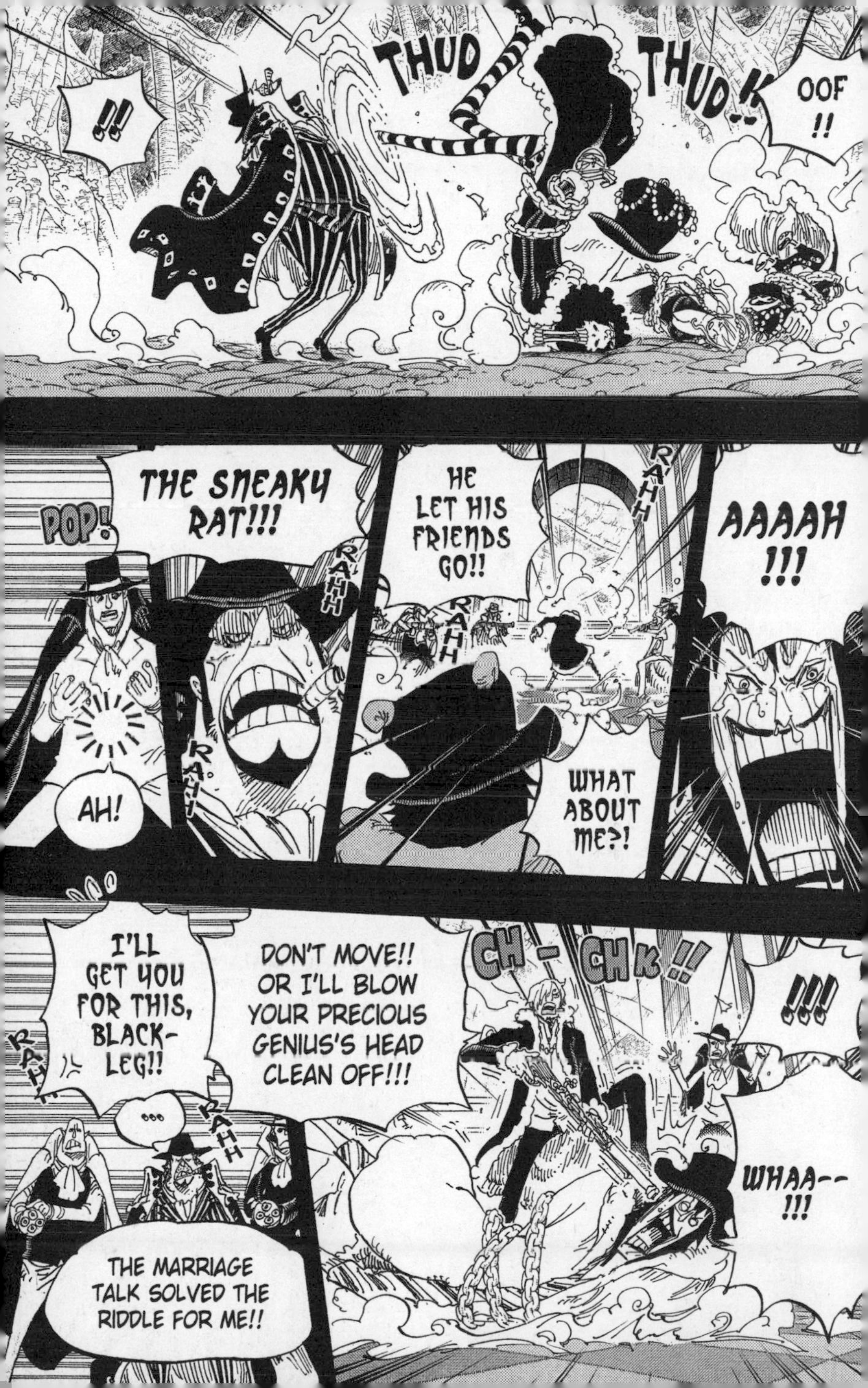
OOF !!
THUD!!
THUD
!!
AAAAH !!!
RAHH
HE LET HIS FRIENDS GO!!
RAHH
RAHH
WHAT ABOUT ME?!
RAHH
THE SNEAKY RAT!!!
RAHH
POP!
AH!
!!!
CH-CHK!!
DON'T MOVE!! OR I'LL BLOW YOUR PRECIOUS GENIUS'S HEAD CLEAN OFF!!!
WHAA-- !!!
THE MARRIAGE TALK SOLVED THE RIDDLE FOR ME!!
RAHH
I'LL GET YOU FOR THIS, BLACK-LEG!!
RAHH
...

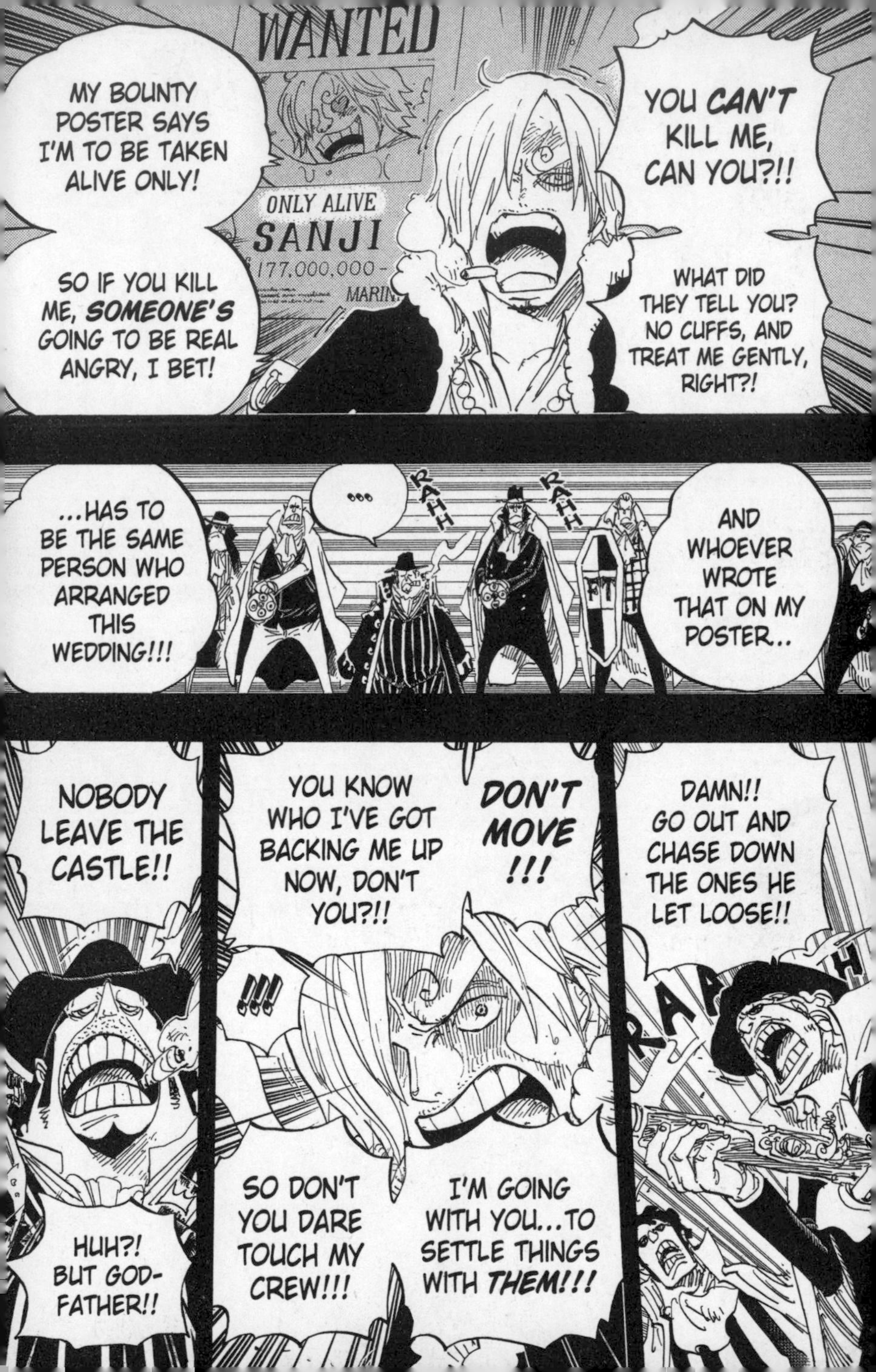
YOU CAN'T KILL ME, CAN YOU?!!
WHAT DID THEY TELL YOU? NO CUFFS, AND TREAT ME GENTLY, RIGHT?!
WANTED
ONLY ALIVE
SANJI
MY BOUNTY POSTER SAYS I'M TO BE TAKEN ALIVE ONLY!
SO IF YOU KILL ME, SOMEONE'S GOING TO BE REAL ANGRY, I BET!
AND WHOEVER WROTE THAT ON MY POSTER..
RAHH
...
RAHH
...HAS TO BE THE SAME PERSON WHO ARRANGED THIS WEDDING!!!
DAMN!! GO OUT AND CHASE DOWN THE ONES HE LET LOOSE!!
DON'T MOVE!!!
YOU KNOW WHO I'VE GOT BACKING ME UP NOW, DON'T YOU?!!
!!!
I'M GOING WITH YOU...TO SETTLE THINGS WITH THEM!!!
SO DON'T YOU DARE TOUCH MY CREW!!!
NOBODY LEAVE THE CASTLE!!
HUH?! BUT GOD-FATHER!!

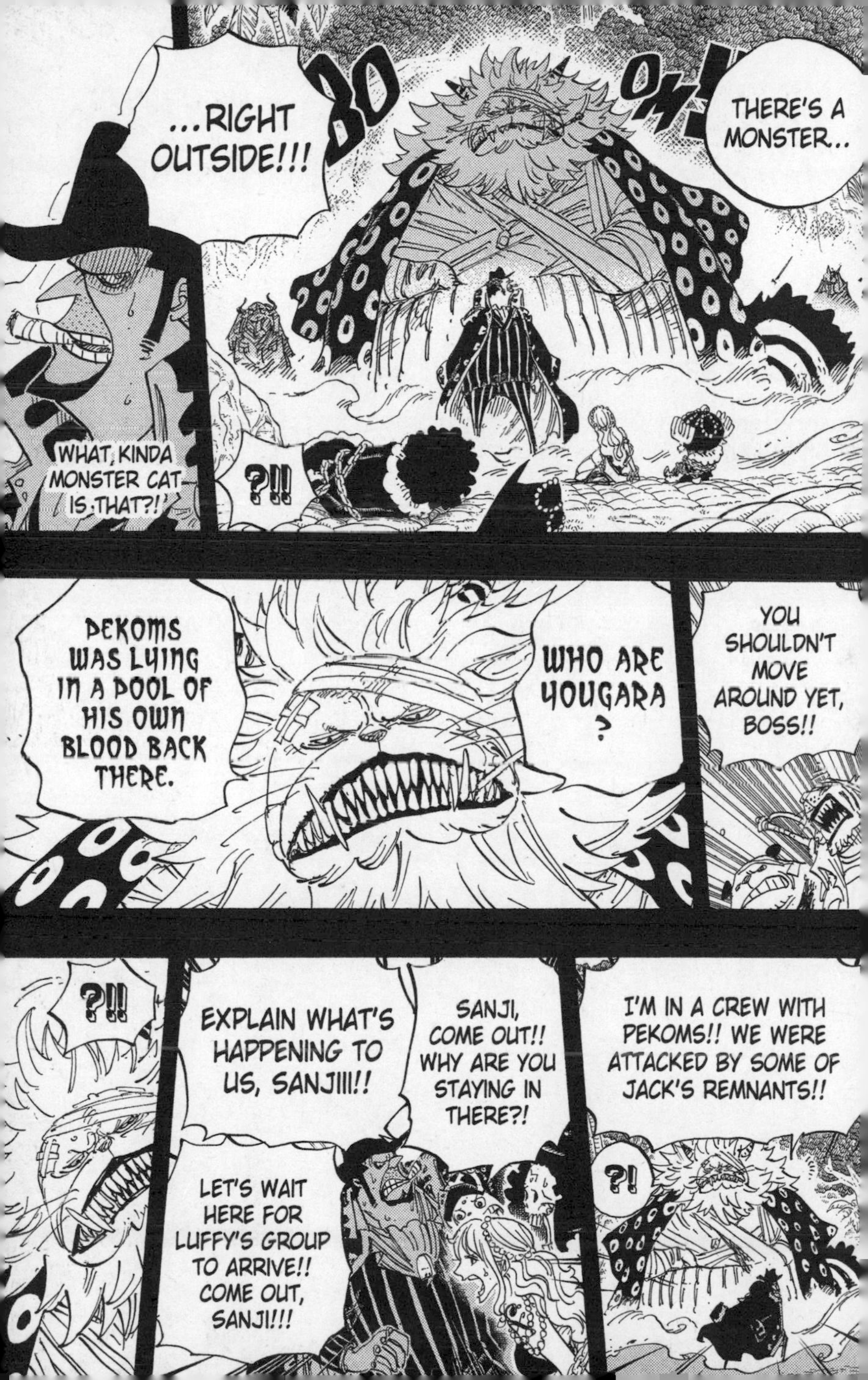
THERE'S A MONSTER...
...RIGHT OUTSIDE!!!
?!!
WHAT, KINDA MONSTER CAT IS THAT?!
YOU SHOULDN'T MOVE AROUND YET, BOSS!!
WHO ARE YOUGARA?
PEKOMS WAS LYING IN A POOL OF HIS OWN BLOOD BACK THERE.
I'M IN A CREW WITH PEKOMS!! WE WERE ATTACKED BY SOME OF JACK'S REMNANTS!!
?!
SANJI, COME OUT!! WHY ARE YOU STAYING IN THERE?!
EXPLAIN WHAT'S HAPPENING TO US, SANJIII!!
LET'S WAIT HERE FOR LUFFY'S GROUP TO ARRIVE!! COME OUT, SANJI!!!
?!!

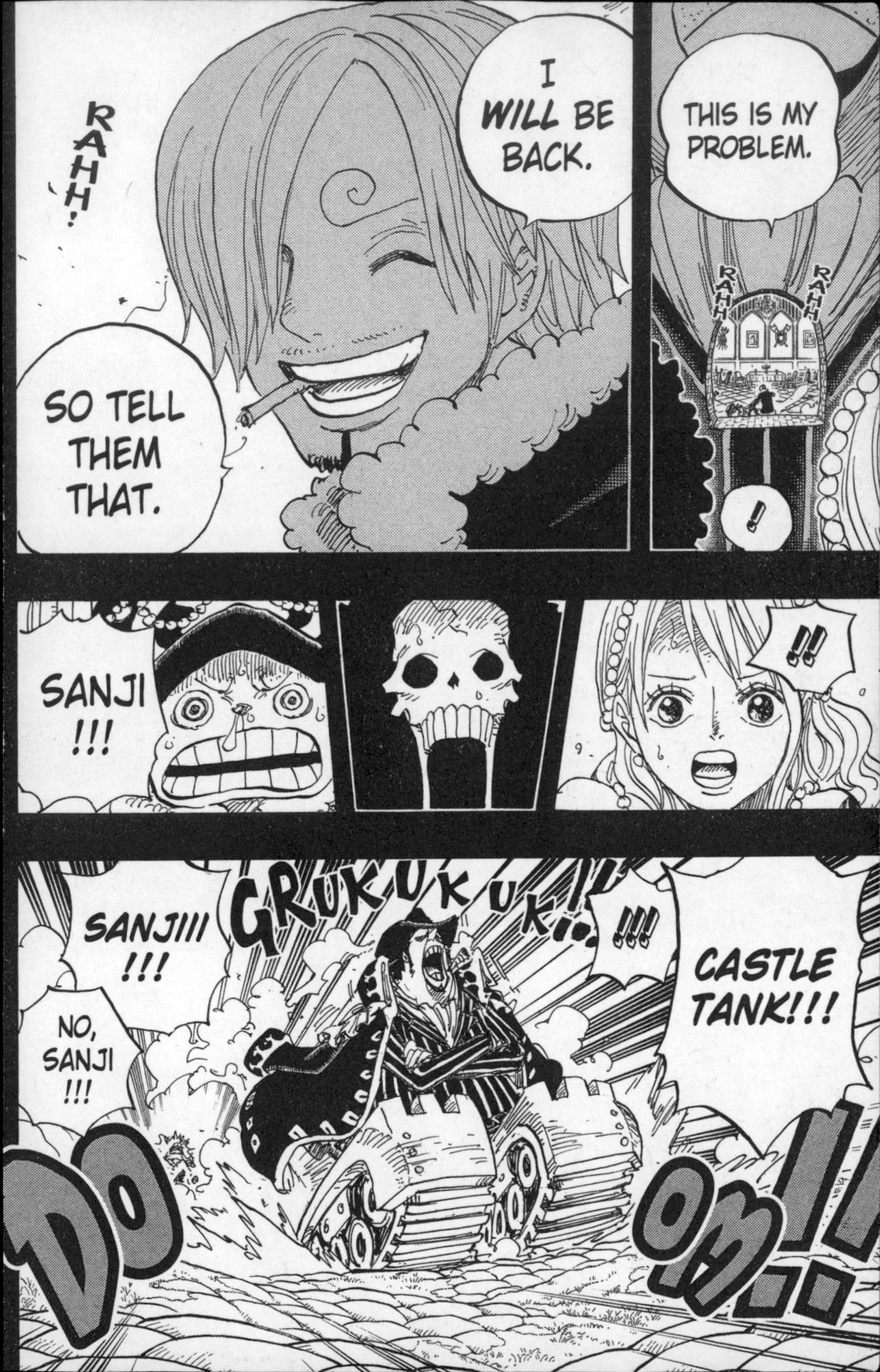
THIS IS MY PROBLEM.
RAHH
RAHH
!
I WILL BE BACK.
RAHH!
SO TELL THEM THAT.
!!
SANJI !!!
CASTLE TANK!!!
!!!
GRUKUKUK..!!
SANJIII !!!
NO, SANJI !!!
DOOM..!!

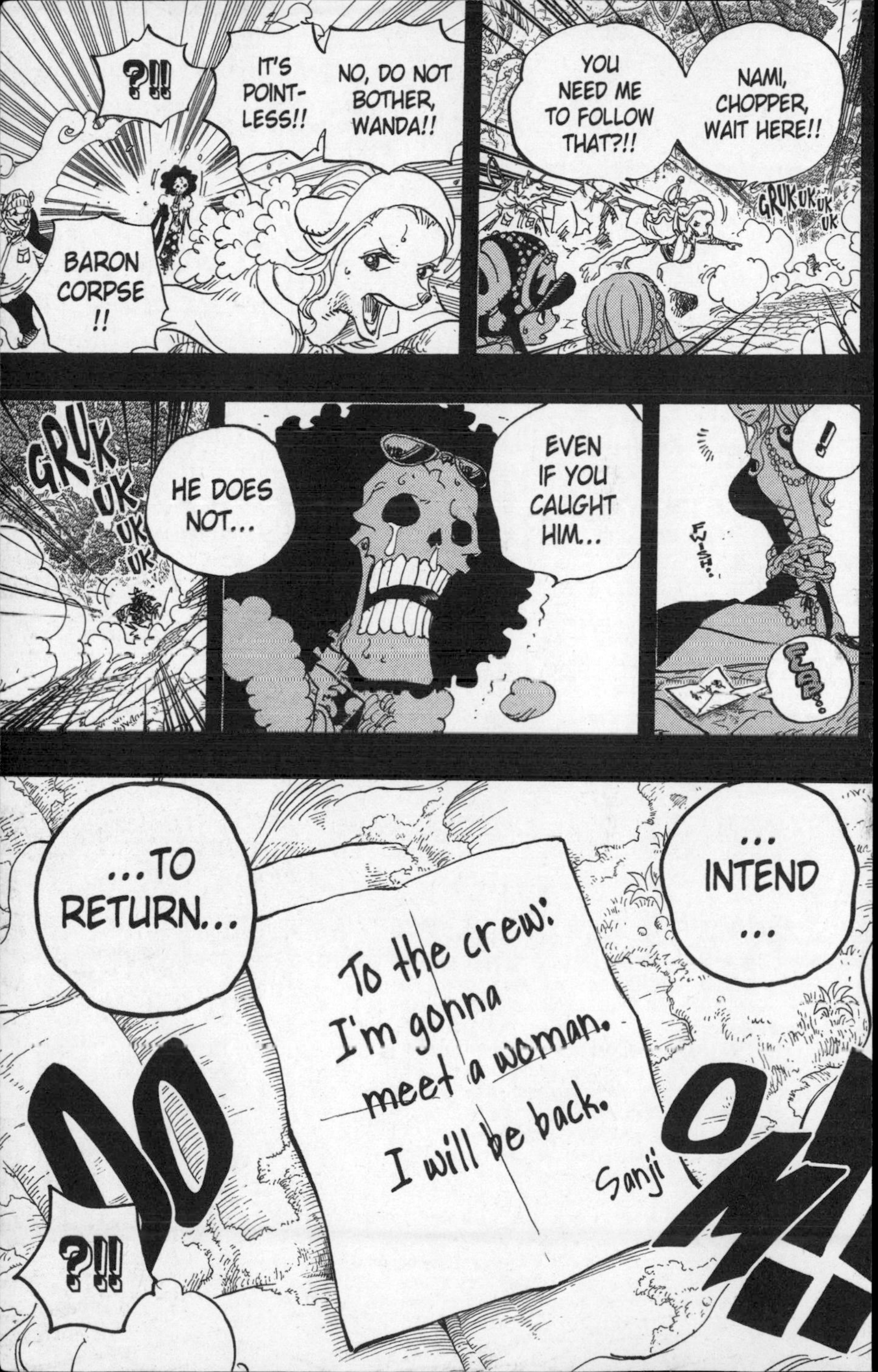
NAMI, CHOPPER, WAIT HERE!!
YOU NEED ME TO FOLLOW THAT?!!
GRUKUKUKUK
NO, DO NOT BOTHER, WANDA!!
IT'S POINT-LESS!!
?!!
BARON CORPSE !!
!
FWISH..
EVEN IF YOU CAUGHT HIM...
HE DOES NOT...
GRUKUKUKUK
... INTEND ...
...TO RETURN...
To the crew:
I'm gonna meet a woman.
I will be back.
Sanji
DOOM!!
?!!

SBS Question Corner

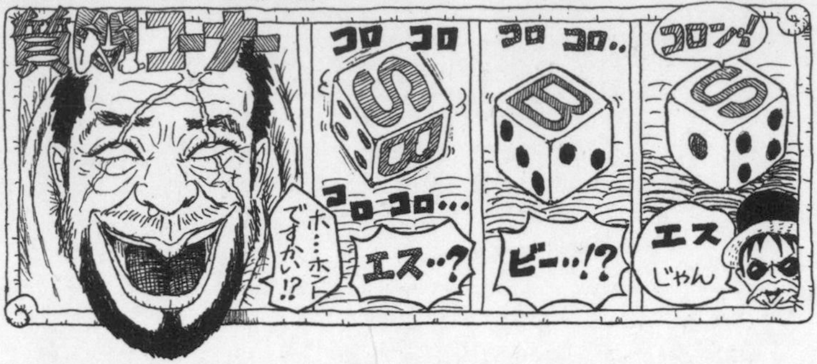
コロン!
エス
じゃん
コロ コロ‥
ビー‥!?
コロ コロ
コロ コロ…
エス‥?
質問コーナー
ホ…ホント
ですかい!?

(Igarashi, Oita)

Q: Tell us what the favorite and least favorite foods of all the big rookies are, aside from Luffy and Zolo. Does Bonney even dislike any kind of food?

--Aneotsu

A: (1) is the favorite, (2) is the least favorite.

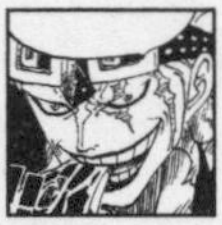
(1) Cabbage rolls
(2) Curry udon

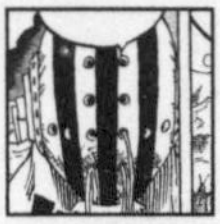
(1) Peperoncino pasta
(2) Curry udon

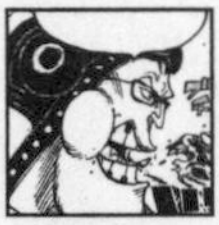
(1) Tom yum kung
(2) Mayonnaise

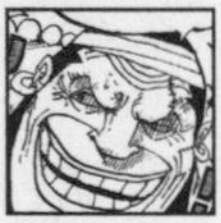
(1) Red beans, pork
(2) Veggies

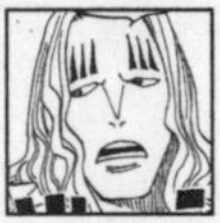
(1) Fortune cookies
(2) Meat

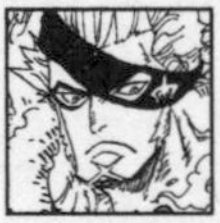
(1) Chicken & rice
(2) Eggs

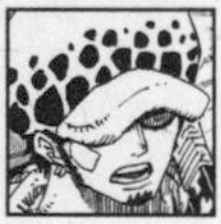
1) Rice balls, grilled fish
(2) Bread, pickled plums

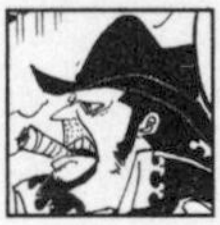
(1) Meat dumplings, tomatoes
(2) Tomato juice

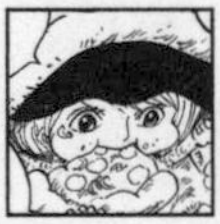
(1) Margherita pizza
(2) Carrots

Q: I would like to be an excellent manga artist like you, Odacchi. So my question is, what do I need to be a manga-ka? Please teach me how to draw. Please, please, please.

--Iku

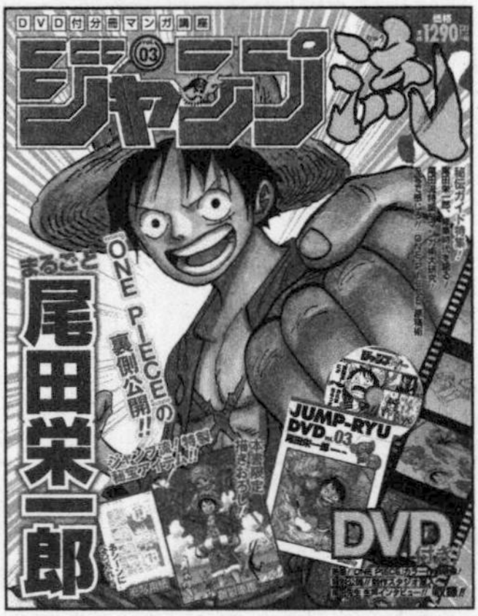
ジャンプ流
まるごと
尾田栄一郎
ONE PIECEの裏側公開!!
JUMP-RYU
DVD 03
DVD

A: Oh, geez, what was that, "excellent"? Can you say it one more time? I just need to hit the "record" button. Anyway, I get a lot of these requests. It's a difficult thing to answer in the SBS, but in Japan recently, they came out with something called Jump-ryu! (Jump Style). They're magazines with DVDs containing footage of artists drawing their manga, which may or may not help you. As a matter of fact, these publications are put together by a former One Piece editor, Habu-yan. If it hadn't been by his request, I never would have allowed them to film such a thing (laughs). It's quite a rare opportunity, and I myself would like to check out some of the other artists involved, so check it out! I'm sorry if it's a little bit too expensive for you, Iku.

Chapter 814:
LET'S GO SEE THE CAT VIPER

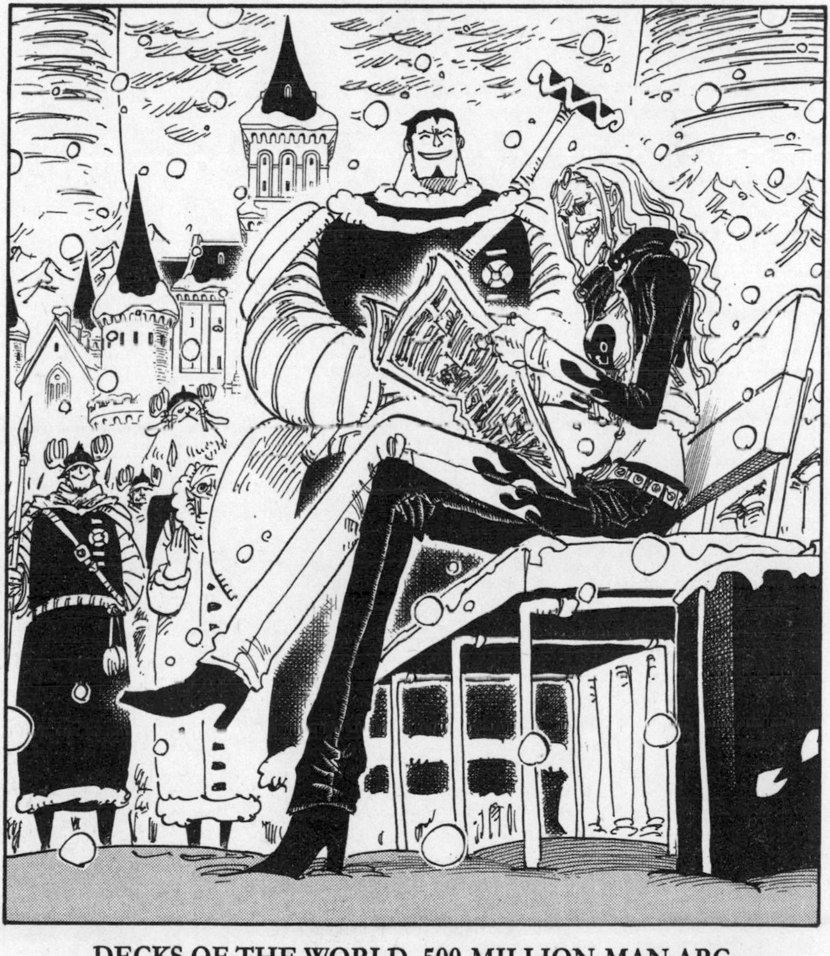

DECKS OF THE WORLD, 500-MILLION-MAN ARC, VOL. 8: "DRUM KINGDOM--NEW DESIGN FOR THE SOLDIERS' HELMETS"

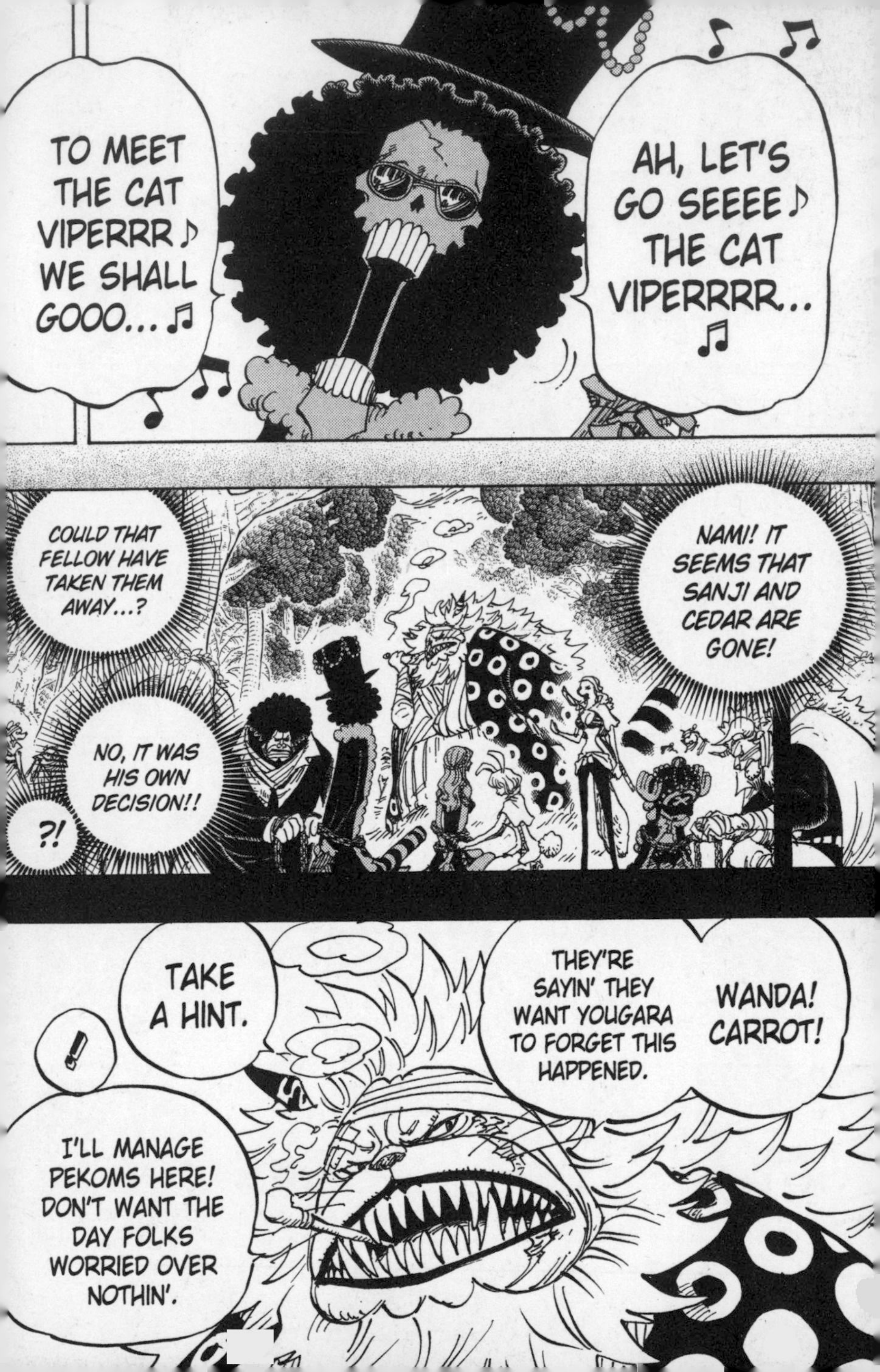
AH, LET'S GO SEEEE♪ THE CAT VIPERRRR...♫
TO MEET THE CAT VIPERRR♪ WE SHALL GOOO...♫
NAMI! IT SEEMS THAT SANJI AND CEDAR ARE GONE!
COULD THAT FELLOW HAVE TAKEN THEM AWAY...?
NO, IT WAS HIS OWN DECISION!!
?!
WANDA! CARROT!
THEY'RE SAYIN' THEY WANT YOUGARA TO FORGET THIS HAPPENED.
TAKE A HINT.
!
I'LL MANAGE PEKOMS HERE! DON'T WANT THE DAY FOLKS WORRIED OVER NOTHIN'.

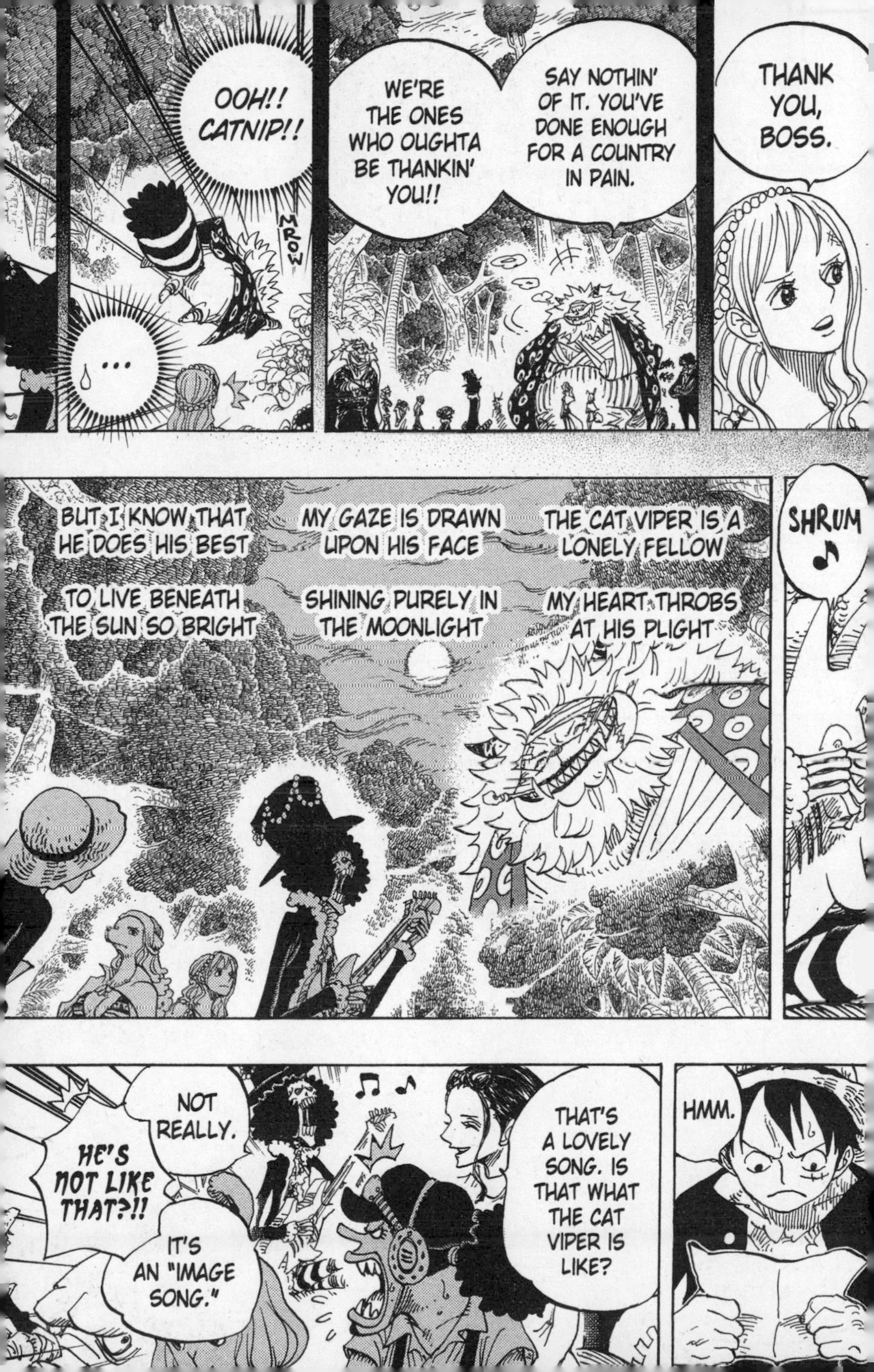
THANK YOU, BOSS.
SAY NOTHIN' OF IT. YOU'VE DONE ENOUGH FOR A COUNTRY IN PAIN.
WE'RE THE ONES WHO OUGHTA BE THANKIN' YOU!!
OOH!! CATNIP!!
MROW
...
SHRUM ♪
THE CAT VIPER IS A LONELY FELLOW
MY HEART THROBS AT HIS PLIGHT
MY GAZE IS DRAWN UPON HIS FACE
SHINING PURELY IN THE MOONLIGHT
BUT I KNOW THAT HE DOES HIS BEST
TO LIVE BENEATH THE SUN SO BRIGHT
HMM.
THAT'S A LOVELY SONG. IS THAT WHAT THE CAT VIPER IS LIKE?
NOT REALLY.
HE'S NOT LIKE THAT?!!
IT'S AN "IMAGE SONG."

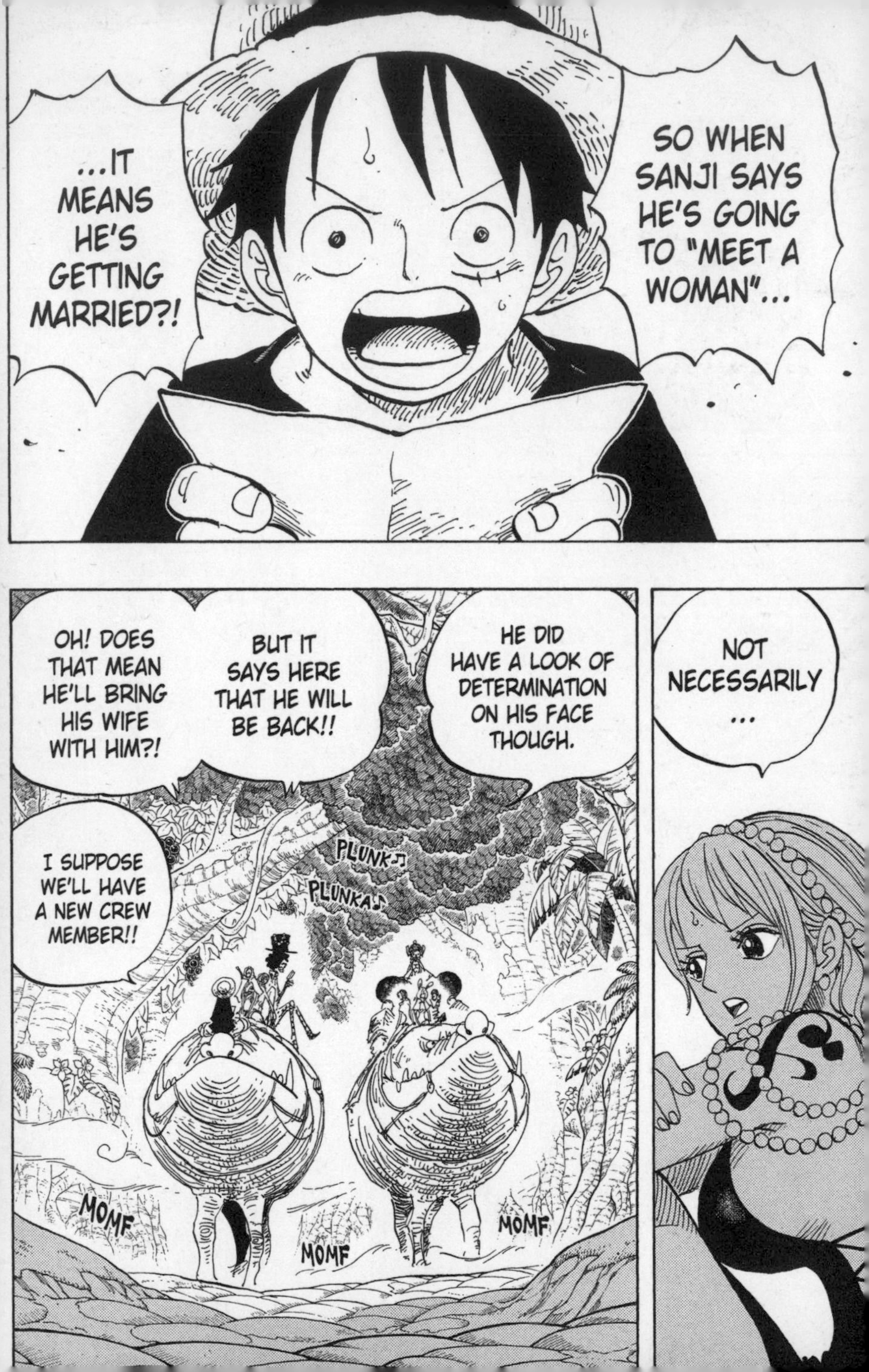
SO WHEN SANJI SAYS HE'S GOING TO "MEET A WOMAN"...
...IT MEANS HE'S GETTING MARRIED?!
NOT NECESSARILY ...
HE DID HAVE A LOOK OF DETERMINATION ON HIS FACE THOUGH.
BUT IT SAYS HERE THAT HE WILL BE BACK!!
OH! DOES THAT MEAN HE'LL BRING HIS WIFE WITH HIM?!
PLUNK♫
PLUNKA♪
I SUPPOSE WE'LL HAVE A NEW CREW MEMBER!!
MOMF
MOMF
MOMF

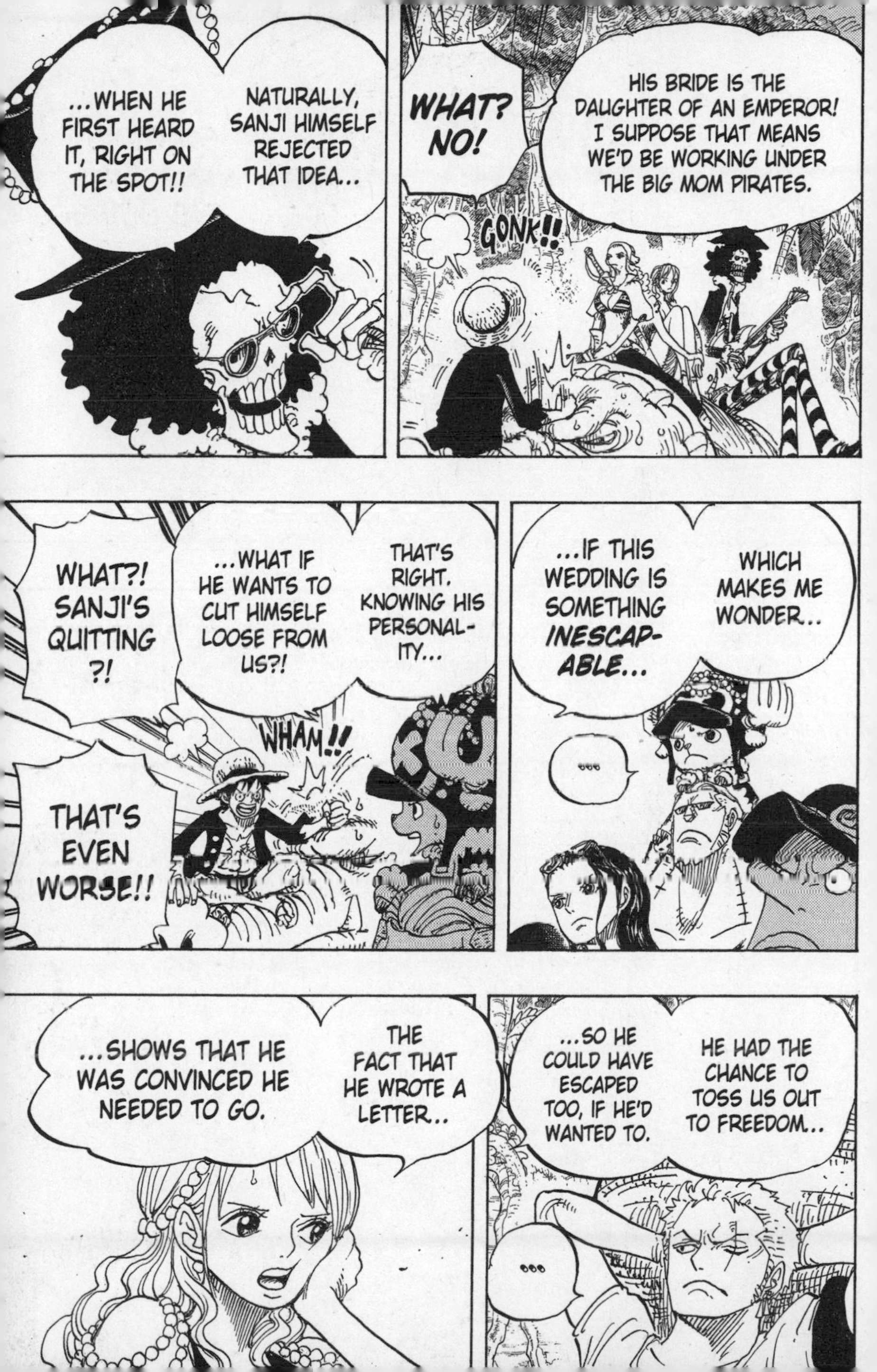
HIS BRIDE IS THE DAUGHTER OF AN EMPEROR! I SUPPOSE THAT MEANS WE'D BE WORKING UNDER THE BIG MOM PIRATES.
WHAT? NO!
GONK!!
NATURALLY, SANJI HIMSELF REJECTED THAT IDEA...
...WHEN HE FIRST HEARD IT, RIGHT ON THE SPOT!!
WHICH MAKES ME WONDER...
...IF THIS WEDDING IS SOMETHING *INESCAPABLE*...
...
THAT'S RIGHT. KNOWING HIS PERSONAL-ITY...
...WHAT IF HE WANTS TO CUT HIMSELF LOOSE FROM US?!
WHAT?! SANJI'S QUITTING?!
WHAM!!
THAT'S EVEN WORSE!!
HE HAD THE CHANCE TO TOSS US OUT TO FREEDOM...
...SO HE COULD HAVE ESCAPED TOO, IF HE'D WANTED TO.
...
THE FACT THAT HE WROTE A LETTER...
...SHOWS THAT HE WAS CONVINCED HE NEEDED TO GO.

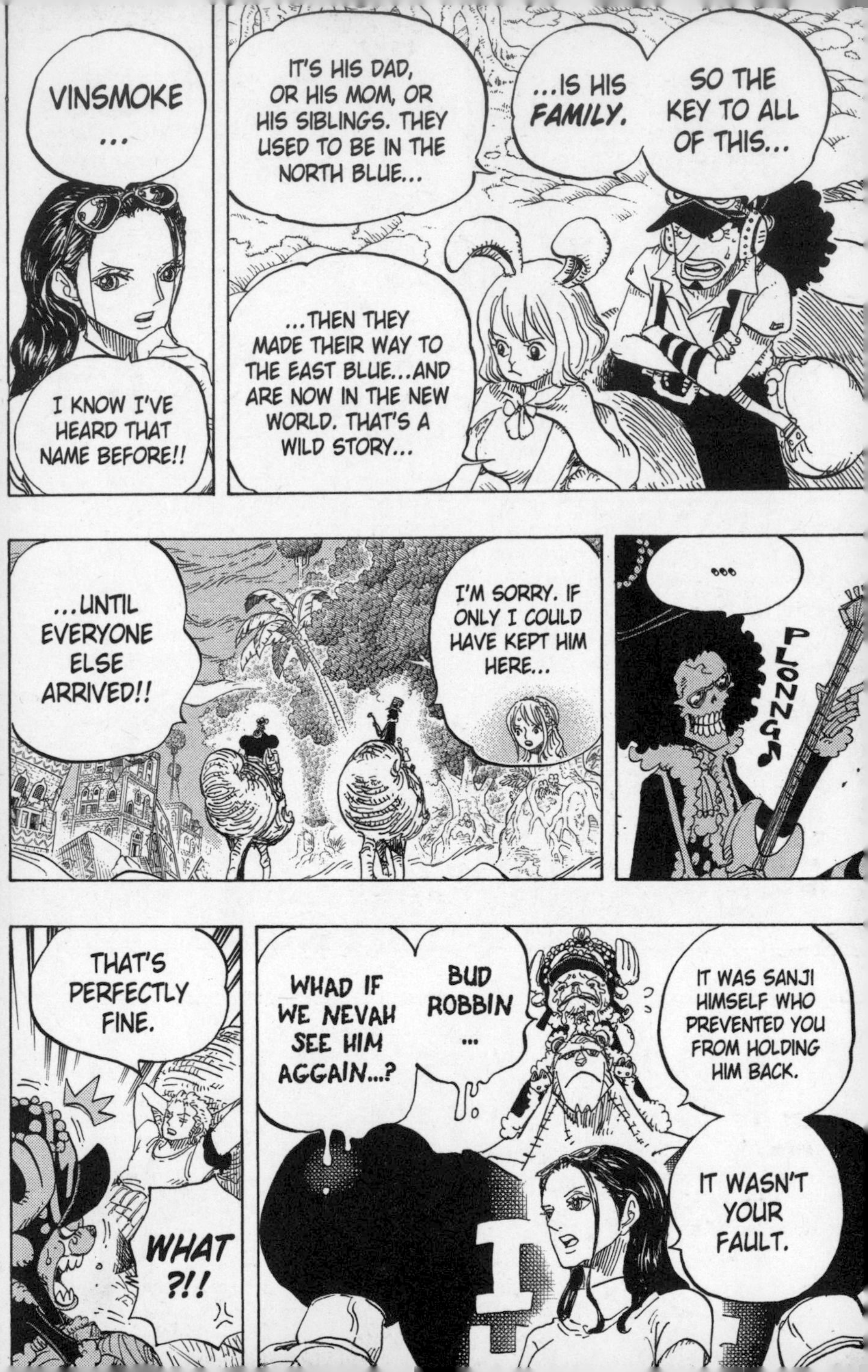
SO THE KEY TO ALL OF THIS...
...IS HIS *FAMILY*.
IT'S HIS DAD, OR HIS MOM, OR HIS SIBLINGS. THEY USED TO BE IN THE NORTH BLUE...
...THEN THEY MADE THEIR WAY TO THE EAST BLUE...AND ARE NOW IN THE NEW WORLD. THAT'S A WILD STORY...
VINSMOKE ...
I KNOW I'VE HEARD THAT NAME BEFORE!!
...
PLONNG♪
I'M SORRY. IF ONLY I COULD HAVE KEPT HIM HERE...
...UNTIL EVERYONE ELSE ARRIVED!!
IT WAS SANJI HIMSELF WHO PREVENTED YOU FROM HOLDING HIM BACK.
BUD ROBBIN ...
WHAD IF WE NEVAH SEE HIM AGGAIN...?
IT WASN'T YOUR FAULT.
THAT'S PERFECTLY FINE.
WHAT?!!

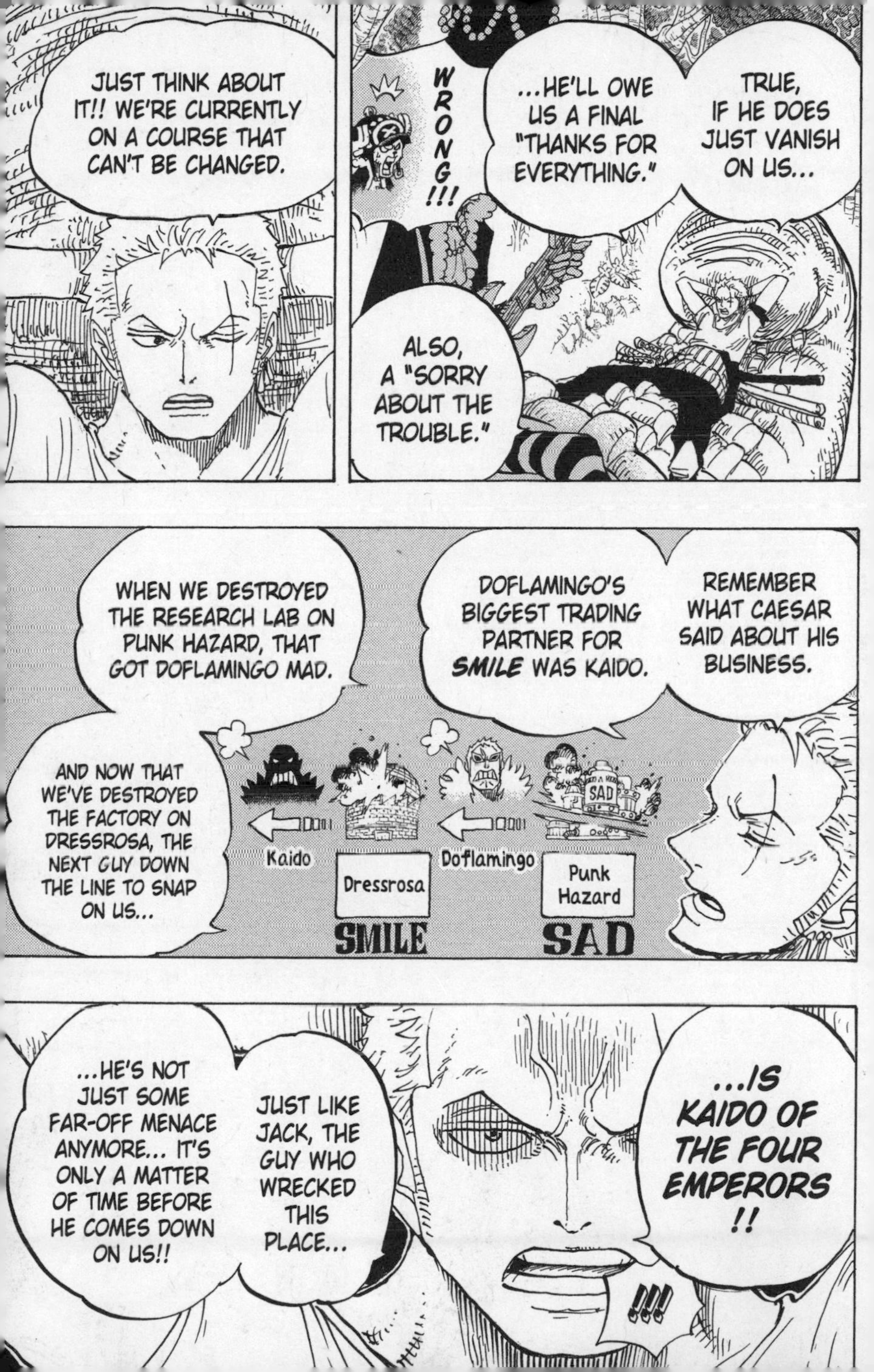
TRUE, IF HE DOES JUST VANISH ON US...
...HE'LL OWE US A FINAL "THANKS FOR EVERYTHING."
WRONG!!!
ALSO, A "SORRY ABOUT THE TROUBLE."
JUST THINK ABOUT IT!! WE'RE CURRENTLY ON A COURSE THAT CAN'T BE CHANGED.
REMEMBER WHAT CAESAR SAID ABOUT HIS BUSINESS.
DOFLAMINGO'S BIGGEST TRADING PARTNER FOR SMILE WAS KAIDO.
SAD
SAD
Punk Hazard
Doflamingo
SMILE
Dressrosa
Kaido
WHEN WE DESTROYED THE RESEARCH LAB ON PUNK HAZARD, THAT GOT DOFLAMINGO MAD.
AND NOW THAT WE'VE DESTROYED THE FACTORY ON DRESSROSA, THE NEXT GUY DOWN THE LINE TO SNAP ON US...
...IS KAIDO OF THE FOUR EMPERORS!!
!!!
JUST LIKE JACK, THE GUY WHO WRECKED THIS PLACE...
...HE'S NOT JUST SOME FAR-OFF MENACE ANYMORE... IT'S ONLY A MATTER OF TIME BEFORE HE COMES DOWN ON US!!

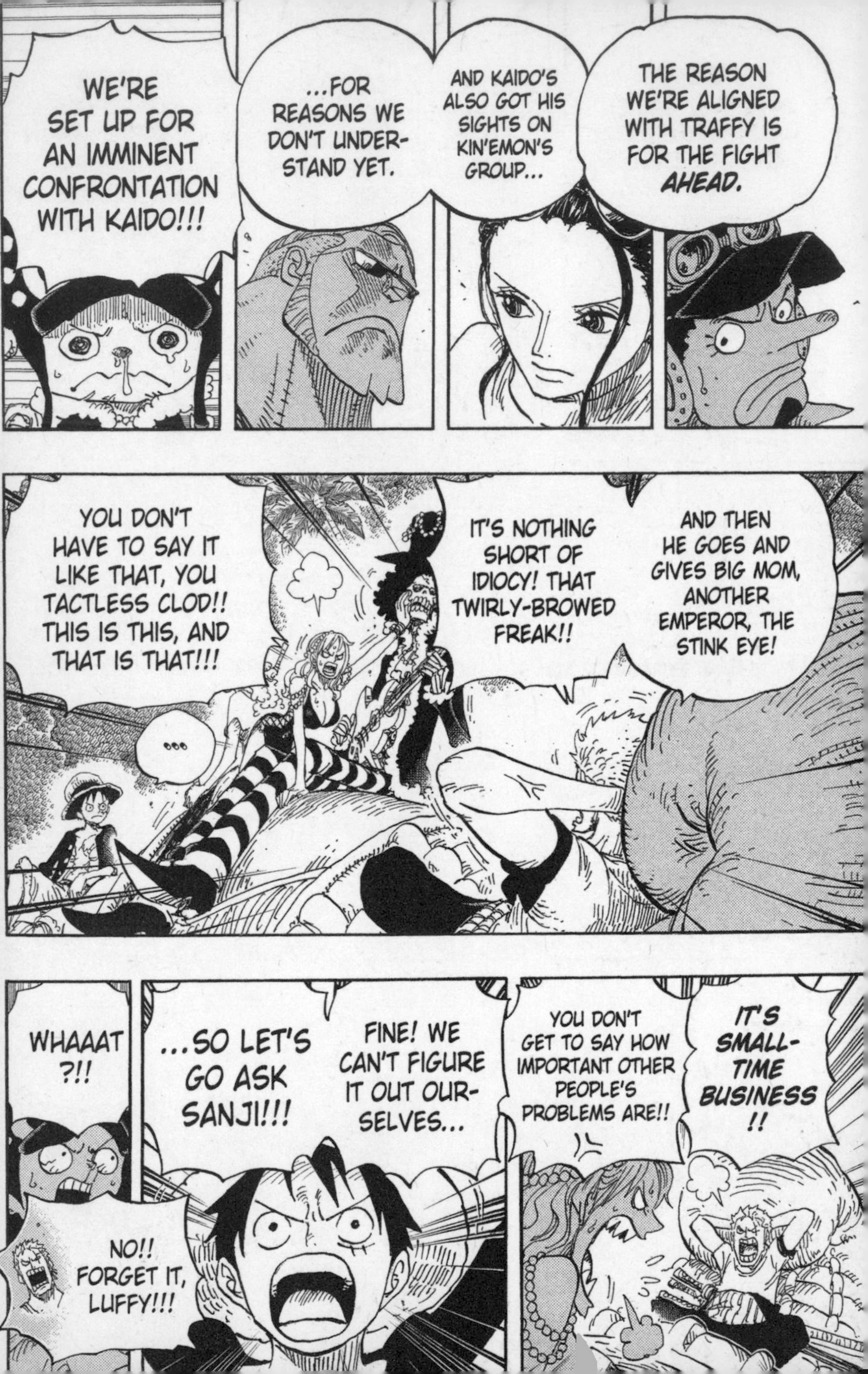
THE REASON WE'RE ALIGNED WITH TRAFFY IS FOR THE FIGHT AHEAD.
AND KAIDO'S ALSO GOT HIS SIGHTS ON KIN'EMON'S GROUP...
...FOR REASONS WE DON'T UNDER-STAND YET.
WE'RE SET UP FOR AN IMMINENT CONFRONTATION WITH KAIDO!!!
AND THEN HE GOES AND GIVES BIG MOM, ANOTHER EMPEROR, THE STINK EYE!
IT'S NOTHING SHORT OF IDIOCY! THAT TWIRLY-BROWED FREAK!!
YOU DON'T HAVE TO SAY IT LIKE THAT, YOU TACTLESS CLOD!! THIS IS THIS, AND THAT IS THAT!!!
...
IT'S SMALL-TIME BUSINESS!!
YOU DON'T GET TO SAY HOW IMPORTANT OTHER PEOPLE'S PROBLEMS ARE!!
FINE! WE CAN'T FIGURE IT OUT OUR-SELVES...
...SO LET'S GO ASK SANJI!!!
WHAAAT?!!
NO!! FORGET IT, LUFFY!!!

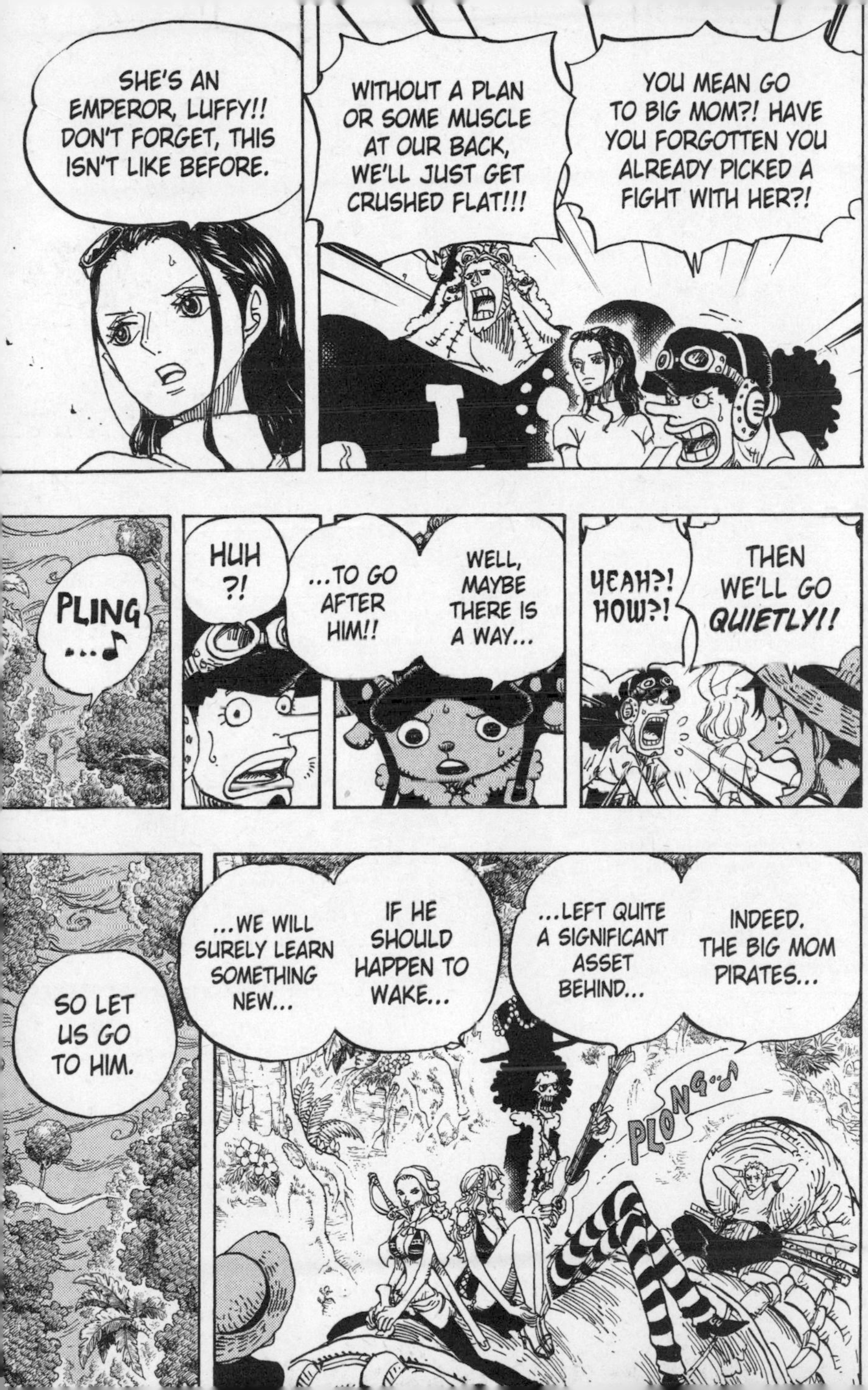
YOU MEAN GO TO BIG MOM?! HAVE YOU FORGOTTEN YOU ALREADY PICKED A FIGHT WITH HER?!
WITHOUT A PLAN OR SOME MUSCLE AT OUR BACK, WE'LL JUST GET CRUSHED FLAT!!!
SHE'S AN EMPEROR, LUFFY!! DON'T FORGET, THIS ISN'T LIKE BEFORE.
THEN WE'LL GO *QUIETLY!!*
YEAH?! HOW?!
WELL, MAYBE THERE IS A WAY...
...TO GO AFTER HIM!!
HUH ?!
PLING ...♪
INDEED. THE BIG MOM PIRATES...
...LEFT QUITE A SIGNIFICANT ASSET BEHIND...
IF HE SHOULD HAPPEN TO WAKE...
...WE WILL SURELY LEARN SOMETHING NEW...
PLONG..♪
SO LET US GO TO HIM.

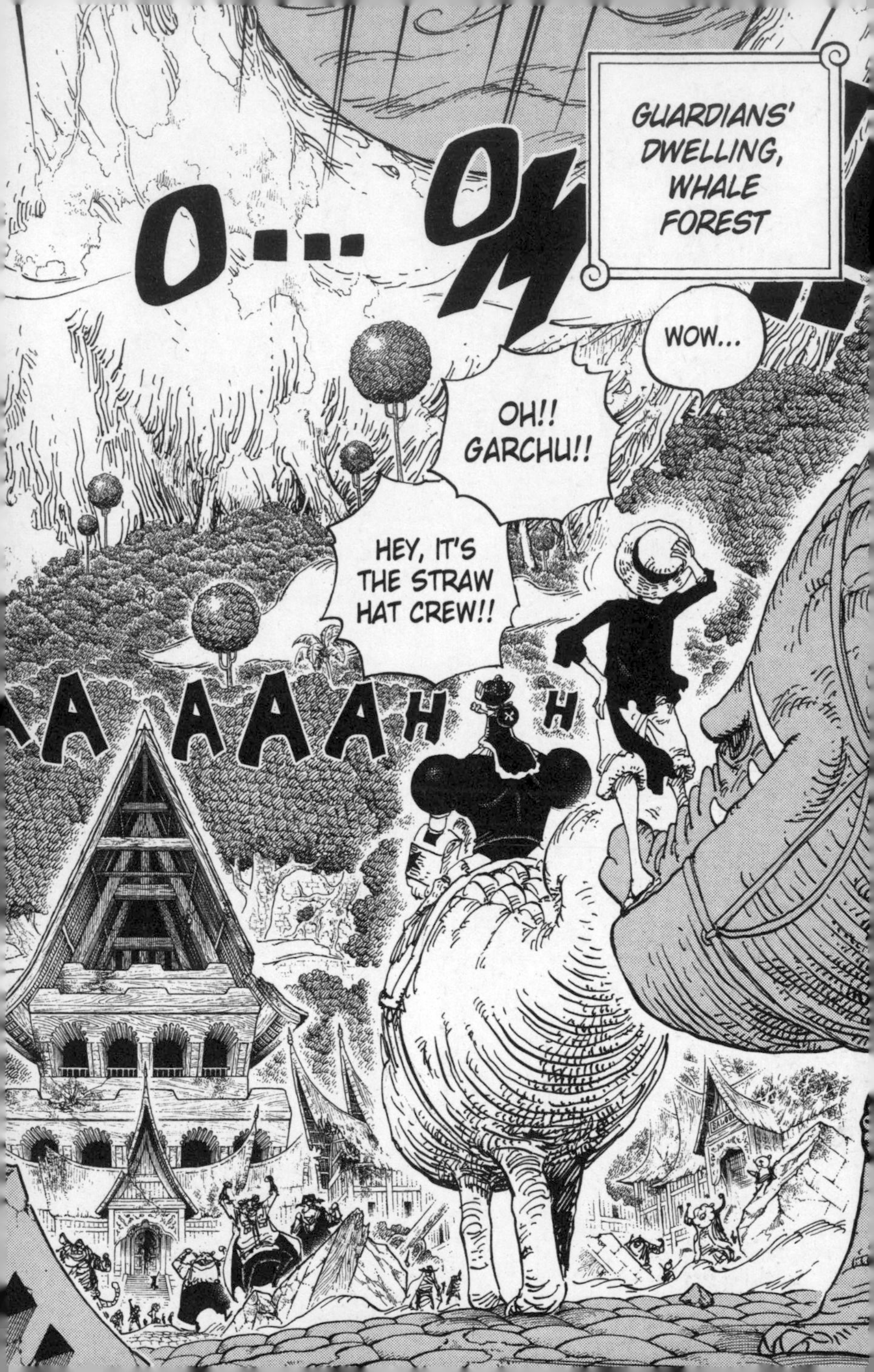
GUARDIANS' DWELLING, WHALE FOREST
O... OM...
WOW...
OH!! GARCHU!!
HEY, IT'S THE STRAW HAT CREW!!
AAAAAHH

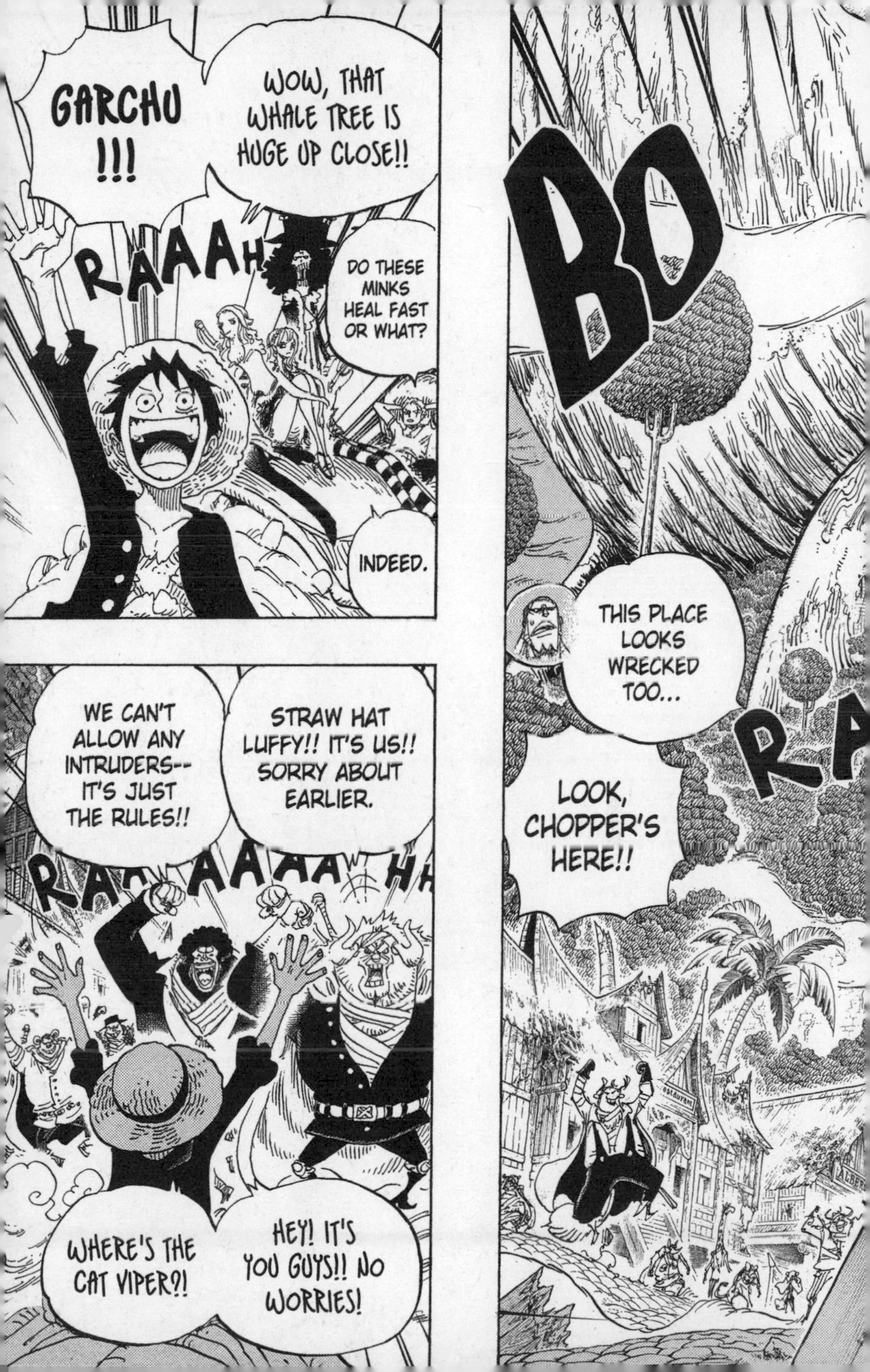
BO
THIS PLACE LOOKS WRECKED TOO...
RA
LOOK, CHOPPER'S HERE!!
WOW, THAT WHALE TREE IS HUGE UP CLOSE!!
GARCHU !!!
RAAAH
DO THESE MINKS HEAL FAST OR WHAT?
INDEED.
STRAW HAT LUFFY!! IT'S US!! SORRY ABOUT EARLIER.
WE CAN'T ALLOW ANY INTRUDERS-- IT'S JUST THE RULES!!
RAAAAAAHH
HEY! IT'S YOU GUYS!! NO WORRIES!
WHERE'S THE CAT VIPER?!

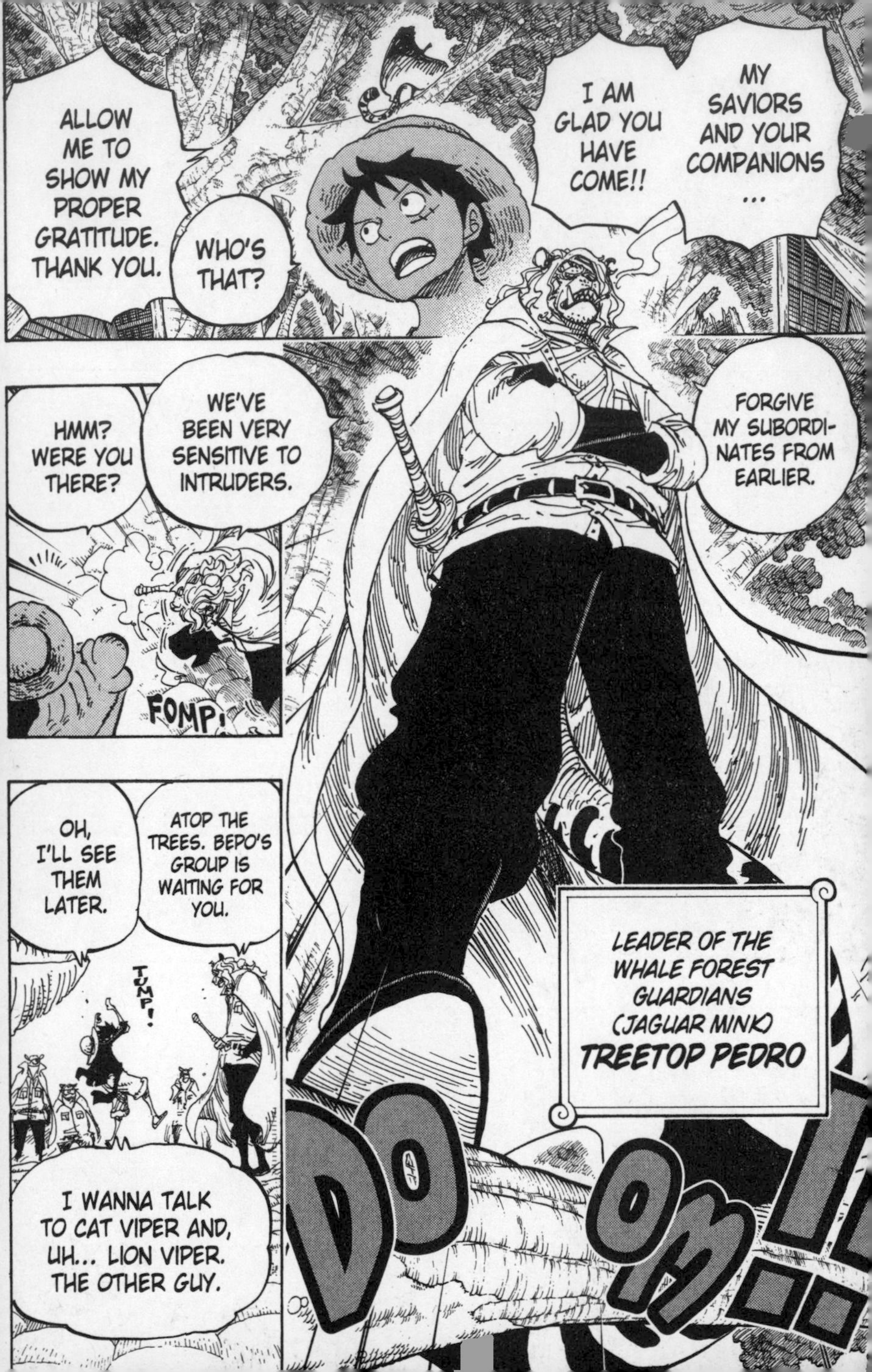
MY SAVIORS AND YOUR COMPANIONS...
I AM GLAD YOU HAVE COME!!
ALLOW ME TO SHOW MY PROPER GRATITUDE. THANK YOU.
WHO'S THAT?
FORGIVE MY SUBORDINATES FROM EARLIER.
LEADER OF THE WHALE FOREST GUARDIANS (JAGUAR MINK) TREETOP PEDRO
DOOM...!!
WE'VE BEEN VERY SENSITIVE TO INTRUDERS.
HMM? WERE YOU THERE?
FOMP
ATOP THE TREES. BEPO'S GROUP IS WAITING FOR YOU.
OH, I'LL SEE THEM LATER.
TUMP!
I WANNA TALK TO CAT VIPER AND, UH... LION VIPER. THE OTHER GUY.

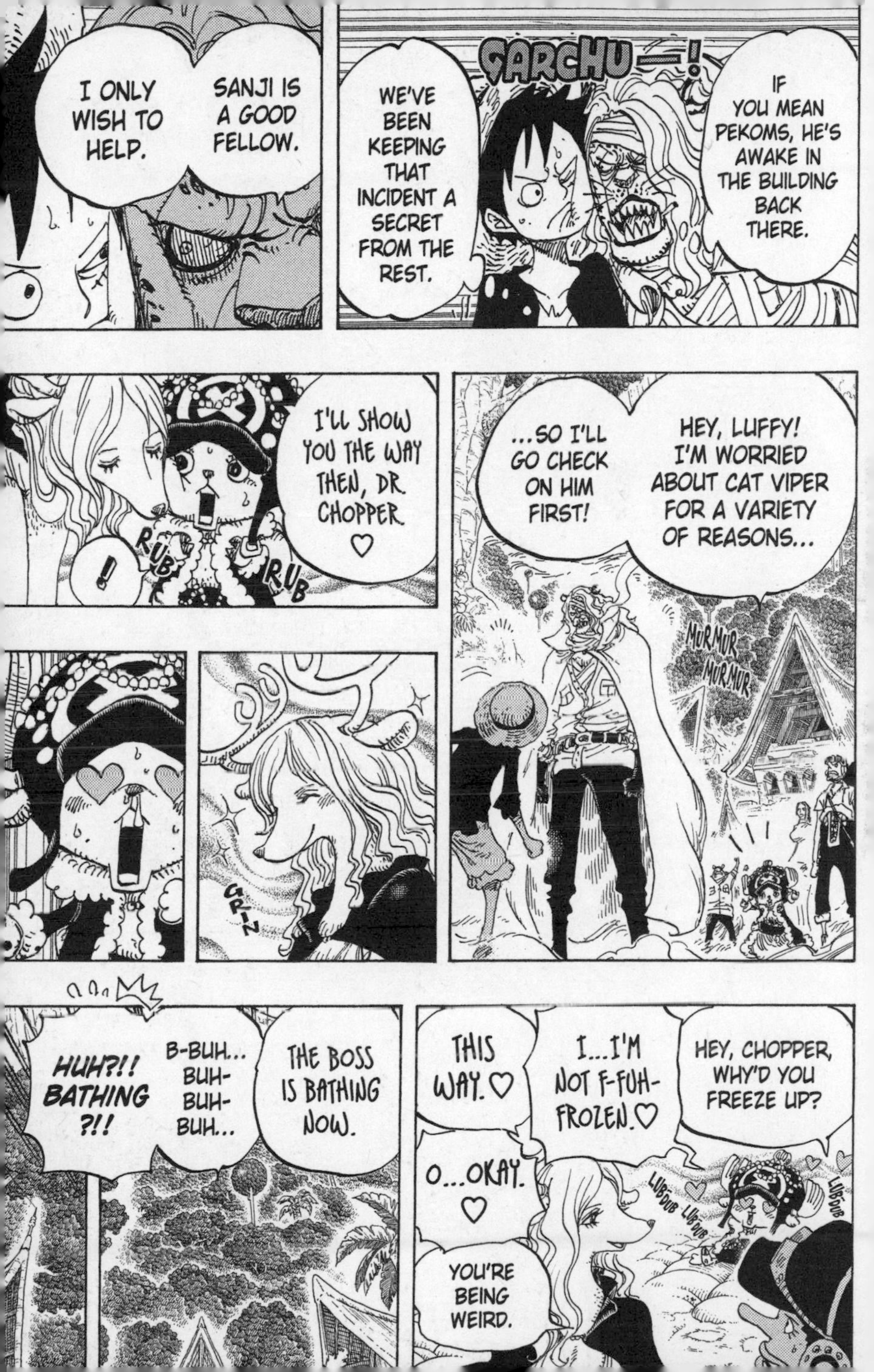
GARCHU—!
IF YOU MEAN PEKOMS, HE'S AWAKE IN THE BUILDING BACK THERE.
WE'VE BEEN KEEPING THAT INCIDENT A SECRET FROM THE REST.
SANJI IS A GOOD FELLOW.
I ONLY WISH TO HELP.
HEY, LUFFY! I'M WORRIED ABOUT CAT VIPER FOR A VARIETY OF REASONS...
...SO I'LL GO CHECK ON HIM FIRST!
MURMUR MURMUR
I'LL SHOW YOU THE WAY THEN, DR. CHOPPER. ♡
RUB RUB
!
GRIN
HEY, CHOPPER, WHY'D YOU FREEZE UP?
I...I'M NOT F-FUH-FROZEN.♡
THIS WAY.♡
LUBDUB LUBDUB LUBDUB
O...OKAY. ♡
YOU'RE BEING WEIRD.
THE BOSS IS BATHING NOW.
B-BUH... BUH-BUH-BUH...
HUH?!! BATHING?!!

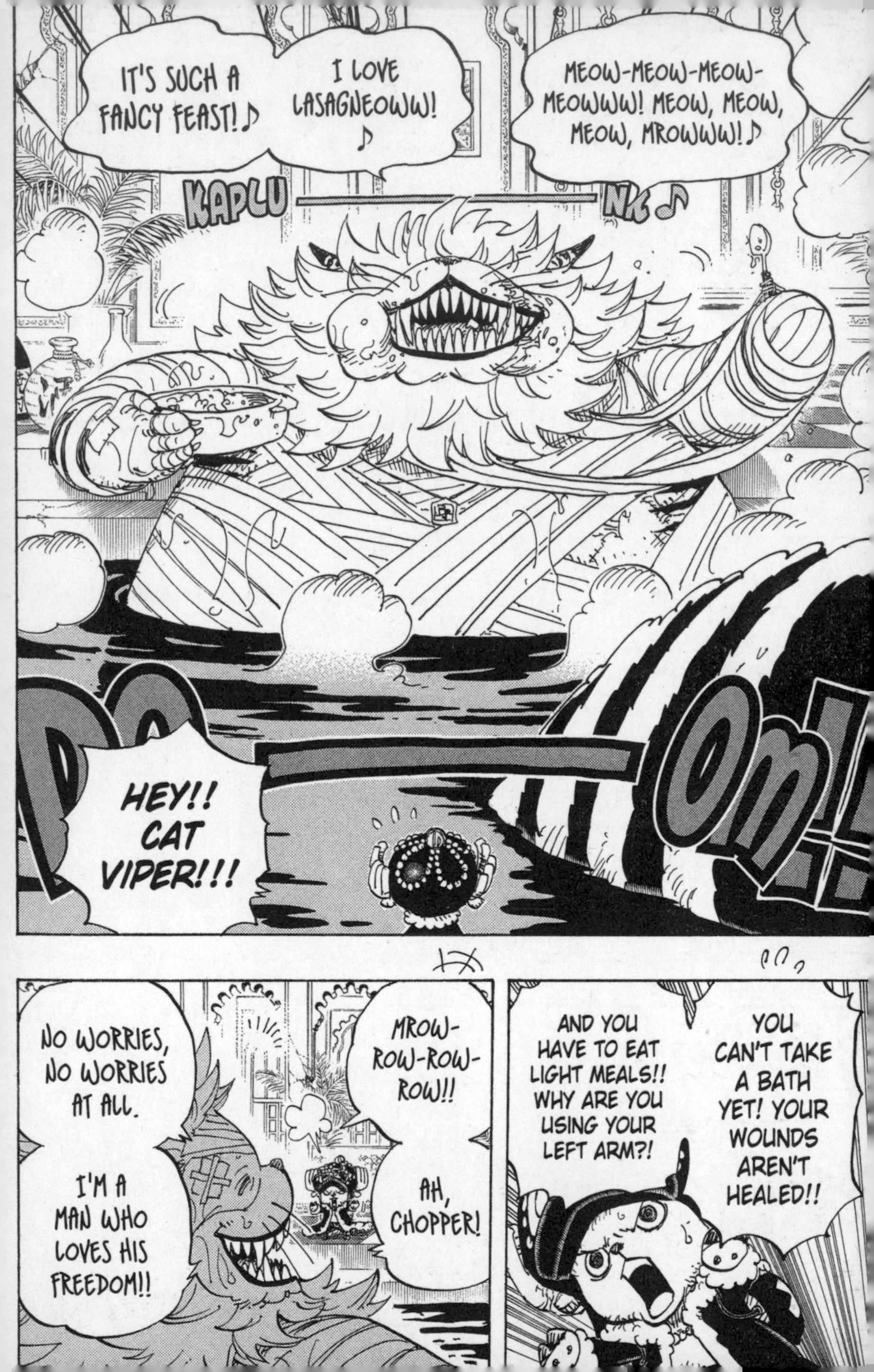

MEOW-MEOW-MEOW-MEOWWW! MEOW, MEOW, MEOW, MROWWW!♪
I LOVE LASAGNEOWW! ♪
IT'S SUCH A FANCY FEAST!♪
KAPLUNK♪
HEY!! CAT VIPER!!!
YOU CAN'T TAKE A BATH YET! YOUR WOUNDS AREN'T HEALED!!
AND YOU HAVE TO EAT LIGHT MEALS!! WHY ARE YOU USING YOUR LEFT ARM?!
MROW-ROW-ROW-ROW!!
AH, CHOPPER!
NO WORRIES, NO WORRIES AT ALL.
I'M A MAN WHO LOVES HIS FREEDOM!!

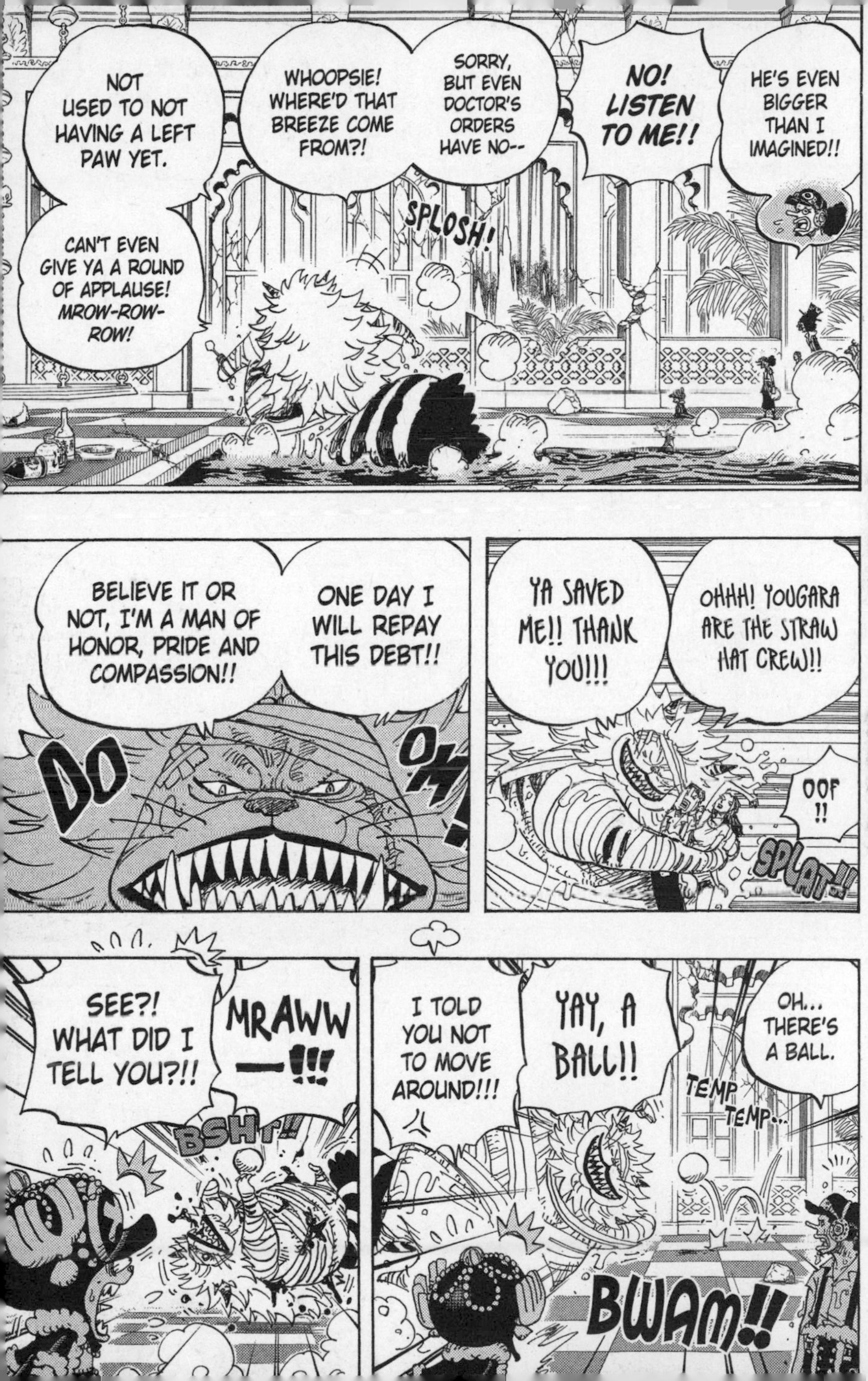
HE'S EVEN BIGGER THAN I IMAGINED!!
NO! LISTEN TO ME!!
SORRY, BUT EVEN DOCTOR'S ORDERS HAVE NO--
WHOOPSIE! WHERE'D THAT BREEZE COME FROM?!
SPLOSH!
NOT USED TO NOT HAVING A LEFT PAW YET.
CAN'T EVEN GIVE YA A ROUND OF APPLAUSE! MROW-ROW-ROW!
OHHH! YOUGARA ARE THE STRAW HAT CREW!!
YA SAVED ME!! THANK YOU!!!
OOF !!
SPLAT!!
ONE DAY I WILL REPAY THIS DEBT!!
BELIEVE IT OR NOT, I'M A MAN OF HONOR, PRIDE AND COMPASSION!!
DO
OM
OH... THERE'S A BALL.
YAY, A BALL!!
I TOLD YOU NOT TO MOVE AROUND!!!
TEMP TEMP...
BWAM!!
MRAWW —!!!
SEE?! WHAT DID I TELL YOU?!!
BSHT!!

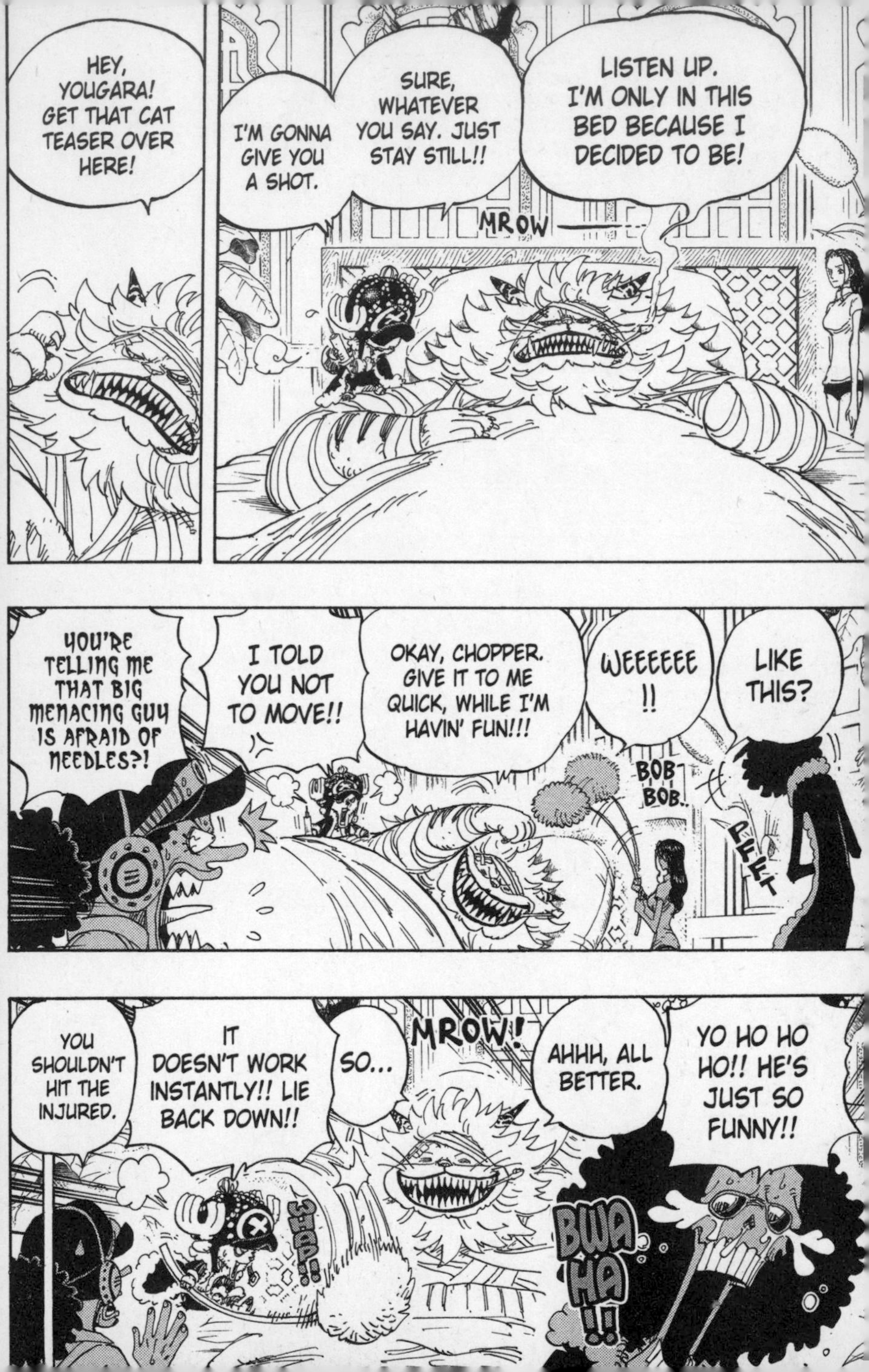
LISTEN UP. I'M ONLY IN THIS BED BECAUSE I DECIDED TO BE!
SURE, WHATEVER YOU SAY. JUST STAY STILL!!
I'M GONNA GIVE YOU A SHOT.
MROW
HEY, YOUGARA! GET THAT CAT TEASER OVER HERE!
LIKE THIS?
WEEEEEE !!
OKAY, CHOPPER. GIVE IT TO ME QUICK, WHILE I'M HAVIN' FUN!!!
I TOLD YOU NOT TO MOVE!!
BOB BOB..
PFFT
YOU'RE TELLING ME THAT BIG MENACING GUY IS AFRAID OF NEEDLES?!
YO HO HO HO!! HE'S JUST SO FUNNY!!
BWA HA!!
AHHH, ALL BETTER.
MROW!
SO...
IT DOESN'T WORK INSTANTLY!! LIE BACK DOWN!!
WHAP!!
YOU SHOULDN'T HIT THE INJURED.

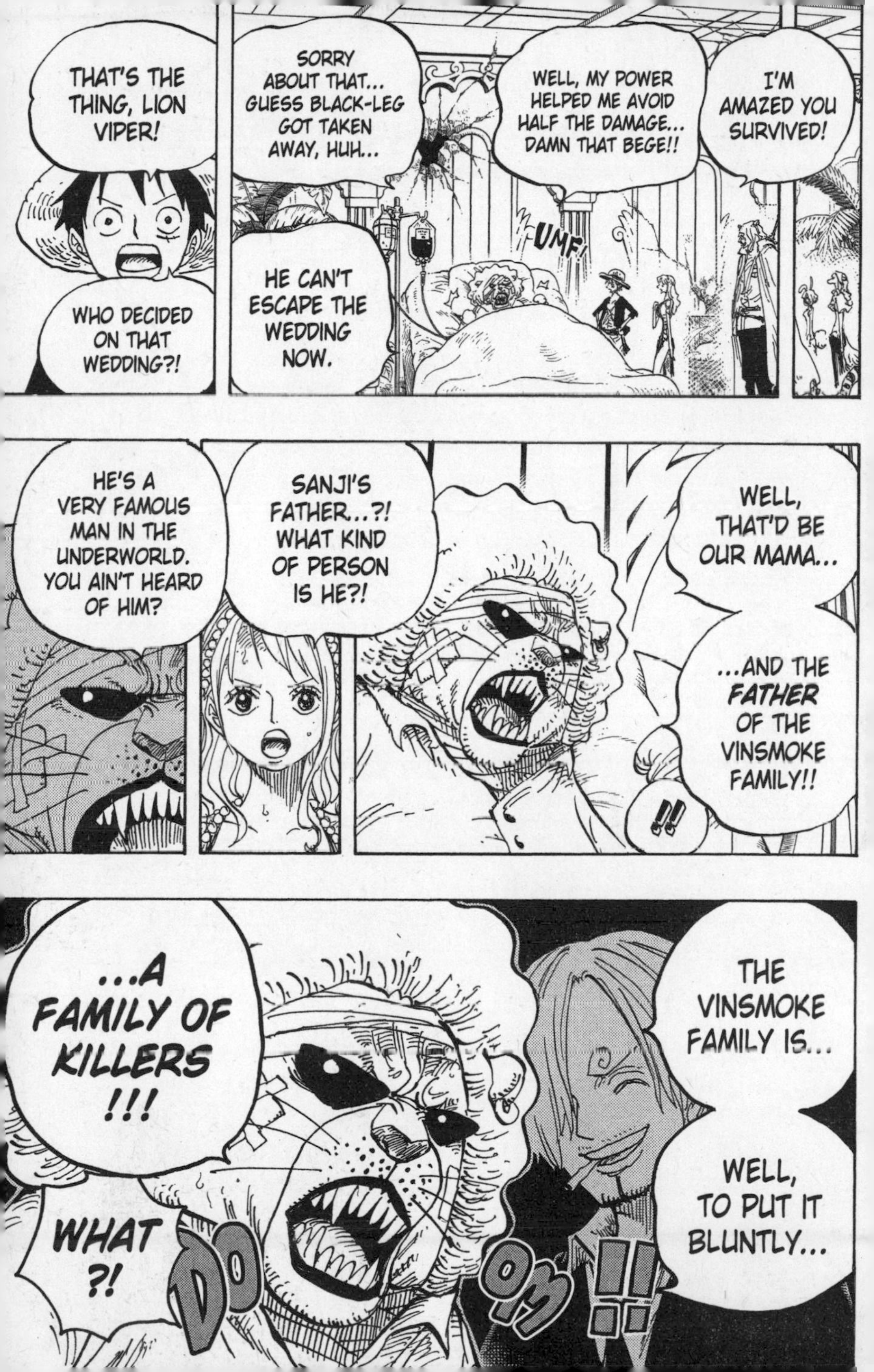
I'M AMAZED YOU SURVIVED!
WELL, MY POWER HELPED ME AVOID HALF THE DAMAGE... DAMN THAT BEGE!!
UMF!
SORRY ABOUT THAT... GUESS BLACK-LEG GOT TAKEN AWAY, HUH...
HE CAN'T ESCAPE THE WEDDING NOW.
THAT'S THE THING, LION VIPER!
WHO DECIDED ON THAT WEDDING?!
WELL, THAT'D BE OUR MAMA...
...AND THE FATHER OF THE VINSMOKE FAMILY!!
!!
SANJI'S FATHER...?! WHAT KIND OF PERSON IS HE?!
HE'S A VERY FAMOUS MAN IN THE UNDERWORLD. YOU AIN'T HEARD OF HIM?
THE VINSMOKE FAMILY IS...
WELL, TO PUT IT BLUNTLY...
...A FAMILY OF KILLERS!!!
DOOM!!
WHAT?!

SBS Question Corner

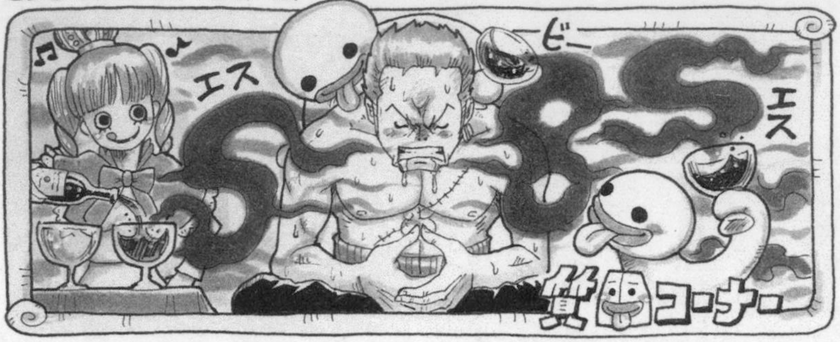
エス
ビー
エス
質問コーナー

(Hippo Iron, Saitama)

Q: Nice to meet you, Odacchi! Is it true that the source for the "Cat Viper" who appeared in Chapter 806 is a song by none other than Cho, the voice actor for Brook? I am a super-super-super fan of his, and I'm so fascinated by this that I can't sleep after 10 o'clock!! Please give Cho all of my best!!

--Puuchan-chan

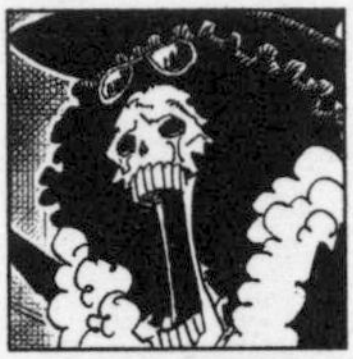

A: Yes. This book contains both the first appearance of Cat Viper, and Brook's song about him. Go ahead and search on YouTube for "Nekomamushi Song" and watch the video. It's sung by Cho, Brook's actor! The melody and lyrics were penned by Choko, his wife. He just happened to have sung this song years ago, and I liked it so much that I asked him, "Can I have Brook sing this song?" With their permission, the Cat Viper has taken life in the manga, although his style is a bit different due to story reasons. I can't wait to hear Brook sing this in the anime (laughs).

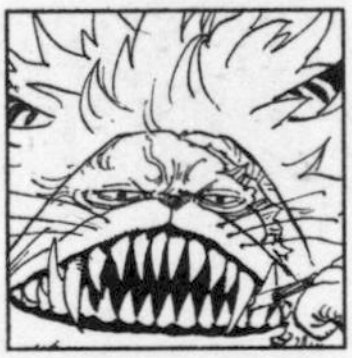

Q: Hello, Oda Sensei. I have counted up the number of times each of the Straw Hats has delivered a verbal smackdown on someone else and ranked them in order.

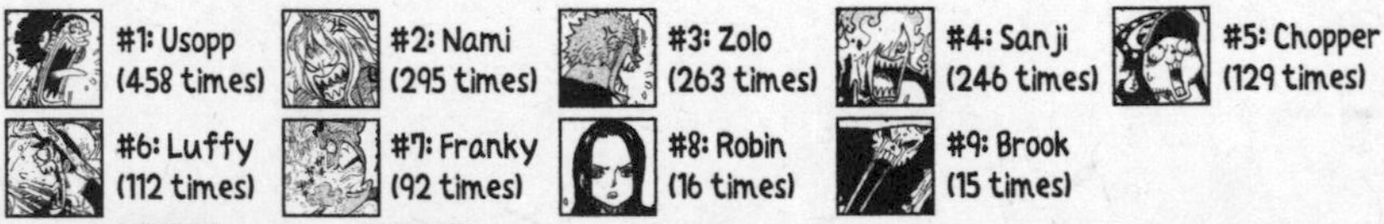
#1: Usopp
(458 times)
#2: Nami
(295 times)
#3: Zolo
(263 times)
#4: Sanji
(246 times)
#5: Chopper
(129 times)
#6: Luffy
(112 times)
#7: Franky
(92 times)
#8: Robin
(16 times)
#9: Brook
(15 times)

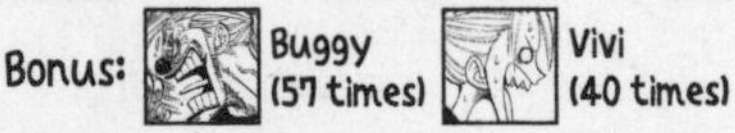
Bonus:
Buggy
(57 times)
Vivi
(40 times)

I covered from Volume 1 to Volume 80. It took me a month and a half.

--Oda Sensei Loves Big Boobs

A: Wow, you must be bored!!! Whap!! Okay, put down one for me... I can't believe you counted these up. Thank you. This is really interesting. I'm surprised how high Zolo ranked.

Chapter 815:
TAKE ME WITH YOU!!

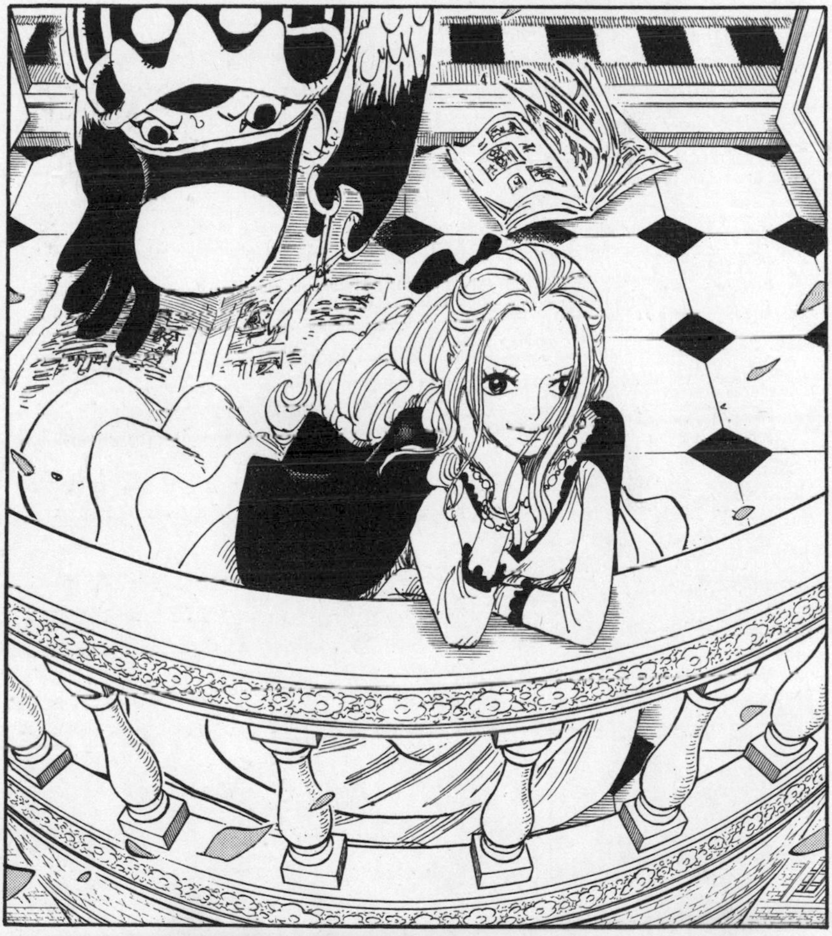

DECKS OF THE WORLD, 500-MILLION-MAN ARC,
VOL. 9: "KINGDOM OF ALABASTA"

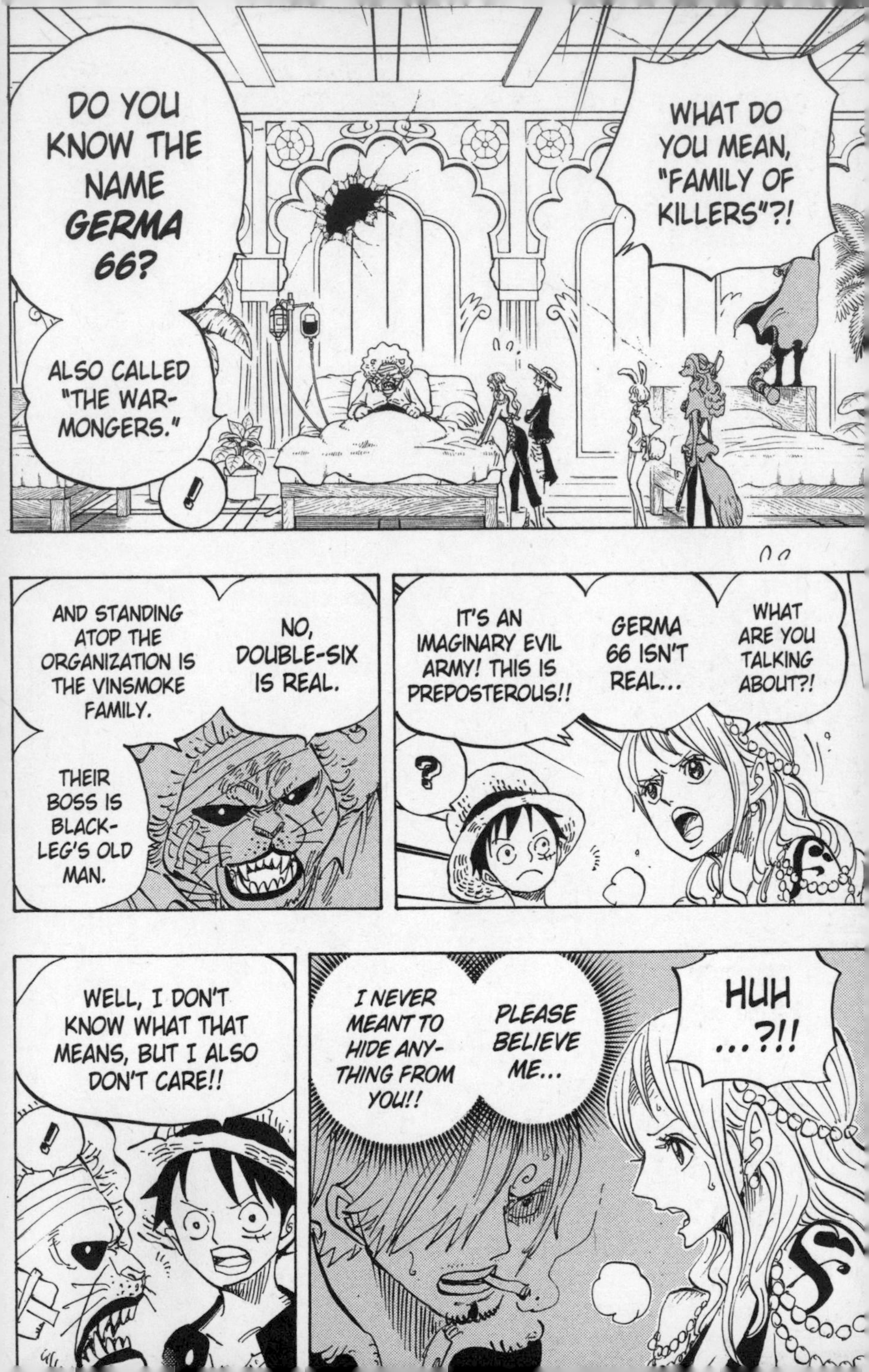
WHAT DO YOU MEAN, "FAMILY OF KILLERS"?!
DO YOU KNOW THE NAME GERMA 66?
ALSO CALLED "THE WAR-MONGERS."
!
WHAT ARE YOU TALKING ABOUT?!
GERMA 66 ISN'T REAL...
IT'S AN IMAGINARY EVIL ARMY! THIS IS PREPOSTEROUS!!
?
NO, DOUBLE-SIX IS REAL.
AND STANDING ATOP THE ORGANIZATION IS THE VINSMOKE FAMILY.
THEIR BOSS IS BLACK-LEG'S OLD MAN.
HUH ...?!!
PLEASE BELIEVE ME...
I NEVER MEANT TO HIDE ANY-THING FROM YOU!!
WELL, I DON'T KNOW WHAT THAT MEANS, BUT I ALSO DON'T CARE!!
!

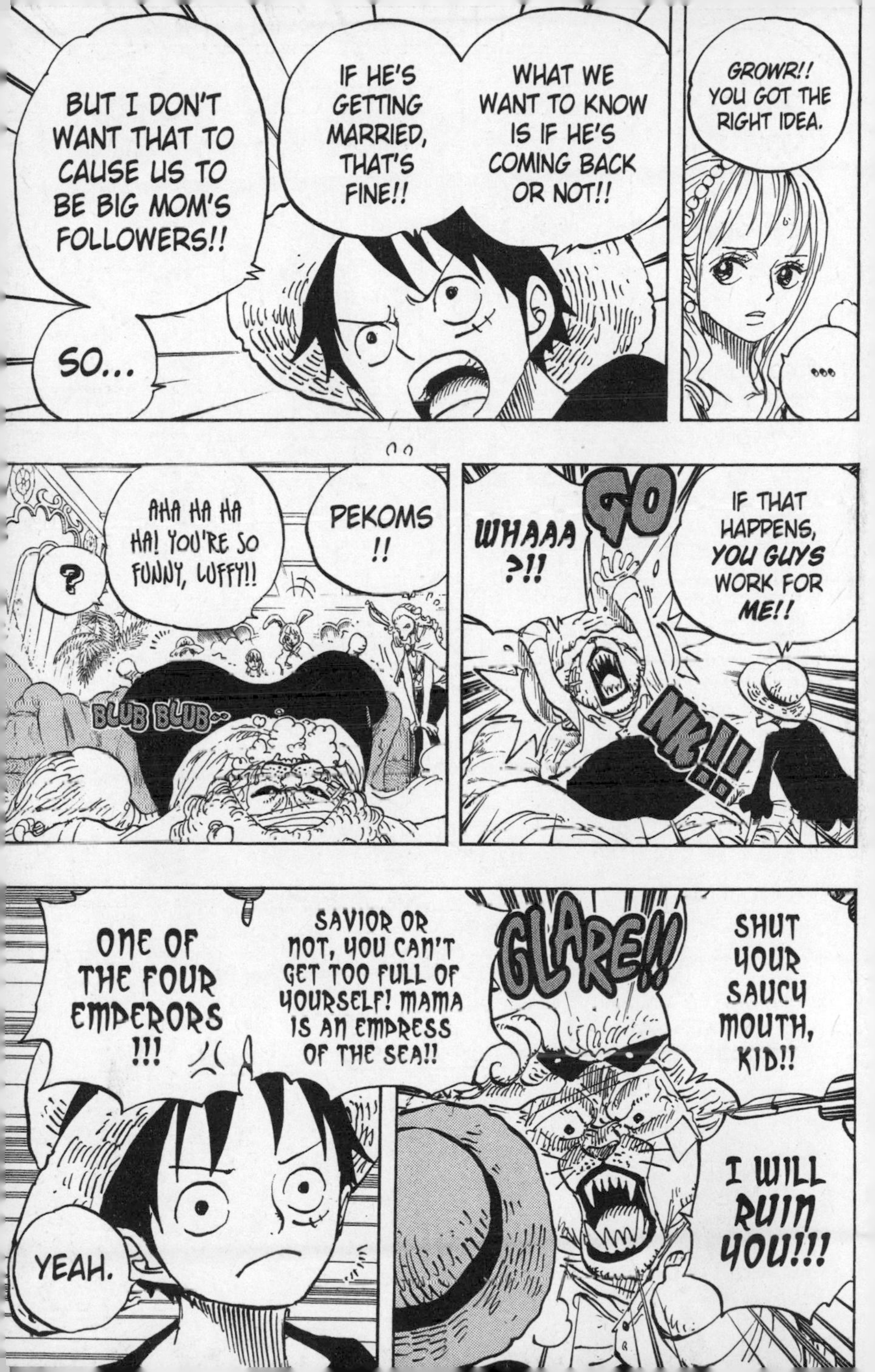
GROWR!! YOU GOT THE RIGHT IDEA.
...
WHAT WE WANT TO KNOW IS IF HE'S COMING BACK OR NOT!!
IF HE'S GETTING MARRIED, THAT'S FINE!!
BUT I DON'T WANT THAT TO CAUSE US TO BE BIG MOM'S FOLLOWERS!!
SO...
IF THAT HAPPENS, YOU GUYS WORK FOR ME!!
GO
WHAAA?!!
NK!!
PEKOMS!!
AHA HA HA HA! YOU'RE SO FUNNY, LUFFY!!
?
BLUB BLUB...
SHUT YOUR SAUCY MOUTH, KID!!
GLARE!!
I WILL RUIN YOU!!!
SAVIOR OR NOT, YOU CAN'T GET TOO FULL OF YOURSELF! MAMA IS AN EMPRESS OF THE SEA!!
ONE OF THE FOUR EMPERORS!!!
YEAH.

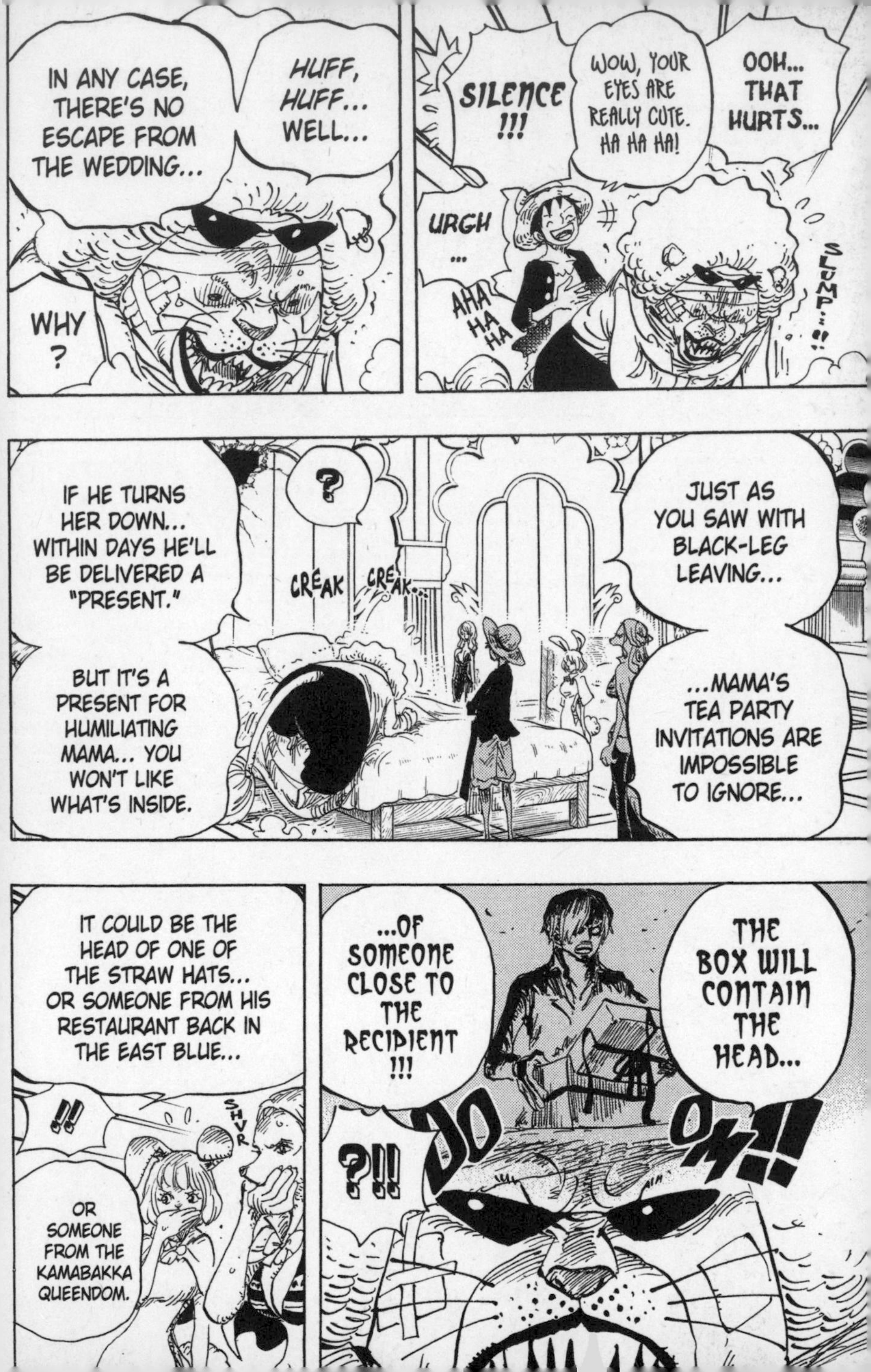
OOH... THAT HURTS...
WOW, YOUR EYES ARE REALLY CUTE. HA HA HA!
SILENCE !!!
URGH ...
AHA HA HA
SLUMP...!!
HUFF, HUFF... WELL...
IN ANY CASE, THERE'S NO ESCAPE FROM THE WEDDING...
WHY ?
JUST AS YOU SAW WITH BLACK-LEG LEAVING...
...MAMA'S TEA PARTY INVITATIONS ARE IMPOSSIBLE TO IGNORE...
?
CREAK
CREAK...
IF HE TURNS HER DOWN... WITHIN DAYS HE'LL BE DELIVERED A "PRESENT."
BUT IT'S A PRESENT FOR HUMILIATING MAMA... YOU WON'T LIKE WHAT'S INSIDE.
THE BOX WILL CONTAIN THE HEAD...
...OF SOMEONE CLOSE TO THE RECIPIENT !!!
DOOM!!
?!!
IT COULD BE THE HEAD OF ONE OF THE STRAW HATS... OR SOMEONE FROM HIS RESTAURANT BACK IN THE EAST BLUE...
!!
SHVR
OR SOMEONE FROM THE KAMABAKKA QUEENDOM.

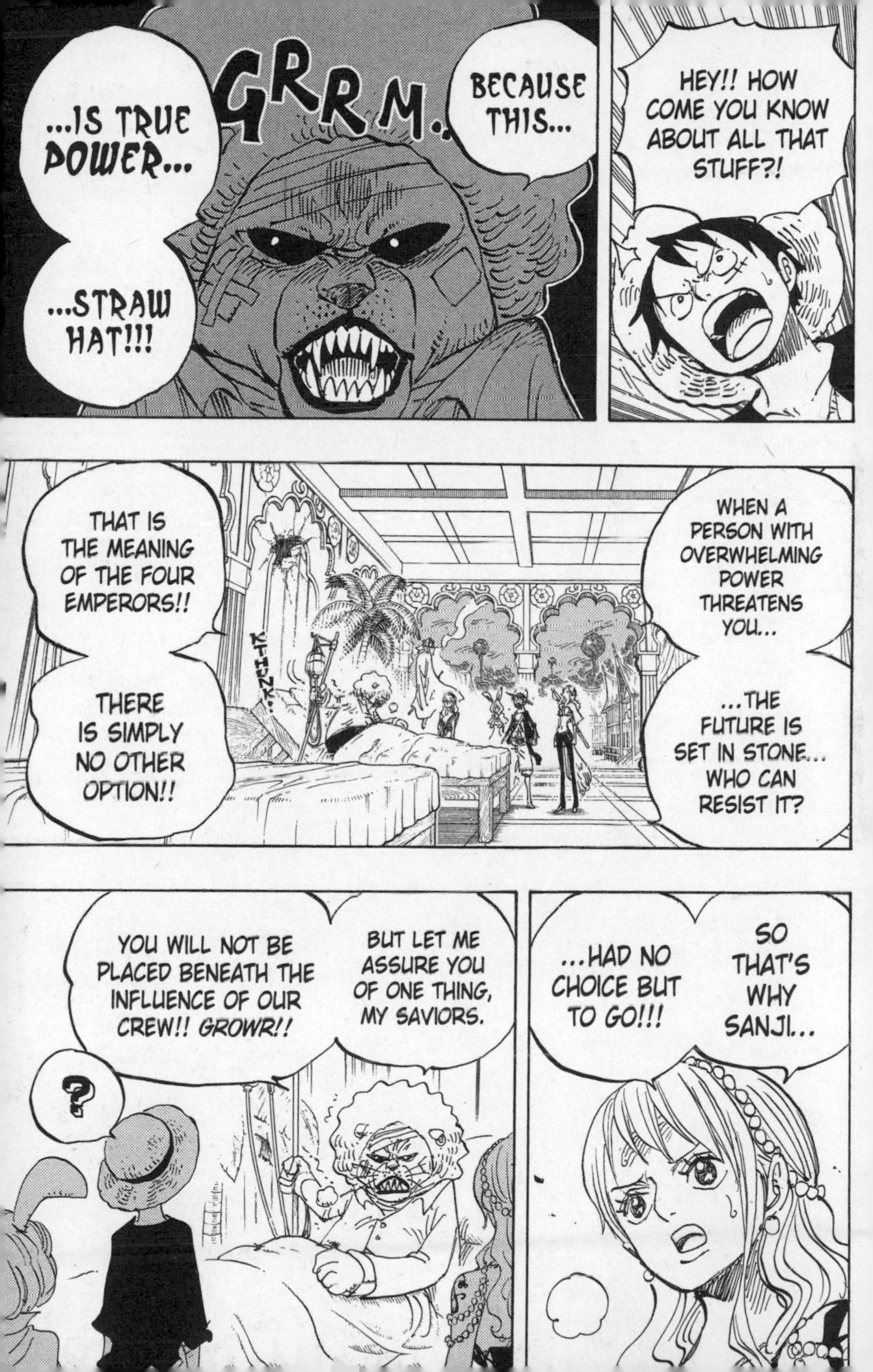
HEY!! HOW COME YOU KNOW ABOUT ALL THAT STUFF?!
BECAUSE THIS...
GRRM..
...IS TRUE POWER...
...STRAW HAT!!!
WHEN A PERSON WITH OVERWHELMING POWER THREATENS YOU...
...THE FUTURE IS SET IN STONE... WHO CAN RESIST IT?
THAT IS THE MEANING OF THE FOUR EMPERORS!!
THERE IS SIMPLY NO OTHER OPTION!!
KTHUNK..
SO THAT'S WHY SANJI...
...HAD NO CHOICE BUT TO GO!!!
BUT LET ME ASSURE YOU OF ONE THING, MY SAVIORS.
YOU WILL NOT BE PLACED BENEATH THE INFLUENCE OF OUR CREW!! *GROWR!!*
?

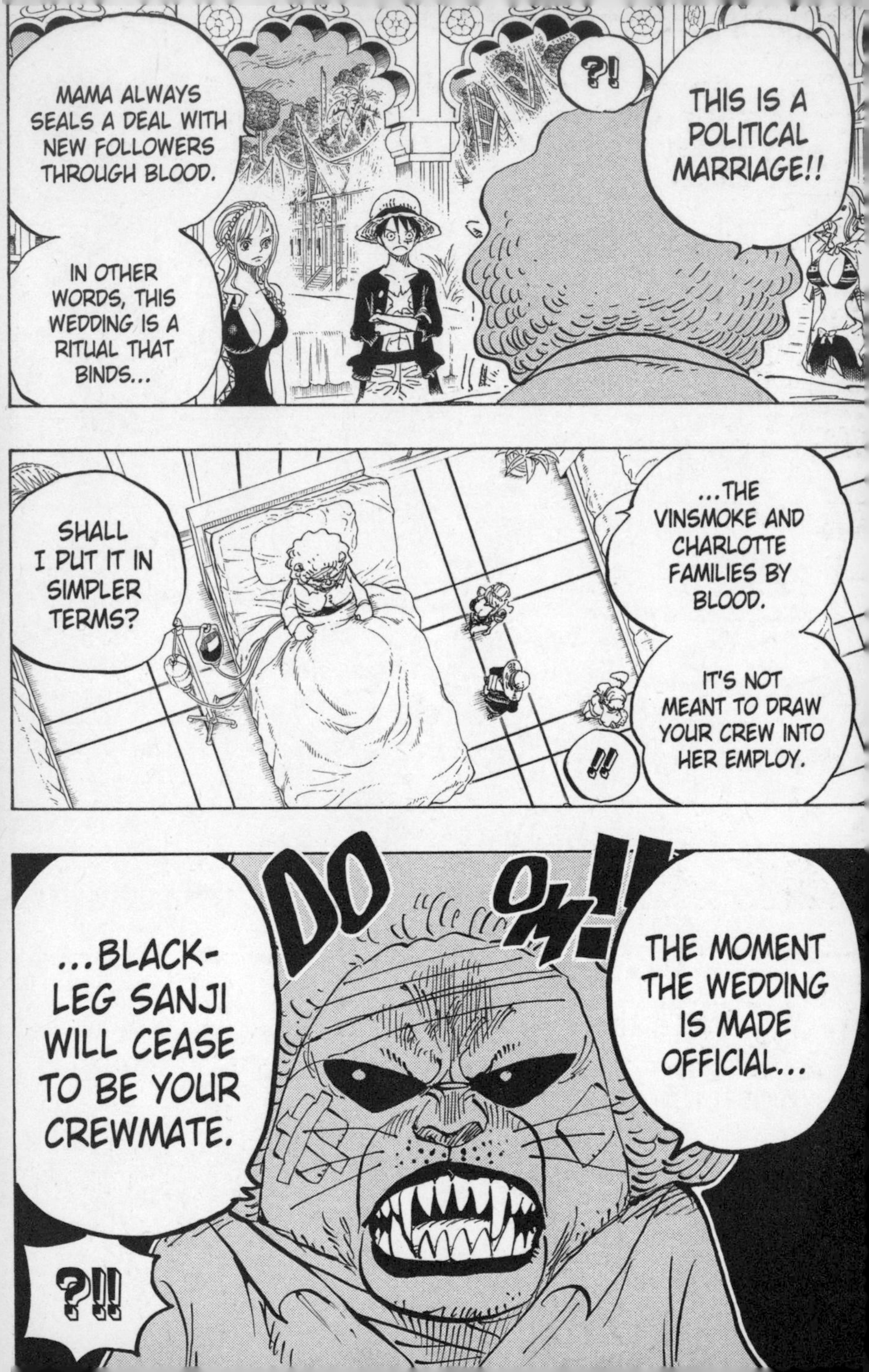
?!
THIS IS A POLITICAL MARRIAGE!!
MAMA ALWAYS SEALS A DEAL WITH NEW FOLLOWERS THROUGH BLOOD.
IN OTHER WORDS, THIS WEDDING IS A RITUAL THAT BINDS...
...THE VINSMOKE AND CHARLOTTE FAMILIES BY BLOOD.
IT'S NOT MEANT TO DRAW YOUR CREW INTO HER EMPLOY.
!!
SHALL I PUT IT IN SIMPLER TERMS?
DOOM!!
THE MOMENT THE WEDDING IS MADE OFFICIAL...
...BLACK-LEG SANJI WILL CEASE TO BE YOUR CREWMATE.
?!!

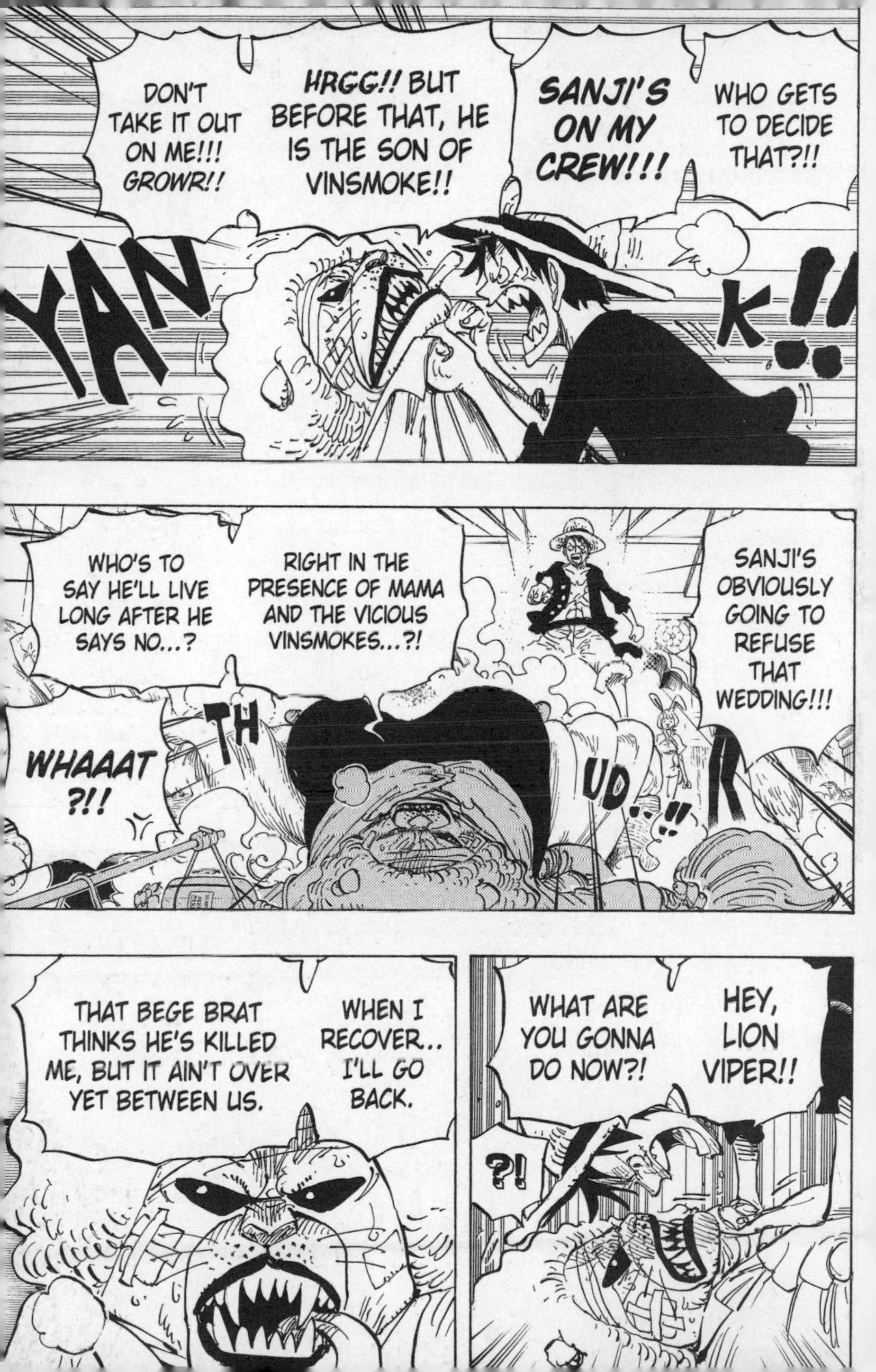

WHO GETS TO DECIDE THAT?!!
SANJI'S ON MY CREW!!!
HRGG!! BUT BEFORE THAT, HE IS THE SON OF VINSMOKE!!
DON'T TAKE IT OUT ON ME!!! GROWR!!
YANK!!
SANJI'S OBVIOUSLY GOING TO REFUSE THAT WEDDING!!!
RIGHT IN THE PRESENCE OF MAMA AND THE VICIOUS VINSMOKES...?!
WHO'S TO SAY HE'LL LIVE LONG AFTER HE SAYS NO...?
THUD!!
WHAAAT?!!
HEY, LION VIPER!!
WHAT ARE YOU GONNA DO NOW?!
?!
WHEN I RECOVER... I'LL GO BACK.
THAT BEGE BRAT THINKS HE'S KILLED ME, BUT IT AIN'T OVER YET BETWEEN US.

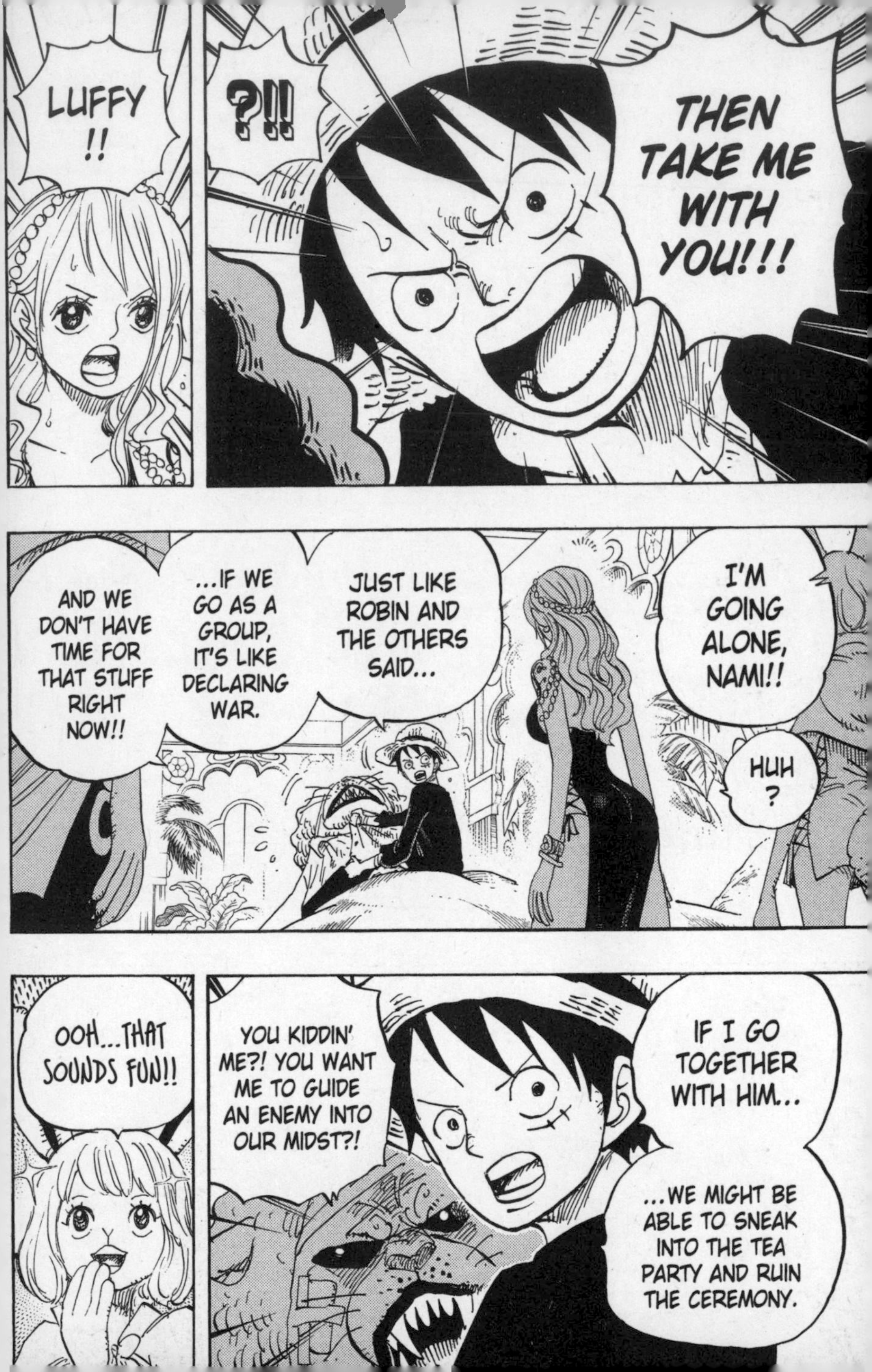
THEN TAKE ME WITH YOU!!!
?!!
LUFFY !!
I'M GOING ALONE, NAMI!!
HUH ?
JUST LIKE ROBIN AND THE OTHERS SAID...
...IF WE GO AS A GROUP, IT'S LIKE DECLARING WAR.
AND WE DON'T HAVE TIME FOR THAT STUFF RIGHT NOW!!
IF I GO TOGETHER WITH HIM...
...WE MIGHT BE ABLE TO SNEAK INTO THE TEA PARTY AND RUIN THE CEREMONY.
YOU KIDDIN' ME?! YOU WANT ME TO GUIDE AN ENEMY INTO OUR MIDST?!
OOH...THAT SOUNDS FUN!!

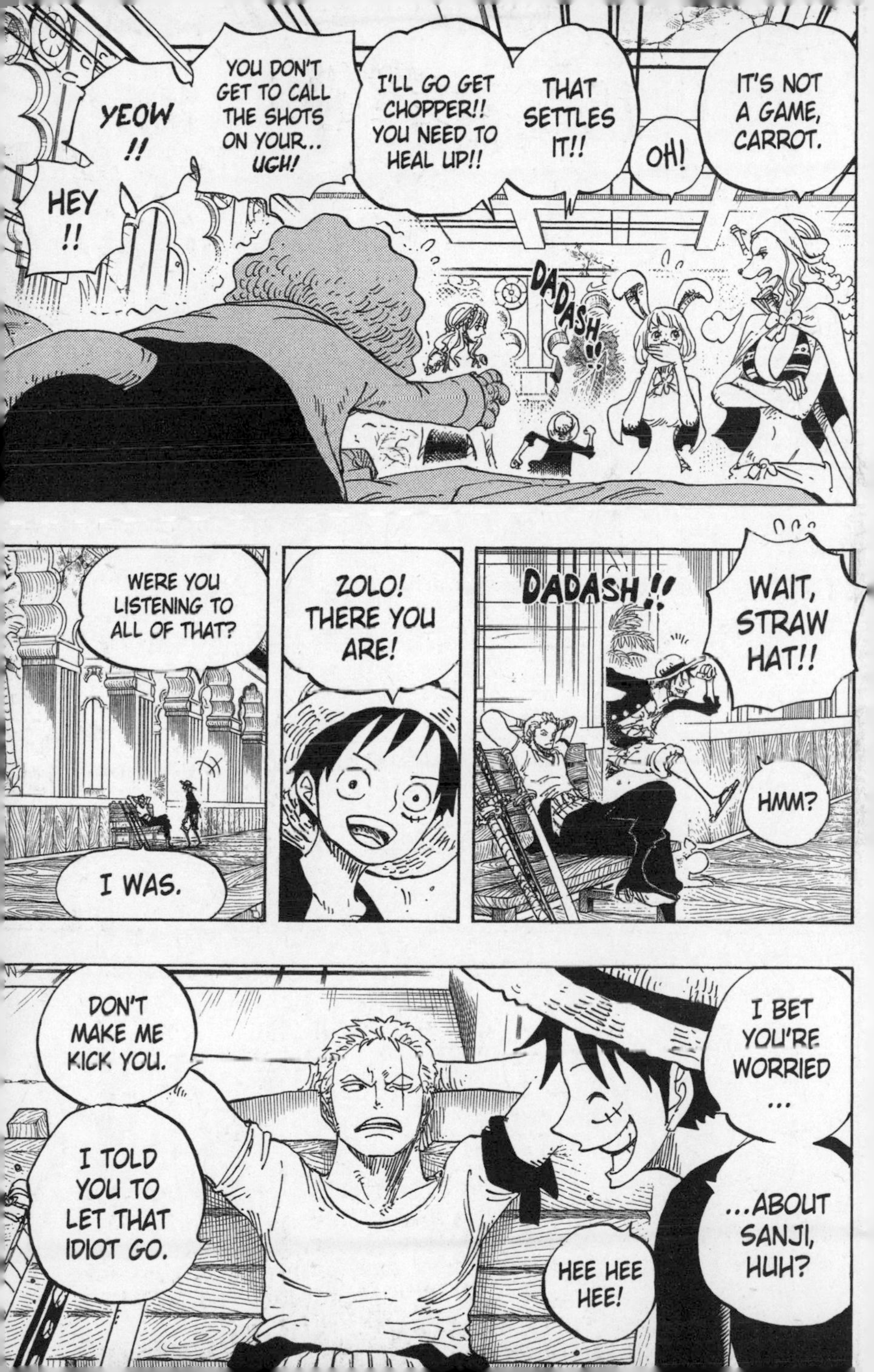
IT'S NOT A GAME, CARROT.
OH!
THAT SETTLES IT!!
I'LL GO GET CHOPPER!! YOU NEED TO HEAL UP!!
YOU DON'T GET TO CALL THE SHOTS ON YOUR... UGH!
YEOW!!
HEY!!
DADASH!!
WAIT, STRAW HAT!!
DADASH!!
HMM?
ZOLO! THERE YOU ARE!
WERE YOU LISTENING TO ALL OF THAT?
I WAS.
I BET YOU'RE WORRIED...
...ABOUT SANJI, HUH?
HEE HEE HEE!
DON'T MAKE ME KICK YOU.
I TOLD YOU TO LET THAT IDIOT GO.

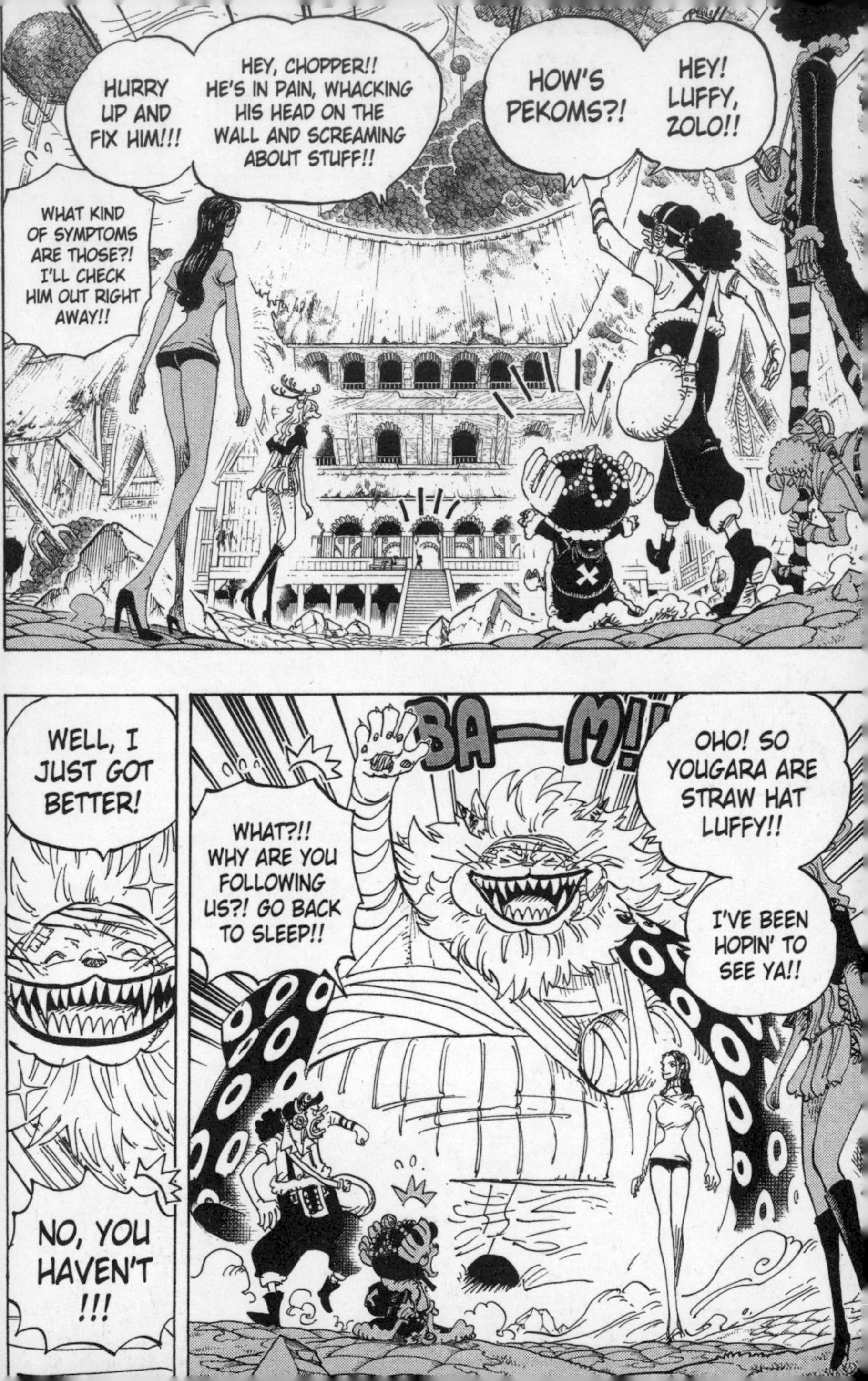
HEY! LUFFY, ZOLO!!
HOW'S PEKOMS?!
HEY, CHOPPER!! HE'S IN PAIN, WHACKING HIS HEAD ON THE WALL AND SCREAMING ABOUT STUFF!!
HURRY UP AND FIX HIM!!!
WHAT KIND OF SYMPTOMS ARE THOSE?! I'LL CHECK HIM OUT RIGHT AWAY!!
BA—M!!
OHO! SO YOUGARA ARE STRAW HAT LUFFY!!
I'VE BEEN HOPIN' TO SEE YA!!
WHAT?!! WHY ARE YOU FOLLOWING US?! GO BACK TO SLEEP!!
WELL, I JUST GOT BETTER!
NO, YOU HAVEN'T !!!

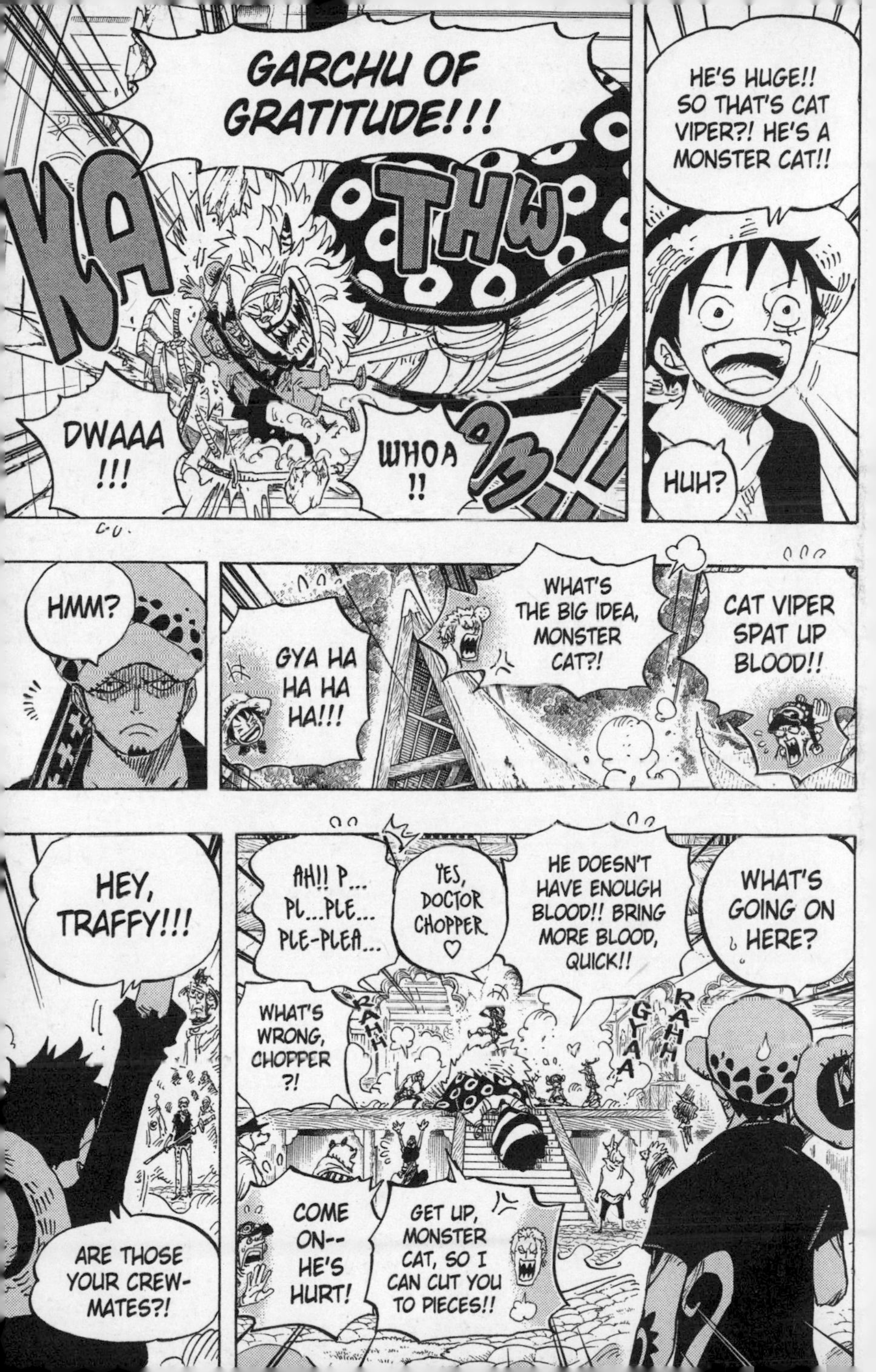
HE'S HUGE!! SO THAT'S CAT VIPER?! HE'S A MONSTER CAT!!
HUH?
GARCHU OF GRATITUDE!!!
KA
THW
AM!!
WHOA !!
DWAAA !!!
CAT VIPER SPAT UP BLOOD!!
WHAT'S THE BIG IDEA, MONSTER CAT?!
GYA HA HA HA HA!!!
HMM?
WHAT'S GOING ON HERE?
HE DOESN'T HAVE ENOUGH BLOOD!! BRING MORE BLOOD, QUICK!!
YES, DOCTOR CHOPPER ♡
AH!! P... PL...PLE... PLE-PLEA...
RAHH
GYAA
RAHH
WHAT'S WRONG, CHOPPER ?!
GET UP, MONSTER CAT, SO I CAN CUT YOU TO PIECES!!
COME ON-- HE'S HURT!
HEY, TRAFFY!!!
ARE THOSE YOUR CREW-MATES?!

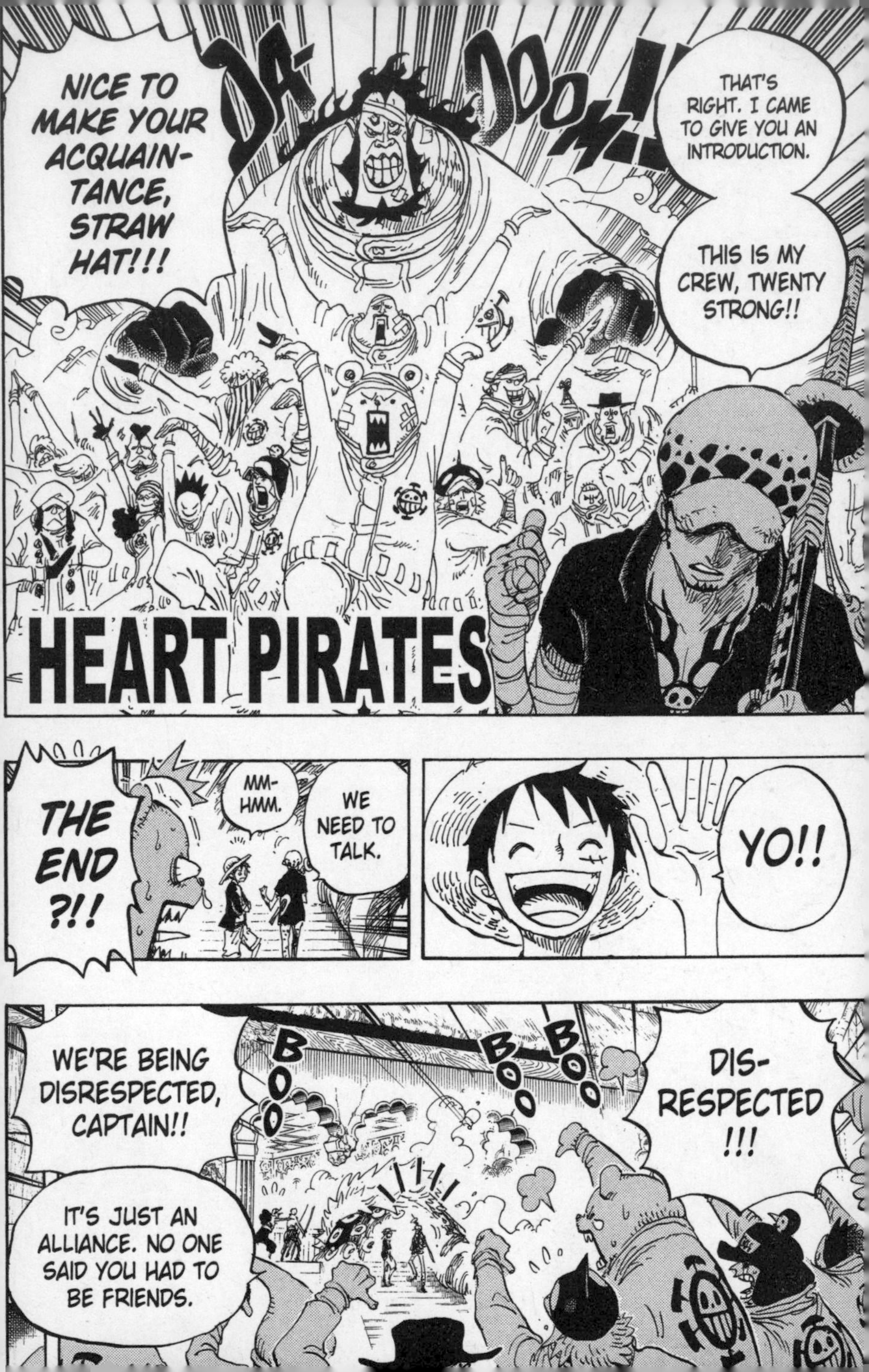
THAT'S RIGHT. I CAME TO GIVE YOU AN INTRODUCTION.
THIS IS MY CREW, TWENTY STRONG!!
DA-DOOM!!
NICE TO MAKE YOUR ACQUAIN-TANCE, STRAW HAT!!!
HEART PIRATES
YO!!
WE NEED TO TALK.
MM-HMM.
THE END ?!!
DIS-RESPECTED !!!
BOO
BOO
BOO
WE'RE BEING DISRESPECTED, CAPTAIN!!
IT'S JUST AN ALLIANCE. NO ONE SAID YOU HAD TO BE FRIENDS.

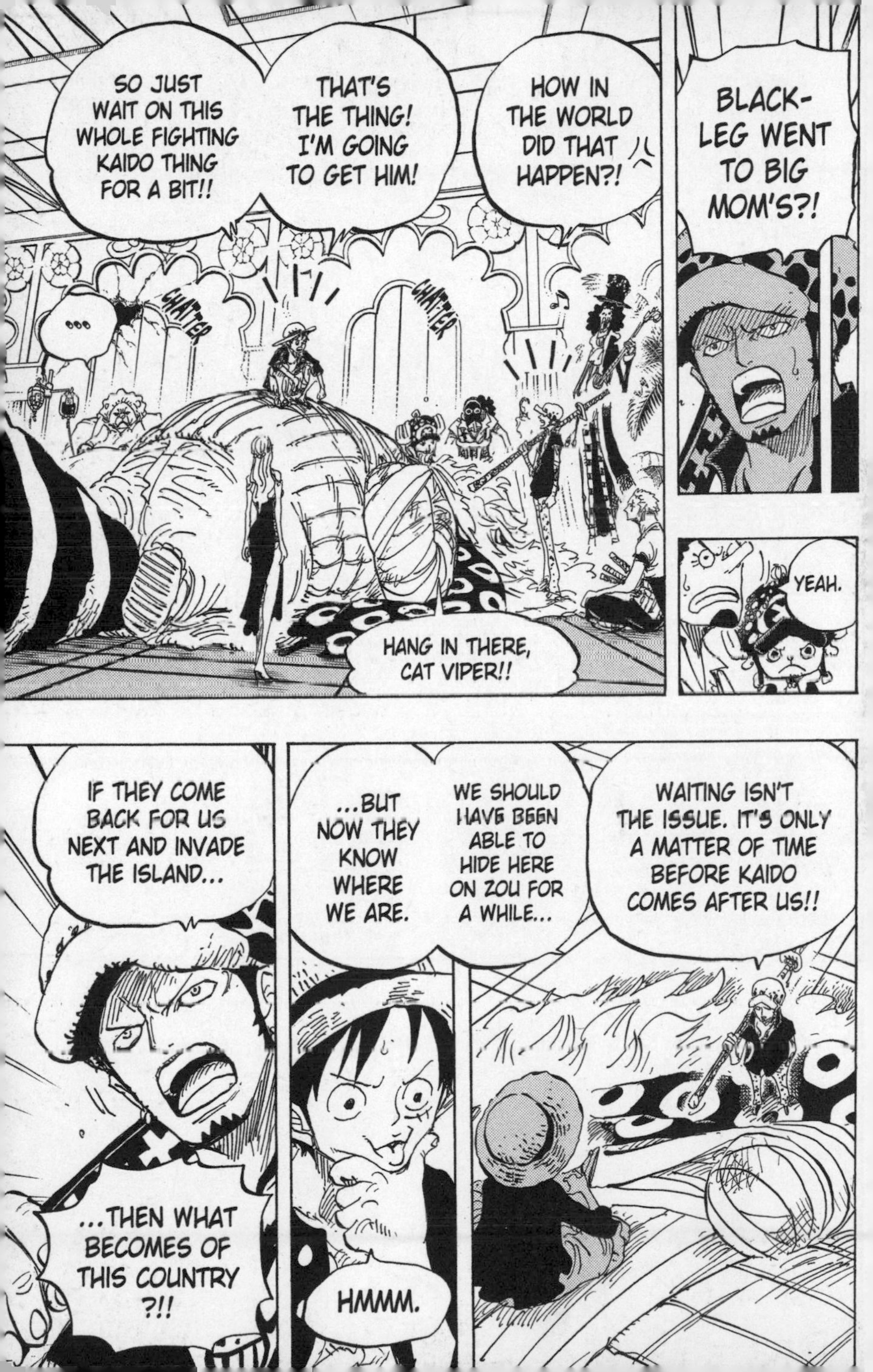
BLACK-LEG WENT TO BIG MOM'S?!
YEAH.
HOW IN THE WORLD DID THAT HAPPEN?!
THAT'S THE THING! I'M GOING TO GET HIM!
SO JUST WAIT ON THIS WHOLE FIGHTING KAIDO THING FOR A BIT!!
CHATTER
CHATTER
...
HANG IN THERE, CAT VIPER!!
WAITING ISN'T THE ISSUE. IT'S ONLY A MATTER OF TIME BEFORE KAIDO COMES AFTER US!!
WE SHOULD HAVE BEEN ABLE TO HIDE HERE ON ZOU FOR A WHILE...
...BUT NOW THEY KNOW WHERE WE ARE.
HMMM.
IF THEY COME BACK FOR US NEXT AND INVADE THE ISLAND...
...THEN WHAT BECOMES OF THIS COUNTRY ?!!

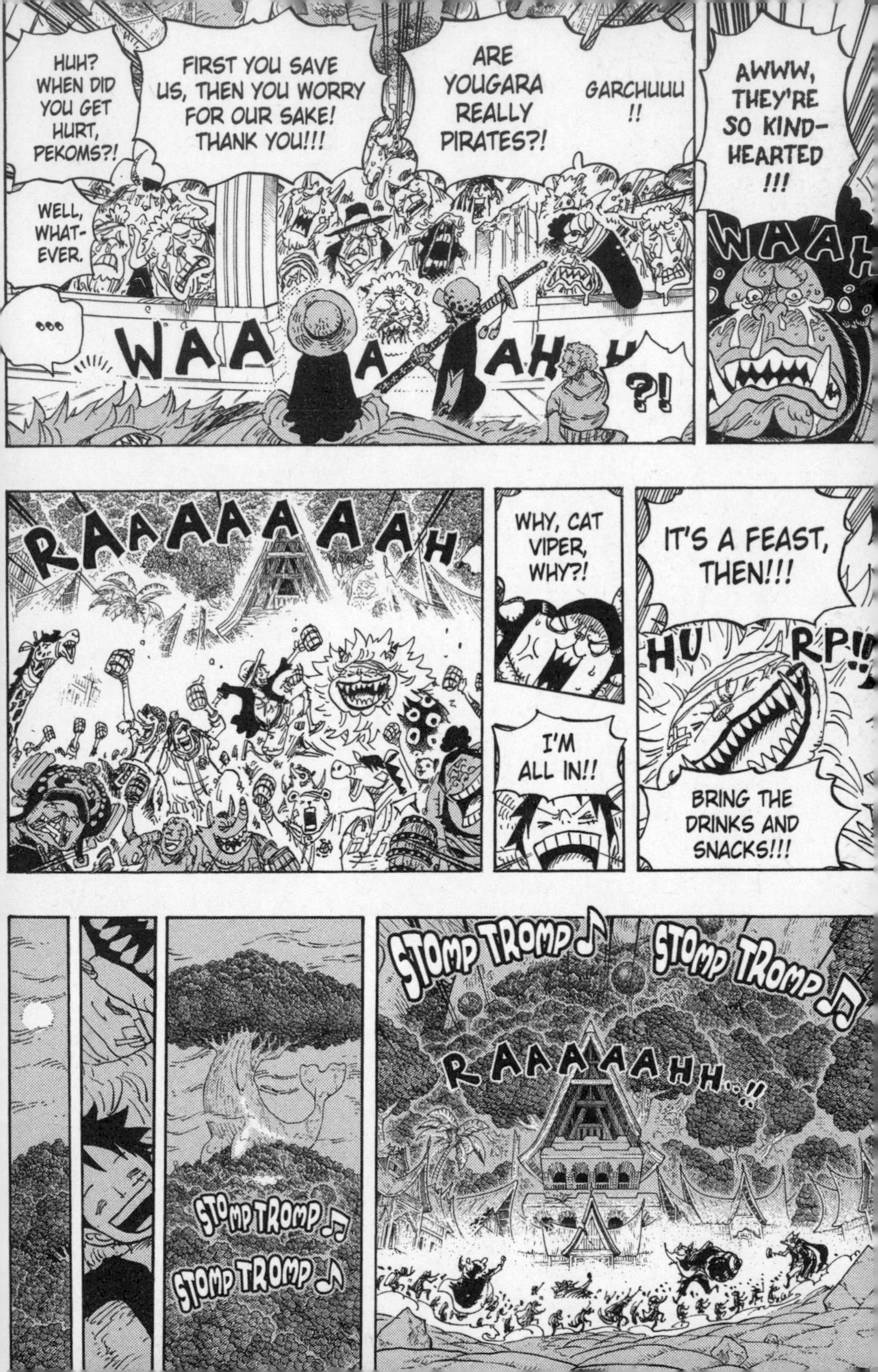
AWWW, THEY'RE SO KIND-HEARTED!!!
WAAAH
GARCHUUU!!
ARE YOUGARA REALLY PIRATES?!
FIRST YOU SAVE US, THEN YOU WORRY FOR OUR SAKE! THANK YOU!!!
HUH? WHEN DID YOU GET HURT, PEKOMS?!
WELL, WHATEVER.
...
WAAAAAH
?!
IT'S A FEAST, THEN!!!
HURP!!
BRING THE DRINKS AND SNACKS!!!
WHY, CAT VIPER, WHY?!
I'M ALL IN!!
RAAAAAAAH
STOMP TROMP ♪
STOMP TROMP ♫
RAAAAAHH..!!
STOMP TROMP ♫
STOMP TROMP ♪

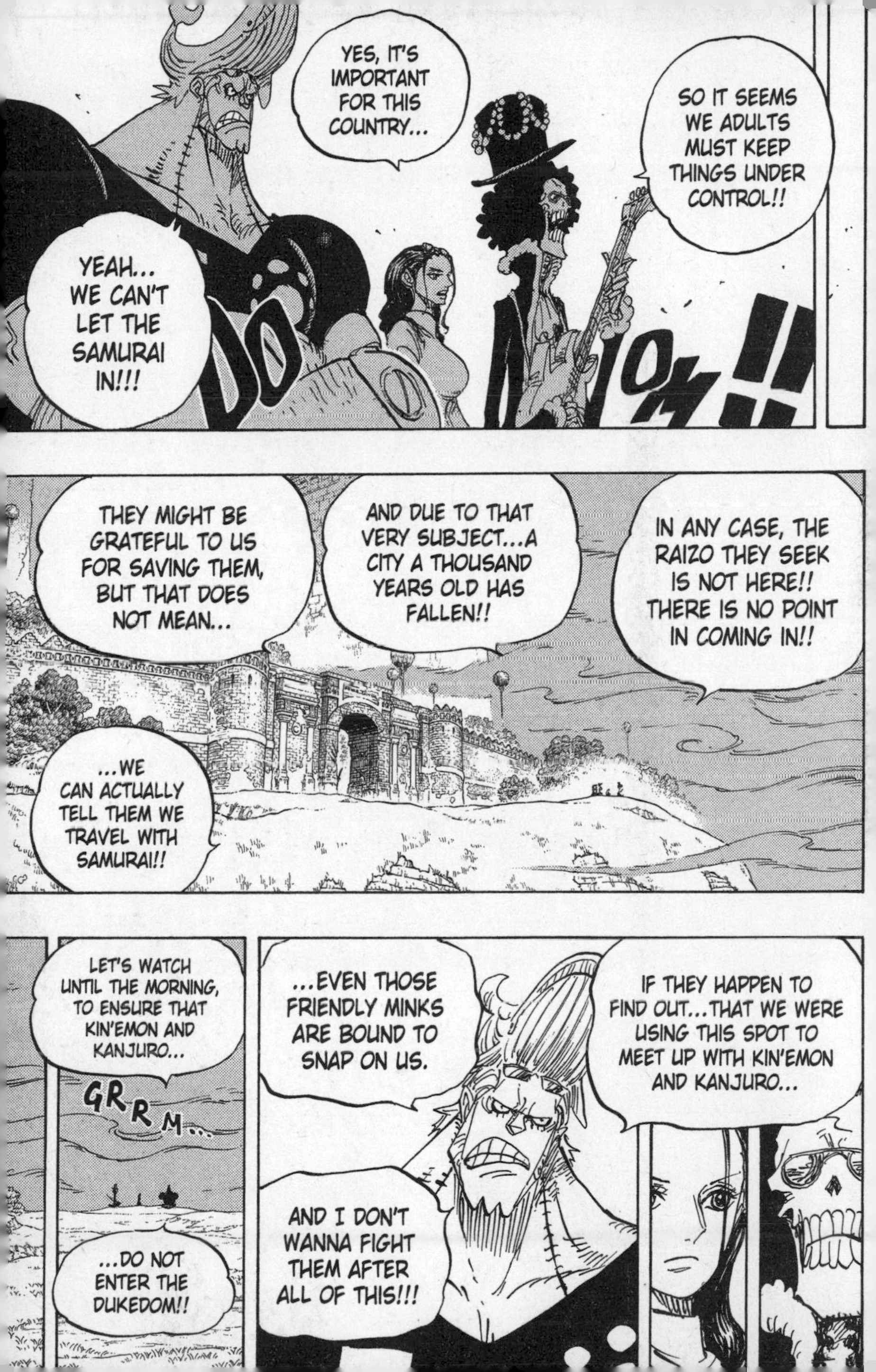
SO IT SEEMS WE ADULTS MUST KEEP THINGS UNDER CONTROL!!
YES, IT'S IMPORTANT FOR THIS COUNTRY...
DOOM!!
YEAH... WE CAN'T LET THE SAMURAI IN!!!
IN ANY CASE, THE RAIZO THEY SEEK IS NOT HERE!! THERE IS NO POINT IN COMING IN!!
AND DUE TO THAT VERY SUBJECT...A CITY A THOUSAND YEARS OLD HAS FALLEN!!
THEY MIGHT BE GRATEFUL TO US FOR SAVING THEM, BUT THAT DOES NOT MEAN...
...WE CAN ACTUALLY TELL THEM WE TRAVEL WITH SAMURAI!!
IF THEY HAPPEN TO FIND OUT...THAT WE WERE USING THIS SPOT TO MEET UP WITH KIN'EMON AND KANJURO...
...EVEN THOSE FRIENDLY MINKS ARE BOUND TO SNAP ON US.
AND I DON'T WANNA FIGHT THEM AFTER ALL OF THIS!!!
LET'S WATCH UNTIL THE MORNING, TO ENSURE THAT KIN'EMON AND KANJURO...
GRRRM...
...DO NOT ENTER THE DUKEDOM!!

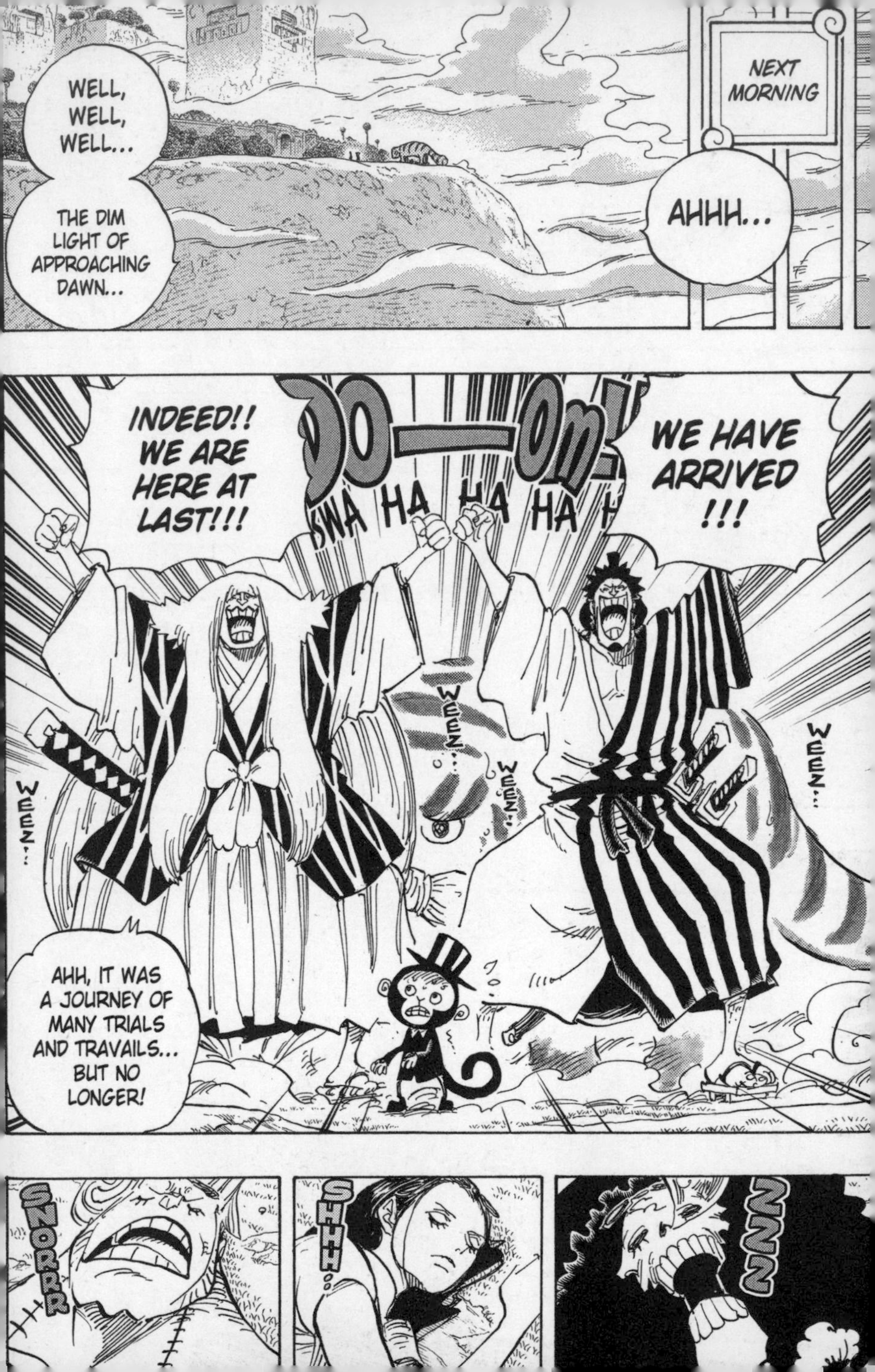
NEXT MORNING
AHHH...
WELL, WELL, WELL...
THE DIM LIGHT OF APPROACHING DAWN...
WE HAVE ARRIVED!!!
DO—OM!
INDEED!! WE ARE HERE AT LAST!!!
SWA HA HA HA
WEEZ...
WEEZ...
WEEZ...
WEEZ...
AHH, IT WAS A JOURNEY OF MANY TRIALS AND TRAVAILS... BUT NO LONGER!
ZZZ
SHHHH...
SNORRR

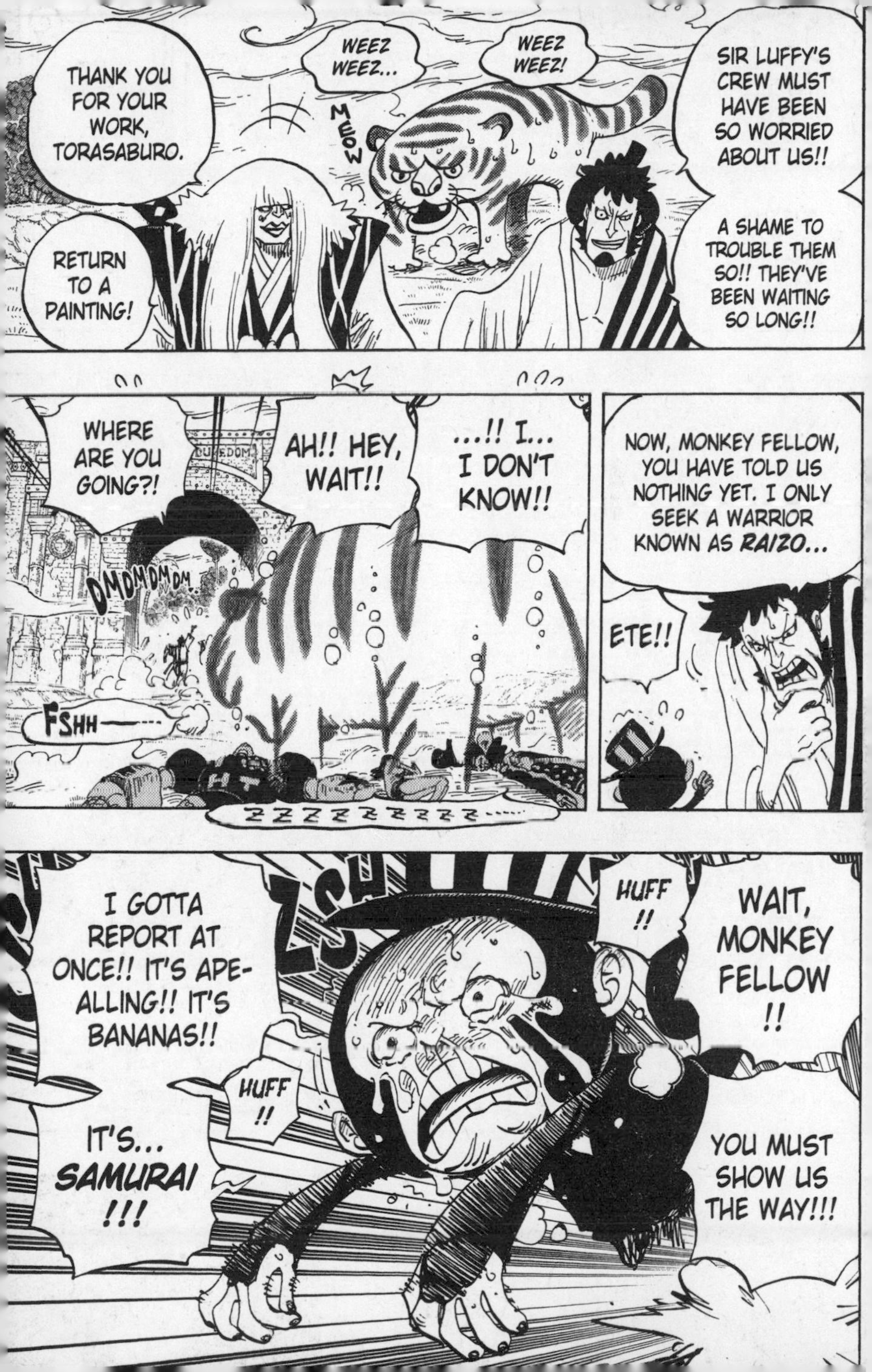

SIR LUFFY'S CREW MUST HAVE BEEN SO WORRIED ABOUT US!!
A SHAME TO TROUBLE THEM SO!! THEY'VE BEEN WAITING SO LONG!!
WEEZ WEEZ!
WEEZ WEEZ...
MEOW
THANK YOU FOR YOUR WORK, TORASABURO.
RETURN TO A PAINTING!
NOW, MONKEY FELLOW, YOU HAVE TOLD US NOTHING YET. I ONLY SEEK A WARRIOR KNOWN AS *RAIZO*...
ETE!!
...!! I... I DON'T KNOW!!
AH!! HEY, WAIT!!
WHERE ARE YOU GOING?!
DMDMDMDM
FSHH———
ZZZZZZZZZZ.....
WAIT, MONKEY FELLOW!!
HUFF!!
YOU MUST SHOW US THE WAY!!!
I GOTTA REPORT AT ONCE!! IT'S APE-ALLING!! IT'S BANANAS!!
HUFF!!
IT'S... **SAMURAI** !!!

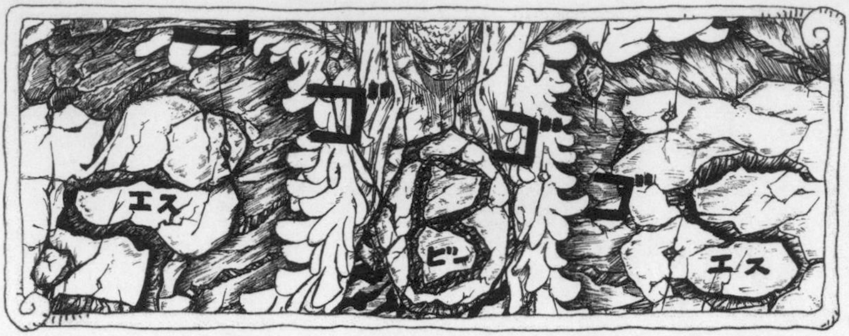
エス
ビー
エス

(Sasaaki, Okinawa)

Q: Please, Sensei, draw us a picture of Gambia's grandma back in the country!! I bet she looks so nice and sweet.
--Aminchi

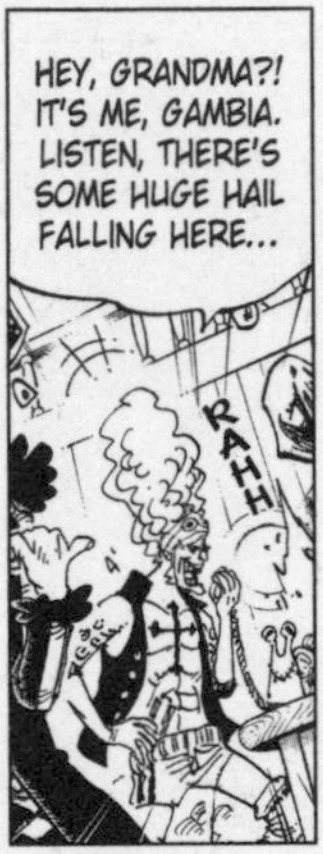
HEY, GRANDMA?! IT'S ME, GAMBIA. LISTEN, THERE'S SOME HUGE HAIL FALLING HERE...
RAHH

A:

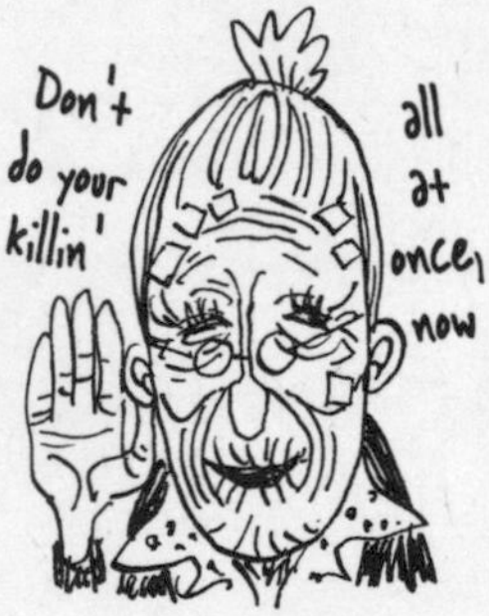
Don't do your killin' all at once, now

Here's Grandma. Technically, she's not related to anyone in the Barto Club. The club is basically just a huge street gang that grew out of a group of old pals that ran wild in the sticks. Eventually they got really obsessed with the Straw Hats, and then the best of the best of them went out to sea. As for Grandma, she owned the local candy shop that they used to hang out at, so they're all very fond of her. Her mind is packed full of folk remedies and wisdom, and she's always been a source of advice for them, given their lack of knowledge about the sea. Sometimes the advice is useful, sometimes not. (Usually not.)

Q: Hello there. In the scene where these ➡ sailors are searching for weapons and bullets, is that one guy, er...searching for his "rounds" down there? Did he find them?
--Boss Keyaki

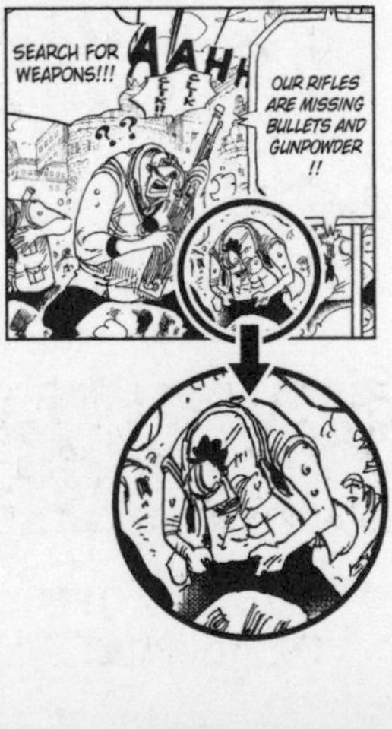
SEARCH FOR WEAPONS!!!
AAHH
OUR RIFLES ARE MISSING BULLETS AND GUNPOWDER !!

A: Have no fear. He found two.
That does it for the SBS! See you next volume!!
There's movie info and an explanation of the "World of One Piece" in the back. Check it out!

Chapter 816:
DOG VS. CAT

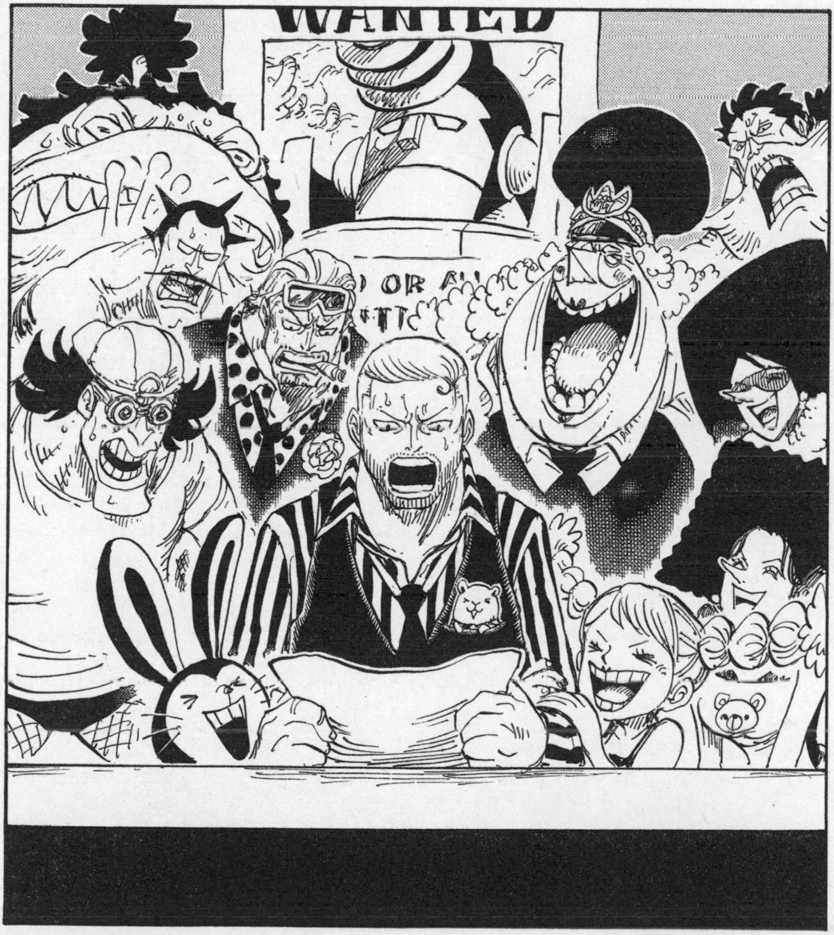

DECKS OF THE WORLD, 500-MILLION-MAN ARC,
VOL. 10: "WATER SEVEN--YOU FINALLY DID IT..."

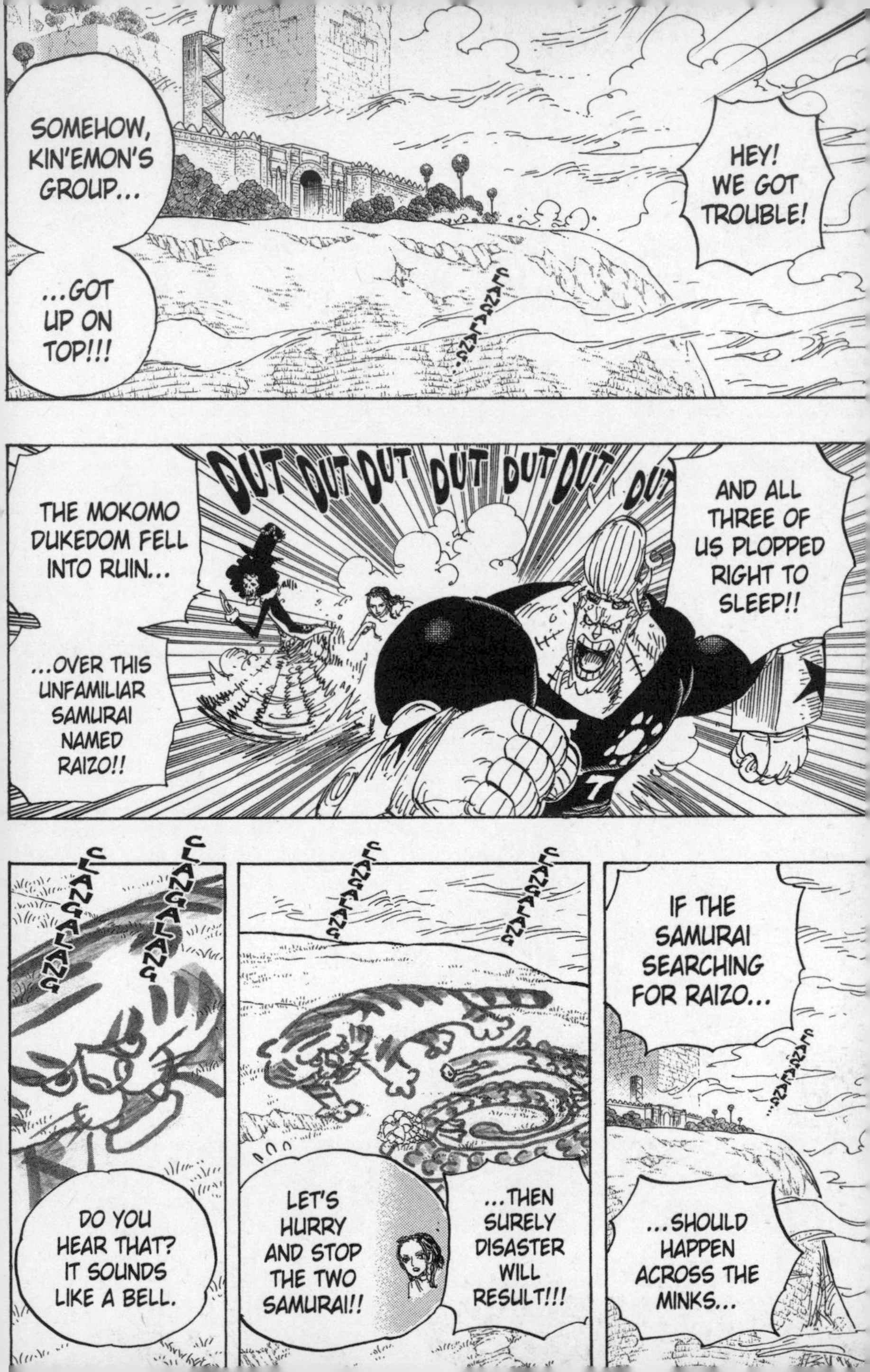

HEY! WE GOT TROUBLE!
SOMEHOW, KIN'EMON'S GROUP...
CLANGALANG...
...GOT UP ON TOP!!!
AND ALL THREE OF US PLOPPED RIGHT TO SLEEP!!
DUT DUT DUT DUT DUT DUT DUT
THE MOKOMO DUKEDOM FELL INTO RUIN...
...OVER THIS UNFAMILIAR SAMURAI NAMED RAIZO!!
IF THE SAMURAI SEARCHING FOR RAIZO...
CLANGALANG...
...SHOULD HAPPEN ACROSS THE MINKS...
CLANGALANG
CLANGALANG
...THEN SURELY DISASTER WILL RESULT!!!
LET'S HURRY AND STOP THE TWO SAMURAI!!
CLANGALANG
CLANGALANG
DO YOU HEAR THAT? IT SOUNDS LIKE A BELL.

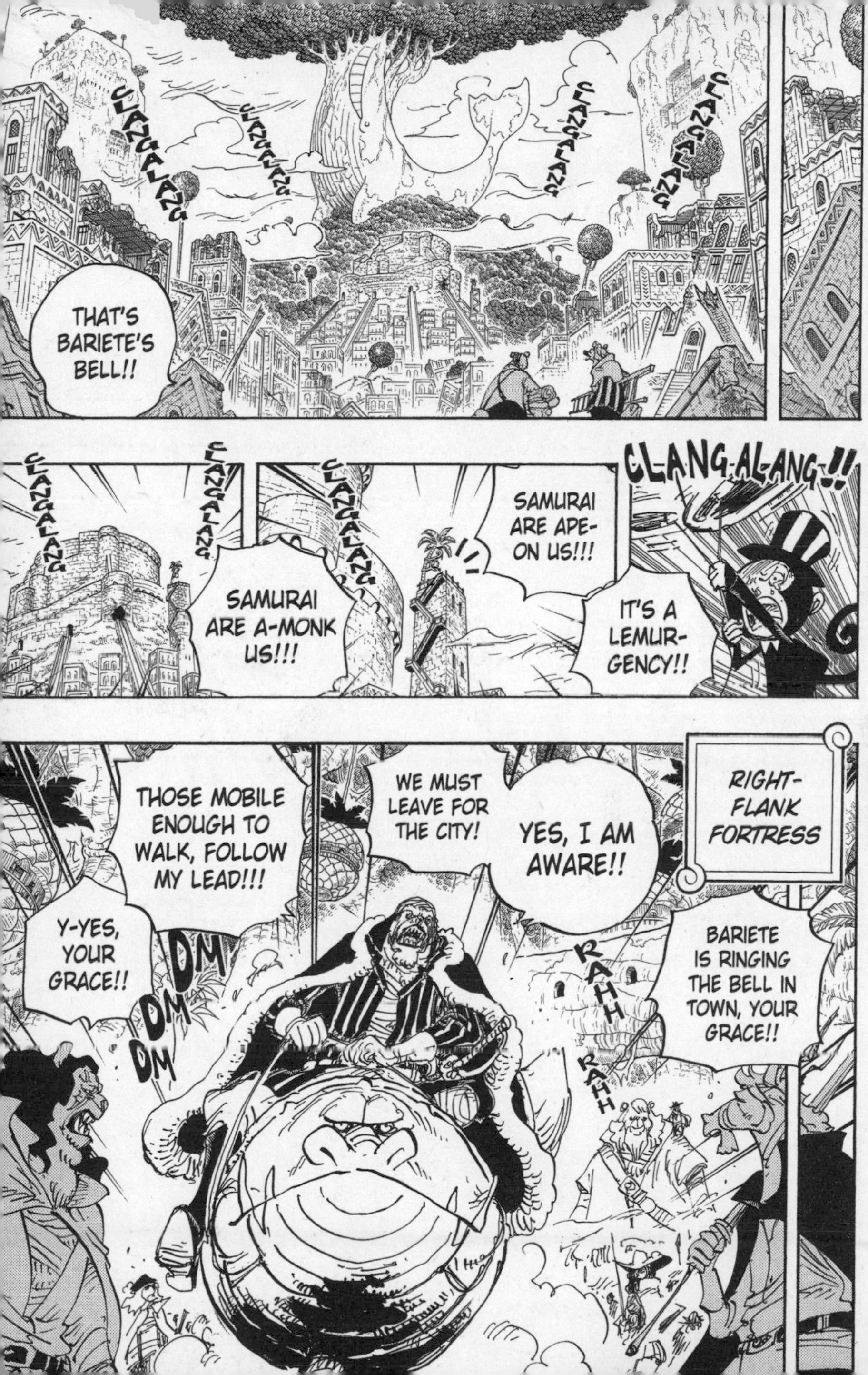
CLANGALANG
CLANGALANG
CLANGALANG
CLANGALANG
THAT'S BARIETE'S BELL!!
CLANG-ALANG!!
IT'S A LEMURGENCY!!
SAMURAI ARE APE-ON US!!!
CLANGALANG
SAMURAI ARE A-MONK US!!!
CLANGALANG
CLANGALANG
RIGHT-FLANK FORTRESS
BARIETE IS RINGING THE BELL IN TOWN, YOUR GRACE!!
YES, I AM AWARE!!
WE MUST LEAVE FOR THE CITY!
RAHH
RAHH
THOSE MOBILE ENOUGH TO WALK, FOLLOW MY LEAD!!!
Y-YES, YOUR GRACE!!
DM
DM
DM
DM

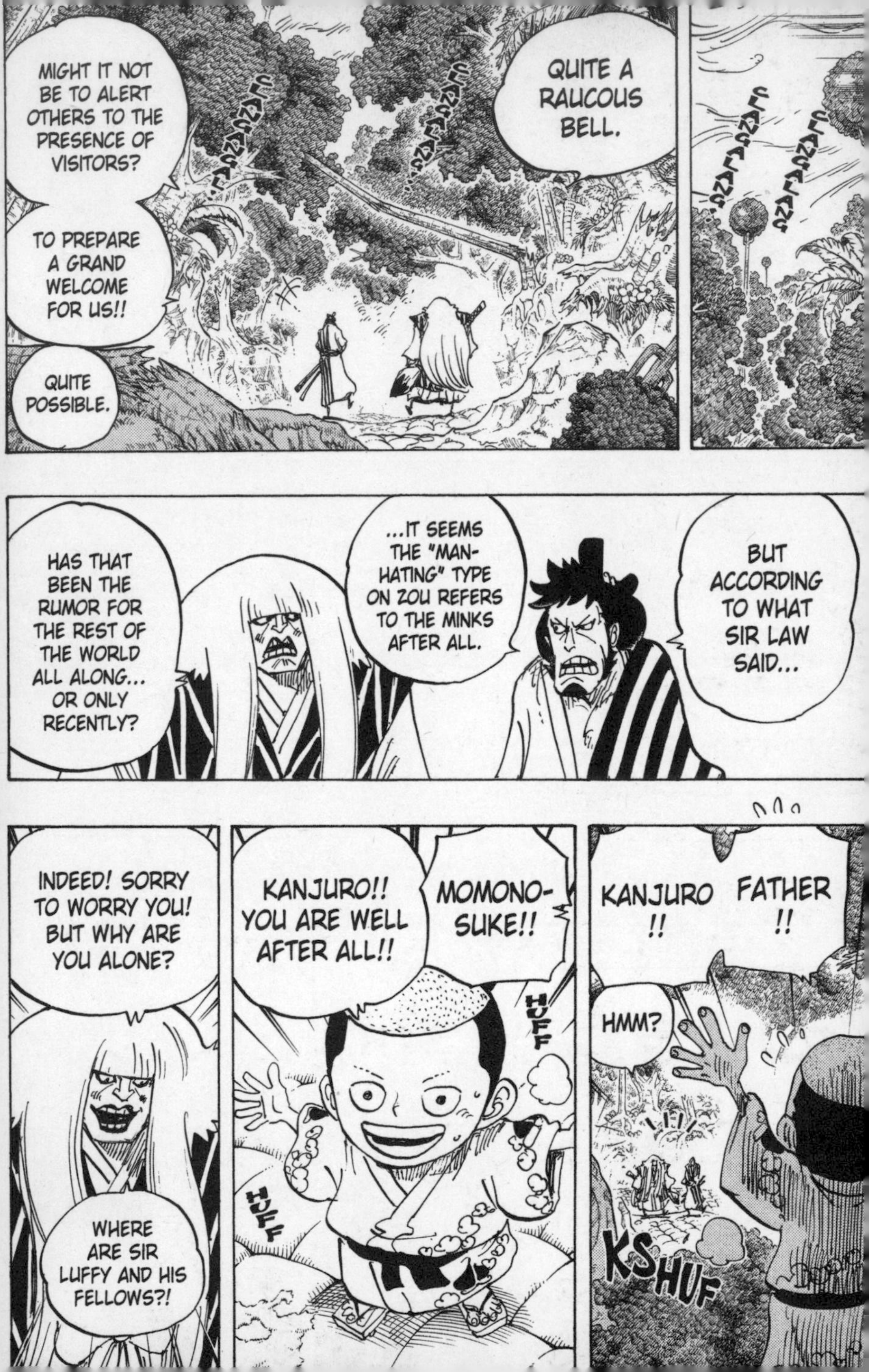
CLANGALANG
CLANGALANG
QUITE A RAUCOUS BELL.
CLANGALANG...
CLANGALANG...
MIGHT IT NOT BE TO ALERT OTHERS TO THE PRESENCE OF VISITORS?
TO PREPARE A GRAND WELCOME FOR US!!
QUITE POSSIBLE.
BUT ACCORDING TO WHAT SIR LAW SAID...
...IT SEEMS THE "MAN-HATING" TYPE ON ZOU REFERS TO THE MINKS AFTER ALL.
HAS THAT BEEN THE RUMOR FOR THE REST OF THE WORLD ALL ALONG... OR ONLY RECENTLY?
FATHER !!
KANJURO !!
HMM?
KSHUF
MOMONO-SUKE!!
KANJURO!! YOU ARE WELL AFTER ALL!!
HUFF
HUFF
INDEED! SORRY TO WORRY YOU! BUT WHY ARE YOU ALONE?
WHERE ARE SIR LUFFY AND HIS FELLOWS?!

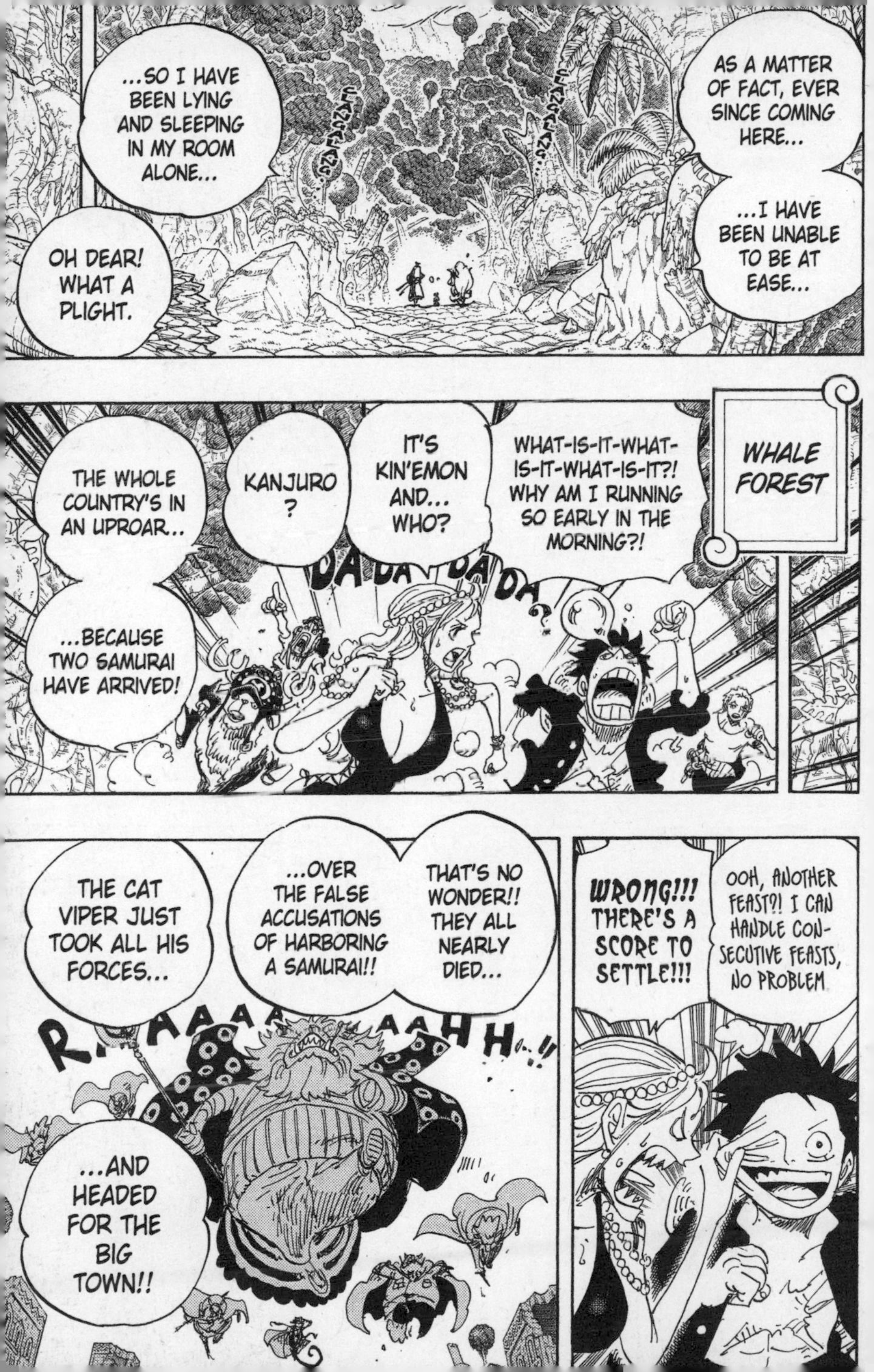
AS A MATTER OF FACT, EVER SINCE COMING HERE...
...I HAVE BEEN UNABLE TO BE AT EASE...
CLANGALANG...
CLANGALANG...
...SO I HAVE BEEN LYING AND SLEEPING IN MY ROOM ALONE...
OH DEAR! WHAT A PLIGHT.
WHALE FOREST
WHAT-IS-IT-WHAT-IS-IT-WHAT-IS-IT?! WHY AM I RUNNING SO EARLY IN THE MORNING?!
IT'S KIN'EMON AND... WHO?
KANJURO?
THE WHOLE COUNTRY'S IN AN UPROAR...
...BECAUSE TWO SAMURAI HAVE ARRIVED!
DA DA DA DA
OOH, ANOTHER FEAST?! I CAN HANDLE CONSECUTIVE FEASTS, NO PROBLEM
WRONG!!! THERE'S A SCORE TO SETTLE!!!
THAT'S NO WONDER!! THEY ALL NEARLY DIED...
...OVER THE FALSE ACCUSATIONS OF HARBORING A SAMURAI!!
THE CAT VIPER JUST TOOK ALL HIS FORCES...
R...AAAAAAAAHH..!!
...AND HEADED FOR THE BIG TOWN!!

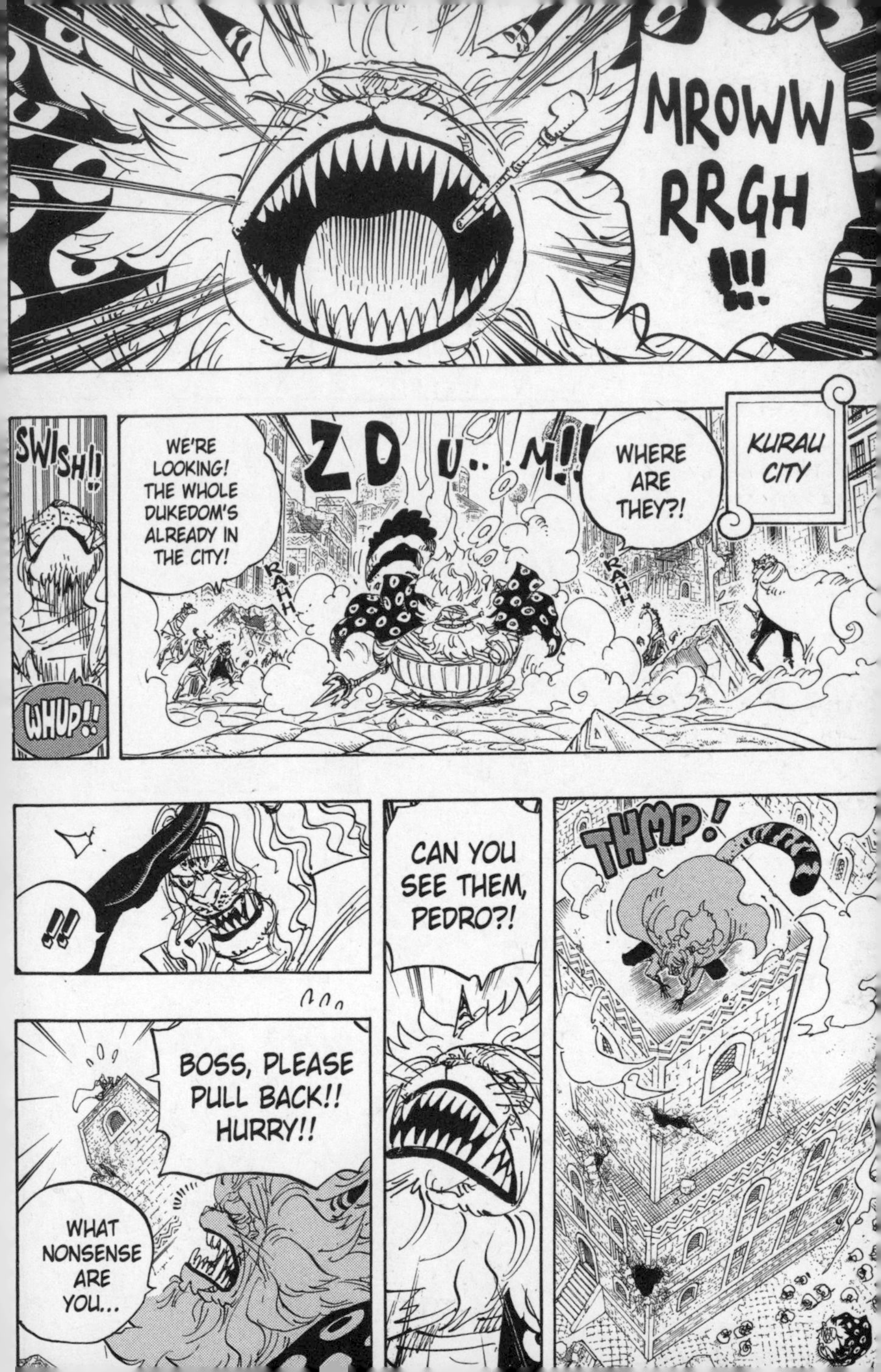
MROWW RRGH!!!
KURAU CITY
WHERE ARE THEY?!
ZD U.. M!!
RAHH
WE'RE LOOKING! THE WHOLE DUKEDOM'S ALREADY IN THE CITY!
RAHH
SWISH!!
WHUP!!
THMP!
CAN YOU SEE THEM, PEDRO?!
!!
BOSS, PLEASE PULL BACK!! HURRY!!
WHAT NONSENSE ARE YOU...

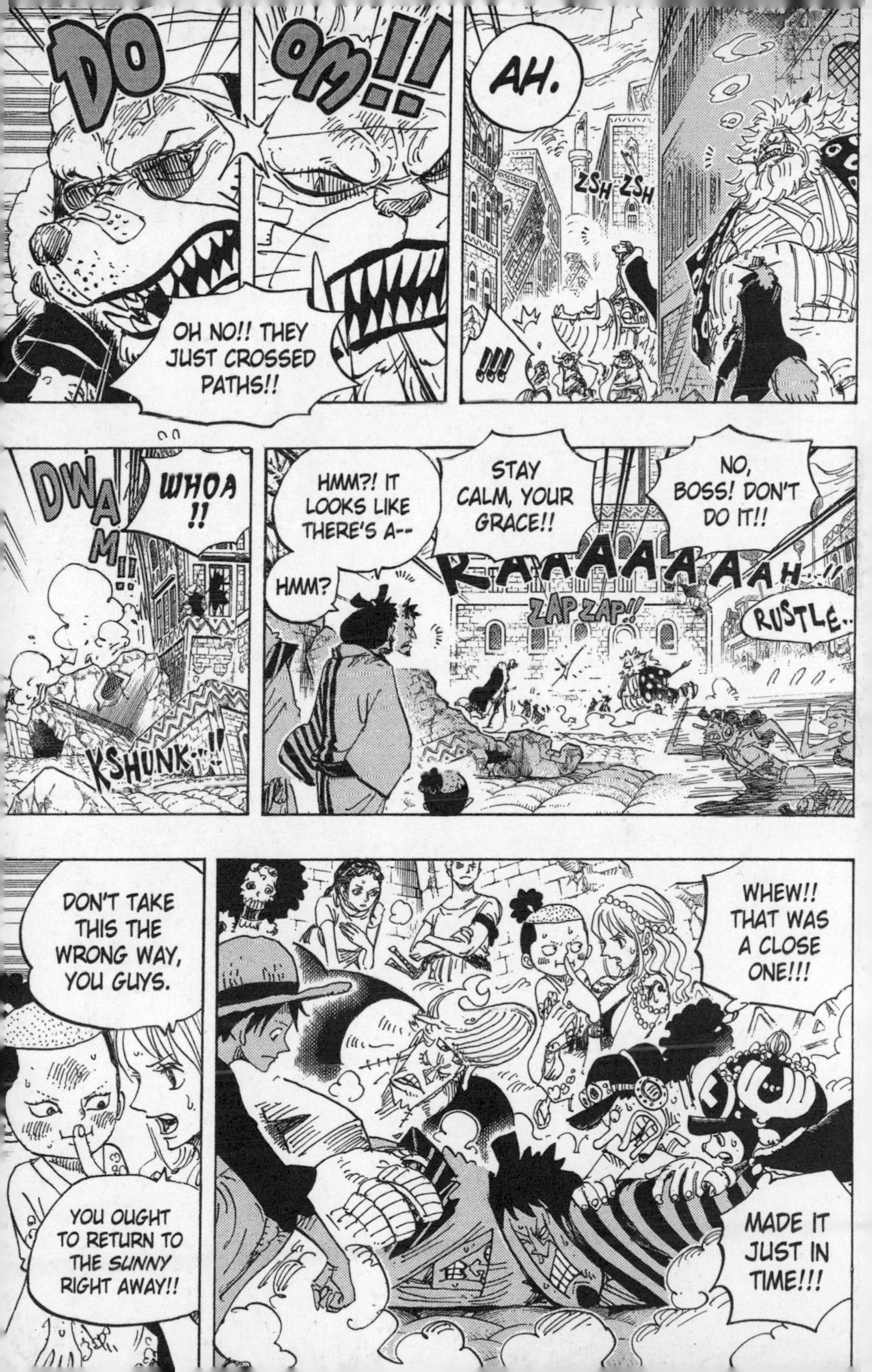
AH.
ZSH ZSH
!!!
DOOM!!
OH NO!! THEY JUST CROSSED PATHS!!
NO, BOSS! DON'T DO IT!!
STAY CALM, YOUR GRACE!!
HMM?! IT LOOKS LIKE THERE'S A--
RAAAAAAAAH!!
RUSTLE...
ZAP ZAP!!
HMM?
WHOA!!
DWAM!!
KSHUNK!!
WHEW!! THAT WAS A CLOSE ONE!!!
MADE IT JUST IN TIME!!!
DON'T TAKE THIS THE WRONG WAY, YOU GUYS.
YOU OUGHT TO RETURN TO THE *SUNNY* RIGHT AWAY!!

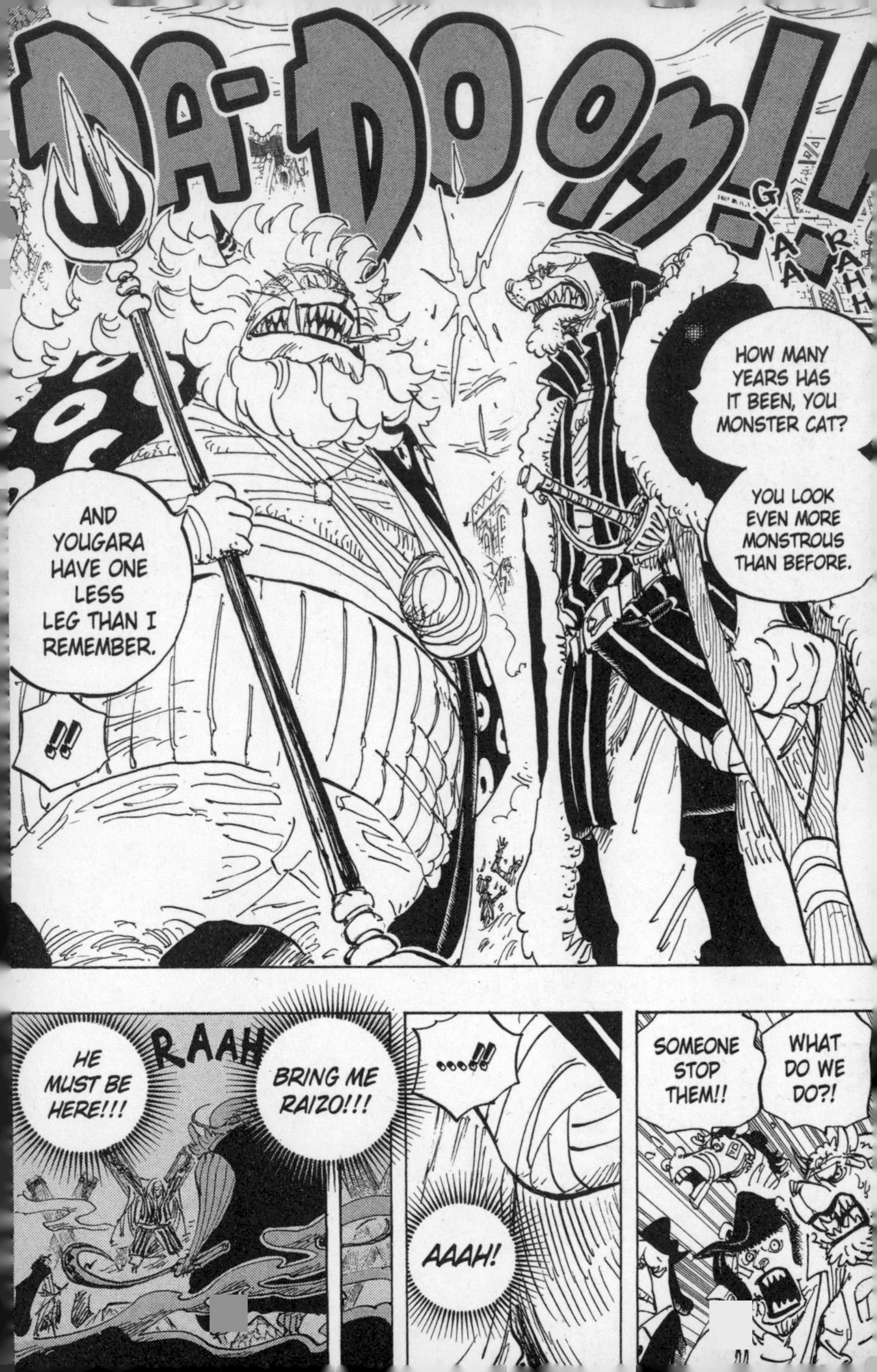
DA-DOOM!!
HOW MANY YEARS HAS IT BEEN, YOU MONSTER CAT?
YOU LOOK EVEN MORE MONSTROUS THAN BEFORE.
AND YOUGARA HAVE ONE LESS LEG THAN I REMEMBER.
!!
WHAT DO WE DO?!
SOMEONE STOP THEM!!
...!!
AAAH!
BRING ME RAIZO!!!
RAAH
HE MUST BE HERE!!!

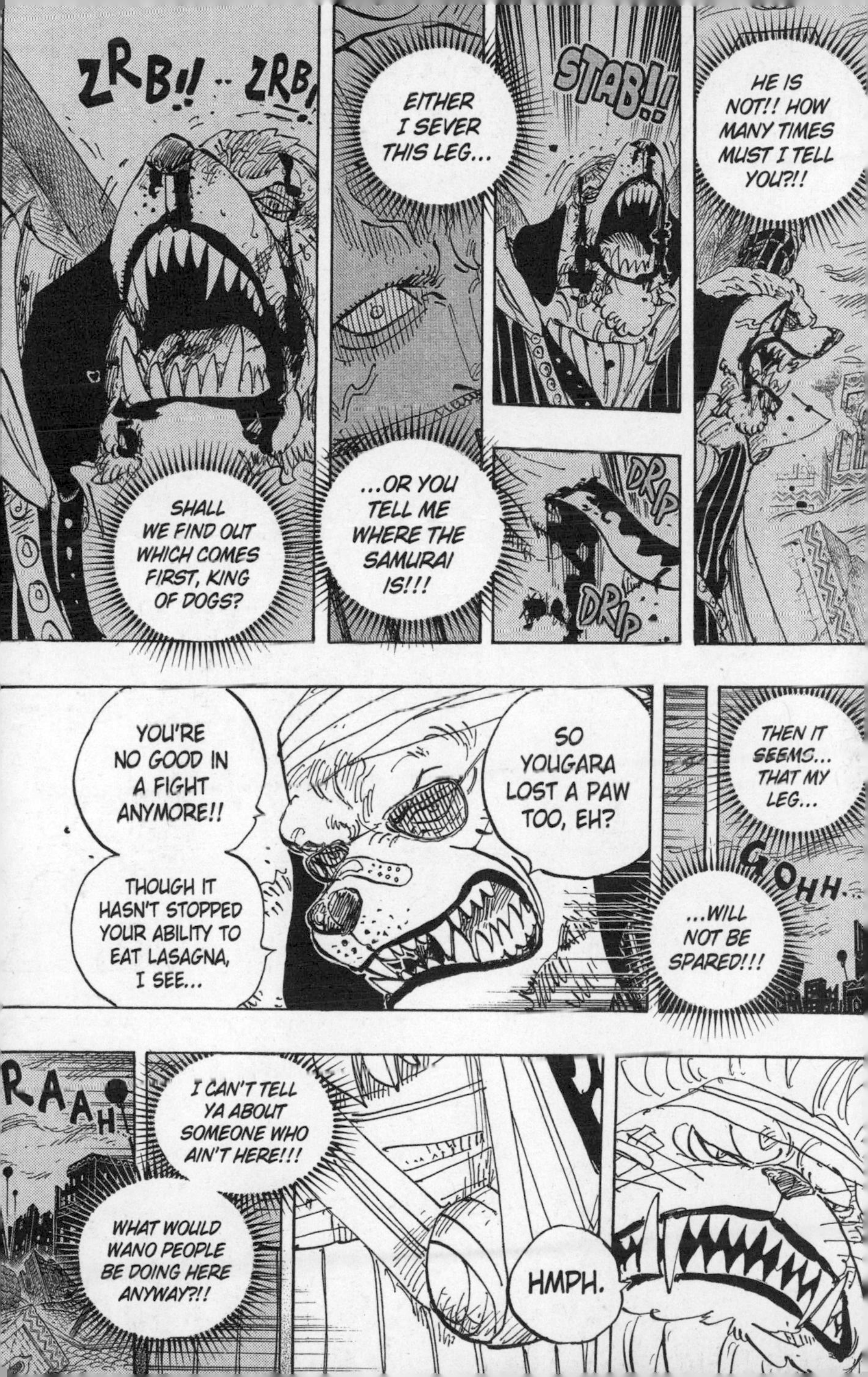
HE IS NOT!! HOW MANY TIMES MUST I TELL YOU?!!
STAB!!
DRIP
DRIP
EITHER I SEVER THIS LEG...
...OR YOU TELL ME WHERE THE SAMURAI IS!!!
ZRB!! .. ZRB
SHALL WE FIND OUT WHICH COMES FIRST, KING OF DOGS?
THEN IT SEEMS... THAT MY LEG...
GOHH...
...WILL NOT BE SPARED!!!
SO YOUGARA LOST A PAW TOO, EH?
YOU'RE NO GOOD IN A FIGHT ANYMORE!!
THOUGH IT HASN'T STOPPED YOUR ABILITY TO EAT LASAGNA, I SEE...
HMPH.
I CAN'T TELL YA ABOUT SOMEONE WHO AIN'T HERE!!!
WHAT WOULD WANO PEOPLE BE DOING HERE ANYWAY?!!
RAAH

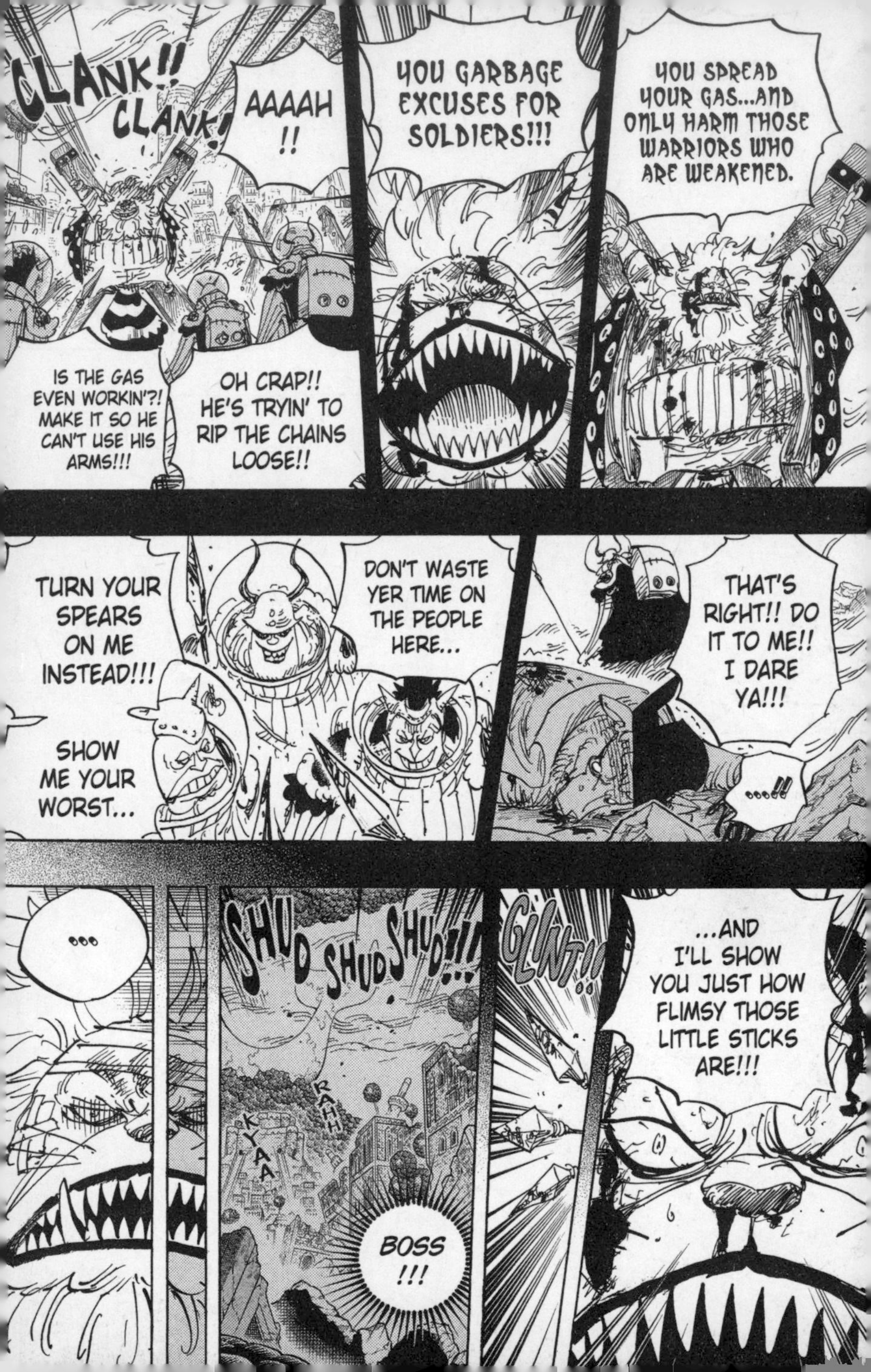

YOU SPREAD YOUR GAS...AND ONLY HARM THOSE WARRIORS WHO ARE WEAKENED.
YOU GARBAGE EXCUSES FOR SOLDIERS!!!
CLANK!! CLANK!!
AAAAH !!
OH CRAP!! HE'S TRYIN' TO RIP THE CHAINS LOOSE!!
IS THE GAS EVEN WORKIN'?! MAKE IT SO HE CAN'T USE HIS ARMS!!!
THAT'S RIGHT!! DO IT TO ME!! I DARE YA!!!
...!!
DON'T WASTE YER TIME ON THE PEOPLE HERE...
TURN YOUR SPEARS ON ME INSTEAD!!!
SHOW ME YOUR WORST...
...AND I'LL SHOW YOU JUST HOW FLIMSY THOSE LITTLE STICKS ARE!!!
GLINT!!
SHUD SHUD SHUD!!!
RAHH
KYAA
BOSS !!!
...

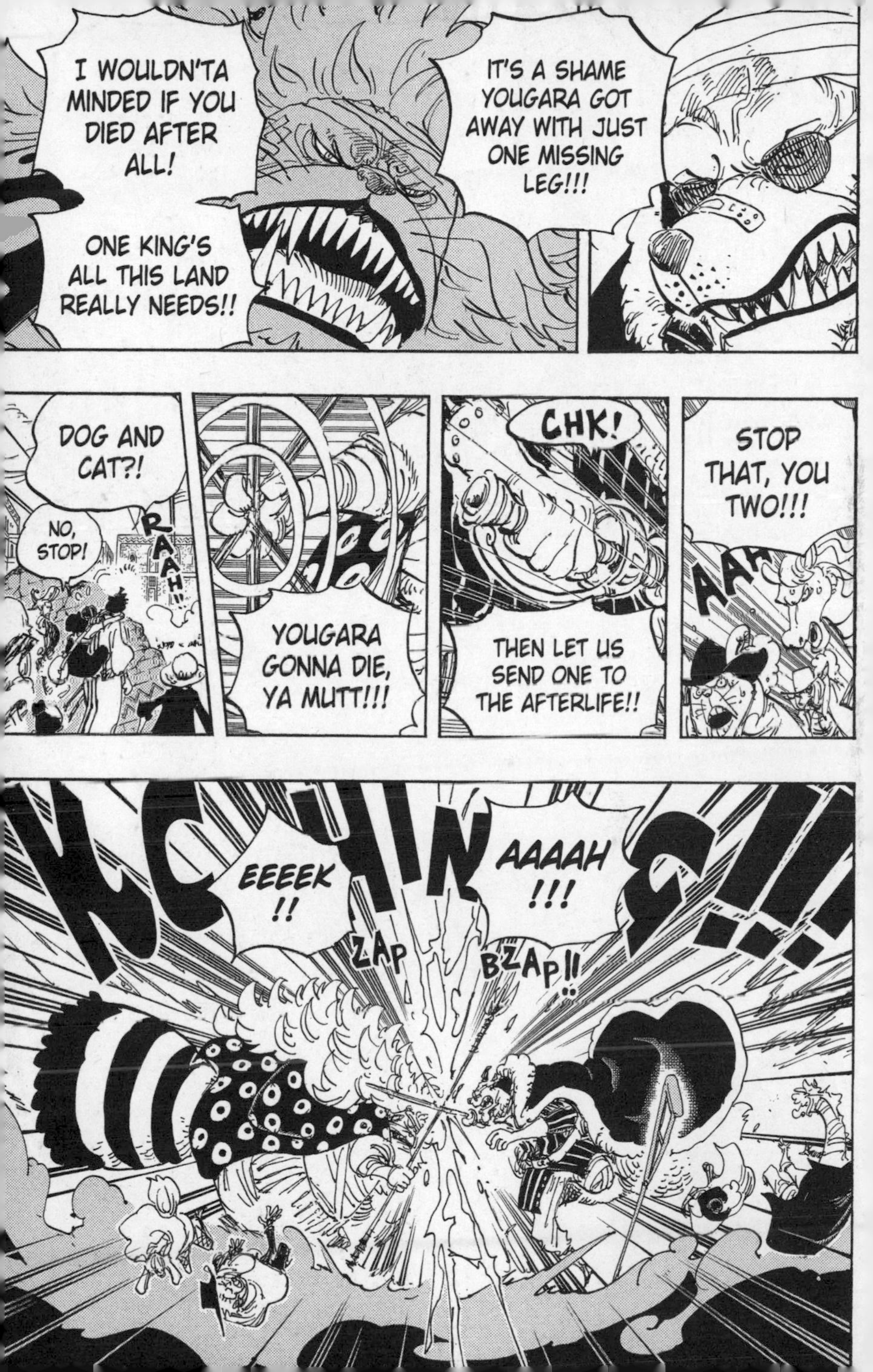
IT'S A SHAME YOUGARA GOT AWAY WITH JUST ONE MISSING LEG!!!
I WOULDN'TA MINDED IF YOU DIED AFTER ALL!
ONE KING'S ALL THIS LAND REALLY NEEDS!!
STOP THAT, YOU TWO!!!
CHK!
THEN LET US SEND ONE TO THE AFTERLIFE!!
YOUGARA GONNA DIE, YA MUTT!!!
DOG AND CAT?!
RAAH!!
NO, STOP!
AAAAH !!!
EEEEK !!
BZAP!!
ZAP

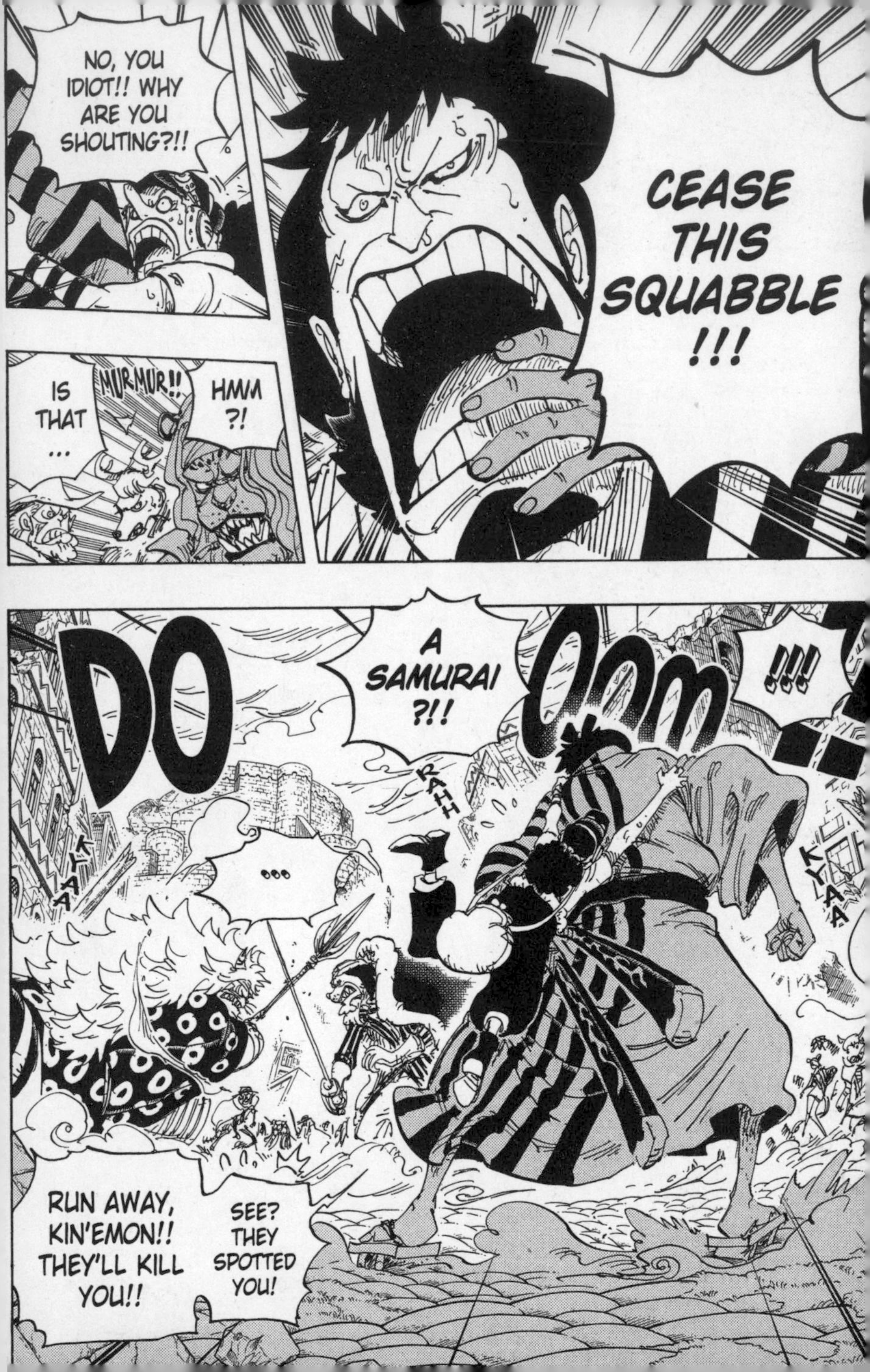
CEASE THIS SQUABBLE !!!
NO, YOU IDIOT!! WHY ARE YOU SHOUTING?!!
HMM ?!
MURMUR!!
IS THAT ...
DO
OOM...!!!
A SAMURAI ?!!
RAHH
KYAA
...
KYAA
SEE? THEY SPOTTED YOU!
RUN AWAY, KIN'EMON!! THEY'LL KILL YOU!!

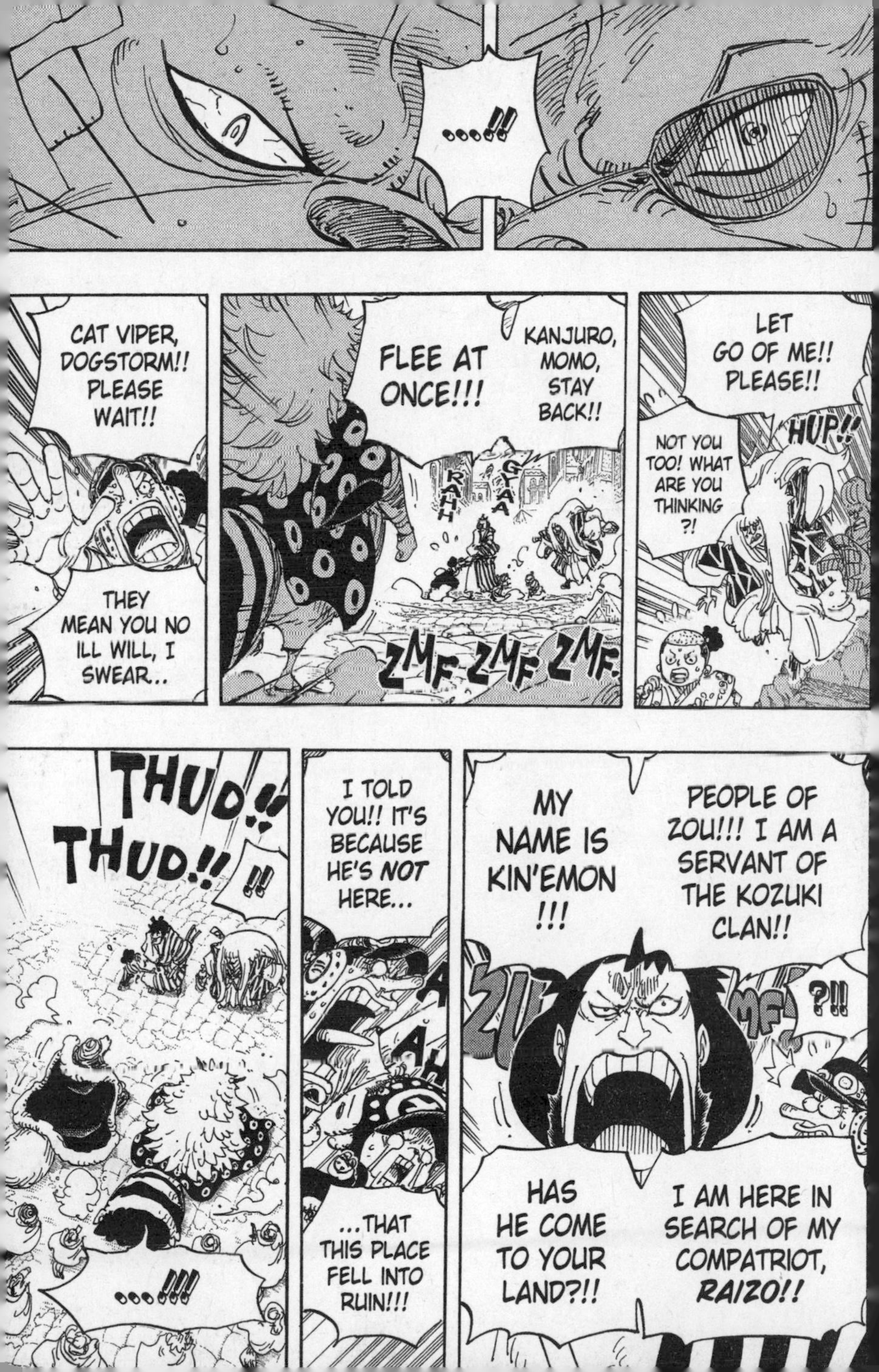
...!!
LET GO OF ME!! PLEASE!!
HUP!!
NOT YOU TOO! WHAT ARE YOU THINKING ?!
KANJURO, MOMO, STAY BACK!!
FLEE AT ONCE!!!
GYAA
RAHH
ZMF ZMF ZMF
CAT VIPER, DOGSTORM!! PLEASE WAIT!!
THEY MEAN YOU NO ILL WILL, I SWEAR...
PEOPLE OF ZOU!!! I AM A SERVANT OF THE KOZUKI CLAN!!
MY NAME IS KIN'EMON !!!
?!!
I AM HERE IN SEARCH OF MY COMPATRIOT, *RAIZO!!*
HAS HE COME TO YOUR LAND?!!
I TOLD YOU!! IT'S BECAUSE HE'S *NOT* HERE...
...THAT THIS PLACE FELL INTO RUIN!!!
THUD!!
THUD!!
!!
...!!!

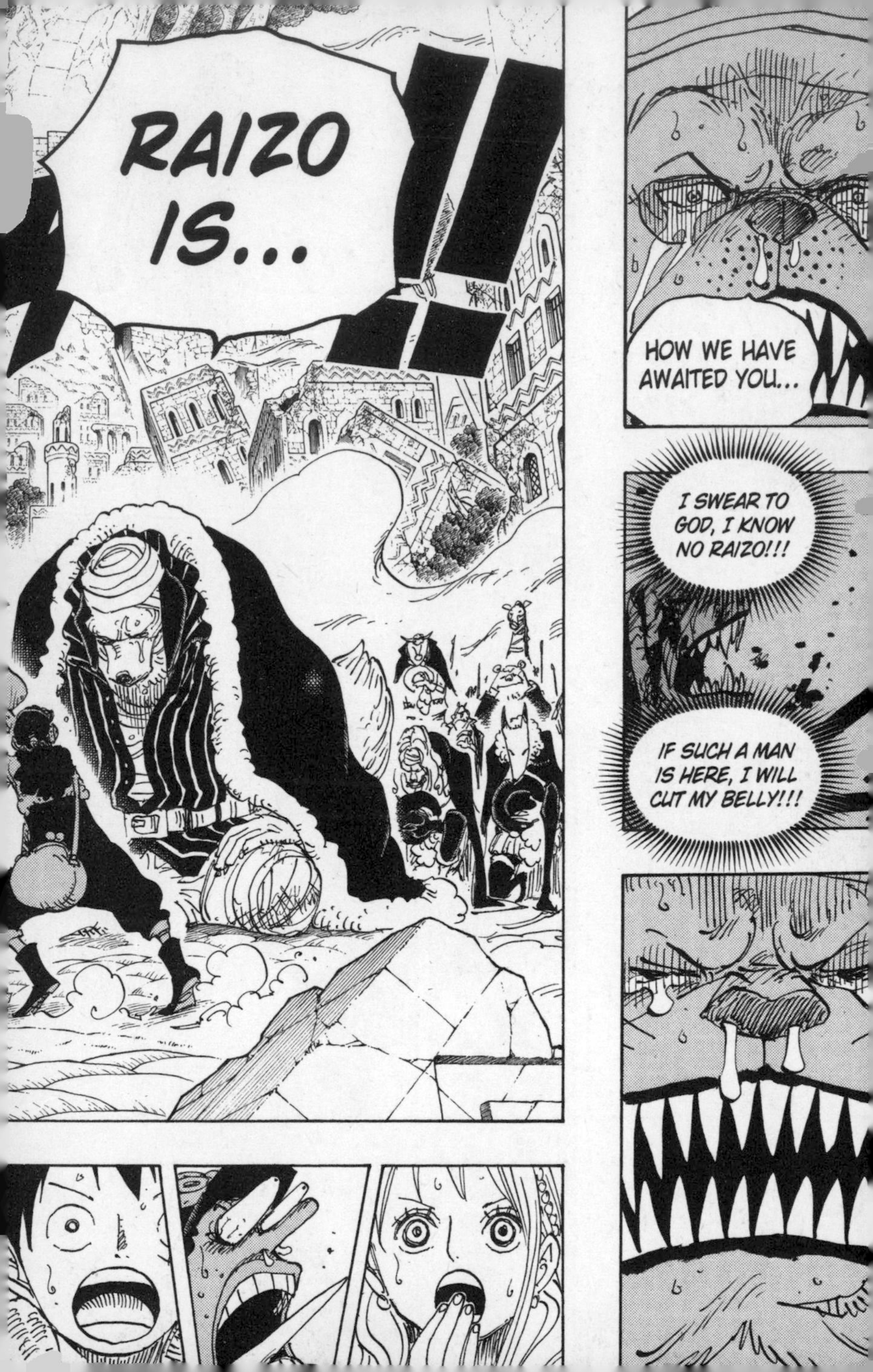
HOW WE HAVE AWAITED YOU...
I SWEAR TO GOD, I KNOW NO RAIZO!!!
IF SUCH A MAN IS HERE, I WILL CUT MY BELLY!!!
RAIZO IS...!!

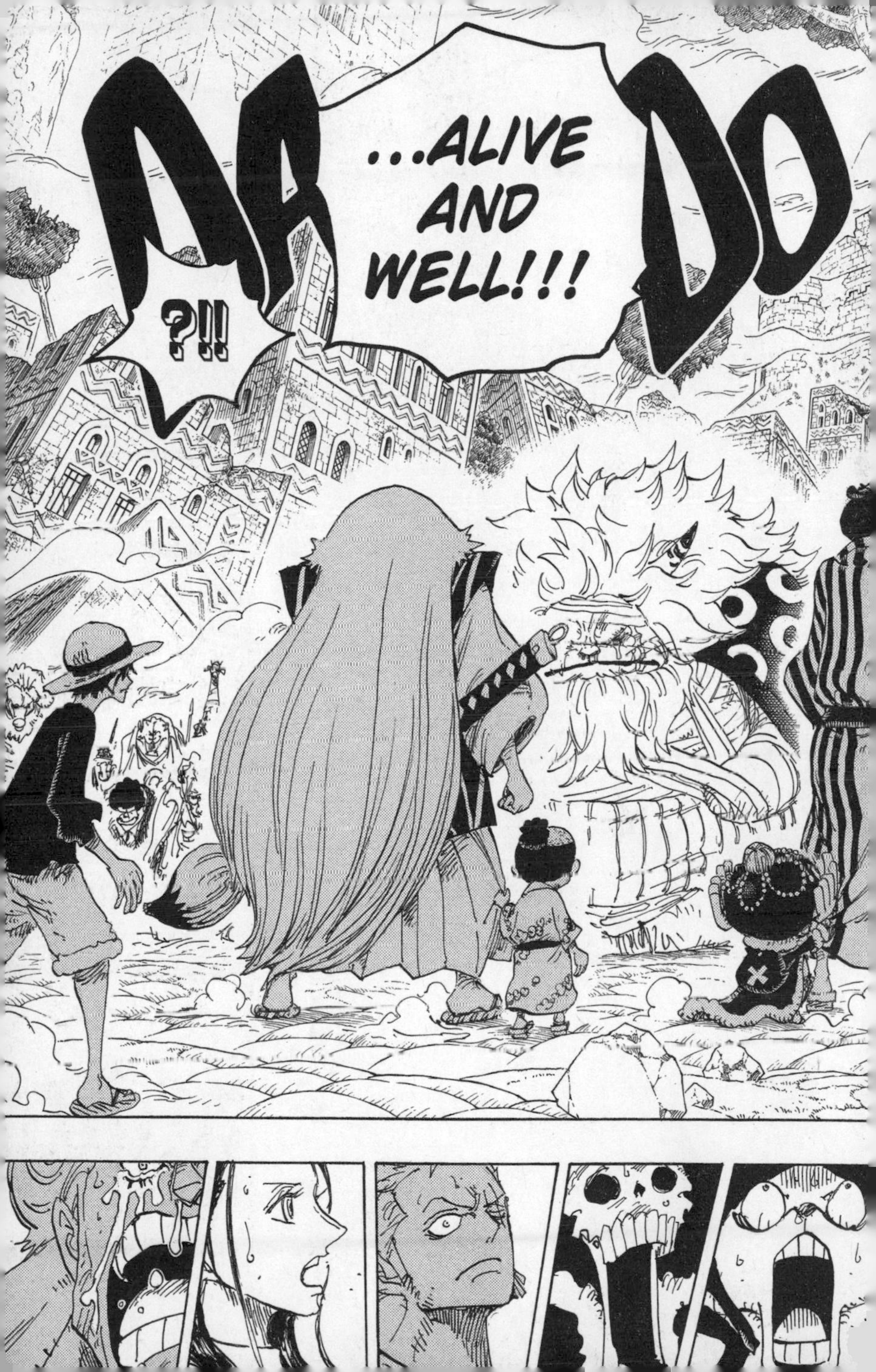
DO
DA
...ALIVE AND WELL!!!
?!!

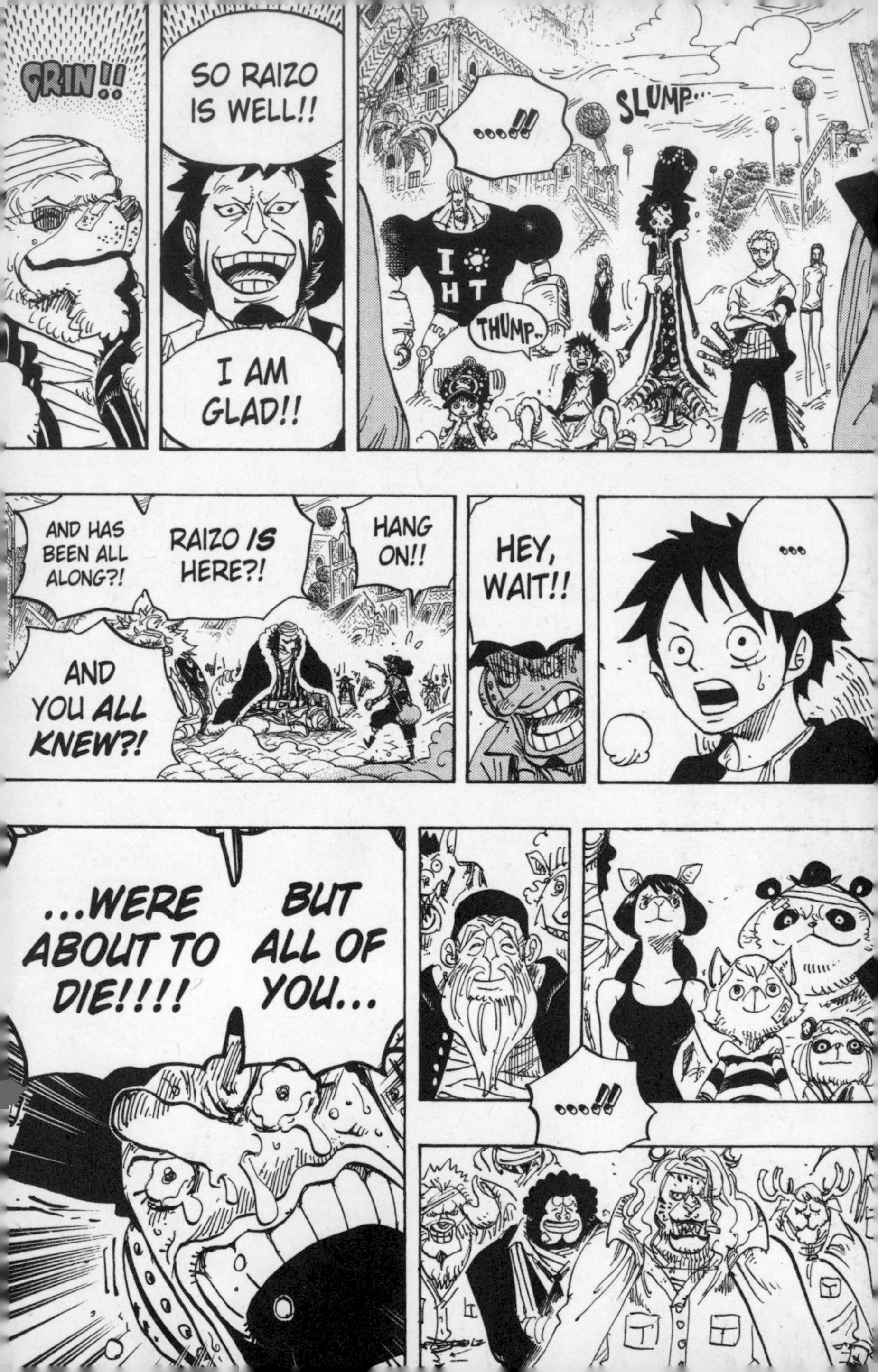
...!!
SLUMP...
THUMP...
SO RAIZO IS WELL!!
I AM GLAD!!
GRIN!!
...
HEY, WAIT!!
HANG ON!!
RAIZO IS HERE?!
AND HAS BEEN ALL ALONG?!
AND YOU ALL KNEW?!
...!!
BUT ALL OF YOU...
...WERE ABOUT TO DIE!!!!

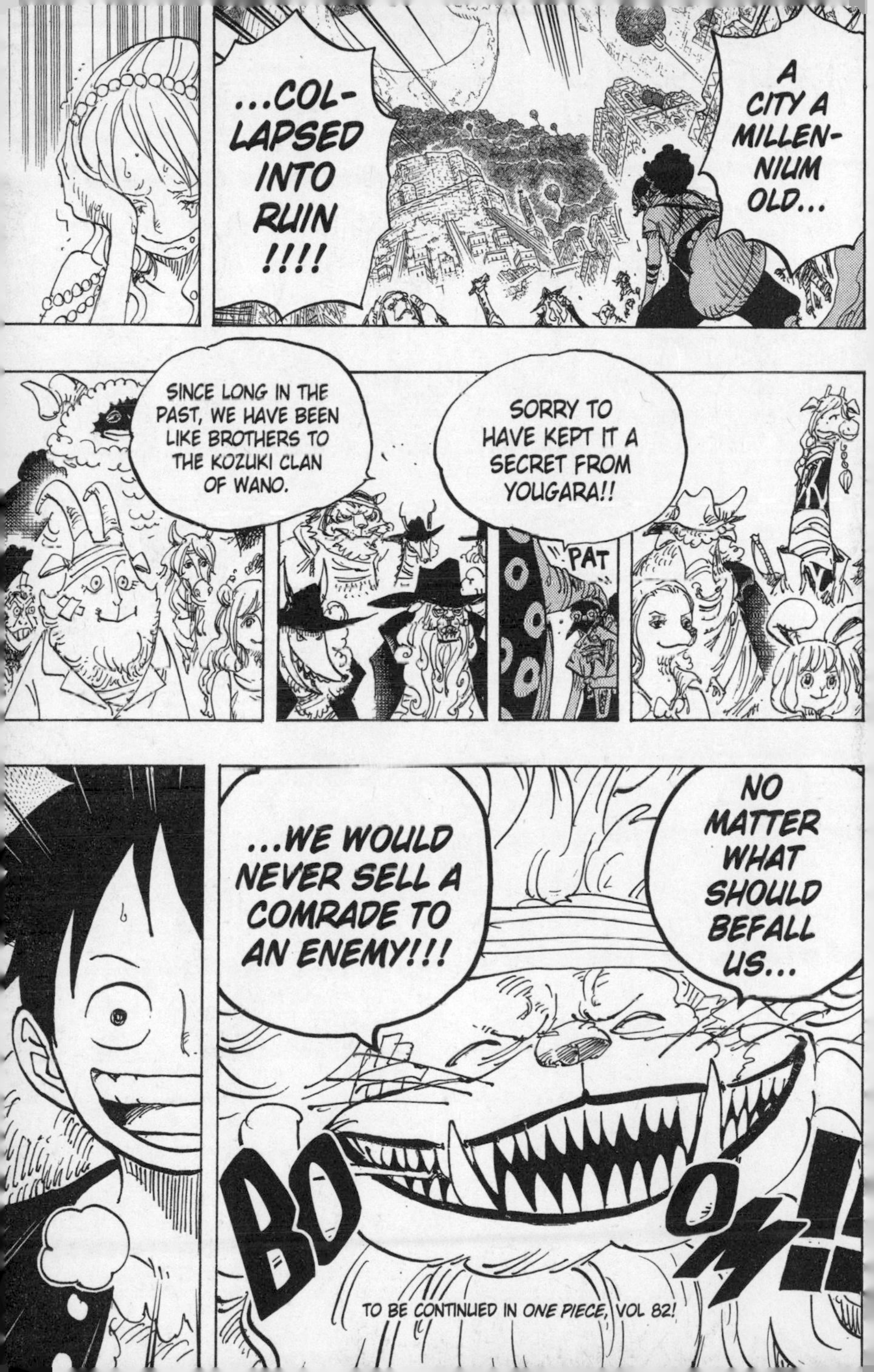
A CITY A MILLEN-NIUM OLD...
...COL-LAPSED INTO RUIN !!!!
SORRY TO HAVE KEPT IT A SECRET FROM YOUGARA!!
PAT
SINCE LONG IN THE PAST, WE HAVE BEEN LIKE BROTHERS TO THE KOZUKI CLAN OF WANO.
NO MATTER WHAT SHOULD BEFALL US...
...WE WOULD NEVER SELL A COMRADE TO AN ENEMY!!!
BOOM!!
TO BE CONTINUED IN ONE PIECE, VOL 82!

Understand the course of adventure!

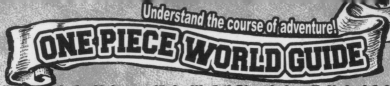

ONE PIECE WORLD GUIDE

You want an explanation of the four seas and the Grand Line that Luffy's crew has been sailing? Look no further!

RED LINE

The enormous continent that cuts the seas into two. At its peak, it pierces the clouds, making it difficult terrain to cross by land.

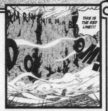

THIS IS THE RED LINE!!!

The Red Line and Grand Line split the water into four seas!!

The perpendicular paths of the Grand Line and Red Line intersect in a way that splits the world into four major seas.

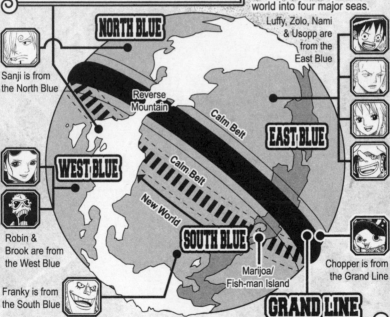

NORTH BLUE
Sanji is from the North Blue
Luffy, Zolo, Nami & Usopp are from the East Blue
Reverse Mountain
Calm Belt
EAST BLUE
WEST BLUE
Calm Belt
New World
Robin & Brook are from the West Blue
SOUTH BLUE
Marijoa/ Fish-man Island
Chopper is from the Grand Line
Franky is from the South Blue
GRAND LINE

Travel through the Grand Line using a Log Pose!!

LOG POSE

A special stretch of sea that runs along all four seas around the world, bordered by the Calm Belt on either side. It features baffling currents and weather patterns - navigation is impossible without a Log Pose.

?
WHUP
WHUP
...!!
SPLASH
SPLASH
SPLASH
SPLASH

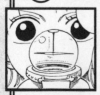

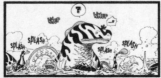

←The Calm Belts that border the Grand Line are home to Neptunians. They're impossible to cross without equipment like the Navy's sea prism stone-lined ships.

A Cheat-Sheet Guide to the Straw Hat Travels!

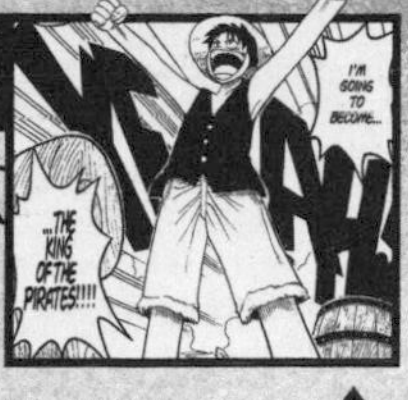
I'M GOING TO BECOME...
...THE KING OF THE PIRATES!!!!

We set sail from Windmill Village in the East Blue!!

Luffy's crew is on the way to Raftel. The journey from Reverse Mountain to Fish-man Island puts them about half of the way to their goal.

East Blue

Zolo joins at Shells Town!!

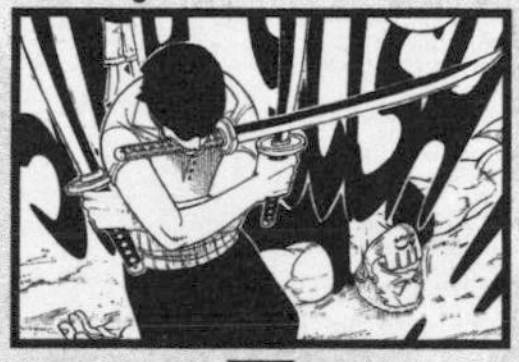

Once freed, Zolo is on board!

Usopp joins at Syrup Village!!

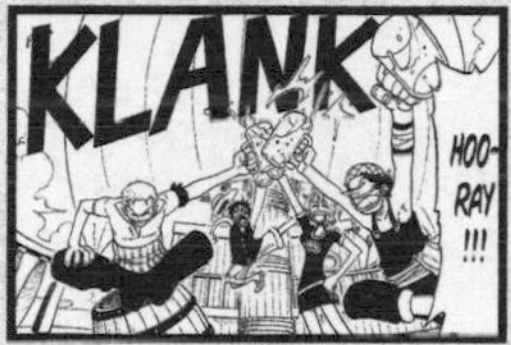
KLANK
HOO-RAY !!!

He brings the *Merry Go* with him!!

Sanji joins at Baratie!!

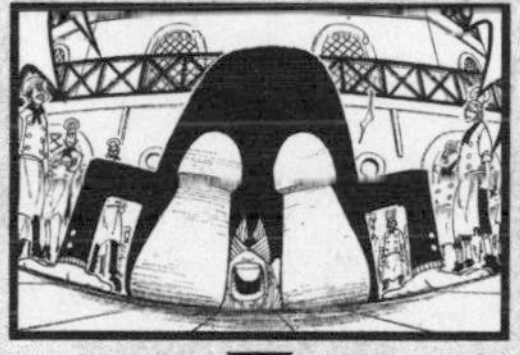

Sanji comes after the battle here.

Nami's officially in at Cocoyashi!!

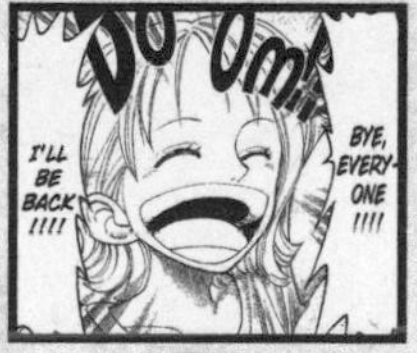
BYE, EVERY-ONE !!!!
I'LL BE BACK !!!!

The defeat of Arlong frees Nami at last.

Cross Reverse Mountain to the Grand Line!!

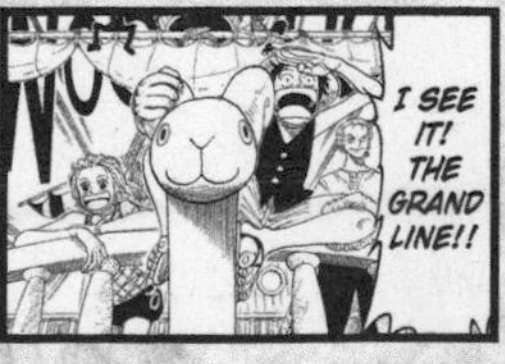
I SEE IT! THE GRAND LINE!!

This is where the Grand Line voyage begins!

Grand Line (First Half)

Chopper joins at Drum Kingdom!!

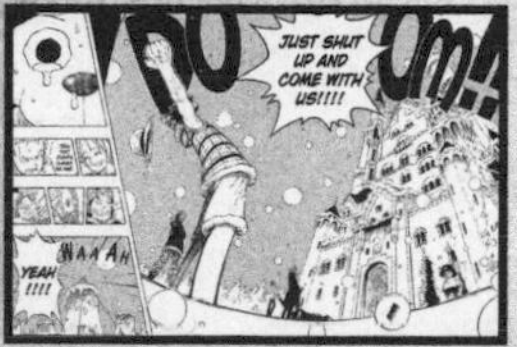
JUST SHUT UP AND COME WITH US!!!!
YEAH !!!!

Inviting Chopper, the doctor reindeer.

Robin joins at Alabasta!!

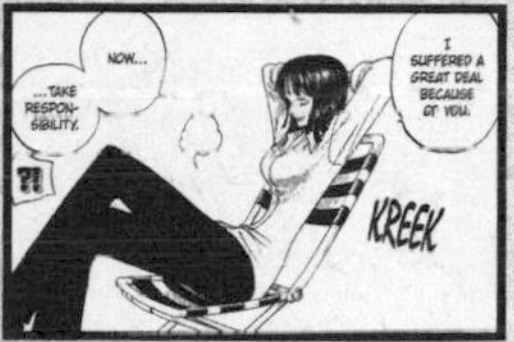
I SUFFERED A GREAT DEAL BECAUSE OF YOU.
NOW...
...TAKE RESPON-SIBILITY.
?!
KREEK

Croco-dile's former partner switches sides.

Franky joins at Water Seven!!

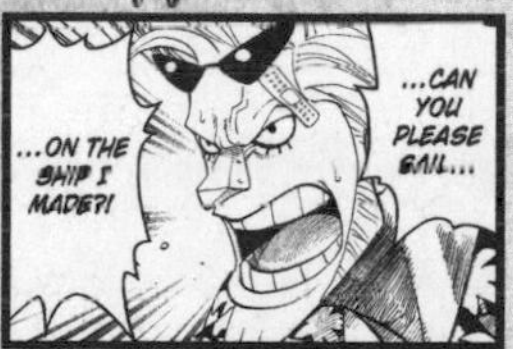
...CAN YOU PLEASE SAIL...
...ON THE SHIP I MADE?!

The ship-wright comes along with the *Sunny*.

Brook joins at the Florian Triangle!!

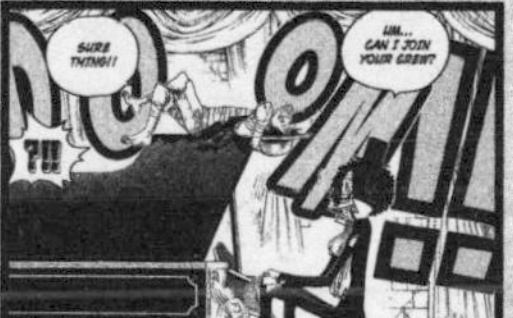
UM... CAN I JOIN YOUR CREW?
SURE THING!!
?!!

Once his shadow is back from Thriller Bark.

New World (Second Half)

And on to the New World!!

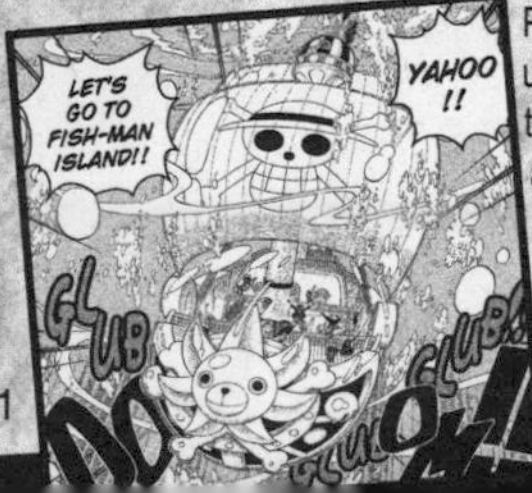
YAHOO !!
LET'S GO TO FISH-MAN ISLAND!!
GLUB
GLUB

Powered up after two years and ready for Fish-man Island!!

KEY

WE'RE PUTTING OUT A MOVIE ON 7.23

A: Saturday, July 23, 2016!! Our first animated film in three years!! July, right during summer vacation! Isn't summer great? How would you like a nice juicy slice of entertainment this summer?! Well, the entire staff is panting and wheezing to bring it to you!! It's called **Gold!!** And this movie is going to be **Cool** and **Gorgeous!!** What is my role in the project? Boom!

Executive Producer: Eiichiro Oda

★ Hey. Hi! I'm a guy who's pretty good at making One Piece!! I'm the secret mastermind behind the movie. I make everyone tea! (Just kidding.) I promise that we'll bring you something cool!! So right off the bat, I want to reassure you all of its quality! Here he is, the life of the film!!

Art Director: Masayuki Sato

★ Yes, it's "Satomasa"!! (Eek!) The adventurer who brought a new breath of life to the One Piece movies!! He has agreed to work with us again!! I put him through so much hell the last two times that I was certain he wouldn't agree to do it again (cries). Thank you so much, I really mean it!! He might look laid-back, but a burning passion hides behind those features!! The power of art!! Watch this movie closely!! Also, check out this fun guy who wrote the script!

Screenplay: Tsutomu Kuroiwa

★ Okay, this part is important too!! It's a very talented writer, the clever Mr. Kuroiwa! Not only does he have an accomplished career, he's a sharp writer with a resiliency that rolls with the punches. He wrote us up a truly dynamic story!! I hope you're excited about Film Gold!! He also put in work on the summer TV special that ties in with the movie! That one's good too! Check it out!!

■ Tsutomu Kuroiwa
Screenwriter. His main credits are the *After-Dinner Mysteries* and *Liar Game* series, and the drama series *Welcome to My Home, Strawberry Night,* and *Samurai Sensei. One Piece Film Gold* will be his first animated feature.

★ Finally, in this movie, the music will play an important role! So we've got to get this part right!! Whom can we turn to for some real big band jazz?! The first name that popped into my head is a genius blues singer I've been following for twenty years!!

Insert Songs: Mayumi Kojima

Yes, we've got her!! When we heard the first demo take, the entire staff said, "Wow! This is it!" Let me tell you, her music and singing are the real deal!! Mayumi Kojima is a monster in the music scene who has mastered jazz, blues, swing, and anything else that catches her fancy. She offered to sing something for a character in the movie, so if you want a preview, check out any of her available music!! My favorites are "Amai Koi" and "Heart ni Hi wo Tsukete," but they're all great.

Genius in the house!!
She's going to rock our opening theme and insert song!!

■ Mayumi Kojima
A girl-pop singer/songwriter who trades in "good-old-days" music. She debuted in 1995 with the single "Marriage Counseling Office." She's released nine albums since then.
http://www.kojimamayumi.com

COMING NEXT VOLUME:

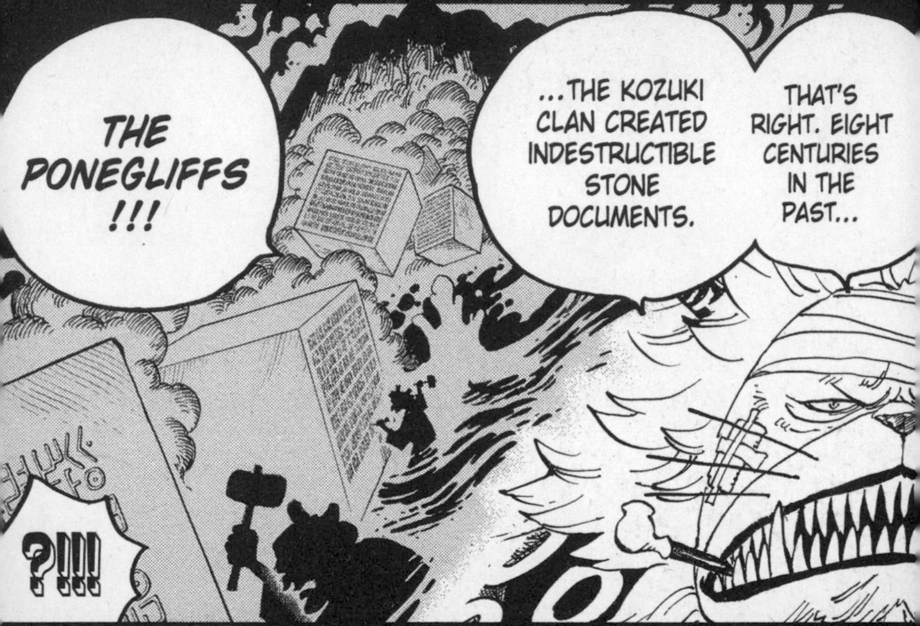
THAT'S RIGHT. EIGHT CENTURIES IN THE PAST...
...THE KOZUKI CLAN CREATED INDESTRUCTIBLE STONE DOCUMENTS.
THE PONEGLIFFS !!!
?!!!

The Minks were hiding mysterious ninja Raizo all along! But who exactly is he and what is the connection between the Minks and the people of Wano? And when all the secrets of Zou are revealed, what will the Straw Hats' next step be?

ON SALE MAY 2017!

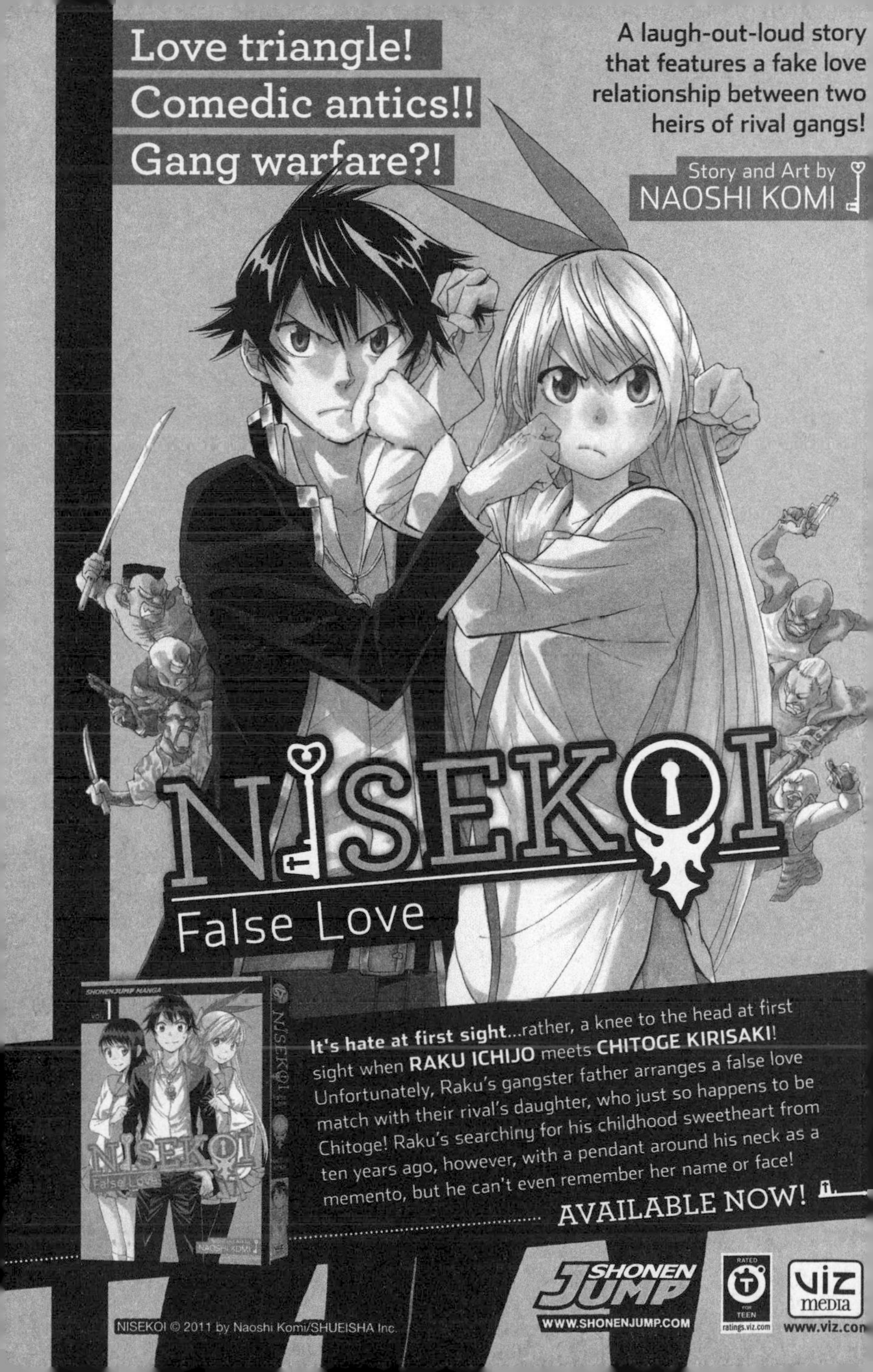
Love triangle!
Comedic antics!!
Gang warfare?!
A laugh-out-loud story that features a fake love relationship between two heirs of rival gangs!
Story and Art by
NAOSHI KOMI
NISEKOI
False Love
It's hate at first sight...rather, a knee to the head at first sight when RAKU ICHIJO meets CHITOGE KIRISAKI! Unfortunately, Raku's gangster father arranges a false love match with their rival's daughter, who just so happens to be Chitoge! Raku's searching for his childhood sweetheart from ten years ago, however, with a pendant around his neck as a memento, but he can't even remember her name or face!
AVAILABLE NOW!
SHONEN JUMP
WWW.SHONENJUMP.COM
RATED T FOR TEEN
ratings.viz.com
VIZ media
www.viz.com
NISEKOI © 2011 by Naoshi Komi/SHUEISHA Inc.

NARUTO

Story and Art by
Masashi Kishimoto

Naruto is determined to become the greatest ninja ever!

Twelve years ago the Village Hidden in the Leaves was attacked by a fearsome threat. A nine-tailed fox spirit claimed the life of the village leader, the Hokage, and many others. Today, the village is at peace and a troublemaking kid named Naruto is struggling to graduate from Ninja Academy. His goal may be to become the next Hokage, but his true destiny will be much more complicated. The adventure begins now!

WORLD'S BEST SELLING MANGA!

www.shonenjump.com   www.viz.com

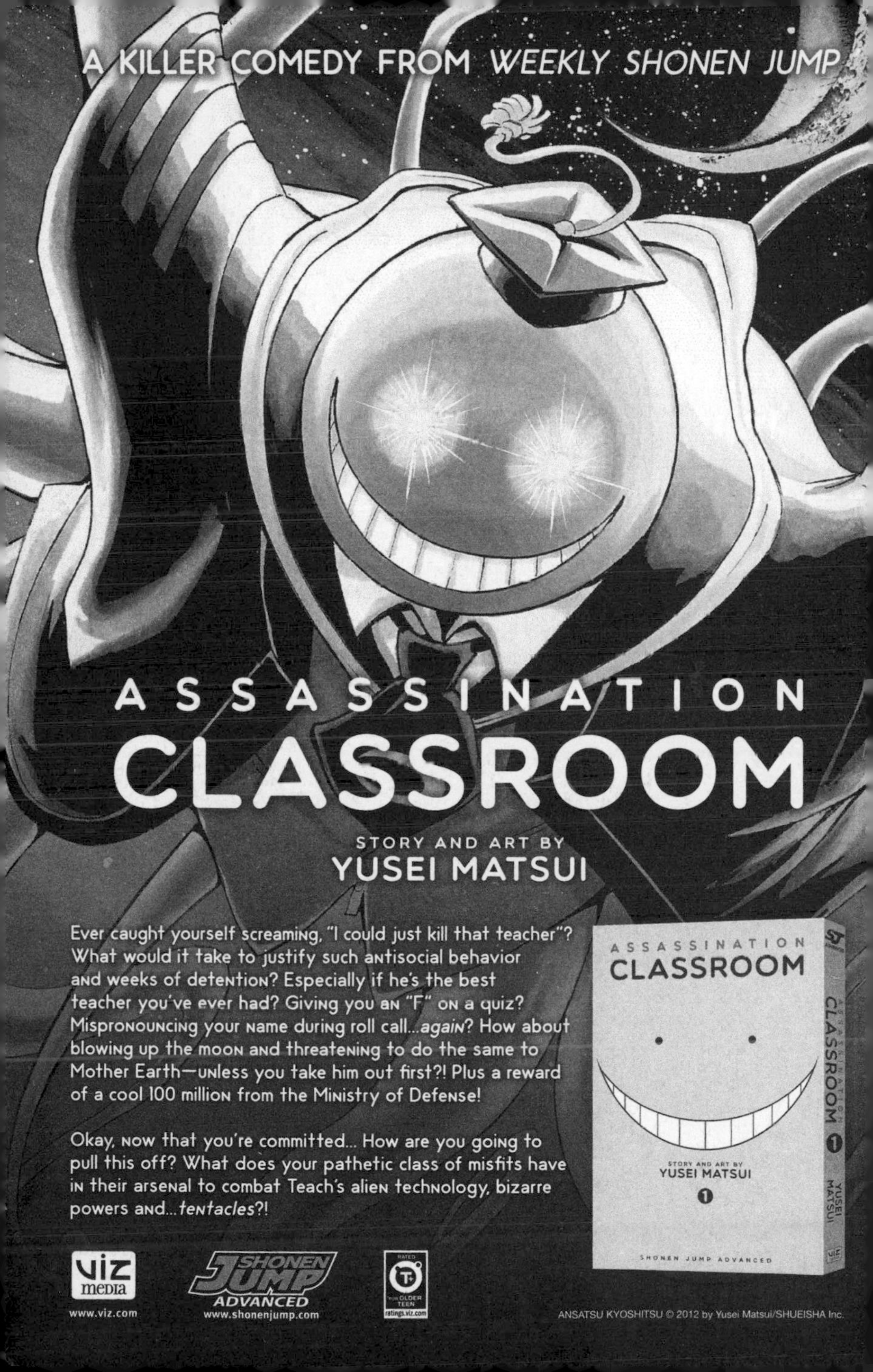
A KILLER COMEDY FROM *WEEKLY SHONEN JUMP*
ASSASSINATION CLASSROOM
STORY AND ART BY
YUSEI MATSUI
Ever caught yourself screaming, "I could just kill that teacher"? What would it take to justify such antisocial behavior and weeks of detention? Especially if he's the best teacher you've ever had? Giving you an "F" on a quiz? Mispronouncing your name during roll call...*again*? How about blowing up the moon and threatening to do the same to Mother Earth—unless you take him out first?! Plus a reward of a cool 100 million from the Ministry of Defense!
Okay, now that you're committed... How are you going to pull this off? What does your pathetic class of misfits have in their arsenal to combat Teach's alien technology, bizarre powers and...*tentacles*?!
ASSASSINATION CLASSROOM
STORY AND ART BY
YUSEI MATSUI
1
SHONEN JUMP ADVANCED
viz media
www.viz.com
SHONEN JUMP ADVANCED
www.shonenjump.com
RATED T+ FOR OLDER TEEN
ratings.viz.com
ANSATSU KYOSHITSU © 2012 by Yusei Matsui/SHUEISHA Inc.

You're Reading in the Wrong Direction!!

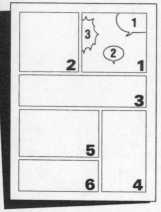

Whoops! Guess what? You're starting at the wrong end of the comic!

...It's true! In keeping with the original Japanese format, **One Piece** is meant to be read from right to left, starting in the upper-right corner.

Unlike English, which is read from left to right, Japanese is read from right to left, meaning that action, sound effects and word-balloon order are completely reversed...something which can make readers unfamiliar with Japanese feel pretty backwards themselves. For this reason, manga or Japanese comics published in the U.S. in English have sometimes been published "flopped"—that is, printed in exact reverse order, as though seen from the other side of a mirror.

By flopping pages, U.S. publishers can avoid confusing readers, but the compromise is not without its downside. For one thing, a character in a flopped manga series who once wore in the original Japanese version a T-shirt emblazoned with "M A Y" (as in "the merry month of") now wears one which reads "Y A M"! Additionally, many manga creators in Japan are themselves unhappy with the process, as some feel the   mirror-imaging of their art skews their original intentions.

We are proud to bring you Eiichiro Oda's   **One Piece**   though, in the original unflopped format. For now,   journey turn to the other side of the book and let the begin...!

    —Editor